'When [Clive Caldwell] died in Sydney in August 19⁊⁊, butes poured in, but only now do we have one worthy of the ma̅.'

Barry Oakley: *The Australian*

'[*Clive Caldwell, Air Ace*] pulls no punches and is very well written—Kristen Alexander is to be congratulated for her first effort—and readers will enjoy her literary style . . . For those interested in key personalities in Australian aviation history, this book is a must. Highly recommended.'

Mark Lax, *Defender*

'Kristen Alexander has written a magnificent book about this enigmatic man . . . the definitive book on a man who loved his country and flew with a passion . . .'

Lt Cameron Jameson, *The Soldiers' Newspaper*

'Kristen Alexander has done a superb job in her approach to chronicling his life . . . A worthwhile book that deserves to be read widely.'

Hugh Collis, *Stand To*

'Kristen Alexander's excellent *Clive Caldwell, Air Ace* is a timely reminder of the breadth and success of Aussie airmen in the air war with all axis powers . . . a fitting testimony to the man, his machines and his times. Read it!'

J.H. Farrell, *Australian & NZ Defender*

'Kristen Alexander . . . has done a tremendous job of describing the war exploits of a most singular man.'

Steve Woodman, *Weekend Herald*

'Kristen Alexander has written a fine biography of Clive Caldwell . . . It will be the standard biography of Caldwell for some considerable time and is highly recommended.'

Ric Pelvin, *Sabretache*

JACK DAVENPORT

· BEAUFIGHTER LEADER ·

KRISTEN ALEXANDER

ALLEN&UNWIN

Allen & Unwin
83 Alexander Street
Crows Nest NSW 2065
Australia
Phone: (61 2) 8425 0100
Fax: (61 2) 9906 2218
Email: info@allenandunwin.com
Web: www.allenandunwin.com

Cataloguing-in-Publication details are available
from the National Library of Australia
www.librariesaustralia.nla.gov.au

978 1 74175 776 7

Maps on pages xxi–xxv are reproduced with permission of
Catherine Gordon. All originally appeared in Ian Gordon,
Strike and Strike Again. 455 Squadron RAAF 1944–45, Banner Books, 1995.

Index by Russell Brooks
Set in 11.5/14 pt Bembo Std by Bookhouse, Sydney
Printed and bound in Australia by Griffin Press

10 9 8 7 6 5 4 3 2 1

Contents

For John and Thérèse Alexander

Foreword

Those who served with Jack Davenport remember him as a remarkable man. The regard in which he was held by those who flew operations in Europe in the Second World War is evident by his invitation to address the eighth annual RAAF Europe Dinner in Melbourne. The first annual speaker had been Hugh Edwards VC, and then before and after Jack, Basil Embery, Douglas Bader, Adolf Galland, Pierre Clostermann, Dennis Smallwood, Johnnie Johnson, Donald C.T. Bennett and Leonard Cheshire VC. Their deeply affecting experiences resonated strongly in the audiences. Such charmed characters and their eventful lives are a challenge to bring forth without loss in the recording. Following her recent portrayal of *Clive Caldwell, Air Ace*, Kristen Alexander's special skill in biography is again apparent in this faithful presentation of history interwoven with penetrating interview material.

An early entrant into the Empire Air Training Scheme, Jack's enthusiasm was rewarded by the achievement of his wish to be a pilot. In Britain he was posted to Australia's first squadron in Bomber Command, No. 455, flying Hampdens. Translocated to Coastal Command, the squadron was re-equipped with Beaufighters and on commencing his second tour of operations he gained its command (one of the first of the Empire Air trainees to command a squadron). His rocket-firing Beaufighter squadron came to mirror his dedication to excellence. He was charmingly boyish yet sure in command, unostentatious and proud of belonging to the RAAF within the RAF, the best service in the world. Finally in October 1944, Air Chief Marshal Sir Sholto Douglas, Commander-in-Chief of Coastal Command, ordered his retirement from air operations to plan those very operations.

Beaufighter strike operations were hazardous. At first it was torpedo dropping which meant holding a steady course into the target under intense anti-aircraft fire. With the change to rockets, engagement became a very close encounter with the pilot releasing the rockets at 150 yards from the target to ensure hits below the water line. In the open sea it was difficult enough but as Coastal Command's war moved from the English Channel into Norwegian waters attacks had to be made in the close confines of harbours and fiords. The hazards were compounded by the appearance of Focke-Wulf FW 190s from German-occupied airfields. To see friend or foe die cruelly is etched on the memory but there is unresolved trauma surrounding those whose death is not witnessed. The mind turns over and over in questing what their fate might have been. In letters to next of kin Jack tried to ease the pain of official notification.

Jack and Sheila's wartime marriage and their settlement in Sydney required a choice between his staying in the air force or a new career. His exceptional service background ensured he would be approached for his leadership and management qualities. Resultant senior business appointments soon escalated to demanding administrative positions. Family time was encroached upon by his readiness to support an ever-widening range of benevolent bodies often as chairman and leader in fundraising activities. He was called upon for service on company boards and counsel on national bodies. Throughout, he remained committed to his former colleagues through the RAAF Association. On Anzac Day he always led his squadron through Sydney and on the previous evening met squadron members at the Cenotaph. On the first Anzac Day after his death, a much diminished group, bolstered by grown children, mourned his passing while waiting beneath the GPO portico in the chill and darkness of Martin Place to lay their wreath. As we stepped forward his ever attentive chief of ground crew passed the wreath into the hands of the next senior officer present.

Of all the fine things said at his funeral in 1996, I most remember Sheila's, spoken to me in her crisp Scottish accent: 'He was a kind man.' Through his own words and actions, and through the eyes of his family, friends and business associates, Kristen Alexander shows that Jack Davenport was, indeed, a kind, compassionate man: a man of great humanity.

Group Captain Peter Ilbery OAM RFD MD

Acknowledgements

Official records and histories provide the bare bones of Jack's military and postwar careers, but personal stories reveal the warmth of his character and personality. My thanks to Jack's family and friends, squadron comrades, business colleagues, employees and neighbours who shared their memories of Jack. I am, in particular, grateful for the assistance of the late Wally Kimpton, Ivor Gordon, Bob Holmes and Hope Gibb.

Although I heard many wonderful accounts from those who knew Jack, much information was buried in official archives. I was fortunate that Ian Gordon, 455 Squadron's second historian, lent me his research material. His old army trunk was a treasure trove of information and I am still overwhelmed at his generosity. I would also like to thank Geoff Raebel, who recorded the squadron's adventures in Russia, for the loan of some of his interview material.

Lack of time always bedevilled me and, so I could concentrate more on reading and writing, I wish to thank Jean Main who retrieved the majority of archival information (that did not come from Ian's trunk!) and patiently responded to my umpteen requests for 'one more file . . . one more fishing expedition'; and Amanda Lomas who transcribed my interviews.

I enjoyed much assistance from my friends in the Military Historical Society of Australia. Thank you Graham Wilson and Ric Pelvin as well as Anthony Staunton and Jim Underwood who read sections of the manuscript relevant to their expertise. My thanks also to Mark Lax for access to an outstanding photo collection, and to David Burrowes and Errol Martyn for information relating to 489 Squadron RNZAF. I am also grateful for the assistance of the National Archives of Australia, Office of Air Force History, Royal Australian Air Force

Association, National Library of Australia, Honours and Awards Secretariat, Government House, Australian War Memorial, Commonwealth Bank of Australia, The National Heart Research Institute, Sydney Boys High School, RSVP column of the *Sydney Morning Herald*, Dundee Central Library and the National Archives of the United Kingdom.

I was privileged to have had close contact with Jack's children, Bruce Davenport and June Ross, as well as Jack's brother, Philip Davenport. I am grateful for all their assistance, comments and criticisms, and access to their private records. Phil graciously lent me his unpublished memoir, 'Things are Seldom What they Seem (Eighty Years of Memories)' which includes many stories of Jack. Through Bruce and June I discovered in many ways how Jack's special qualities translated to the second generation. Bruce, in particular, took up his father's role as a mentor and I greatly appreciate his constant encouragement.

Many people have helped me over the last few years but a small group offered love, support and technical assistance. It is not too much of an exaggeration to say this book would not have been written without their help. I wish to thank Lex McAulay and Peter and Marianne Ilbery who were there from the beginning, offering advice and moral support and providing a sounding board to my ideas. Lex and Peter also 'volunteered' to read early drafts and I am grateful for their technical assistance and constructive comments. I was fortunate that a number of Jack Davenport's friends also 'volunteered' to read sections of the manuscript and my profound thanks go to the late Bruce Daymond, Alan Bowman, John Ayliffe, the late Jack 'Bluey' Collins, the late Ron Warfield, Bill McFadden, Lyn Shaddock, Scott Milson, Dick and Mary Mason, and Ron and Rosemary Duncan. I wish to thank Jill Sheppard for her thoughtful observations on the manuscript, Joanne Holliman for her expert editorial guidance, and Karen Gee for her eagle-eyed copyediting. As before, I enjoyed the continuing love and support of my husband, David, my aunt, Zanna Cahill, and my friend Jill.

Thank you, all.

Author's word

My father died unexpectedly in July 2005. I had just posted the manuscript for *Clive Caldwell, Air Ace* to Allen & Unwin and, for the first time in over three years, was at a loose end. There was nothing to distract me from my grief. Perhaps realising this, Lex McAulay, who had helped me so much with the Caldwell biography, started emailing suggestions for a new book. Every few days, he would send the name of another unsung Second World War pilot of great skill and interesting deeds. Despite their worthiness, none sparked my interest.

Knowing how I tick, Lex pulled out the big 'selling' guns when he mentioned Jack Davenport. He told me Jack had been well decorated during the war, had been revered by his men, looked like a film star and had led the dangerous strikes at the head of the squadron. Film star looks? Dangerous strikes? My curiosity was piqued. I Googled and discovered the bare bones of Jack's air force career. He certainly seemed fascinating.

Unbeknownst to me, Lex had been talking to Peter Ilbery, who had also helped me with *Clive Caldwell*. The next thing I knew, Peter was also emailing me about Jack. I admire Peter and Lex more than I can possibly say and value their opinions. Before I knew it, and with the support of Jack's children and brother, I was delving into Jack Davenport's life.

As is so often the way—with me at least—confidence levels fall, doubts set in and I wondered if I was doing the right thing. I confess that there were times when I felt too daunted to continue with my research. Jack Davenport had had an extraordinary life and I was not sure I could do it justice. As friends had set me on the path, so too was a friend instrumental in ensuring I kept on it.

I first met Alan Righetti, a former fighter pilot with 3 Squadron RAAF who had spent much of the war in Stalag Luft III, while I was working on *Clive Caldwell*. When I told Alan I was researching Jack Davenport's life it was during one of my dark, insecure periods. He told me how much he admired Jack and he wished he could help but could not contribute anything as he had met Jack only once, at a RAAF reunion dinner many years ago. Alan recalled that Jack was the guest of honour and had spoken modestly about his war service, paying tribute to his flying mates. He also talked about the charities he supported. Everybody was totally absorbed. Afterwards, Jack visited each table. He and Alan talked for only a few minutes, and Jack kept the conversation to his interest in Alan—what and where he had flown, Stalag Luft III and Alan's postwar life. Then Alan mentioned that, if I wanted, I could have copies of some articles about Jack he had kept. This astounded me. What was it about Jack that not only brought about total admiration in such a short time, but led someone to keep a collection of articles about him for almost ten years after his death?

Alan then introduced me to his friend Cyril Johnson who also had only met Jack once, many years after the war. Cyril had had friends on 455 Squadron who had told him about Jack's wartime exploits and, from those tales, he had developed a deep admiration for a great pilot and leader. He talked about Jack's actions as if he had been on the squadron, and when he told me how Jack had saved a pilot from a burning aircraft, his account was so vivid it was as if Cyril had witnessed it himself. Cyril's stories were second-hand, but the impact Jack had made on him, even from such a distance, was genuine. I resolved to complete Jack's story so others could read of his great contribution to Australia's war effort and postwar life. I wanted others to see what it was about Jack that engendered such high regard in Alan and Cyril. Thanks to them, my path now had light.

Some of the impact Jack had on people stemmed from his great humanity; he was a man of true compassion. He also possessed unerring, unassailable integrity. These, as well as his ambition to prosper in life and provide security and stability for his family, were at the heart of his character and personality. So too were loyalty, friendship, dedication and duty. Much of what made Jack, came from within—his own singular qualities. But there was something outside Jack that contributed to his exceptional nature. It was his wife Sheila.

She was his passion, his friend, his support and his business helpmate. Their marriage grew with love and strength for over fifty years. Naturally, as I learned more of their lives and love, I recalled my parents' love. My father's death was the starting point for my involvement in Jack's story and I've dedicated this book to my parents, John and Thérèse Alexander.

General note

In researching this book I have drawn on many written and oral primary sources. For the main part, extracts appear as originally recorded. However, in the interests of consistency and readability, where appropriate I have corrected spelling, 'improved' punctuation and cut out repetition and digressions.

Where possible, I have included the given names of Jack Davenport's squadron friends and wartime associates. This was an easy task for Australians because of the online Second World War nominal roll at www.ww2roll.gov.au. Unfortunately, squadron records and other sources did not always record given names so non-Australian squadron members were more difficult to fully identify. In these cases I have included just initials and surnames.

The term 'observer' was used until March 1942, when it was dropped and replaced by 'navigator'. For ease of reading, I have simply used 'navigator' throughout. For the same reason, although used within the air force, I have not used the 24-hour clock.

Measurements

Measurement conversions in the text are always messy, especially in quoted text so, for ease of reading, weights and measurements are given in imperial form. The exceptions are some types of armament.

Length

1 inch = 25.4 millimetres = 2.54 centimetres
1 foot = 12 inches = 30.48 centimetres
1 yard = 3 feet = 91.44 centimetres
1 mile = 5280 feet = 1.61 kilometres

1 nautical mile = 1.151 statute miles = 1.852 kilometres

Speed

1 knot = 1 nautical mile = 1.151 statute miles = 1.852 kilometres per hour

Weight

1 pound = 16 ounces = 0.454 kilograms
1 ton = 2240 pounds (the metric tonne is virtually equal)

Prologue

'we all need heroes to look up to and to emulate'

Some years after the Second World War, eight-year-old Pam Watson came home from school and told her parents she had to write an essay about a famous person, but did not know who she should choose. Did they have any ideas? This was the 1950s and there were many famous people Ted Watson and his wife Madge could have suggested—sporting legends such as Don Bradman, war heroes such as Roden Cutler VC, or Antarctic explorer Douglas Mawson. Ted did not contemplate even one of them. He immediately suggested Pam write about 'Uncle Jack'.[1]

Ted had first met Jack Davenport in mid 1943 at a torpedo training unit where Jack was one of his instructors. At the end of his training, Ted was posted to 455 Squadron which Jack would soon command. Jack and Ted had much in common and soon became friends. Like Jack, Ted was an old boy of Sydney Boys High. Jack loved music and singing and Ted was accomplished on saxophone and banjo, with musical interests ranging from Mozart and Beethoven to jazz. The two men also shared a love of sports, especially golf. There was much to talk about and they would meet whenever their careers allowed.[2]

Both Pam and her brother Geoff remember visits to the Davenports. Geoff, in particular, recalled piling out of their black Humber Hawk, and later the blue Ford Customline, Jack and Sheila embracing his parents and sister with welcoming hugs, and Jack giving him and his younger brother, Ian, manly handshakes. The young Watsons went off with the young Davenports, eating great slabs of watermelon and running riot. Their parents stayed up late, chatting and laughing, long after the children were put to bed. Even as a boy, Geoff could see the special bond between his father and Uncle Jack: a bond that had survived the trials of war and was now strengthened by laughter, friendship and common interests.[3]

Ted Watson well knew of Jack's wartime experiences. He knew of the time, about six weeks before the end of Jack's operational training, when Jack had a 'shaky do'. From 6500 feet his aircraft spiralled out of control. He told his crew to bale out and the wireless operator did so successfully, but the navigator could not. Jack did not abandon his navigator but stayed in the cockpit. He finally recovered from the spin and made a successful landing. Ted also knew of the time Jack saved the life of one of his pilots. The Beaufighter's petrol tanks had burst, it was a mass of flames with exploding ammunition, but Jack managed to pull the trapped pilot through the blaze to safety. Ted knew that Jack Davenport was a dedicated and courageous leader who flew the dangerous strikes, of which there were many, at the head of the squadron, and later at the head of the strike wing. It was only natural then that Ted suggest Jack to Pam for her essay, and Pam, who had grown up with stories about her Uncle Jack, decided that yes, he did fit the bill as a famous man. Borrowing her mother's pink note paper, she wrote about the man who had always been a hero to her family.[4]

Pam may have considered Jack a hero, but Jack certainly did not consider himself as anyone special. On one occasion, he was lauding Australia's contribution to Bomber Command where he had had his earliest operational experiences. Although he had displayed the same quiet courage as any of those whom he praised, he did not include himself as one of those whose actions should be extolled.[5] Jack's friend and business consultant, Wilfred Jarvis, recalled that Jack was always reluctant to talk about his wartime achievements and protested that he only did what any member of the service would do in the circumstances. Jack emphatically rejected the title 'hero'.[6]

Jack Davenport may not have claimed the title, but he was a hero, displaying the true heroism which encompasses sacrifice, courage, honour and bravery in the first instance, and duty, humanity and genuine compassion in the second. He was a hero every time he climbed into his cockpit. No matter how scared he was of anti-aircraft fire, coning and night-fighters, he continued to fly. He led his squadron on operations he knew were flawed and had little hope of success. Thinking nothing of his own safety, he saved lives.

Those qualities of heroism translated to Jack's postwar life. His wife, Sheila, testified to his great moral courage and his brother, Phil, considered Jack's life 'was remarkable for achievement, integrity and compassion'.[7]

In March 1993, Jack retired from the board of Alcoa of Australia Ltd. Alcoa's chairman, Sir Arvi Parbo, recognised Jack as a man of extraordinary personal character who had touched many lives. As he handed Jack his retirement gift of an elegant pen and pencil set, he urged him to use them to write his life story:

> We all need heroes to look up to and to emulate, to stretch our horizons and to set targets which will make us reach out. The young people in Australia today particularly need this. Your story, Jack, is a wonderful example for them and for us all. Please make sure it is recorded.[8]

Jack had no real inclination to write his own story, and even if he wanted to, he was not afforded the time. But Jack's story has not been lost.

Maps

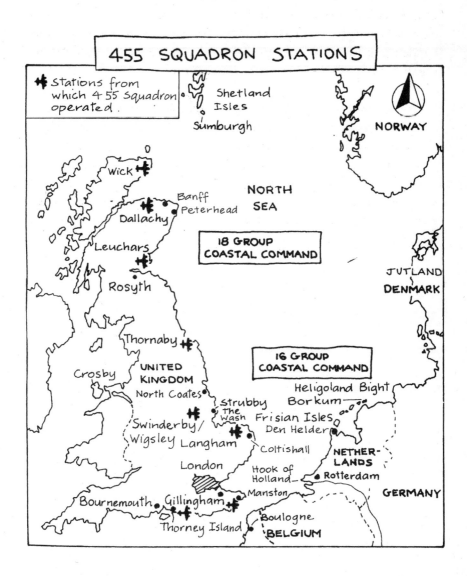

455 SQUADRON STATIONS

⊕ Stations from which 455 Squadron operated.

Shetland Isles
Sumburgh

NORWAY

Wick

Banff
Peterhead
Dallachy

NORTH SEA

Leuchars

18 GROUP
COASTAL COMMAND

Rosyth

JUTLAND
DENMARK

Thornaby

16 GROUP
COASTAL COMMAND

Crosby

UNITED KINGDOM

North Coates

Strubby
the Wash

Heligoland Bight
Borkum

Frisian Isles
Den Helder

Swinderby/
Wigsley

Langham

Coltishall

NETHER-LANDS

London

Hook of Holland

Rotterdam

GERMANY

Bournemouth

Gillingham

Manston

Thorney Island

Boulogne
BELGIUM

Courtesy Catherine Gordon

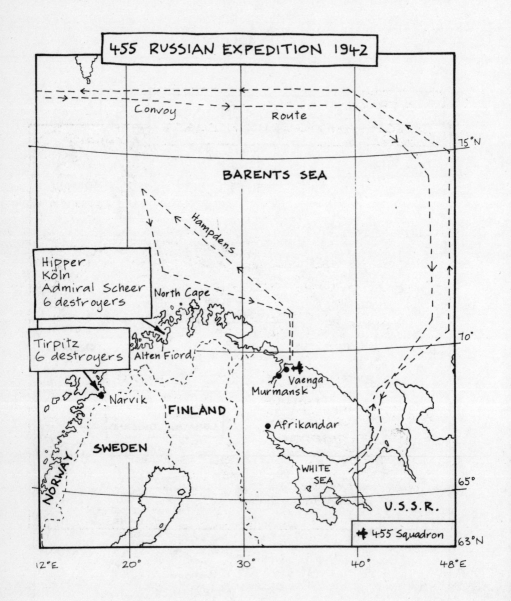

455 RUSSIAN EXPEDITION 1942

Convoy   Route

75°N

BARENTS SEA

Hampdens

Hipper
Köln
Admiral Scheer
6 destroyers

North Cape

70°

Tirpitz
6 destroyers

Alten Fiord

Vaenga
Murmansk

Narvik

FINLAND

Afrikandar

SWEDEN

WHITE
SEA

65°

NORWAY

U.S.S.R.

✈ 455 Squadron

63°N

12°E   20°   30°   40°   48°E

Courtesy Catherine Gordon

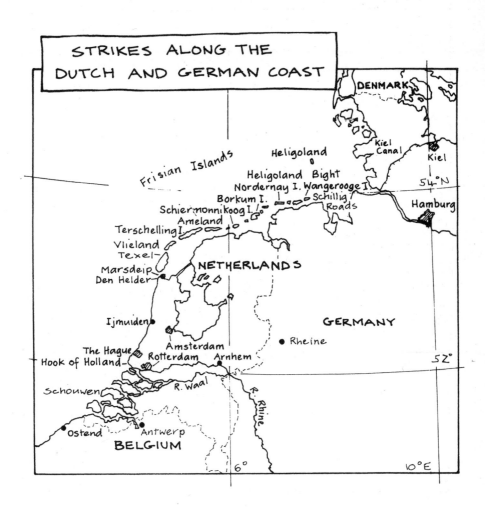

STRIKES ALONG THE
DUTCH AND GERMAN COAST

DENMARK

Frisian Islands

Heligoland

Kiel
Canal

Kiel

Heligoland Bight
Nordernay I. Wangerooge I.
Borkum I. Schillig
Schiermonnikoog I. Roads

54°N

Hamburg

Ameland

Terschelling I.

Vlieland
Texel

NETHERLANDS

Marsdeip
Den Helder

GERMANY

Ijmuiden

Rheine

The Hague
Hook of Holland

Amsterdam
Rotterdam Arnhem

52°

Schouwen

R. Waal

R. Rhine

Ostend Antwerp

BELGIUM

6°

10°E

Courtesy Catherine Gordon

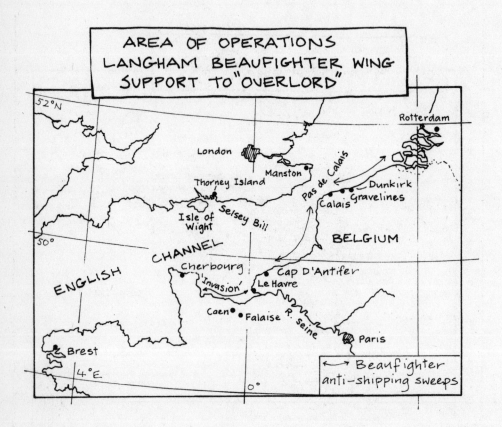

AREA OF OPERATIONS
LANGHAM BEAUFIGHTER WING
SUPPORT TO "OVERLORD"

Courtesy Catherine Gordon

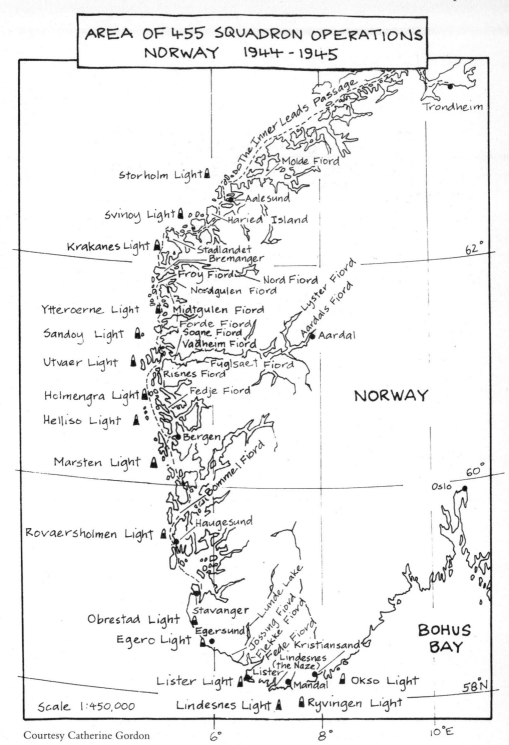

AREA OF 455 SQUADRON OPERATIONS
NORWAY 1944 - 1945

Trondheim

The Inner Leads Passage

Molde Fiord

Storholm Light

Aalesund

Svinoy Light

Haried Island

62°

Krakanes Light

Stadlandet
Bremanger

Froy Fiord

Nord Fiord

Nordgulen Fiord

Lyster Fiord

Aardals Fiord

Ytteroerne Light

Midtgulen Fiord

Sandoy Light

Forde Fiord
Sogne Fiord

Aardal

Utvaer Light

Vadheim Fiord

Fuglsaet Fiord

Risnes Fiord

NORWAY

Holmengra Light

Fedje Fiord

Helliso Light

Bergen

Marsten Light

Bommel Fiord

60°

Oslo

Rovaersholmen Light

Haugesund

Lunde Lake

BOHUS
BAY

Obrestad Light

Stavanger

Jossing Fiord

Egero Light

Egersund

Flekke Fiord

Fede Fiord

Kristiansand

Lindesnes
(the Naze)

Lister

Lister Light

Mandal

Okso Light

58°N

Scale 1:450,000

Lindesnes Light

Ryvingen Light

Courtesy Catherine Gordon

6°

8°

10°E

PART 1

Childhood and training

1

Depression era childhood

'no home; nowhere to go'

Grace Hutton and Roy Davenport were living in Adelaide when they first met.[1] They were both Anglican, albeit non-practising, with English-born fathers who died leaving their mothers widowed in middle age, and they were both one of seven children. There the social similarities ended. Grace was the youngest of her siblings, Roy was the second born. Grace, born in 1892, was a little older than Roy. She was tall, slim with a gentle personality that had hidden depths of strength. Grace's father, Henry, was a plate layer with the South Australian Railways and the family lived in many different towns before he died in a railway accident.[2] Grace's mother, Louise, was only forty when her husband died, leaving her with no income and seven children ranging in age from two to nineteen. Louise took her children to Mile End, a suburb of Adelaide, to start anew.

Roy's life and character were very different from Grace's. He was good looking, full of charm, socially at ease and a confident conversationalist. He was also well dressed and meticulous in maintaining a smart appearance. His father, William Davenport, had been a hotel owner and, when he died in 1915, his wife Annie, at 51, was left in comfortable circumstances.[3]

Roy was 22 when his father died. He had had a good education at Prince Alfred College, a leading boys' school. He had gone on to study wool classing at the well-respected South Australian School of Mines and Industries and was working at William Haughton & Co., a wool broking and shipping agent firm that had branches throughout Australia as well as in Canada and London. Two of his brothers had joined the war effort: Victor had joined the 27th Battalion and Leslie

3

the 32nd Battalion. Although Roy was of military age, he did not serve. He never spoke of his reasons but he was plagued with problems with his feet and would suffer serious bouts of pleurisy a few years later, so it is likely that his health excluded him from war service.

It is not certain how Grace Hutton and Roy Davenport met, but soon after they agreed their joint future lay in Sydney, where Roy would take up a position in William Haughton's Sydney branch. Accompanying Grace to Sydney were her brother Bob and her mother. Roy and Grace were married at St John's Anglican Church, North Sydney, on 28 June 1916. Roy's career with William Haughton was short-lived. Sometime after the birth of their first son in May 1918, Roy, Grace and baby Philip moved to the Northern Club Hotel in Sydney's Haymarket area.[4] Roy, who had recently resigned as a wool classer, had been granted the hotel's licence.[5]

The Northern Club's location favoured busy trade. Roy played host, sharing a glass or two with his patrons and pulling beer when needed. Grace diligently washed glasses, did all the housework and the bookkeeping and still managed to care for young Phil. Her brother, Bob Hutton, had been employed as a steward before the war and now helped Roy out behind the bar.[6] Taking his cue from Roy, Bob was generous when measuring spirits and the hotel soon became popular.

Grace soon fell pregnant again and her second son, Jack Napier Davenport, was born on 9 June 1920.[7] The year heralded much that would resonate throughout Jack's life. On the day of his birth, Captain George Matthews and Sergeant Thomas Kay, veterans of the Australian Flying Corps and two of Australia's earliest military aviators, arrived in Australia. They had been employed by the Sopwith Aviation Company and the next day the *Sydney Morning Herald* told its readers about their game attempt to fly from England to Australia in the Greatest Air Race.[8] Matthews' and Kay's adventures were not the only aviation portent for Jack. Throughout 1919, Great Britain had been despatching aeroplanes and equipment which would form the basis of Australia's own independent air force. Just the month before Jack's birth, the first of the 'Imperial Gift' machines, a De Havilland DH 9A, made its maiden flight at Point Cook, and the Royal Australian Air Force formally had its own birth the following year. Interestingly for someone who would serve with distinction on the board of Qantas for ten years, Jack was born in the same year that also saw the birth of Australia's own airline.

The Davenports did not stay long at the Northern Club Hotel. Roy suffered a serious bout of pleurisy and was so weakened he was no longer able to keep up with the demands of a busy hotel. This began a long period of hardship during which, Phil recalled: 'The devil debt was either with us or soon to arrive.'[9] The family were to move nineteen times before the next war and Jack experienced his first move in late 1920 when they moved to Port Hacking and then to a share flat at Coogee. Roy slowly recovered and in early 1923, while Grace was pregnant with their third child, Roy was granted the licence for the Commercial Hotel in Coonamble, on the western plains of north-west New South Wales.

The Commercial was larger than the Northern Club and boasted a dining room. As in their former establishment, Grace was responsible for the bookkeeping and now also organised staff, planned menus and ensured the table and bed linen were changed daily and laundered pristinely. Grace's mother and brother Bob accompanied the Davenports to Coonamble, moving to a small farm just outside town. It proved an exciting place for Jack and Phil to live when Grace returned to Sydney for the birth of their brother Keith. There was always something happening on the farm. The boys would run down to the train tracks to wave to the passengers whizzing by, they would enjoy the smells and noises of shearing time and they would experience grandmother Louise and Uncle Bob's concern when a brown snake invaded the kitchen.

After the birth of Keith, Grace returned to Coonamble and resumed her duties in the Commercial, combining them with her responsibilities as a mother of three boys under the age of five. As Jack and Phil played in the garden, or snuck out on a rare unsupervised excursion to the banks of the Castlereagh River, they had little idea that life for their parents was becoming increasingly more difficult. The clues were there: the dry river bed, left thirsty from the lack of rain; the stinking, rotting kangaroo carcasses; the bleached skeletons they witnessed as they travelled to and from the farm in Uncle Bob's sulky; their mother and grandmother preparing rabbit, shot by their father, for the hotel's menu. Drought combined with the debt of unpaid brewery accounts resulted in the family's departure from the Commercial.

By 1924, the Davenports were back in Sydney. The sojourn in Coonamble may have been far from successful for his parents, leaving, especially for his mother, a bitter memory as she recorded the worst drought in years, but the time in Coonamble sparked an enthusiasm for the bush that stayed with Jack all his life. He treasured the poetry of Banjo Patterson and Henry Lawson, and with little encouragement would start spouting Lawson's 'The Teams'.[10] His strong sense of the land influenced him to purchase his first property in the New England area in 1966.

The years following their return to Sydney were some of the most difficult for Jack's family. Roy's fortunes waxed and waned. At one time he was driving a model T Ford and connected with a business that imported tractors from Germany but his involvement ceased when he was crippled by the months-long agony of an abscess on the bladder. He required constant nursing from Grace but, despite the difficulties of caring for an ill husband and raising three boys, she would not accept charity or handouts and only rarely sought assistance from her Adelaide relations, preferring to struggle to keep up appearances.[11] Grace's independent spirit and quiet dignity bound the family together as she fought to make ends meet. There were many times when the Davenports did not know where the next meal would come from and Grace often went hungry herself so her children could eat, even if it was only bread-and-dripping.[12]

There was some light, however, during this difficult time. Like many other mothers in New South Wales, Grace gained some financial respite after Jack Lang's government passed the *Family Endowment Act* of 1927 as part of its social welfare reforms. Eligible mothers were entitled to five shillings a week for each legitimate child, up to the age of fourteen.[13] Fifteen shillings a week would not stretch far, but it would make a great difference to the family when Roy was not working. The children were protected as much as possible from the stresses of this time and had little awareness that life was so difficult.[14] They saw only adventure when they were sent to Uncle Bob's little shack out in the then countryside of Turramurra for visits, when, in reality, Bob was helping Grace by taking the boys off her hands for a few days. Despite support from her mother and brother, things became too much for Grace. The constant caring for her ill husband and looking after three active boys, combined with the never-ceasing effort to make ends meet, the succession of share houses and cramped rooms with family and friends, wore her down and in 1928 her sister came and whisked Phil off on an extended visit to Adelaide.

During Phil's absence, Roy recovered sufficiently to rejoin the workforce. Unemployment, however, was on the rise—in 1926 it was at 7 per cent, and by 1928 it had risen to 11 per cent. Recently ill and with a patchy track record, Roy would have had difficulties gaining employment. Preferring self-employment, he had decided that, after leaving William Haughton, he would always be his own boss.[15] He thought he was onto a winner when he found out about a new type of polishing mop. He leased an empty shop amid other empty shops in Newtown. He was enthusiastic that this venture might see his fortunes turn, but he was starting a new business with little capital behind him. His family lived in the flat above the shop and Grace's mother slept in the basement. There were but a few sticks of furniture and he and Grace and the children all slept on the floor as there was no money for beds. Roy put what little they had into a few hardware odds and ends, but the shop was only sparsely stocked and no-one had the money for, or any interest in, a new type of mop when their old ones were serviceable enough.

With Phil in Adelaide, Jack assumed the responsibilities of the oldest child. He rarely spoke of this time and would only hint at his family's suffering when he brushed off Phil's enquiries by saying: 'You were away; you don't know what went on.'[16] Perhaps the worst day was when the bailiffs came. Roy had almost given up on the mop enterprise; rent was owed with no way to pay it. As the Depression gained momentum, the Davenports were not the only family to face the bailiffs. Many evictions took place in Sydney and ugly scenes from organised, violent anti-eviction rallies and riots did much to focus attention on the plight of those who had no work, no wages and no rent money. There was no violence from the crowds the day the bailiffs came to King Street, but it was not a peaceful encounter.

Roy and Grace were out and Grace's mother Louise was looking after the boys. The bailiffs came to the front door of the shop but it was locked. They then headed towards the back lane where they encountered Jack and Keith. The young boys furiously fought off the bailiffs with sticks; they shouted at them to go away and fiercely kicked them. Louise grabbed her grandsons and pushed them inside. She then rushed upstairs and threw buckets of water down onto the hapless men. Soaked, and to the cheers of the neighbours, the bailiffs departed. The inevitable could not be delayed, however, and within a few days, shortly after Phil's return from Adelaide, the family was evicted. They moved to Bondi for a few months, but the bailiffs returned. This time, there was no place to go and Phil well recalled the deflated feeling, the desolation, shared by all in the family, 'of having no home; nowhere to go'.[17]

Roy and Grace Davenport gathered together their children and meagre possessions and Roy talked a friend into letting them spend the night in a tiny flat in Roscoe Street, Bondi Beach. Luck was briefly on their side when they were presented with the opportunity to look after a boarding house for a few weeks. It was not just a kindness: Roy worked in the garden and Grace kept the house clean and tidy for guests, as she had done in the Northern Club and Commercial hotels.[18] From there, the Davenports moved to a flat in Tamarama. Phil had started at Sydney Boys High School in 1931 and, on top of everything else, the family had to meet the expenses of a new suit and bus fares to and from Moore Park—at thirteen, Phil had to pay full fare, not the child's penny fare. Many school boys could not pay their fares in those Depression years and kindly bus or tram conductors would turn blind eyes and let them on for free. One day, Phil did not have enough money so, after climbing aboard, he and Jack offered pennies. The conductor asked Phil his age and he replied 'eleven'. The conductor then asked Jack how old he was, and Jack also said 'eleven'. The conductor looked at the two boys. Phil was much taller than Jack so the conductor was not convinced. He asked Jack if they were brothers but Phil quickly answered that they were cousins. The conductor relented and took their pennies.[19]

There was a rare glimmer of hope for the Davenports. Early in the morning of 2 April 1931, when many of its passengers were still in their night attire or breakfasting, the Burns Philp motor ship, *Malabar*, struck the rocks off Miranda Point. The passengers and crew all found their way safely to shore but the *Malabar*'s cargo was not saved and much was washed up on nearby beaches. The next day was the Good Friday holiday and thousands of pleasure-seekers made their way to nearby vantage points to view the final break-up of the stricken vessel. As well as sightseers, the crowd included looters and the beach was soon cleared of the *Malabar*'s sodden cargo. Some of the cargo drifted northward and some washed ashore on Tamarama Beach where, under the bright light of the full moon, the Davenports joined the hopefuls and the sheer desperate on the sand in search of salvage. Phil was the first to claim a prize, a large tin of butter. Quickly, they grabbed other much needed spoils, including a sack of flour, wet on the edges but perfectly dry in the middle. There were many times when the family did not know where the next meal would come from so the butter-spread scones that became their Easter treat were a far cry from the bread-and-dripping that usually made its way to their table.[20]

The Davenport family's many moves and struggle against poverty affected Jack's schooling. It is not clear exactly when Jack started school; it is certain, however, that he was attending North Bondi Public School when he did his qualifying certificate in 1931.[21] He was eligible for Sydney Boys High School, a prestigious selective school in the Greater Public Schools system. This school had a top academic and sports tradition and, even better for the Davenports, it was state funded.

In June 1932, Grace Bros advertised uniform specials in *The Record*, the school's magazine, emphasising their long-lasting qualities[22] but the Depression was biting very hard at this time and many could not even take advantage of these sale prices. Recognising that many families were battling, the school was flexible in its interpretation of school uniform and allowed all sorts of variations. This is seen clearly in Jack's 1935 class photo where only a few boys were wearing the school's blazer. Jack was not one of them and his jacket looks a little tight. Nor was Jack one of the few who wore the school tie and, like the majority of his classmates, he could not afford the school lapel badge. Even so, he was neat and tidy, and a credit to his mother as he proudly held the class plaque.[23]

Jack embraced high school life and the sporting opportunities offered by Sydney Boys High. Whenever he had the chance, he would energetically throw himself into whatever game was organised at school or elsewhere, whether baseball with the local lads or, after he left school, cricket with the Kyle Bay team and grade rugby with St George.[24] Jack donned the chocolate and blue with enthusiasm, joining the school rugby team. In 1933, his sixth grade team was highlighted as a team of good individualists and Jack was cited as one of those who had done well. In 1934, his fifth grade team were premiers, winning their division for the first time in a decade. In

Jack's final year his third grade side won the high schools' competition. He scored six points during the course of the year and was one of those boys whose sporting achievements were frequently applauded loudly at school assemblies.[25] Although class groups kept much to themselves, there was always a certain amount of mixing between those who played sports and Jack was one of the few older boys who socialised with the younger ones off the sporting fields.[26]

Roy Davenport's circumstances improved as the 1930s advanced. He went back into the wool trade, managing his own wool business in Young Street, Sydney, and his family moved to Bellevue Hill. Sometime after this Louise and Bob Hutton moved into a small, two-bedroom weekender at Kyle Bay, near Blakehurst. The Davenports visited on weekends and the waterfront cottage was soon extended, almost doubling in size, so they could move in.[27] Louise and Bob kept the original bedrooms; Grace and Roy shared a tiny one and Phil had his own room, both in the extended part; and Jack and Keith took over the veranda sleep-out. It was cramped but it was their first real home.

Jack spent four years at High, repeating his first year. His school records do not indicate why, but perhaps his enthusiasm for the rugby field had something to do with it; it was likely the sportsmaster had had a say in the matter, wanting Jack to stay in the junior rugby team.[28] Whether the reason was academic or sports-related, Jack's results before his intermediate exam show he was above the class average in only English, Maths I and Maths II. He was below average in Latin, French, Science and German. Even so, he was made class prefect in 1935, a position that usually went to a boy of high academic standing.[29] When he sat for his intermediate certificate, his only A pass was in Maths I; he gained B passes in the rest of his subjects.[30] Although in a more stable job by this time, Roy's income was not high and Jack, like Phil the year before, left school to seek employment without obtaining his leaving certificate.[31]

Sydney Boys High School was proud of its students and displayed a moving brand of school spirit during the war years as it noted which of its old boys had joined the services, those who had fallen, whether on active duty or in accidents, and those who had been awarded for their deeds. Jack featured in a number of wartime issues of *The Record*, including when he received the Distinguished Flying Cross and George Medal.[32] In its June 1946 issue, *The Record* published the Roll of Honour, acknowledging its many former students who had laid down their lives. The roll included Bruce Elder, one of Jack's classmates who, along with the entire ship's complement was lost when HMAS *Sydney* was sunk by the German Raider *Kormoran* in November 1941; and William Charlton, one of Jack's team-mates in his sixth grade rugby team, who had been posted to 460 Squadron RAAF.[33] In 1946, Jack was invited to High's Empire Day celebrations. The entire school filled the assembly hall to hear Jack speak of his wartime experiences and held the boys' interest from beginning to end. Looking back years later, and with many speeches under his belt, Jack thought this speech was one of the best he had ever made.[34] The wartime actions of his friends and other former pupils were formally commemorated by the school in 1951 when the Old Boys Union and its Ladies Auxiliary presented an honour board to the school. Jack was invited to participate in the dedication ceremony, reading out the names of some of those young men who had lost their lives.[35]

2

30th Battalion

'we were all very young . . . the major consideration was to get there and become involved'

The Depression years were difficult for the Davenports, but Jack only rarely spoke of that time. He was not one to dwell on the past or what he could not change, and there was a sense he wanted to forget and move on. Even so, those years left their mark. His brother Phil recalled that, throughout his life, Jack 'continued to enjoy his bread-and-dripping snacks. For him, a slice of bread-and-dripping in the kitchen tasted better than caviar at a cocktail party in the lounge.'[1] The years of poverty left a more significant legacy for Jack: they defined his sense of security. Throughout his young life, Jack and his family had experienced great turmoil as a result of Roy Davenport's attempts at self employment. As a consequence, Jack wanted a job that offered stability and opportunity for advancement but there were few such jobs in the mid 1930s. Jack's first job after leaving school at the end of 1935 was in a warehouse,[2] which was low paying and offered few prospects, but he was only marking time.

In a country that was coming out of the worst years of the Great Depression, a job in the bank—with attractive conditions of service including regular salary increases, sick leave, recreation leave, long service leave and pension entitlements—was considered highly secure. One of the largest banking employers at the time was the Commonwealth Bank of Australia. It was not until September 1945 that it introduced entrance examinations, and in Jack's day all a boy had to do was telephone head office in Martin Place and make an appointment for an interview with a senior man in the staffing section.[3] About a week after his interview, Jack received a letter stating he would be employed on probation for six months, and if assessed as suitable, would then be admitted to staff. It was welcome news: he felt proud to be selected for a job at the Commonwealth Bank.[4]

Jack started at the Sydney branch on 23 March 1936. His annual gross salary was £70, paid fortnightly, from which he contributed to his family's income. This ceased when he went overseas in 1941 but, ever mindful of his obligations, Jack arranged for an allotment to his mother from his military pay.[5] He was transferred to the Rockdale branch and by September he was carrying out the duties of the check sheet clerk. The branch manager was pleased with Jack's progress and, on 23 September, judged him as being 'keen to learn' and noted that he was 'progressing favourably in typewriting'. He recommended that Jack be admitted permanently to staff, and his salary increased to £100 per annum. In August 1937 Jack was considered a 'junior showing good progress' and in February 1939 he was promoted to savings bank ledger keeper and assessed as a 'good type of junior. Ambitious.' Jack certainly had aspirations. The Bankers' Institute of Australasia conducted courses in banking at intermediate and advanced levels. It was not compulsory for staff members to undertake any of these courses, but it was acknowledged that it was in their best interests to do so. Jack enrolled in the institute and passed his intermediate exam in 1939. His next promotion was on 1 May 1940, when he took on the duties of the general bank ledger keeper. He was now earning £170 a year.[6] His next step up the banking ladder, after he turned 21, would be a teller, but Jack was never promoted to this more senior position as he took extended military leave.[7] He enjoyed working at the Commonwealth Bank and believed the skills learned there would be good training for anything the future would bring.[8]

Despite British prime minister Neville Chamberlain's declaration of 'peace for our time' after he signed a non–aggression pact with Germany in September 1938, the following months showed all too clearly that war was imminent as German troops occupied the Sudetenland in October 1938 and then took Czechoslovakia in March 1939. As Germany's aggression strengthened, Jack and three fellow Commonwealth Bank officers agreed that their part in Australia's preparations for conflict lay with the militia. The Commonwealth

Bank had generous military leave provisions[9] and, on 5 July 1939, Corporal Anthony Nugent, who also worked at the Commonwealth Bank, introduced Jack, Anthony Booth, Duncan MacRae and Roy Beveridge, one of Jack's school friends, to A Company of the 30th Battalion, New South Wales Scottish Regiment.[10]

The 30th Battalion had a proud tradition. It had battle honours from South Africa 1900–1902 as well as important Great War battles such as the Somme, Bullecourt, Menin Road and Passchendaele. It had re-formed in July 1935 and was affiliated with the famous Black Watch and its striking tartan formed a memorable part of the battalion's battle dress.

Jack and his friends regularly attended the Millers Point drill hall but their first real taste of battalion life came when they attended the October 1939 training camp at Rutherford, west of Maitland. One of the first things the trainees had to endure on arrival were typhoid inoculations and then they started their training: basic military and defence skills, trench digging, route marches, field training, river crossing and tactics training. They had extensive weaponry training with the Lewis light machine guns that had seen service in the First World War and, having no vehicles, made use of horse transports. Jack also participated in the three-month Greta camp, commencing in September 1940. As well as the training activities, there were many games and athletics events and Jack proved himself a good athlete in a number of events including the triple jump.[11]

In the late 1930s, Jack met a man who became a significant influence in his life, a mentor and almost a surrogate father. Phil Davenport first met Clement Shaddock around 1937, soon after the Shaddocks had moved to Connells Point.[12] Phil loved sailing and had taken to the water from a young age on all sorts of makeshift vessels. Now he was working he could afford a proper sailing boat and his small skiff, *Mischief*, was his pride and joy. One day, Phil and a friend were sailing around Connells Point when *Mischief* tipped over in front of Clem Shaddock's large waterfront house. Clem, who was on the water that day, quickly headed over to the stricken boat and fished the young sailors out. Phil and Clem hit it off immediately. They shared a love of sailing and together formed the Connells Point

Sailing Club. Phil introduced Jack and Keith to Clem and they all developed a good relationship with him.[13]

Jack spent much time with Clem before he went overseas. Their personalities differed in some ways—Jack was social, an extrovert, Clem was more of an introvert—but they both loved music and sport and had ambition and great drive. Over the years, Clem would influence Jack's leadership style and impart an almost visionary aspect to Jack's future planning.[14] Jack loved his own father, but Roy's inability to provide a secure and stable life for his family created a tension between the two that was never fully resolved. In some ways, Jack saw Roy's charm and social savoir faire, combined with his lack of consistency in providing for his family, as a sign of irresponsibility.[15] He had inherited his father's charm and social ease but he had displayed a strong sense of responsibility from an early age. He recognised this important trait in Clem and was drawn to him. Like Roy, Clem had an entrepreneurial streak but, unlike Roy, he had enjoyed a successful business career. He had managed St George Lime and Cement through the Depression and founded Cement Linings Limited, a company which used a patented system of cement linings to triple the life of water mains.[16] In Clem, Jack found a person from whom he could learn, a sounding board, and someone who influenced the direction of his military career.

As 1940 progressed, Jack's maturity and competence were noted by his commanding officers in the 30th Battalion. He rose through the ranks, firstly to corporal and finally to sergeant. In mid 1940 he was one of those selected to train recruits for the 7th Division AIF.[17] Reminiscent of his own training at Rutherford, Jack taught marching, drills and basic weapon handling. Those destined for overseas service were not the only ones trained by Jack. At one time, Jack's colonel came to him and told him he had 'volunteered' for extra duty. He would still be required to drill recruits, but these were different: they were women. Jack later recalled that at first 'they were impossible. Wolf whistles when I arrived and great backchat.' Handsome Sergeant Davenport must have seemed too good to be true as an instructor. Despite their initial irreverence, Jack soon found that the women trainees were much better at drill than the men, achieving a high standard in half the time.[18]

Jack was well liked within the battalion, respected as a soldier and trainer.[19] Edward Amaral was one of those whom Jack trained and he was impressed by Jack as his platoon sergeant. He followed Jack's career in the RAAF and considered 'his exploits, combined with leadership and courage awarded him honours he richly deserved'. He felt it was an honour to have known Jack and every year on Anzac Day, when he joined his friends from the 30th Battalion, he 'made it a personal duty to meet Jack and his mates in 455 Squadron'.[20]

The 30th Battalion was keen to carry on its fine battle tradition so, when war was declared, it volunteered for overseas service. It was denied this as militia units were designated for home service only; the government had decided to raise the Second Australian Imperial Force (AIF) to serve overseas. Many from the 30th Battalion wanted to fight for the Empire rather than help defend the seemingly safe Australian shores, so they joined the AIF and the air force. Jack, too, was eager to join the overseas war effort: 'We were all very young and . . . the major consideration was to get there and become involved.'[21] In joining the militia, however, Jack had committed to three years' service in Australia, unless sooner lawfully discharged, dismissed or removed. Even so, he requested a release but he had become such a valuable member his commanding officer would not let him go.

Jack was determined to go overseas but he did not enlist in the AIF. Like many young men of the time, he was attracted to flying: to the 'excitement, it was something new, I think we all look up to the air, even today, and see aeroplanes and think, isn't it wonderful the way they stay up. I liked the thought of it.'[22] Certainly, growing up in the 1920s and '30s, Jack heard of many thrilling events in Australia's rapidly expanding aviation industry; aerial exploits were covered in the press with great enthusiasm and talked about constantly. The country was 'air-minded'[23] and it would have been hard not to be inspired by the daring deeds of a small band of pilots, many with experience over the Great War battlefields. As well as listening to and reading about the aerial achievements of the interwar years, Jack was influenced by the battlefield experiences of Clem Shaddock and his Uncle Bob.[24]

Clem had enlisted in the AIF on 27 July 1915. He was a reinforcement to the 13th Battalion and served in Egypt, Belgium and France. During its illustrious career the 13th Battalion experienced much bloody trench warfare. It saw its first major action at Pozières in France in August 1916, when Clem was not much past his nineteenth birthday. On 11 April 1917, as part of the 4th Brigade of the 4th

Division, it attacked strong German positions at Bullecourt without the promised armoured support and with casualties of 21 officers and 546 other ranks.[25] It fought at Messines and Passchendaele and later advanced to the Hindenburg Line, and in March and April 1918 played its part in halting the German spring offensive. It also participated in the fighting near Amiens on 8 August 1918 which was perhaps the greatest single day's success on the Western Front. The 13th Battalion suffered 1090 killed and 2128 wounded, including many who were gassed. Clem only suffered minor wounds during his service but he was well aware of the suffering and misery of trench warfare and furious battle.[26]

Bob Hutton had enlisted in August 1915 at the age of 41, when the general enlistment age for the Australian Imperial Force was nineteen to 38.[27] He was only of slight build and had a gentle disposition; he did not have to serve, but he did so as it was his duty. He left Australia in December 1915 as a 3rd Battalion reinforcement, joining it on the Western Front in June 1916. On 20 July, the battalion marched toward Albert, France, to take part in the capture of Pozières, the Australian 1st Division's first major operation in France. An attack was launched on the night of 22–23 July, with the 3rd Battalion attempting to storm a line immediately south and parallel to the main Albert–Bapaume road. Bob missed the main attack as he had been wounded in the left arm by enemy small arms fire, possibly as he moved to the start line. He was one of the battalion's 350 other ranks who were wounded during the period 22–29 July 1916. His injury was not serious but he was evacuated to the Australian General Hospital in Rouen. Bob recovered well and returned to the battalion but contracted trench foot, caused by the prolonged exposure of the feet to the damp and cold. Bob served with the 3rd Battalion through its continued operations in the Somme Valley and in the difficult conditions around Ypres in Belgium until he was invalided to Australia in September 1917 with a double inguinal hernia, from which he never fully recovered.[28] His experiences revisited him each fortnight as he received his war pension and set off to visit his army friends. The lifelong legacy of his service was a metal back brace and limp, and in later years he used a walking stick.

Bob was never strong of limb, and did not have a great deal of energy, but he was strong in family loyalty and his nephews had a great love and affection for him. Both Clem and Bob would occasionally

17

talk of their war experiences, underplaying their suffering. Although Jack could not fully understand the horrors his uncle and Clem Shaddock had endured—'for those that did not experience that era, to me, it is hard to visualise such stark, purposeless misery of static trench warfare'—he was well aware of the effects of their wars.[29]

Jack applied to join the Royal Australian Air Force (RAAF) during May 1940, about two weeks after his brother Phil.[30] Applicant numbers at that time were overwhelming. Jack, like many others, was put on the reserve list and received his reserve badge and an instruction book which contained brief details of aircraft engines and airframes, elementary navigation, meteorology, theory of flight and other subjects that he would cover in more depth when training formally commenced.[31] It was recognised that, although keen, a large proportion of these men did not have adequate educational qualifications and would probably struggle with the technical coursework in the initial training schools. Jack was not the only one to have left school to contribute to the family income. In 1939, only 16.4 per cent of men between the ages of eighteen and 28 held a state intermediate certificate or better. To address this, the RAAF devised night and weekend courses to provide trainees with a consistent technical knowledge. These courses were commonly known as the 'twenty-one lessons' and they included mathematics, basic navigation, aerodynamics, King's regulations, air force administration and law and Morse code.[32] Jack was no stranger to study. He had passed his exams for promotion in the 30th Battalion and in 1939 had received his intermediate certificate from the Bankers' Institute of Australia. Jack worked diligently and had no difficulty with the 'twenty-one lessons'. He was well prepared for the technical work he would undertake when his training commenced.

Jack was not the only one of the group of Commonwealth Bank friends to leave the 30th Battalion. Corporal Nugent and Anthony Booth joined the AIF in May 1940; Duncan MacRae was called up to the RAAF on the same day as Jack and Roy Beveridge joined in April 1941. While Jack forged a fine service career, his friends were not so fortunate. One by one they fell. The first was Anthony Nugent. Now a lieutenant with the 2/13th Battalion, he was killed in action on 29 November 1941 when the battalion was carrying out a counterattack at El Duda, south of Tobruk.[33] Jack's old school friend, Pilot Officer Roy Beveridge, was posted to 4 Squadron RAAF and died on 1 May 1942 when his Wirraway struck a tree near Howlong, east of Wodonga, apparently during a forced landing approach. Beveridge and his navigator, Sergeant Bruce Smith, were killed instantly and the aircraft was destroyed.[34] Corporal Anthony Booth, a driver with the 9th Division Carrier Company, contracted malaria shortly after disembarking at Milne Bay in August 1943. It reoccurred in December and was followed by a bout of scrub typhus. He died on 9 February 1944.[35] The last to die of Jack's Commonwealth Bank friends was Flying Officer Duncan MacRae, who was posted to 118 Squadron RAF. On 23 August 1944, MacRae had been one of four pilots detailed to carry out a formation and cine-camera exercise. Attempting to avoid bad weather, MacRae had flown into cloud and lost control. About a minute later, his Spitfire dived into the sea off Peterhead, Scotland.[36] Anthony Nugent, Roy Beveridge, Anthony Booth and Duncan MacRae were four of the 307 Commonwealth Bank staff members who died in service. All have been included on the bank's Honour Roll.[37]

3

Bradfield Park, Narromine and Macleod

'I insisted that I wanted to be a pilot'

There was much positive news about Australia's war involvement as 1940 drew to a close. General Wavell, Commander-in-Chief Middle East, had launched his planned offensive against the Italians with a combined British, Indian and Australian force. Within days, Sidi Barrani and Sollum in the Western Desert were captured, thousands of Italians were taken prisoner and Australian troops had consolidated around Bardia. Australia's Lieutenant General Thomas Blamey was appointed as General Officer Commanding AIF, and 3 Squadron RAAF's tally against the Regia Aeronautica, the Italian air force, was mounting. Against this backdrop of military success, Jack's papers from RAAF recruitment arrived, advising that he had been called up for enlistment as an Aircraftman Class II and requesting that he report to 2 Recruitment Centre, Woolloomooloo at 8.30 a.m. on 6 January 1941.[1] Phil Davenport also received his papers about the same time, but reported two days earlier than Jack, and was off immediately to 1 Initial Training School, Somers, Victoria.

After all the formalities were completed, including medical exams and X-rays, the short arm parade, the swearing-in, and the issuing of the air force numbers that would identify them for the duration of the war and beyond, the brand new airmen were driven to 2 Initial Training School, Bradfield Park at Lindfield on Sydney's North Shore. It is not likely any of the recruits expected a warm welcome when they arrived at the school, but they probably did not expect the first words they would hear as they approached the main gate would be the shouts of 'You'll be sorry!' from those who had started an earlier course.[2]

Jack and his fellow trainees were still wearing civvies at this stage, as their uniforms would not be issued for a few more days. If anyone had any illusions about the air force, thinking life in the services would be a glamorous joke divorced from death, they would have been quickly disillusioned when they received their identification disks. Known as 'dead meat tags', the recruits had to hammer their name, service number and religion onto them.[3] If their bodies were rendered unrecognisable by battle or accident, these tags would probably still be readable, so they could be identified.

Shortly after he arrived, Jack was told he would be trained as a wireless operator/air gunner. This was not welcome news: 'I insisted that I wanted to be a pilot. They said that if I did well on my wireless operator's course that I'd be remustered as a pilot.'[4] Jack applied himself during the month-long course and attained first place in his exams: 'I did well and was remustered.'[5]

Jack soon met Bruce Daymond and Allan Ada.[6] Bruce's was a very different background from Jack's. His father was a successful manufacturer with business links throughout Australia and overseas and the family lived in affluent Haberfield and Vaucluse before moving to Mosman in 1934. Bruce attended the prestigious Scots College in Bellevue Hill and, after taking his leaving certificate in 1935, studied economics at Sydney University. Before he enlisted, he worked in the accounts department at Qantas. Allan Ada lived in Drummoyne. Like Jack, he had attended Sydney Boys High, but was seven years Jack's senior. After gaining his leaving certificate, Allan enrolled at the Metropolitan Business College and Sydney Technical College. He was employed as a delivery clerk in a furniture factory when he enlisted.[7] Despite the age and social differences, the three clicked. Allan possessed a quiet reserve that was appealing, and Jack and Bruce were drawn to him. Jack and Bruce had their own fair share of commonsense. They were not hell raisers, they knew how to have fun, but they also displayed a quiet maturity that appealed to Allan. Jack and Bruce nicknamed Allan 'Pop', and they spent much of their spare time together.

Jack was at Bradfield Park for another month after he transferred from the wireless operator/air gunner course. There was plenty of time to spend with his new friends, but the technical work was demanding and the physical training just as challenging in its own way. Jack and his course mates were subjected to regular drills, route marches and exercises. Jack was already fit from sporting activities and the militia, and had experienced the army's particular brand of discipline, so he had few surprises from the Bradfield Park curriculum. He worked hard and achieved first place in his exams. Bruce and Allan passed their exams as well and, along with the entire course which crowded the school's gymnasium, listened expectantly to the announcement of their new postings. All three heard they were bound for 5 Elementary Flying Training School at Narromine in western New South Wales.

Jack, Bruce and Allan arrived at Narromine early on 6 March 1941. It was a bitterly cold autumn morning and, almost before they could find their bearings, Jack and his fellow 10 Course trainees were divided into flights; Jack and Bruce Daymond were in A Flight.[8] Soon, they were shown the controls of the school's De Havilland DH 82 Tiger Moths, dual controlled aircraft that could be flown from either seat. In practice, however, the trainee sat in the rear cockpit and his instructor in the front.

The next day, Jack and his fellow trainees were out of bed at the crack of dawn. After a quick breakfast of tea and toast, they headed to the flight offices. Early morning was the best time to fly, when the air was usually still, and the first flying slots were always reserved for new students. If it became too windy, flying would be cancelled as the new boys were not skilled enough to cope with the bumpy air. With experience, they would fly later in the day, taking whatever the weather brought. The cold wind whipped around corners and through their heavy-duty blue overalls, known as goon skins, as Jack and his friends huddled around their instructor while he briefed them on the drill for starting the Tiger Moth: chocks secure, petrol on, throttle set, contact, swing the propeller and flick the switch. Bruce Daymond took his first familiarisation flight that morning, but Jack was not so lucky. His instructor, Sergeant Ivan McSparron, explained the Tiger's controls and allowed him to feel them, but that was all. But Jack did not have long to wait. On 8 March 1941 he climbed into the rear cockpit of Tiger Moth N9266 for his first flight. Finally, he was in the air; the dream was real. Sergeant McSparron showed Jack the boundaries of where A Flight pilots were allowed to fly. He explained the effects of the controls and let Jack handle them briefly.

That first flight was 50 minutes long and seemed to be over before it began. Even so, it heralded 'two months of intensive flying training on Tiger Moths'.[9]

Jack, Bruce and Allan shared a hut and spent much of their rare spare time together. On weekend passes Jack and his friends would go into Narromine to have a drink and meal at the Court House Hotel or to meet the locals. With his easy manner and ability to draw people out in conversation, Jack soon made a number of other friends among the trainees, including John Martin, Ian Morse, Ian Thomson, Rex Marre, Charlie Lark, Ken May, Jim Kearns, Bill Campbell, Bill Clark and Gordon 'Stumpy' Lee. Most were young men, all with uncertain futures and they would occasionally cut loose in the huts with pillow fights or races around the bunks, or head off to the pub or the occasional woolshed dance on a nearby property. Jack enjoyed the lighter moments of friendship with the larger group, but it was with Bruce Daymond and Allan Ada that he developed the closest bond. He was never one to waste words and so the simple note in his diary that 'they are great pals'[10] tells much more than a few wordy paragraphs.

Jack made his first solo flight on 19 March 1941 in Tiger Moth A1725 and it was not long before he was flying six days a week— climbing and steep turns, side slips, aerobatics, forced landings and how to prepare to abandon the aircraft, as well as long flights and low-flying exercises. By the time he made his last flight in A1789 on 26 April, the day after his final assessment, he had flown 29 hours dual and 25.10 hours solo and was assessed as above average. Jack was always very modest and when he noted his achievement in his diary, he simply stated he had 'scraped a pass of 88 per cent . . . luckily being first on course at flying'.[11]

Jack, Bruce and Allan were all recommended for multi-engined aircraft—bombers.[12] This was what Jack wanted. While many young men had been influenced by the exploits of the Great War fighter aces and Battle of Britain veterans, Jack did not want to fly fighters. He relished the potential for personal challenge and thought the demands on a bomber pilot were greater than those in a single-engine aircraft.[13] He also 'thought you were flying with somebody else for whom you were responsible and who had some responsibility towards you.'[14] Accepting this responsibility was a commitment that would last even until death—if an aircraft was damaged, on fire, or under devastating attack, the pilot was expected to stay at the controls until all his crew had baled out.

Jack and his friends reported to 2 Embarkation Depot, Bradfield Park, on 7 May 1941. Canada was soon confirmed as their destination and, on 16 May, they were told they would be embarking soon. Their days had been full of drill and physical training so, knowing they had a long voyage ahead of them, they came up with a plan for a different, much more congenial, form of exercise.

Bill Campbell and John Martin, two of the 10 Course graduates from Narromine, were members of Elanora Country Club. It was a beautiful, clear day, perfect for enjoying the advantages of the club which, at its highest point, boasted a commanding view of the coastline from the Hawkesbury River in the north, right down past South Head. The lure of a day in the sun away from Bradfield Park was too much to resist and a group of eager golfers was soon recruited. Some had leave passes. Ian Thomson, another Narromine graduate, had forgotten his, but at least he had had one in the first place. Jack, Allan Ada and Bruce Daymond, however, would be absent without leave. Jack later good-naturedly accused Bruce of leading him astray that day but it seems he was a willing participant; they thought the day out would be worth the risk.[15]

The boys put their goon skins over their uniforms and snuck out in a couple of cars. Ian Thomson drove one of them, with Jack hiding under a blanket on the floor of the back seat, and Bruce risking asphyxiation in the boot. They drove past the guard with ease and were soon on their way, after a brief stop so Bruce and Jack could emerge from their uncomfortable positions.[16]

The pale blue water glistened as they viewed it from Elanora's heights and Jack enjoyed the day. He later recalled that 'the golf was hilarious' and he had much trouble extracting himself from the bunker on the eighteenth.[17] He maintained fond memories of that illicit game of golf: 'It was a happy occasion . . . and it is significant that every occasion at [Elanora] has been a happy one for me ever since—despite my golf.'[18]

Jack's day on the golf links and his final hours with his family on Monday 19 May 1941 were some of his last carefree moments before embarkation. After final parade on 20 May, a draft of 244 officers and airmen climbed into the four awaiting double-decker buses.[19] Despite the sense of the great adventure ahead, and many of his fellow trainees hanging out the windows waving gleefully to the passers-by, Jack travelled quietly to Darling Harbour where they boarded RMMS *Aorangi*, a 17,491 gross tonnage passenger ship of the Canadian–Australasian Line.[20]

Early next morning, Jack and Bruce went up to the deck. They were only partly dressed and it was still dark, with a chill in the air. As the *Aorangi* glided under the Sydney Harbour Bridge, escorted by HMAS *Adelaide*, they heard a woman's plaintive cry: 'Goodbye, Charlie. I love you. Come back soon.'[21] It was an unsettling start to the voyage but even so Jack did not consider that he and his friends might not return: 'One didn't contemplate the possibilities of anything happening to you.'[22] Jack and Bruce stayed on deck as the *Aorangi* and her escort passed through the heads. Later that day, the commanding officer, Pilot Officer White, made Jack flight commander of 1 Flight, who was responsible for a variety of administrative tasks during the voyage, including compiling the watch rosters, posting reliefs and conducting inspections.

Shipboard life was pleasant. There were the inevitable lectures and physical training, but there was ample time to relax. Films were shown, there was plenty of swimming, table tennis, deck games and sports, and opportunities to sneak into the out-of-bounds first-class lounge abounded. There were also plenty of chances to let off steam, including cabin raids, 'some scamperings round the deck' and, on one occasion, the forcible and totally hilarious removal of eleven moustaches. There were many quiet times on board where Jack could play bridge, read, lounge about, keep up with the inevitable mending and washing or write the first of many letters home. There was usually something to do to crowd out the occasional melancholy moment, but not always. On 28 May 1941, the sea was rough and Jack was assailed by loneliness: 'Today seems to be a day of reflections as I keep thinking of everybody at home . . . [and] wish to see them again.' However, Jack would not let himself succumb to despondency: he set off to bed early 'to rid myself of that idea'.[23]

The highlight of the voyage was the RAAF concert. Friendships that had developed at Narromine were cemented aboard the *Aorangi*. It was all laughter as Jack, Bruce, Allan, John Martin, Ian Morse, Ian Thomson, Rex Marre, Charlie Lark, Ken May, Jim Kearns and

Gordon 'Stumpy' Lee, billing themselves as the 'Narromine Choir', prepared their skit for the show that was to take place on 9 June 1941, Jack's 21st birthday. After the Narromine Choir's final rehearsal Jack was 'lured' into the first-class smoking lounge. Awaiting him was a tray of fancy biscuits, courtesy of their steward, and the one and only bottle of champagne on board, which the boys had somehow scavenged. Cork popped, Jack's friends all drank his health. As the Narromine Choir waited to take their place on stage, an announcement was made and Jack was pushed to the front of the stage to receive the congratulations of the entire ship's complement.

After joining in the opening number, Jack, gifted with a clear baritone, lined up as one of 'The Terrible Three' performing *Three Little Pigs*. The Narromine Choir took another turn on stage singing an old Australian favourite, 'Waltzing Matilda'. Before they knew it, it was time for their feature item, *Corroboree*, a send up of the Haka, which the New Zealanders had performed at their earlier concert. The crowd applauded appreciatively and it was a festive, riotous night of much laughter.

The *Aorangi* sailed into Vancouver Gulf at sunset on 12 June 1941. After an informal gathering where many autograph books were signed, Jack packed, did some washing and went to bed early. He was woken by Pilot Officer White to 'dig out seven chaps to transfer . . . to single-engine planes'. When the seven were selected, Jack went on deck to watch as the *Aorangi* tied up at Victoria. They had arrived in Canada. It was all very quiet, but the peacefulness of his first Canadian night did not last. Before he had a chance to return to his cabin, he:

> Discovered quite by chance that Bruce and I had been transferred to single-engines so bolted and saw the [commanding officer] who heard my tale of woe and said not to worry, and adjusted the matter for us. Only thirty-six chaps went to multis while sixty-four went to singles. Bruce and I were very relieved when the adjustment was made.[24]

The next morning, the RAAF contingent marched ashore, straight to the railway station to begin the journey to their training stations. They sped along to Calgary, in Alberta where Jack and those destined for bombers left the train. The would-be fighter pilots would travel on to Ottawa, the navigators to Toronto and the gunners to Winnipeg.

Only eight from Narromine were destined for 7 Service Flying Training School, Fort Macleod, Alberta, which had been established in December 1940 as part of Canada's commitment to the Empire Air Training Scheme (EATS), known in Canada as the Commonwealth Air Training Plan.[25] Jack's group would be part of 31 Course, the school's eighth course. It was a difficult break for Jack and he was overwhelmed by sadness as he farewelled fellow members of the Narromine Choir.[26]

After six hours' leave in Calgary, Jack, Bruce Daymond, Allan Ada and the others about to embark on bomber training climbed aboard the train to Fort Macleod, arriving at about 10.30 p.m on 14 June 1941. Tired as he was, and wanting a long overdue meal and a good night's sleep, Jack found a moment to take notice of the station's Avro Ansons, and thought they seemed 'quite formidable after Tigers'.[27]

When the trainees were introduced to the station commander, Wing Commander Arthur L. James, the Chief Instructor, Wing Commander Mair and the Chief Ground Instructor, Squadron Leader Bawlf, Jack discovered a great difference between the ethos at Macleod and that at Bradfield Park. There, the EATS trainees had often been the victims of resentment by pre-war RAAF staff who addressed them roughly and often called them 'scum and everything lower'.[28] Here, they were called 'gentlemen' and treated with respect. Nothing seemed too much trouble. Jack thought Wing Commander James and his instructors 'seemed great coves . . . They seem rather casual and yet treat us as men'.[29]

The Royal Canadian Air Force (RCAF) did not stint on facilities for its trainees. Jack and his friends soon found themselves in large, well-insulated wooden huts with internal bathrooms, all centrally heated to protect against the cold. The facilities were a strong contrast to Bradfield Park with its bare huts, wire beds all in a row and outside ablution blocks and toilets.[30]

The huts hosted trainees from Canada, Australia, Great Britain, Singapore and Ceylon. There was not always harmony and, in particular, there were some tensions between the Australians and Canadians. On one occasion, Jack encountered congestion in the showers from all the first-light risers rushing to take their wake-up shower. He snidely noted, however, that it was only the Australians as the Canadians never seemed to wash.[31] The Canadians also preferred their huts to be warm at night while the Australians preferred things a little cooler: 'We'd switch the heating off, they'd switch it on. We'd switch it off, they'd switch it on. So we solved that problem by putting a boot through the window.'[32]

Jack's early opinion of the Ansons was soon confirmed and they seemed 'even more formidable at close range'.[33] He took his first training flight on 21 June 1941 in Anson 6484 and, on 24 June, his first Anson solo in 6348. He considered that he 'flew quite well except the last landing was a bit on the nose'.[34]

After lunch was a talk by the medical officer and their first lecture, then the trainees elected their section seniors. Jack's sense of responsibility had been recognised by his militia superiors and this was acknowledged when he was chosen to represent Red Section. He was also elected senior pupil of his course out of 45 trainees, which meant he was responsible for the welfare and performance of his fellow trainees, and in charge of organising their social activities—he started off by scheduling a concert party for the next weekend. Bruce Daymond had early on recognised Jack's qualities and was not surprised at Jack's election. Nor was he surprised when Jack went on to more senior positions in his air force career.[35]

With his love of sport, Jack had developed many skills needed by a pilot—agility, physical strength, good hand–eye co-ordination, mental alertness and the ability to 'read the game' and make split-second decisions—but he needed much more before he could receive his wings. As at Narromine, there were frequent lectures, flying practice as often as possible and constant exams. Jack wanted to do well and appreciated that the success of any future operation and the safety of his crew would depend on honed skills, meticulous care and attention to detail. He studied constantly and revised his coursework assiduously, and if he could not fly he would be under the hood in the Link trainer, which was used to train pilots to 'fly blind' at night or in cloud.[36]

As Jack was training on multi-engined aircraft, it was likely his posting would be to Bomber Command with nightly bomb runs. His first night flying session was on 15 July 1941. First, he did a couple of circuits under dual control, then went solo and 'had some fun. It is great flying and went quite well considering.'[37] Over the next few nights he carried out a number of night flying exercises, some more successful than others. That of 17 July was marred by a bad cross wind but 19 July saw good flying with a rare treat at the end: 'It certainly is a great sight to see the dawn break when up in the air.' He notched up his first ten night-flying hours on 22 July, after a low-flying effort from which he saw the lit-up streets of Lethbridge with the townsfolk looking upwards at his Anson: 'So ended my first ten hours night flying. It is a great experience and [I] felt [it] to be quite an accomplishment.' Jack's high did not last long when, two nights later, he was fined for taxiing with flaps down. Apart from that, he thought his first cross-country exercise had gone well. Fortunately, so did his instructor and he was rated 'satisfactory'.[38]

Jack thought the training at Macleod was of better quality than at Narromine[39] but he could not say that about one of the instructors, Flying Officer Weimer. Luckily, Jack did not strike him often but the times he did were memorable. Weimer, an American who had joined the RCAF, was the instructor from hell. On 26 June 1941, Jack had a 'terrible fifty minutes' with Weimer. He was 'yelling and screaming ceaselessly from [the] time we left the ground till we returned. He did not allow me to go solo and I was justifiably ropable'.[40] Jack did not hide his anger. He fumed into the pupils' room after the flight and told Bruce Daymond that Weimer had whinged constantly from the moment they had taken off.[41] If Weimer proved a prime example of how not to train new pilots, Flying Officer Angus MacLean, who was the officer in charge of C Flight, showed Jack how it should be done. Jack's first impression, that he seemed to be 'a very nice chap', was borne out.[42] MacLean's pupils found him a supportive and skilled instructor and Jack took his example of equanimity to his future instructional duties.

Time passed in a blur of lectures and instruction on instruments and navigation, flights in the warm weather with its ideal flying conditions, and constant cramming and revision. All too soon, Jack's training at 7 Service Flying Training School was nearly over. By the time he did his wings test on 21 August 1941, Jack thought he was 'flying like a veteran'.[43] As Jack and his friends awaited their wings parade, the occasion that marked the successful completion of their service flying training, they participated in a local fundraising event. Starting a pattern of community involvement that lasted all his life, Jack and his friends performed in a 'Carnival of Music' program to raise money for the swimming pool fund, singing for over 1000 people. The concert was later reported as a great success.[44]

Jack considered that 30 August 1941 was *the* day of his air force career: it was the day on which he received his wings, the symbol of dedication, status and qualification that he was a pilot. It was a proud day and he was quietly pleased to learn he had come top of the course, obtaining the highest average ever obtained at Macleod.[45] Years later, when asked how he rated himself as a pilot when he had received his wings, Jack modestly replied 'not as well as the instructor did.'[46]

Two days later, they were all lined up and the commissions were read out: 'Pilot Officer Davenport' was the first. Jack was pleased when Bruce Daymond was commissioned, but 'it was quite a disappointment that "Pop" Ada missed out'.[47] Jack and his friends experienced their first rank-imposed separation when, after receiving the white armbands denoting their new status, he and his fellow officers were called up before the commanding officer who congratulated them and then escorted them to the officers' mess. The separation of close friends was further enforced soon afterwards when they began their next train trip across Canada. Allan, like the other sergeant pilots, was excluded from first class.

It was a long trip east with a number of stop-offs. They arrived at Fairview, near the Halifax embarkation depot, on 9 September 1941, where Jack and Bruce met up with Allan Ada. The next day, they encountered old friends from Narromine also stationed at Fairview as they awaited their next postings. Finally, after a few days kicking up their heels in town, dining at good restaurants, buying gifts for loved ones and much needed luggage items, and then scuffing their toes on an unwelcome route march, Jack and his friends learned their next destinations—Jack and Allan Ada to the United Kingdom for operational training and Bruce Daymond to Charlottetown, Prince Edward Island, for a general reconnaissance course.[48]

Before they went their separate ways, they organised what they called their 'separation dinner' at the Nova Scotia Hotel.[49] As well as Jack, Bruce and Allan, that farewell meal was shared by a large group of Australians bound by the ties of nationality, duty, training experiences and friendship. There were so many they could not sit at the same table. It was a good night with a fine meal, laughter and shared memories. They pushed on to a show after dinner, cramming as much fun and companionship as they could into those last precious hours. Jack, Bruce and Allan in particular felt the keen sadness of parting from those to whom they had grown close. They had shared much over the last few months and were now to be separated by geography and rank. Jack, an officer, and Allan, a sergeant, could not travel together. Jack did not usually confide deep emotions to his diary and later wrote simply that 'it was quite a break' when Bruce left for Charlottetown.[50] Recalling their separation many years later, Bruce Daymond said it all: 'I was busting up from my two chums. You made other friends of course but we'd become pretty close. We'd done a lot together.'[51]

4

Operational training

'there were lots of hazards'

Jack boarded the *Umtalia* on 15 September 1941 and caught his first glimpse of land while he was on watch during the evening of 28 September. The *Umtalia* travelled up the Firth of Clyde, dropped anchor at Greenock and before he knew it, Jack was whisked away by train to London. Then to Waterloo by RAF bus where he caught the train to Bournemouth, on the English coast, about 100 miles from London, and the RAF reception centre where thousands of airmen awaited processing to their next stage of training.

As the *Umtalia* sailed up the Clyde, Jack had seen 'one crater and a wrecked building or two', his first signs of a nation ravaged by enemy bombing.[1] He experienced his first air raid alert at a Bournemouth cinema, but he ignored the siren warning and stayed to watch the show. His blasé attitude soon disappeared, however. The next evening, he was having a drink at the Bath Tap, one of the local hostelries, when he heard two loud explosions. The windows smashed and the patrons flung themselves down. When he realised what was happening, he too dropped to the floor.

Jack's three weeks at Bournemouth were a period of marking time and he filled the days as best he could: weekends with host families courtesy of Lady Frances Ryder and Miss MacDonald of the Isles Dominion Hospitality Scheme,[2] leave in London where he toured the Tower of London and saw the bomb damage to Westminster Abbey, drinks sessions at the Bath Tap, local day trips, evenings at the cinema, billiards, the RAF v the Pay Corps football match, reading, walking, and always writing letters home. Despite enjoying many of England's attractions, Jack felt much frustration as there was 'still no sign of a posting'.[3] He may have chafed at the delay, but his hiatus from training had one highlight when he met Pilot Officer Alan Bowman.

Alan was a Queenslander, born in Boonah in 1914. Like Jack, he had served in the militia during the inter-war years and was a white-collar worker, employed as a shipping clerk for ten years before enlisting in the air force in October 1940. After initial training at Bradfield Park, Alan did elementary training at 8 Elementary Flying Training School, Narrandera, where he was mustered as a pilot. He was scrubbed from pilot training when he failed because of inadequate training from an instructor who had gone absent without leave.[4] Remustered as a navigator, he travelled to Canada for further training. When he arrived at Bournemouth, he was still wearing his airman's uniform as he awaited his officer's uniform. He wasn't even wearing sergeants' stripes. Jack, already proudly wearing his officer's uniform, noticed the inappropriately attired Australian in the officers' mess and chided him for it. Jack soon realised Alan had every right to be in the officers' mess and laughed at the mix-up.[5] Jack was again drawn to the apparent stability and maturity of an older man and they soon became good friends.

On 23 October, Jack was told he was posted to 2 Central Flying School, Church Lawford, Warwickshire, to become an instructor. This was not what he expected; he wanted an operational posting and 'did not want to miss all the fun instructing'.[6] One of Jack's new friends, who was married and had children, was posted to Bomber Command. Although he would do his duty as directed, the ties of a husband and father were strong. When Jack mentioned he was to be an instructor, they decided to ask the commanding officer if they could swap their postings.[7] He was amenable and four days later Jack was posted to 14 (Bomber) Operational Training Unit at Cottesmore, Rutland, to train on Handley Page Hampdens.

Cottesmore was a permanent RAF station. Its runway was simply a grass field, flat and stable when dry but boggy when wet. Jack was impressed by its brick buildings, comfortable messes and his modern quarters. He was surprised by the number of instructors wearing Distinguished Flying Cross ribbons and was amazed at how young they were. They were veterans, tour-expired survivors of 30 operations or more. Their experience was displayed on their chests and seen in their eyes. Ironically, Jack would not be much older when, just before his 23rd birthday, he would be awarded his own Distinguished Flying Cross which, shortly after, he wore as an instructor at 1 Torpedo Training Unit, Turnberry.

It was some time before Jack's mail caught up with him after the move to Cottesmore but, when it arrived on 3 November, it was not the treat he had expected. One of his letters gave him the sad news that his grandmother had died. For many years, Louise Hutton had relied on her inner strength to battle against circumstance. At long last, life had improved and she enjoyed a number of years of stability and security in her Kyle Bay home with her son, daughter, son-in-law and grandchildren. In recent months, she had succumbed to ill health and had to move from the comfort of her family to a nursing home. On 27 August 1941, with her youngest grandson Keith present, the woman who had been such a support to Jack's family passed away.

As is often the way, grief can be assuaged by occupation. Jack was made captain of his squad and was put into A Flight but, because of the inclement weather, he was denied the very activity guaranteed to set aside all thoughts of home, his family and the loss of his grandmother. Jack's last solo flight had been back at Macleod on 28 August. After such a long break from flying, Jack was concerned about losing his skills. After morning lectures on 18 November 1941, he carried out two circuits on dual control and then went off solo. He completed fourteen circuits and bumps and thought that he had 'never landed the old Anson better'.[8] This appears to have been an achievement as the grassy landing area, subject to landings from trainees of many different calibres, 'was terrible, all holes and bumps and one great hollow and [the Anson] bumped like blazes on take-off'. Jack was pleased with his first solo at Cottesmore, 'it restored all my confidence'.[9]

Jack and his fellow pilots soon felt the pressure to 'crew up'. Usually, airmen were thrown into a room and told to form crews. Amazingly, this more often than not proved successful and men of many disparate tastes, experiences, backgrounds and personalities formed strong and cohesive bonds. John Pearson recalled they were all milling around with seemingly little purpose when Jack 'picked on me'. Pearson did not have the chance to fly with Jack as he came down with pneumonia shortly afterwards and his operational training was deferred until he recovered.[10] Jack's first choice for navigator may have been haphazard but his second was not. Alan Bowman was a navigator without a pilot so, as they had clicked as friends, they decided to team up.

Jack's first flight with Alan was a navigational exercise on 25 November 1941. It was a cloudy day and visibility was so bad Jack had to fly under the clouds, at about 300 feet. They still missed one of their landmarks but managed to return to base with little trouble. Despite the visibility problems, it was a good flight and Jack later indicated he did not regret his decision to crew up with Alan.[11] Their next trip, however, was not as successful. Again, visibility was bad and they became lost, eventually finding their way without having to resort to radio communications with base. Jack still considered it a good trip as several others had failed to return in good time.[12]

Jack repeated his early success in the Anson on a number of occasions and on 9 December 1941 was deemed ready to take his first familiarisation flight in the Hampden. The British Handley Page HP.52 Hampden was a twin-engine medium bomber with a crew of four. It was powered by two Bristol Pegasus XVIII radial engines, had a single stage blower and used three-bladed De Havilland controllable-pitch propellers. It had a maximum speed of 265 miles per hour at 15,500 feet and a cruising speed of 217 miles per hour at 15,000 feet. It was armed with six .303-inch machine guns, one of which was operated by the pilot.[13] Jack knew 'it was a big change to go from the Anson to the Hampden, a very different aeroplane, a much more powerful aeroplane, despite its age'.[14]

The Hampden was already obsolete, or at least obsolescent, but Jack thought it 'a lovely aircraft to fly. You had to not be afraid of it and be prepared to throw it around'; he had 'a grand time' flying it.[15] Despite his fondness for the Hampden, he recognised 'there were lots of hazards' and disadvantages.[16] With its long, narrow fuselage— only about 3 feet wide, which led to it being dubbed the 'flying suitcase', the 'flying pencil' or the 'flying coffin'—the Hampden was extremely uncomfortable for the pilot, who could not move from his seat while in flight, even if wounded.[17] It was also notoriously difficult to learn to fly. It tended to stall and was prone to a vicious swing to port if the correct airspeed had not been attained when taking off.

•

Many young pilots lost their lives while on operational training—out of every 100 airmen who arrived at a Bomber Command operational training unit, 51 would be killed on combat operations, twelve would be killed or injured in non-operational accidents and twelve would be taken prisoner of war. Only 25 would survive.[18] Despite the chilling possibilities, no-one dwelt on them. Jack, however, was confronted with a devastating loss on 13 December 1941. The day started innocuously enough, with early morning Link training and an hour on circuits. That afternoon, he enjoyed an 'away' football match against a team from a nearby RAF station. He damaged his toes by wearing boots that were too small, but he still thought it a good game with its eight–all result. When he returned to the station, he learned that one of his friends had been killed.

After the Narromine Choir had gone their separate training ways, Jack had become friends with Pilot Officer Anthony 'Tony' Webb, a member of the Royal Air Force Voluntary Reserve who, like Jack, had trained at Fort Macleod. Tony's wife lived locally and Jack and Tony had spent much time together over the last weeks, touring the local countryside or sharing meals as Joan Webb fussed over them in their little cottage.

Tony and Sergeant Kenneth Thornton had been killed while practising single-engine flying. During this exercise, the pilot would shut off one engine to simulate flying after an engine failure. As one engine then had to do the work of two, more power had to be added to keep the aircraft flying with control pressures at rudder and ailerons altered to cope with the loss of power on one side and more on the other. Care was needed as much could go wrong and, on this occasion, it did. Tony's aircraft had gone into a spin known as a 'stabilised yaw'.[19] With its long, thin tail and small-surfaced tail fins, the Hampden had limited stability. If the rudder was used coarsely, coupled with insufficient bank, a flat turn could suddenly become a terrifying sideways skid that rendered the ailerons useless and locked the rudders.[20] The only way to recover from a yaw was to have height. At about 6000 or 8000 feet, the pilot could put the Hampden's nose down and gradually pull out.[21] Tony had the height and was able to regain control but his Hampden stalled. He plummeted to the ground, crashing in flames.[22]

On this occasion Jack broke from his practice of not putting his emotions onto paper and noted in his diary that he 'went to [a] show in [the] evening to try and forget it'.[23] It was impossible to forget, however, and the next day he went to see Tony's wife, Joan. He stayed with her for some time, giving her comfort and friendship. She gratefully gave Jack Tony's tobacco pouch as a memento which, although he felt uncomfortable about it, he 'just had to take it'.[24] Over the next few days, Jack did what he could for Joan Webb. He returned Tony's bike and helped with the funeral arrangements. He had single-engine flying practice on the morning of the funeral and was pleased with the results, but he was fully aware of the irony that later that day he would be burying someone who had not been as successful as he at this exercise. Jack escorted Tony's father to the funeral service which he thought was impressive, celebrating the life of someone who had been prepared to die for his country. For him, it 'was sad saying farewell to Tony for the last time' and that night, grief mingling with homesickness, he read quietly for a time and wrote some letters.[25]

Jack was already familiar with the Hampden's many good qualities but soon he too would experience its deadly vice. With Alan Bowman as navigator and Sergeant Les Jonas as wireless operator/air gunner, Jack was practising steep turns over Spalding on 28 January 1942, six weeks before the end of his operational training. They had been scheduled for night flying and were taking Hampden P1205 for a daylight test to ensure it was serviceable and were also doing map-reading exercises. Jack had already flown with Alan on a number of exercises and this was the second time that Jonas had been with them.[26] There was an art to steep turns: the pilot had to keep the aircraft level. Alan would always good-naturedly criticise Jack when he executed a less-than-perfect turn and this occasion was no exception. With their final assessments due within a few weeks, Jack tried another, but in the opposite direction.[27] This time, so much pressure built up that the Hampden's nose perspex cracked and dislodged. Air rushed in, Jack lost control and the Hampden plunged into an almost vertical spin. Alan's navigational instruments went haywire, and pieces of perspex and anything not tied down were flying everywhere. Jack tried to regain control but could get no response from aileron and he felt as if the right rudder had come off. He told the crew to bale out and kept repeating this message over the intercom.[28]

Jonas jumped successfully, but Alan, in his position down in the Hampden's nose, had not heard Jack as his intercom had come out of its socket during the spin.[29] As the Hampden spun down, Alan was flat on the floor, unable to climb out of the nose because of the centrifugal forces. Even if he could, he was not wearing his parachute so would not have been able to jump unless he could struggle against the centrifugal forces to retrieve it from the stowage compartment.[30]

As the Hampden continued to plummet, the wind and centrifugal forces also affected Jack. His senses were overwhelmed and he was disorientated. He could not raise Alan on the intercom and could not see the escape hatch from his position. He had no way of knowing if Alan had already jumped or was still on board but injured. Jack finally spotted Alan through the vista panel so, even if he had entertained the idea of following Jonas out of the aircraft, he 'had to stay with it'.[31] Alan was able to grab his parachute and struggle into it. He was about to jump when he looked up and saw Jack's feet still on the rudder pedals. Jack had not baled! There was still a possibility Jack could regain control so Alan decided to stay.[32] At 4000 feet, Jack made a partial recovery 'using bags of rudder and aileron' but, 'owing to rudder locking on she span again the same way and I thought I'd "had" it'.[33]

Finally, at about 1500 feet, the Hampden responded to Jack's attempts to stabilise it. He pulled it out of the spin, but thought it was still flying badly. The Hampden was certainly in poor shape with no perspex, no bomb door, no brake pressure, the wireless operator's door open and the side of Jack's cockpit cover torn up. But that did not matter, they were safe. After circling to locate Jonas, Jack made a successful landing.[34] Jonas was eventually picked up after suffering his own shaky do—he'd been accosted by a shotgun-wielding local, fearful of an enemy invasion.[35]

After three months at Cottesmore, Jack had piloted the Hampden on 24 occasions, a total of less than nineteen hours. This was not much experience at the best of times and certainly not in a seemingly never-ending aerial plunge. For Jack, this was his 'closest shave so far', but there was no time to panic, no time for fear to set in.[36] He had only seconds to react and regain control of the Hampden and he did. But there was something other than reflexes instilled by discipline acquired over months of training that guided Jack's actions that day. He stayed at the controls because of his innate responsibility towards his crew. Alan might still be on board, and Jack was responsible for Alan's safety. Jack had originally wanted to fly multi-engined aircraft because of the challenge they offered and the sense of responsibility for a crew. His actions on this day proved he had made the correct choice and that he was a man of selfless courage and commitment.

Good training, quick responses and a cool head had paid off for Jack, and Alan Bowman recognised that his pilot was a skilled one. Many years later, Alan recalled how Jack 'acted automatically; automatic responses'. He may have criticised Jack's turns but Alan recognised good piloting had saved them from a tragedy that too many other crews had experienced.[37] Even so, Jack was still lucky. One in seven of Bomber Command losses occurred at training units[38] and Jack had already seen for himself the high death rate at Cottesmore with the loss of Tony Webb and many others during his short time there. It was a sobering day. After sharing the 'gen on what the Hampden does in a spin', Jack spent a quiet evening in the mess and then retired early, but the events of that day were not put to bed.[39] The *Daily Mirror* soon heard about Jack's save and, in an article headlined 'Stuck to plane for mate's sake', reported Jack's actions as 'one of the stories of heroism which come out of the war'.[40]

PART 2

First tour

Fresher Pilot, 455 Squadron, Bomber Command

'I was absolutely petrified of the searchlights'

Jack and Alan Bowman completed their final assessments a month after the stabilised yaw incident. Like many young men who had finished their training, they were anxious to take their turn at the enemy, especially at a time when the war was not progressing well for the Allies. There was the good news that, with the German invasion of Russia and the attack on Pearl Harbor, the Russians and Americans had now joined the Allies, but elsewhere the war news was bad. Australians were devastated to hear that HMAS *Sydney* had been lost with her entire complement, including Jack's school friend Sub-Lieutenant Bruce Elder; Hong Kong, as well as Singapore, the supposedly impregnable fortress, had fallen; Rommel had launched a counterattack in North Africa in late January, taking the British and Commonwealth forces by surprise; the Japanese had penetrated to the Australian mainland with the Darwin raids; and the evacuation of Rangoon was about to take place. Of particular interest to air force trainees in the United Kingdom, the British Navy and RAF had recently suffered embarrassment when the German battleships *Scharnhorst*, *Gneisenau* and *Prinz Eugen*, which had been penned up in Brest for some time, had escaped from under their noses through the English Channel and dashed off to their home ports.

By 1 March 1942, Jack had flown 155 hours 20 minutes and received an 'above average' assessment from the chief flying instructor. As modest as ever, even in his private moments, he noted in his diary that he was 'quite pleased'.[1] Many of his fellow trainees had already been posted and Jack spoke with the station adjutant about joining the same Australian squadron but nothing had yet eventuated.[2] So, with their clearances out of the way, Jack and Alan fixed some leave passes and headed off.

Their first stop was London, where they overnighted in a suite at the Mayfair, and then to Sway, where they stayed with one of Alan's cousins. While Alan enjoyed time with his relations, Jack went to nearby Bournemouth to meet his brother Phil, who had recently arrived in England.[3] After completing his initial training Phil had sailed to Rhodesia for elementary flying training at 26 Elementary Flying Training School, Guinea Fowl, service flying training at 22 Service Flying Training School, Thornhill, and a navigation reconnaissance course at the General Reconnaissance School, George, South Africa.[4]

Although not yet 22, Jack appeared to have matured beyond his years and, despite being pleased to see Jack after so long, Phil was nonplussed when his younger brother called out to him in greeting, 'Hi ya, son.'[5] For Jack, it was good to see his brother again after so much time apart.[6] They spent a few days together, relaxing and catching up. When he returned to Cottesmore, Jack was advised he had been posted to 455 Squadron RAAF.

455 Squadron RAAF was an Empire Air Training Scheme squadron that had had two separate formations. The first, with mainly ground crew, was at Williamtown, New South Wales on 23 May 1941. The second, with mainly RAF personnel, came into existence at Swinderby in the United Kingdom on 6 June 1941. The squadron was part of 5 Group, one of Bomber Command's six operational groups. Equipped with Hampdens, it was the first Australian Bomber Command squadron, participating in the strategic bombing campaign against Germany and carrying out a number of mine-laying sorties in dangerous waters. The squadron's first bombing raid was to Frankfurt on 29–30 August 1941 when it became the first Australian squadron to bomb Germany.[7] The 'firsts' did not stop there: it was generally believed it had been the first squadron to send an all-Australian crew—Pilot Officer Henry 'Mickey' Martin, Pilot Officer Jack Leggo, Sergeant Bertie 'Toby' Foxlee and Sergeant Tom 'Tammy' Simpson—on a raid over Germany on 21 February 1942.[8]

455 Squadron was administratively and operationally under the control of RAF Station Swinderby in Lincolnshire, but was located

about 7 miles away, at Wigsley, in the county of Nottinghamshire. It was surrounded by flat countryside and, although it had long concrete runways, the aircraft did not have hangars and were a long way from the flight buildings. To make matters worse, the accommodation huts were some distance from the mess. Jack thought Wigsley 'a grand 'drome with good runways' but he was not impressed with the distances or the facilities.[9]

While at Cottesmore, Jack and Alan Bowman had trained with an assortment of wireless operators. Now, on an operational squadron, they needed a complete crew of four. Although the squadron considered itself Australian, there was a shortage of Australian wireless operator/ air gunners, so many of these positions were filled by Royal Air Force airmen. RAF sergeants Ernest Smith, known as 'Ernie' or more often as 'Smithy', and Clifford Harrison, known to all as 'Harry', had been at the squadron for some time before Jack and Alan arrived and had already flown separately with other crews. Jack's diary does not record how Smithy and Harry joined his crew but in an interview many years after the war he indicated that, contrary to the usual practice of crews picking themselves, they had been allocated to Jack.[10]

Within days of arriving at 455 Squadron, Jack flew his first exercises with his complete and permanent crew of Alan as navigator, Smithy as wireless operator/upper gunner and Harry as lower rear gunner.[11] His verdict was 'they were all very good'.[12] The four personalities gelled and they worked together well in the Hampden's confined space under both easy and stressful circumstances. In the RAF, crew members usually addressed each other formally while on operations: 'pilot to navigator', 'gunner to navigator' and so on. But the four men agreed early on to use their first names and nicknames. Despite the informality, they all had great respect for each other and their abilities. Even though the officers and sergeants messed separately, they still shared a good friendship and developed a bond that lasted many years.[13]

Alan thought Jack was a 'first class' pilot[14] but there was at least one occasion when that belief was tested. Shortly after they took off on a cross-country exercise on the night of 25 March 1942, the flare path had to be changed to another runway.[15] The changeover had not been completed by the time they returned so Jack was diverted to nearby Waddington. He landed there and, when the changeover finished, returned to Wigsley. As he approached, Jack noticed the flare path was in almost the same direction as Waddington's. Being only a fifteen-minute flight from Waddington, he assumed the wind was in the same direction as at Waddington.[16] On his first approach, the aircraft seemed to hold off for a long time, so he tried again. When he finally touched down, it was halfway along the runway so he applied the brakes as soon as he could, but the aircraft crashed through a hedge and into a ditch at the end of the runway. Jack and his crew walked away unharmed but the Hampden was written off. So, too, was Jack's reputation for some time.

The problem was not that Jack had crash-landed, but that he had landed downwind. Pilots landed into the wind, as the airflow kept control surfaces powerful. If the pilot landed downwind, the airflow was lessened, and the aircraft 'floated' over the ground instead of settling. Official reports indicate the duty traffic controller, who was responsible for watching out for all arrivals, ensuring they were coming into the correct runway, had flashed the red signal from his hand-held Aldis lamp on both of Jack's approaches to show there was a problem with his landing. In addition, the revolving device known as the 'T', which indicated wind direction, had been illuminated and the Chance light, another visual signal to aid pilots when landing, was also switched to red. Jack saw none of these. He later suggested the Aldis 'was not directly focussed on me' and noted Alan Bowman had only seen the light as they touched down on the second approach.[17] Not having seen any of these signs, Jack had no idea he was approaching downwind, but ignorance was no excuse. As far as the squadron commander, Wing Commander Grant Lindeman, was concerned, Jack 'was guilty of Gross Carelessness in this matter and should be the subject of disciplinary action'.[18]

There were two legacies of Jack's downwind incident. Almost immediately, Jack became known as 'Downwind Davenport'. As far as the squadron was concerned, Jack was still naught but a 'sprog', new and inexperienced. (Sprog is air force slang derived from 'frog spawn' which, like a recruit, is very, very green[19] and a pilot had to be very green if he committed the cardinal sin of landing downwind.) Luckily, an unflattering nickname is something one can outgrow and 'Downwind Davenport' was eventually replaced by 'Davo' (pronounced 'Davvo') as respect for Jack's piloting and leadership skills grew.

Wing Commander Lindeman reported the episode to the Swinderby station commander and the report soon found its way to the Air Officer Commanding at 5 Group headquarters, who took 'a very serious view of the act of Gross Carelessness which led to this accident'. Jack's log book was endorsed in red ink, and his promotion delayed for three months.[20] Jack noted the verdict in his diary, commenting wryly 'rather tough I thought'[21] but this disguised his true feelings: he told Alan Bowman he was devastated.[22]

The downwind incident did not stop Wing Commander Lindeman scheduling Jack for his first operation the next day. As far as Jack was concerned, it was about time. It had been just over a year since his first solo and he had been with the squadron for ten days. He had completed his familiarisation exercises and was keen to do the work for which he had signed up. He looked with 'something like awe' at those who were already on operations. 'I was very keen to get cracking . . . I guess it was a matter of testing yourself.'[23] His chance had now arrived.

A crew's first operation, or 'op' (and from that, the expression 'on ops') was known as a fresher, a sort of a warming up exercise for the new boys to show them the type of procedure to carry out on raids. Jack's first op over enemy territory was a 'nickel' over occupied Paris where, rather than bombs, propaganda leaflets were released. Before Jack and the three other fresher crews tasked with leaflet dropping took off, they sat through the mandatory briefing. Lives could depend on the information imparted in the smoke-filled briefing room. As they nervously awaited take-off time, the airmen were instructed on the weather, the target, expected defences and their plan of 'attack'. They were then trucked to the dispersed aircraft.

Jack flew Hampden AE296, and the conditions could not have been better for his first operation: good moonlight, no cloud and visibility of 6–7 miles.[24] His crew aboard, Jack climbed into the pilot's seat, strapped himself in and ran up the engines. Smithy and Harry were in their positions and Alan sat behind Jack, with his legs dangling below the pilot's seat. The Hampdens then taxied out one after another. Jack grasped the brake lever, pushed the throttles to full, let off the brakes and felt the Hampden's tail lift before the whole aircraft was airborne. Once in the air, Alan slid down feet first under Jack's seat into his position in the nose.

The leaflets were bundled together, and while Jack concentrated on flying and Alan did his navigation calculations, Smithy and Harry were supposed to untie the bundles of leaflets so they would flutter down, spreading broadly over the target area. Jack noticed that it was extraordinarily quiet behind him, but did not think too much about it, as he concentrated on flying safely to France. They reached Paris after about two-and-a-half hours, successfully evading the anti-aircraft fire, also known as 'flak', a term derived from *Flugabwehrkanones*, aircraft defence cannon. Flak might appear beautiful at a distance as its colourful explosions filled the sky like fireworks but it was intimidating close up and could result in fatal damage to aircraft and crew.

In the moonlight they saw the Eiffel Tower and, shortly after, Jack was above the target at about 7000 feet. He was about to order the leaflet drop when he heard a great kafuffle down the back of the aircraft. Then Smithy called out, 'wait a minute, we're not ready yet', so Jack circled the target. Finally, Smithy and Harry were ready and they fed the leaflets through the flare chute.[25] Task accomplished and pumped full of adrenaline, Jack triumphantly made a series of steep turns around the Eiffel Tower and flashed the 'V' victory sign with the navigation lights. All on board returned from Paris singing 'The last time I saw Paris' at the top of their voices.[26]

Their exhilaration was as real as if they had dropped live bombs over their target instead of just propaganda pamphlets. But, in a sense, Smithy and Harry thought they had dropped bombs, even if not live ones. Jack did not know it at the time but, instead of loosening the leaflets so they fluttered down, Smithy and Harry had tied the bundles together with wire in hopes that they would be an effective deadweight if they landed on someone's head.[27] Despite their keenness to strike some sort of blow to the enemy, the slipstream would probably have made the reinforced bundles collapse into leaflets.

The Hampden choir, led by Jack in his clear baritone, displayed an almost devil-may-care and thoughtless attitude as they returned to base. Nothing could prepare a crew for the reality of heavy defences and Jack later confessed he and his crew had no real understanding of the problems they could have encountered: 'In the initial stages of joining the squadron, one was full of ignorance and survival was more a matter of chance than anything else.'[28]

The war might not have been going well for the Allies generally, but for a budding bomber pilot, March–April 1942 was a good time to join 5 Group, though it might not have seemed so at first. In the months before, bomber activity had been reduced for a number of reasons. One was the same reason that saw the cancellation of any number of Jack's training flights at Cottesmore—bad weather. In addition, the recent embargo of American supplies to the Allies so the United States could quickly gain a solid war footing after the Pearl Harbor attack, along with the British commitment to maintaining its munitions supplies to Russia and reinforcements to the Middle East, meant the RAF had been directed to conserve its resources.

Perhaps the most significant reason, however, was the general restriction on Bomber Command activities after a disastrous raid on the night of 7–8 November 1941, which saw 37 aircraft lost in wicked weather conditions. During that period of restriction, high-level debates had occurred about the way Bomber Command would carry out its future operations. Some favoured a tactical approach, some a more strategic bombing campaign to bring the war to civilian populations, a great departure from the earliest policy of bombing only military targets.[29] On 14 February 1942 the decision was made: Bomber Command would focus its attacks on built-up areas in an attempt to break the morale of enemy civilians, and in particular industrial workers.[30] Eight days later, Air Marshal Arthur 'Bomber' Harris was appointed to head Bomber Command and he embraced the concept. By the time Jack took his fresher flight, the new policy had been bedded down and, with ten operational Hampden squadrons, two of Manchesters and two non-operational squadrons, 5 Group was Bomber Command's most powerful group.[31]

On 29 March, Jack's and four other freshmen crews were tasked with a 'gardening' expedition off the Frisian Islands, a group of islands along the Dutch and German coastlines. 'Gardening' referred to the relatively easy task of mine-laying near enemy ports or in shipping channels, a duty often reserved for the newer crews. It would be Jack's first operation with live ordnance.

5 Group had been laying out mines since 1940. It was earlier recognised that it was difficult to destroy enemy shipping by aerial attacks so the magnetic mine was developed. The large, cylindrical mines were attached to parachutes and dropped from a height of about 300 feet into the deep water of enemy shipping channels or harbours. Air Marshal Harris had been so impressed by early results he decided in March 1942 that Bomber Command's heavy and medium bombers should be equipped for gardening expeditions and set a target of 1000 mines a month. This was soon exceeded, with an average of 1113 mines a month.[32]

Jack's first gardening expedition was in the area between the Dutch Frisian island of Vlieland and the German coastal town of Wilhelmshaven. In AE296, Jack took off at 7.30 p.m. laden with a 1900-pound mine and two 250-pound bombs under the wings. Alan Bowman plotted the course to Terschelling, the largest of the Frisian Islands off the Netherlands' coast, which were well defended with anti-aircraft guns and radar and wireless stations. There were patches of cloud at 6000 feet, and a slight sea haze. The moonlight was bright and Jack ran in from the east end of Terschelling. Alan located the target and 'laid' the mine. Jack's 250-pound bombs, however, were not released because no suitable target could be found. Despite returning with two bombs, this was another dream run. They did not encounter flak and no ammunition was fired in defence.

April opened with a large raid consisting of 34 Wellingtons and 22 Hampdens, including three from 455 Squadron, which targeted docks and shipping at Le Havre on 1 April 1942.[33] The weather was bad, the trip extremely bumpy and Jack gained as much as 500 feet height per bump. Sixty mile per hour winds meant that Jack, flying P2065, arrived over the target ten minutes early, so he 'stooged round until time'.[34] Their 250-pound bombs were then dropped 'bang on target' over the docks, 'pranged and observed'.[35] He experienced some flak, which, although it was close to the mark, 'wasn't too bad'.[36]

The flak was worse the next night at Quiberon Bay, on France's Biscay coast. Again in P2065, Jack struck several patches of flak as well as the inevitable searchlights on the way over. After successfully laying the mine and bombing an aerodrome with two 250-pound bombs, Jack put his aircraft's nose down to gain speed and leave the target area as fast as he could.[37] During the intelligence debriefing, he learned that Pilot Officer John Maloney, who had taken off one minute before Jack, had not returned. 455 Squadron had notched up a number of firsts in its career, and this loss was another. It is believed Maloney's was the first all RAAF crew to die in Bomber Command.[38]

There was little rest for Jack over the following two days. Ops were cancelled on 3 April but Jack carried out an air test and then participated in a fighter co-op, also known as 'fighter affiliation', with two Hurricanes. Here, he was able to practise evasive techniques, as if he were pitted against deadly Luftwaffe fighter aircraft. Those corkscrew manoeuvres could prove vital on a future bombing trip but, for the moment, it was all 'good fun'.[39] He was on the ops program again the next day but instead of the planned evening run the operation was brought forward because of weather conditions. Flying AE296, Jack and his crew headed off on a 'mole', a daylight mining trip, to Ameland, one of the West Frisian islands. About 40 miles from the target the cloud cover dissipated, revealing a blue sky. Standing orders were to turn back if the weather cleared so Jack returned with his 1500-pound mine.

Jack was briefed for a 'very big show' at Cologne on 5 April 1942.[40] Take-off was scheduled for after midnight but, after many hours hanging around, Jack discovered his aircraft was unserviceable. He was on the ops program again on both 6 and 7 April but, other than the five most experienced crews taking off for a raid on Essen on 6 April, operations were cancelled because of bad weather.[41] Jack's next raid was to Hamburg on 8 April. By now, fifteen days from his fresher trip, Jack and his crew were considered experienced. No more mollycoddling, no more gradually easing into the swing of things. If Jack had any residual feelings of euphoria or the devil-may-care attitude of his Paris leaflet run, they were gone by the time he completed this trip. Operations were not about joyful singing and jubilant turns, they were about foul weather, dropping bombs and retreating from the target area without delay, and the ever-constant threat of enemy defence.

A record number of aircraft powered towards Hamburg that night—272, consisting of 177 Wellingtons, 22 Stirlings, thirteen Manchesters, twelve Halifaxes, seven Lancasters and 41 Hampdens, including ten from 455 Squadron. Icing and electrical storms plagued the trip across Europe. Visibility was so bad Jack had not seen a thing by the time they reached the Danish coast. Then, the usually reliable

AE296's port motor started sputtering. Jack continued to the target area, through 'hundreds of searchlights' and several artificial targets known as 'dummies'.[42] To Jack, those created targets:

> were amazing. [The Germans would] have places out in the forest where they had great lights and flares and all sorts of things. When a bombing attack started, they'd switch all these things on and you'd home on to this great conflagration thinking that the target's already been hit. If you weren't careful you'd be bombing the wrong target, perhaps several miles away from the target you were after.[43]

Despite the dodgy motor, Jack had to stay in the target area for over an hour. The cloud cover seemed impenetrable and Alan Bowman could not pinpoint the target. Finally, using the estimated time of arrival (ETA), as a guide, Alan dropped the landmine and two 250-pound bombs.[44] They encountered flak and searchlights, so Jack dived low to avoid them: 'I think I was probably as low as two thousand, two-and-a-half thousand feet, which was ridiculous—but that's because I was absolutely petrified of the searchlights.'[45] This was a common fear but training and steely determination gave the majority of aircrew the courage to persevere. With the searchlights successfully evaded, Jack then turned his attention to the flight home. The port motor came and went and it seemed a long trip to the English coast. Blessed coast finally sighted, Jack made arrangements to land at Coningsby, which was much closer than Wigsley.[46]

Jack had not heard the last of this night's efforts. Every time bombs were dropped, he would take a photograph so the intelligence officers could see how close the bombs were to target:

> There was a competition held by [5] Group every month about the best photograph, and I was suddenly called to Group and I thought 'here's the best photograph; I've won something'. When I arrived at Group I discovered that the target that I'd taken the photograph of was Hamm when we were, in fact, going to Hamburg. It was a very good photograph, but I was asked to explain how I'd got to Hamm.[47]

Jack really must have been befuddled by the dazzle of the searchlights because he confused Hamm, one of the largest and most significant of the Ruhr's marshalling yards, with the large port of Hamburg, located on the Elbe, about 400 miles away. It was perhaps not so surprising. In August 1941, the RAF had conducted a study of photos taken on 100 night raids in June–July 1941. Out of those crews who claimed to have reached their target, only one in four managed to fly within 5 miles of it. Over the Ruhr, with its dense blanket of smog, the proportion was one in ten. Even worse, one third of crews failed to drop their bombs within 5 miles of the target.[48] Jack's mix-up was just one of many.

6

Ruhr operations

'that hell hole Essen'

The trip to Hamm was bad but, as so often happens, worse was yet to come. On the night of 10 April 1942, the real dangers of night flying were clearly brought home to Jack in perhaps his worst experience with Bomber Command. That afternoon, Jack had taken Hampden P1145 on an exercise and its port motor had seemed 'a bit crook' but it was all right by the time he had finished so the aircraft stayed on the ops list.[1] Jack and his crew boarded again at about 9.30 p.m. for a large raid on Essen which lay at the heart of Germany's great industrial conglomeration, the Ruhr. Harry Harrison was not flying with Jack this time; the lower rear gunner was Sergeant C.F. Marshall.

The Ruhr provided Germany with most of its coal, almost half of its electricity and had numerous mills and factories continuously producing iron, steel and chemicals to fuel Germany's giant war effort. Its many cities, clustered along the Rhine river system, were densely populated with industrial workers and their families as well as the many ancillary service providers. Essen was a favoured Bomber Command target but the Ruhr was protected by a massive concentration of anti-aircraft defences and a great expanse of protective searchlights which was about 20 miles wide and extending for miles. There was no way to avoid the defences and they were most active around important towns. In addition, Essen was almost perpetually covered by a dense cloud of industrial haze. All this combined to make Essen one of the most difficult and dangerous targets in Germany and, as far as Jack was concerned, 'it was one of the toughest targets of the Ruhr'.[2]

A short while previously, the RAF had introduced the TR 1335 radar aid commonly known as 'Gee'. Three transmitters would send pulses to a cathode ray tube carried on board the aircraft and the navigator could calculate the exact location. It was a line-of-sight device and its range was directly related to the aircraft's height and range. If the aircraft flew below 20,000 feet, or was more than 400 miles from base, the Gee signals would be lost because of the curvature of the Earth. The Ruhr, the Rhineland, Bremen, Emden and Wilhemshaven were within Gee range but, even for those areas outside its limits, Gee could be useful in the early stages of the flight and on the return journey.[3]

It would take some time for all aircraft to be fitted with Gee so the 'shaker' technique was devised to make the best use of those that were. The bombing force was split into three sections—the illuminators, target markers and followers. Wellingtons, which were fitted with Gee, would arrive over the target first and drop bundles of flares upwind of the target and then bomb it with high explosives. The idea was that the target would be obvious from the long trails of the burning flares. This would then guide the second wave of bombers, also fitted with Gee. They would hit the target with loads of incendiaries, creating a huge area of concentrated fire, a clear target for the followers with their high explosive bombs. 455 Squadron had participated in the first shaker attack to Essen on 8–9 March 1942 but this was Jack's first raid using the new technique.

Jack 'had rather a hot trip in' with flak and searchlights. He climbed to 9000 feet but experienced icing, so dived to 3000 feet. Still proving a good flak target, he climbed again to 6000 feet.[4] Visibility was poor as they neared the target. As well as the smog, at 3000 to 7000 feet there was near total cloud cover and it was impossible to bomb the primary target, so Alan Bowman directed Jack to the secondary target. With the satisfying crump, crump, crump sound of the dropping bombs just behind the fuselage, Alan told Jack, 'Let's get out of here', and Jack, nose down to gain speed, headed home.[5] On the way back, a number of 455's Hampdens encountered an active searchlight belt that seemed to be co-operating well with the ground defences.[6] Cones, where the light beams intersected, were thrown up about every 400 yards and Jack's Hampden was caught in their blinding glare three times. Jack discovered the Hampden's manoeuvrability as he dodged the lights but, as he ducked and dived to avoid their brilliant blaze, he kept flying off course. In an attempt to escape the potentially deadly coning, Jack would fly higher, but the higher he went the heavier the flak. He had to try to find the right course in between the heavy and light flak. At one point, he plunged the Hampden to 50 feet above the ground. He dived into one of the searchlights, aiming directly at it with his fixed .303-inch machine gun, shouting: 'Take that you, bastards.'[7]

They eventually flew safely out of the deadly belt but this proved a 'very shaky do' for even more reasons than the dangerous coning and flak.[8] Jack recalled years later that:

It's very difficult to see when you are in searchlights, you can't see anything. It's very hard to see your cockpit, very hard to see your instruments, and sometimes you wouldn't know whether you are flying straight and level or turning sideways.[9]

With all the flak dodging, Jack was drifting further off course. This was a serious problem that had been going on for some time. Not for the first time, Alan tried to direct Jack back on course, but Jack kept saying 'look at all the flak'. They had many fierce arguments[10] but Jack had the immediate safety of his crew and Hampden in mind as he tried to dodge flak and searchlights. There was no doubt he was an excellent pilot, and, as far as target location was concerned, he improved quickly. Many years later, Jack credited Alan with saving him and their aircraft on many occasions[11], including the times he tenaciously argued Jack back on course as they dodged through the deadly flak and dazzling searchlight belts. Looking back, Alan Bowman offered no criticism of Jack's early operational efforts. He recognised they were all green and had much to learn.[12]

As he always did, Jack experienced 'great relief, great relief' when the bombs fell and the flak had been successfully evaded. 'All you were thinking about then was getting back.' One of the first things he noticed was how dry his throat had become because 'you obviously hadn't swallowed for quite a long time. But as soon as you headed home, there was a great relief.' Then he had to concentrate on reaching the coast: 'I think that was a false barrier . . . you hoped that if you got through that, everything would be all right.'[13]

Jack's troubles, though, were not over and even that false barrier seemed far away. The port motor had appeared dodgy that afternoon but now the starboard engine, which had been sputtering on the way to Essen, stopped about 230 miles from the English coast. Finally, Jack sighted the coastline. 'Usually this was fairly clear, even on a dark night, because of the waves . . . the white of the waves. And when you got back to base there was always a great welcome.'[14]

Jack and his crew landed safely after a terrible night's experience, but not all from 455 Squadron were so fortunate. Of the eight crews who flew to Essen, two did not return. Flying Officer Seth Manners (with whom Jack had flown during training exercises at Cottesmore) and Pilot Officer Robert Roberts, both Australians, and their crews, failed to return. This was 455 Squadron's last loss with Bomber Command.[15]

Jack had known real fear that night, and perhaps had come closer to death than at any time in his air force career. The combination of harshly bright searchlights, anti-aircraft fire and the explosion of shells rocking the aircraft, proved a real test to Jack's ability to take advantage of the manoeuvrability of the Hampden. He passed that test, but would never again be as complacent as when he had returned from Paris singing at the top of his voice. The memory of this night stayed with him and, years later, he confessed that he 'feared the searchlights more than any other aspect of the flight because they were relentless . . . there'd be hundreds of them, and they'd light up acres of the sky'.[16] Jack never forgot those bombing raids:

> the incredible Guy Fawkes display [of] flak making the peacetime displays cheap unspectacular comparisons; the grasping, needling fingers of searchlights, their tenacity and refusal to let go when they [caught] an aircraft in their beams. Glaring blindness. The warning shout of a rear gunner as the enemy night-fighter comes in for the kill—diving and weaving—contortions borne of some panic. The glorious darkness as the cone of lights is shaken off. The cold, the freezing of the sweat of fear, the smell of flak, the blazing wrecks hurtling, apparently quite remotely, downwards. Fire and destruction.[17]

It has been said that 'fear is the inevitable companion of the flyer. It never leaves him . . . but it is the conquest of fear that sets the flying man apart from other mortals.'[18] Jack conquered his fear. Adrenaline took over as he dodged the lights and flak, anger against the enemy boiled up as he shouted 'Take that, you bastards', and duty and responsibility came to the fore as he nursed his damaged aircraft back to base and safely returned his crew to briefing room and bed. There are many degrees of courage and in continuing to fly despite his fear Jack, like so many others, displayed inordinate and seemingly limitless amounts of steely, determined courage.

Ops were cancelled because of bad weather on 11 April 1942 but, after an early rise for two air tests the following day, Jack heard he was again on the program to 'that hell hole Essen' as part of another large force.[19] Flying AE379, Jack was one of 171 Wellingtons, 31 Hampdens, 27 Stirlings, thirteen Halifaxes and nine Manchesters. As on their last trip to Essen, visibility was poor and Alan Bowman had trouble identifying Essen's main square so he dropped the landmine on the alternative target. Jack headed home via Zuider Zee and encountered active searchlights and flak, 'striking some bother' at Amsterdam.[20] Jack was not the only one who had difficulties identifying the Essen target that night. Crews from 173 aircraft claimed they had hit the primary target but photographs indicated many had bombed other Ruhr sites. This concluded the series of less than satisfactory raids on Essen and was the last of the Gee raids. Of the 1555 aircraft dispatched, only 1006 crews had reported bombing Essen. Of these, only 212 bombing photos showed ground detail, and Essen's records indicated industrial damage occurred on only two occasions, there was only a modest amount of residential damage and 63 civilians were killed.[21] In addition to problems operating the Gee equipment there was great opposition from searchlights, flak and dummy flares.

Although it had gone relatively smoothly, Jack's second Essen trip was tiring. He had been up early that day and, after 8 hours 4 minutes in the air, landed at 5.31 the next morning. He then had to endure the debrief before he could fall into bed, where he slept until tea-time. Still exhausted, he awoke to find that, mercifully, ops had been scrubbed, but not so the next day. On 14 April, Jack was back over the Ruhr Valley in Hampden AE156. They were briefed for Dortmund's main square but ended up attacking Dortmund town, the alternative target. This trip was another difficult one. On the way over, Jack saw a fighter but 'luckily going in [the] opposite direction'. He arrived at the target but the anti-aircraft artillery, the ack-ack barrage, 'was terrific and searchlights were very numerous and active. There were terrific fires everywhere.' Jack managed to dodge the cones and attacked from the south-east. He then turned out the same way and went round to the east. He watched as another aircraft was caught in the searchlights and was shot down.[22] Within about ten minutes of their ETA, Alan released the landmine from 9000 feet. They saw it burst, as well as lots of fire on the ground.

On this occasion, Jack had more success evading German defences. He 'crept round the main flak' and glided 'to very good effect against searchlights'. He had a good trip back and was the first to return to base.[23] This was Jack's last operation with Bomber Command. He was tired but, as was the way after an operation, he could not go straight to bed to lose himself in blissful sleep because 'the intelligence officers would be waiting for you'.[24] Debriefing over, there would be a meal and then, finally:

> Everybody would get to bed just as quickly as they could because in that time . . . there were more aircraft than there were people, and the drill had you getting to bed at perhaps three, four, o'clock in the morning—you'd been on a seven hour, eight hour, flight—and you'd be up again before lunch to do a flight test to fly the next night. It was very demanding.[25]

Many crews had been lost through sheer exhaustion and Jack's fatigue was becoming debilitating. He had had only four hours' sleep after his return from Dortmund and was expecting to commence leave, but found it had been cancelled and he was scheduled for ops again. It was too much: he 'felt far too tired' to continue.[26] The constant tension and strain of ops, as well as standby and cancellation, had caught up with him.

In the beginning, when he did not really know what to expect, it had been easy to cope with the stress, but now, after almost consecutive nights on ops and seriously rationed sleep, Jack found he was not always concentrating: 'If you weren't careful you'd find yourself, when you were really tired, nodding. It took effort.'[27] Including his fresher run to Paris, Jack had flown nine long, night-time operational sorties within twenty days, some of which were over the most heavily defended targets in Europe, but he had been scheduled for fifteen ops. Whether the operation went ahead or not, he still had to spend many hours at the flight offices before and after briefings. When he did fly, he would be awake for hours afterward as he was debriefed. Sometimes, when he tumbled into bed in the early hours, he was physically drained; other times he suffered the natural wind-down period, waiting for the adrenaline, coursing through his body, to subside. Now, the strain had become intolerable; equilibrium was elusive. Scheduled for ops again, Jack realised he could not go on.

This was not uncommon. From an early stage, squadron medical officers had been provided with instructions for dealing with fatigue.[28] It was well recognised that the stresses of constant operations took their toll. Aircrew were, for the main part, fit and healthy and usually built up good psychological defences against the overwhelming demands of their jobs. Sometimes, however, sheer tiredness played havoc with their natural ability to cope. Jack went to see Flight Lieutenant John Bilton, the squadron's medical officer, who recognised Jack's exhaustion as something very real. Jack had never been, and never would be the type of person to shirk his duty. At no point did fear consume him to the extent he could not take the pilot's seat. He enjoyed flying and flew on every possible occasion, but was now losing the battle against fatigue.[29] It was all too apparent to Bilton that Jack was not fit enough to fly, so he ordered him to bed.[30] But Jack did not go to bed, he went straight to London.

While Jack was clocking up operational hours, his brother Phil had been languishing in Bournemouth waiting for a posting. So too, had Bruce Daymond, Jack's friend from their training days. After completing his general reconnaissance course in Canada, Bruce had arrived in England on New Year's Day.[31] There was not much for Phil and Bruce to do until their postings came through so, when it seemed as if Jack could take a few days' leave, they all agreed to meet in London. Phil and Bruce booked into the Regent Palace Hotel and, when Jack arrived, it was a joyful reunion. Phil had brought along a friend, Dave Laurenti, a South Australian who, like Phil, had trained in Rhodesia and was waiting for a posting. Jack, Phil, Bruce and Dave were sitting in the Regent Palace's lounge the next morning 'when in walked Allan "Pop" Ada. Bruce and I nearly wrecked the place reaching him and created quite a disturbance, but it was great to see him.'[32] It was the first time Jack, Allan and Bruce had been together since they had parted in Canada. Allan had had a short posting to 51 Squadron and only days before had transferred to 58 Squadron but had yet to make his first operational flight with his new squadron.

There was much catching up as the Davenport brothers swapped stories and the close friends from training days made up for lost time. They wandered about town and did a little shopping and sightseeing. They went to a dinner dance at the Liberal Club and later tried to gatecrash the Embassy Club but were politely asked to leave as they were not members. Jack considered London was, 'as ever, dull and dismal and very expensive'[33] but Bruce Daymond remembers it as 'a wild leave'.[34] Regardless of their differing perceptions, it was a memorable visit.

On their last day together, they slept in late and had breakfast in bed, a real luxury for Jack after a series of hurried meals grabbed before pre-op test flights. After lunch in a Chinese restaurant, they went to see a film, then there was a great rush to Waterloo station, where Jack almost missed his train. The five friends assembled at the front of the station for a photo to record their brief reunion. There were but a few minutes for farewell. Jack was rushing for his train to Liverpool en route to a few days in Symington and Allan was off to St Eval in Cornwall, where 58 Squadron was stationed. Bruce, Dave and Phil were to return to Bournemouth.

After converting to Catalinas, Bruce would be posted to 209 Squadron RAF, based in East Africa and tasked with patrolling the Indian Ocean. Soon, Phil and Dave would be posted to 461 Squadron RAAF flying Sunderlands. The squadron, which would become operational on 1 July 1942, would spend the rest of the war hunting U-boats. The five would never meet again. Within a few short months, Allan Ada and Dave Laurenti would be dead. First was Allan, less than three weeks later on 6 May 1942, on his third operation with 58 Squadron, an anti-submarine patrol of the Bay of Biscay. 58 Squadron flew obsolete Whitley twin-engine medium bombers and Allan, the only Australian, was second pilot on Whitley Z-9426 which failed to return. All were later confirmed dead.[35] Next was Dave Laurenti. Like Allan, Dave was also lost in the Bay of Biscay but he was not on an operational flight. He was one of the crew who flew with 461 Squadron's commanding officer, Wing

Commander Neville Halliday, on a search operation for a ditched Wellington. On 12 August 1942, after spotting a dinghy, Halliday landed his Sunderland flying boat on the rough surface of the sea. The sea was choppy, it was a bad landing, and the Sunderland broke up with an engine bursting into flames. One by one, the crew tried to escape. The navigator, Flying Officer John Watson, was trapped in the astrodome but Dave Laurenti shoved him through, thus saving his life. Somehow, five of the crew managed to swim to their floated dinghy but it was overloaded and sprung a leak. Treading water, they decided to try for the dinghy that they had seen from the air. But no one had the strength. After he had recovered from swallowing a lot of seawater, Watson impulsively decided to try for it. He was weak and it was some time before he finally reached it. It was a tremendous effort to drag himself into the dinghy. Exhausted—even passing out for a time—he waited, but no one else joined him. Halliday, who had been commanding officer for only two months, Dave Laurenti and those other crew members who had participated in the thwarted rescue operation, all succumbed to the relentless chop of the Biscay waves. John Watson was the only survivor.[36]

Death is indiscriminate; it makes no distinctions as to whom it claims next, but perhaps there is something in the belief that some were marked for death. Even 'Bomber' Harris recognised it: 'They were in fact—and many knew it—faced with the virtual certainty of death, probably in one of its least pleasant forms.'[37] Many years later, Jack recalled 'a funny little incident' that had stayed with him for more than half a lifetime. There was no flying because of widespread fog so Jack and his friends decided to cycle to the local. Without any signposts or bicycle lamps, and not being able to see much beyond the ends of their noses, they were not sure if they were even on the right road. They stopped an old lady who was walking past and asked her the way. She looked straight at them and said: 'Ah, you boys are from the air force. I always know you fly boys. You have a certain look, a sad look. I always say to my hubby, here today, gone tomorrow.'[38]

The old woman may have seen something of death about the young airmen, but Jack survived. He spent his operational career with one squadron and during those years many friends and compatriots died on ops and in accidents. Through those last hectic weeks on Bomber Command operations, 455 Squadron had lost five crews.

Since it had formed in August 1941, it had lost 21 aircraft, including three written off in accidents.[39] Death was always with Jack; it was something he became familiar with, and accepted. He would initially note the deaths of companions in his diary but, as time passed, and death became a part of operational life, he ceased to record his personal loss. Death 'was a great difficulty and it became . . . so common that you built a mechanism to cope with it. It put a pall over the place consistently . . . it was a terrific strain.'[40] Somehow, Jack and his friends learned to deal with the death of their companions. One of their coping mechanisms was to take advantage of every rare free moment—to relax, laugh, tear around the mess, play pranks, have fun; do whatever they could to put all thoughts of operations, and fear, and the inevitable loss of their friends aside:

> There were two groups of people. There were those that were very quiet and withdrew into themselves, but the great bulk of people were prepared to have fun at the drop of a hat . . . All sorts of intriguing activities went on. We played a lot of billiards and snooker . . . There was not anywhere near as much drinking as most people have suggested, people were fairly restrained, but we had a lot of fun.[41]

Some of that fun was instigated by Pilot Officer Rupert 'Jeep' Patrick, who had an unusual but very mirthful talent—he could hypnotise chooks:

> That gave us a great deal of pleasure . . . He held them—he had a canny knack—he could catch chooks much easier than anybody I know in a chook yard. And then he'd get a match and stroke its comb in a particular fashion, and the chook would lay down flat and wouldn't move, just blink its eyes. It was amazing.[42]

Laughter, however, was not always a salve to loss. Usually, they just had to carry on: 'You had the opportunity of going to bed and coming back the next day and having to do things, and having to get involved again and that, I think, helped.'[43]

Jack may have coped but he never forgot the friends and fellow flyers who died. Their memory stayed in his heart and he commemorated their loss formally and informally throughout his life. His sentiment towards his fallen confrères was constant but, over the years, his feelings towards his former adversaries changed. At the time, Luftwaffe pilots were very much the enemy:

> When I was on an operation my objective was to do exactly what I'd been asked to do and, if possible, a little bit more. The Germans did horrific things to many parts of England—London, Coventry . . . [I] had seen a lot of it. I guess that revenge was something that we felt—or I felt—was very important; we had to stop it . . . We had a very strong feeling that we had to get rid of the Germans.[44]

Those strong emotions took some time to recede. In his speech for the 1978 RAAF Europe Dinner, Jack spoke eloquently about the 'horror of the war years' and the 'arrogant huns' who cruelly 'imposed their will on countries and people'.[45] By 1987, however, Jack's feelings had changed. He now felt 'a real association, an affinity almost, with them'.[46] In 1987, he was invited to join the board of Munich Reinsurance Company of Australia, a fully owned subsidiary of Münchener Rückversicherungs-Gesellschaft in Germany, one of the largest reinsurance companies in the world. Every four or five years, the parent company would invite directors of its foreign subsidiaries and their wives to a meeting at the Munich head office. On one occasion, Jack observed quietly to Sir Arvi Parbo, the chairman of the Australian subsidiary, that the last time he had been to Munich was at 10,000 feet above, dropping bombs.[47] It was totally beside the point that Jack never flew to Munich on a bombing operation—he may have bombed Germany in the past, when it was his duty to do so, but all enmity had been put aside and the former foes were now friends.

Perhaps not on that day, but during another of those large international gatherings, Jack enjoyed a spirited conversation with a former Messerschmitt pilot. No doubt remembering the occasion on which he was relieved to see a German fighter flying away from him[48], Jack and the former Luftwaffe pilot chatted about their respective war experiences, re-fought old battles and discussed the relative merits of Hampden and Messerschmitt. It was a lunch where there was much laughter and friendship between business colleagues, some of whom had served on both sides of a long-ago conflict, who had many years since put aside any feelings of hostility.[49]

7

Coastal Command

'Intelligence . . . thought our raid was a marvel'

After his much-needed leave, Jack returned to Wigsley on 22 April 1942. Almost immediately, he heard the squadron had been transferred from 5 Group to 18 Group, Coastal Command.[1] As well as transferring to a new command, 455 Squadron would soon relocate to RAF Leuchars in Fifeshire, on Scotland's east coast.

These great changes, which would have significant impact on 455 Squadron as a whole and on Jack's military career in particular, all came about because of a disastrous event on 11 February 1942. On that day, the *Scharnhorst, Gneisenau, Prinz Eugen* and a number of smaller enemy ships broke out from Brest, via the English Channel, in an attempt to return to their home bases in Germany. They left Brest at 9.15 p.m. and, amazingly, managed to escape detection for more than twelve hours. Eventually, their 'channel dash' was noticed but, despite attacks by Coastal Command and later Bomber Command and coastal artillery, all of the ships reached their destination safely.

The 'channel dash' proved a great embarrassment to Coastal Command as it clearly highlighted its weaknesses. The inquiry following the fiasco determined that urgent consideration should be given to the development of a powerful and highly trained torpedo bomber strike force. Coastal Command's resources were already stretched, with shortages of aircraft and crews. Because of the priority given to Bomber Command for resources, it was decided that two of its squadrons would be transferred to Coastal Command. For some time, 5 Group squadrons had been in the process of converting from Hampdens, through Manchesters, to Lancaster heavy bombers. As 144 RAF and 455 squadrons still had not converted to Manchesters, it was decided they would be transferred to Coastal Command and their Hampdens converted to torpedo bombers.[2]

Coastal Command was responsible for defending the United Kingdom from naval and U-boat threats, as well as the protection of Allied convoys and the destruction of German shipping. It carried out anti-U-boat operations in home waters and the Mediterranean, and anti-shipping strikes in the English Channel and later off Holland and Norway. Despite its important work in the war at sea, Coastal Command never gained due recognition during the war, whether in receiving a fair share of resources or from the public who were more familiar with the glamorous actions of the 'fighter boys', or the solid but deadly work of Bomber Command. Some Coastal Command work is reasonably well known—most people have heard about its anti-U-boat campaign—but the anti-shipping campaign became almost a forgotten offensive.[3] Forgotten maybe, but Coastal Command contributed greatly to the war effort by destroying much of the German U-boat fleet and merchant shipping, protecting British home waters and ensuring enemy war materiel was kept in short supply.

455 Squadron's service in Bomber Command had been brief—just over seven months of operations—but it was worthy of accolade. In the first three months of 1942 it was lauded as the most accurate Hampden squadron.[4] Its transfer to Coastal Command would not be a simple business. Originally, the squadron was advised that the only persons to transfer were the commanding officer, Wing Commander Lindeman, the adjutant, Flight Lieutenant John Lawson, the medical officer, Flight Lieutenant John Bilton, gunnery officer Flight Lieutenant Flemming and the flight commanders of A and B flights, Flight Lieutenant Jimmy Catanach and Squadron Leader Dicky Banker, and their crews, and ground crew for the establishment of a much smaller two-flight squadron.

5 Group wanted to keep the best crews, but Coastal Command wanted an intact squadron so high-level arguments ensued and Wing Commander Lindeman enjoyed a measure of success in securing twelve more of his crews for the transfer, with as many RAAF personnel as possible. But these were not his most experienced crews because, to prevent the almost total destruction of his squadron, Lindeman agreed to exclude all those who had over 50 operational hours.

Jack had tallied over 50 hours so, strictly speaking, he should have been posted to another Bomber Command squadron. He had only joined 455 Squadron on 15 March 1942 but had crammed half a lifetime's experience into those short but frenetic weeks. He was not yet 22 but had grown from a green sprog to a pilot who had gained the trust of his crew and had quickly learned that operational flying was a serious business where people who relied on their pilot's skill could die if he failed. He had recovered from the ignominious downwind episode and had proven to be a mature and able pilot and a well-liked member of the squadron. Lindeman argued successfully to retain Jack and his crew.[5]

RAF Leuchars was a former Royal Naval Air Service station. It was large, well established and close to RNAS Crail, a naval air torpedo training base. Leuchars hosted a number of units—a photographic reconnaissance unit, a beam approach training flight, a gunnery training school, an intelligence school, the semi-civilian air service to neutral Sweden—as well as 42 Squadron, which flew torpedo-carrying Beauforts, and now 455 and 144 squadrons, which were converting to torpedo-carrying Hampdens.

Leuchars had good station amenities and much to recommend it from a social perspective as it was convenient to Dundee and the Royal and Ancient Golf Club of St Andrews, which, founded in 1754, was the oldest golf club in the world. Of particular interest to many of the young men was Leuchars' contingent of the Women's Auxiliary Air Force, whose members were invariably and affectionately referred to as 'WAAFs'. The WAAFs enjoyed good relationships with the squadron boys and were welcome guests at dances and social evenings.

As invariably happens, romantic sparks were kindled and a number of squadron members fell in love and later married. Romance with the WAAFs, however, did not always lead to marriage and, occasionally, the results of these romances became all too apparent with many a young WAAF having to leave the service. During Jack's period as 455 Squadron's commanding officer, an edict was issued about the high number of WAAF pregnancies, noting that it usually takes 'two to tango' and that it was a commanding officer's responsibility to ensure the situation did not continue. Jack called the station's chief WAAF and asked her how many within her ranks were pregnant. Not at the time realising the consequences of his next statement, he then informed her: 'I will have you know that I am responsible for every one of them'. Jack repeated the story—often in the presence of his laughing wife—on many occasions over the years.[6]

Squadron life in those early days at Leuchars was very different from the last hectic days with Bomber Command. Now Jack had time for regular squash matches, snooker challenges and games of golf. Soon after arriving at Leuchars, Jack, Flight Lieutentant Bob Holmes and Pilot Officer Frank Dick all became members of St Andrews. Many RAF and RAAF airmen joined the club during the war years and it was commonly held that, as St Andrews was in Leuchars' low-flying area, the club encouraged them to join on the proviso that they did not fly over the golf courses and disturb the members.[7]

Jack and his friends played their first game as honorary members on 7 May 1942 but 'local knowledge was lacking'.[8] Jack, Holmes and Dick played many games at St Andrews. Looking back, Bob Holmes didn't know if any of them were any good, but he recalled that they had had a lot of fun![9] They made friends with some of the older members and enjoyed their companionship over many an indifferent meal brought about by the rigours of rationing and, on at least one occasion, their elderly companions enjoyed a little fun at the young Australians' expense:

We joined five old members for dinner about once every three or four weeks . . . Rationing was severe and while we brought food from time to time it became clear to us that in that lovely clubhouse, dinner was to our friends largely an excuse to reach [for] the port . . . On one occasion, with some trepidation, we asked if we could provide the port for our next dinner. This idea was accepted with enthusiasm. Our station . . . mess was managed by Withers, a civilian with a vast experience and background in food and wine. I approached him and asked did he have any Australian port in the cellar. 'Good God, no sir!' I was rebuffed and downcast. A couple of days later, Withers approached me in a somewhat secretive manner. Looking around to ensure that no-one could hear, he explained that he had found a bottle of Australian port in the cellar. It really was an apology . . . The meagre dinner proceeded very well. We came to the port and . . . the decanter proceeded around the table to the left. Number One said 'Hmm, hmm'. Number Two said 'Hmm, yes'. Number Three said 'Hmm, a vintage'. Number Four said 'Hmm, yes a vintage 1927, I think'. Number Five said 'Hmm, I agree, 1927'. We were pleased. Delighted. On our return to our station

I found Withers waiting. I, slightly smugly, told him that the port had been acclaimed by our hosts. He expressed surprise and asked what they had said. I advised him that they said it was a vintage port and had reached agreement that it was a 1927 vintage. 'Did you say 1927, sir? But sir! 1927 was the greatest catastrophe of the port industry!'[10]

At that stage, 22 and 42 squadrons RAF had been carrying out torpedo operations flying Beauforts for some time. Their success rate, however, was less than satisfactory because they had been using tactics developed for naval Swordfish aircraft, with First World War-designed torpedoes. Many aircrew died because of ineffective techniques and equipment. The loss in Beaufort squadrons had been so great it was said that when Wing Commander Lindeman had walked into the mess for the first time, he was greeted by a young flight lieutenant who solemnly wished him luck in his new role as a torpedo leader: 'I've been in torpedoes three weeks and have had three commanding officers so far'.[11]

Coastal Command headquarters recognised the need to develop torpedo techniques that could adapt to moving targets. It also recognised that squadrons trained in bomber techniques would require specific torpedo training, so 455 and 144 squadrons were taken off-line. Much of their training would be carried out at RNAS Crail. When he first arrived at Leuchars, Wing Commander Lindeman had hoped to learn tactics from 42 Squadron but he soon found that that squadron had nothing useful to pass on. Their usual plan was to arrive at the target together, and then, on an 'each man for himself basis', just drop the torpedoes when it seemed appropriate.[12] The squadrons were fortunate to have the assistance of Lieutenant Commander Harland who worked with Lindeman and Wing Commander James McLaughlin, the commanding officer of 144 Squadron, to develop tactics especially suited to the Hampden.

Within a few weeks, Harland, Lindeman and McLaughlin determined that the basic tactical unit consisted of a flight of three aircraft. The squadron would initially fly in tight formation and then, as the aircraft approached the target, the groups of three would fly line astern—in a line, with the leader in the rear—stepped downwards. This process of 'stringing out' would be effected by making turns as required.[13] With the aircraft flying abreast and widely spaced, they would present three separate targets to the enemy defences, making it easier for at least one of them to strike with their torpedo.[14]

The new tactics were difficult and would prove dangerous. They were a vast change from the Bomber Command night raids where they flew as high as possible and then dropped their bombs over what they hoped was the target. Now, they would have to fly low to within a few hundred yards of a fully armed enemy vessel. The torpedoes then had to be dropped from a height between 800 and 1100 yards:

And 'aimed off' to allow for the speed of the boat . . . That required the design of special sights, which we made from bits of wood and nails. On top of that, the torpedo had to hit the ship under the water line, the deeper the better. Since each class of enemy ship had different under-water dimensions, we had to know what class of ships we were attacking before we left for the strike so the torpedoes could be set for the correct depth. This meant that our intelligence was very important for success in strikes.[15]

After launching the torpedo at the vessel, their wide turning circle would bring them directly under the bows of the attacked vessel before they could fly clear.[16] Over the next few weeks the budding torpedo crews honed their new skills, regularly practising formation flying, dropping dummy torpedoes and 'attacking' Royal Naval vessels.

Although 455 Squadron had been taken off-line for some months it still carried out patrols, mine-laying operations and bomber strikes in Hampdens that had not yet been converted.[17] Jack only participated in one of these operations, a special strike on the airfield and barracks of the military strong point of Kristiansand, on the southern tip of Norway.

3 May 1942 had already been a long day for Jack, with an early rise for more torpedo tactics lectures at RNAS Crail, practice runs on ships and a night flying session. Flying AE435, and loaded with four cans of incendiaries and two 250-pound general purpose bombs with fuses set to detonate instantly, he was the first to take off at 11.25 p.m. Bombing from 4500 feet, they attacked the German military barracks. 'We started a terrific fire and saw several huge explosions

Grace Davenport (standing), Louise Hutton (sitting), Phil, age 8 (standing at rear), Jack, age 6 (standing at front) and Keith, age 3. c 1926.

(COURTESY PHIL DAVENPORT)

Class 3D, Sydney High, 1935. Jack, a prefect, is holding the class plaque.

(COURTESY BRUCE DAVENPORT)

Jack in uniform of 30th Battalion, New South Wales Scottish Regiment, 1939. (COURTESY PHIL DAVENPORT)

Sergeant Jack Davenport, A Company, 30th Battalion.

(COURTESY BRUCE DAVENPORT)

Jack arrived at 5 Elementary Flying Training School, Narromine, New South Wales, on 6 March 1941. A few days later, new trainees were issued with the white insert for their forage caps, which indicated they were aircrew trainees. (COURTESY BRUCE DAVENPORT)

Jack is climbing into A17-86, one of 5 Elementary Flying Training School's De Havilland DH 82 Tiger Moths. (COURTESY BRUCE DAVENPORT)

Jack and Pilot Officer Alan Bowman, his first navigator. Jack noted on the reverse of this photo that 'we still feel cold despite all the clothes'. January 1942.
(COURTESY BRUCE DAVENPORT)

Waterloo Station, London: 'The end of a wild leave in London'. 17 April 1942. Standing, from left, Bruce Daymond, Allan Ada, Jack. Sitting, Dave Laurenti, Phil Davenport.
(COURTESY BRUCE DAYMOND)

Close up of the smiling white skull and crossbones that was painted on the port side of Hampden P1287, B–Beer. Jack sent this photo home, with the caption on reverse: 'Wizard isn't it.' August 1942. (COURTESY BRUCE DAVENPORT)

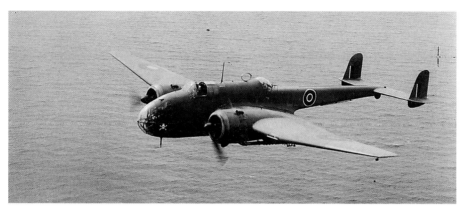

Jack's Hampden, B–Beer, which he flew to Russia in August 1942.
(COURTESY PHIL DAVENPORT)

From left: Jack, Squadron Leader Jimmy Catanach, Wing Commander Grant Lindeman, the squadron commanding officer, Flight Lieutenant Les Oliver, and Squadron Leader Bob Holmes. August 1942, just before 455 Squadron flew to Russia.
(COURTESY TONY OLIVER)

During the Russian sojourn, 455 Squadron was stationed at Vaenga on the western side of Kola Inlet. It was bitterly cold and Jack and his friends were soon wearing the Soviet navy-issue fur caps and waterproof leather jerkins. Jack is also wearing his thick flying gloves. September 1942.

(COURTESY BRUCE DAVENPORT)

Vaenga suffered almost daily bombing raids. Stints in the trenches were not normally laughing affairs but, here, Jack and Frank Dick smile for the camera. September–October 1942.

(COURTESY PHIL DAVENPORT)

Relaxing in front of their Russian billet. Sitting in front, from left: Sergeant Gordon Dun, Flying Officer Alan Bowman, Flying Officer Bill Lovell, Sergeant Clifford 'Harry' Harrison, Jack's lower rear gunner, and Jack. Sergeant Ernest 'Smithy' Smith, Jack's wireless operator/upper rear gunner, is behind Jack, concealed. The three standing are unidentified. September–October 1942. (COURTESY JACK COLLINS)

in their midst.'[18] Flak was light and inaccurate but AE435 was struck in the port flap. Machine-gun fire, with the muzzle waving about in the general direction of the target, spewing a stream of bullets out in a wave—known as hose-piping—was just as inaccurate. To make it even easier for the raiders, there was limited searchlight activity. Other crews reported imprecise and ineffective tracer from the aerodrome and practically no heavy flak. Most of 455 Squadron's bombs were seen to explode and the fires caused much damage.[19] Jack later recorded that 'Intelligence . . . thought our raid was a marvel'.[20]

Jack was progressing well on torpedo tactics. On 4 May he was made deputy flight commander of A Flight. As well as carrying out his own training in torpedo tactics, he now had many new responsibilities. In addition to administrative duties, he would occasionally stand in for Squadron Leader Jimmy Catanach as flight commander and took on the training of pilot officers Archer 'Arch' Broughton and Malcolm 'Dick' Humphrey, who had recently joined the squadron. Looking back, Dick Humphrey recalled that Jack was a good airman, a competent instructor and socially at ease with all ranks.[21]

On 23 May Jack was advised that he had been promoted to acting flight lieutenant with effect from 27 April 1942, just over a month from the downwind landing, and only 22 days after the Air Officer Commanding's determination. Jack's substantive promotion to flying officer came through on 27 July, twelve days after Wing Commander Lindeman had carefully pasted over the red ink endorsement in Jack's log book. Alan Bowman had seen first-hand how Jack had developed as a pilot over the last few weeks, becoming 'damned good' and considered his promotions were well deserved.[22]

The ground crew had been working diligently to convert the Hampdens to torpedo bombers. P1287, B-Beer, which was ready on 12 May 1942, became Jack's aircraft and he gave his verdict of 'quite OK' after his first test flight.[23] Many pilots personalised their aircraft with an insignia or a name and Jack was no exception. A local girl visited the squadron on 12 June carrying a paint tin and brush and daubed a smiling, white skull and crossbones on the port side of B-Beer's nose.[24] Some thought Jack had chosen this design because it was his sailing insignia from his days on Sydney Harbour.[25] Although Jack loved the water, he was not a sailor and never owned a boat. His brothers were sailors, spending many days on the harbour in *Mischief*, with its skull and crossbones insignia. Phil and Keith adopted it for their sailing kit, and looked rather sinister in their dark jerseys with their macabre emblem proudly displayed on their backs. Jack had chosen the design in homage to his two brothers. [26]

Jack's 22nd birthday rolled around all too soon. There were no lectures or training scheduled and he spent the morning of 9 June 1942 with his new pupils. It was a very windy day so they could not fly, but there was still plenty to keep them occupied. In the evening, he carried out an air test and on his return, he flew low and fast over Dundee. When he returned late that night 'the boys had a little celebration for my birthday'.[27]

Jack had come a long way since his 21st on the *Aorangi*. He had completed operational training; had just over 50 operational hours in Bomber Command; had been promoted to deputy flight commander and was responsible for training new pilots. His maturity and competency were becoming more evident as he demonstrated sound flying, instructional and administrative skills. He did not overindulge in the birthday festivities as it would be an early day on the morrow. Squadron Leader Catanach was away and Jack 'had the baby'—he was in charge.[28]

Torpedo training was progressing well. New crews continued to be posted to the squadron after the transfer from Bomber Command and its full complement of 21 was reached in June. On 1 July 1942 all aircrew transferred to RAF Wick, at the extreme north of Scotland, to carry out tactical exercises with the Royal Navy.[29] After the amenities of Leuchars, Jack found Wick to be desolate and, despite it never really getting dark during the northern summer, the mess rather morbid.[30]

Before training had a real chance to bed down, a 'flap'—air force slang for a panic, disturbance or enemy raid—was on. There had been reports about a major German vessel sighted off Norway; they did not know it at the time, but this was the *Lützow*. Despite not completing formation attack training and having no experience in anti-fighter tactics, Group ordered all available aircraft to be fitted with warhead torpedoes. The most practised crews were put on standby but were stood down after three hours. The flap continued however and, on the afternoon of 5 July 1942, they were told they were on a strike.

Twelve aircraft, in two formations of six, prepared to fly to the Norwegian coast. Jack was briefed to lead the second formation, but his aircraft, Hampden P1287, had been ready early, so he led the second three in the first formation. Wing Commander Lindeman, leading the first formation, took off at 4.00 p.m. The second took off some time later.[31]

Jack had had some training in leading formation attacks and now had the opportunity to put that to the test. 'The weather going out was shocking and we really had to work as it was alternate rain and heavy fog or low cloud.'[32] It was so thick and heavy that Jack's group of three, flying underneath Wing Commander Lindeman's group, could barely see the Hampdens above. As they approached the Norwegian coast, however, the weather cleared. They flew in sight of the coast for almost two hours, before turning around about 20 miles north of Trondheim Fiord and heading back down the coast. They were flying low in tight formation to avoid coastal radar and to maintain the element of surprise as they approached enemy shipping lanes.[33] Jack had to hold the controls all the time, to ensure the nose did not go down. It was a long trip, the enemy did not appear to be on the water or in the sky, and Jack was becoming tired. He was tempted to turn on the automatic pilot but Alan Bowman would not let him. It was too risky to use automatic pilot in close formation or while flying low along the enemy coast in case the aircraft made a sudden dive.[34] They argued, as they often did, but Alan would not let Jack fall to temptation.[35]

They were on their way home when they were attacked by two Messerschmitt Bf 109E fighters.[36] The German fighters attacked about a dozen times over 30 minutes before breaking away. Even so, the Hampdens maintained tight formation and kept steadily on course. Sergeant William 'Tango' Martin was on Jack's left and his Hampden was hit. Sergeants Henry Pearson and Kenneth Applekamp, Martin's navigator and rear gunner, both sustained flesh wounds in their legs. Sergeant Lincoln Lord, who was on Lindeman's left in the top three, was also hit. None was seriously wounded. Jack's Hampden, as well as three others, received hits from cannon and machine gun.

The Hampdens continued home in 'very dirty weather and thick cloud which broke up the formation'.[37] Alan was having difficulty plotting a course and, to make matters worse, there was no radio assistance because of bad interference. Wick had closed down so Alan asked Smithy to obtain a bearing for the Orkneys, but Smithy could not raise anyone there. He kept trying and, a little later, passed a bearing to Alan who assumed it was Sumburgh, in the Shetland Islands, and plotted his course accordingly. All was in darkness below and they had no idea where they were. Jack circled and flashed the colour of the day. The station lights came on and they recognised RAF Dyce where, almost out of fuel and with the aid of searchlights, they eventually landed.[38] Despite the weather, wounds and damaged aircraft, all aircraft landed safely after a nine-hour operation and sergeants Pearson and Applekamp, although wounded, 'were in quite good condition'.[39]

Although 455 Squadron did not sight the *Lützow*, its first operation as a torpedo bomber squadron was looked on in a favourable light.[40] Jack, however, thought it 'was a crime sending us on this trip. Our aircraft were incomplete and definitely not operational. Guns had not been harmonised for daylight ops and we were still under training.'[41]

The squadron scribe indicated disappointment that the target had not been sighted.[42] Perhaps it was just as well because Captain F.W. Walton, the commanding officer of RNAS Crail, later reported that, although the new torpedo tactics were largely satisfactory there was a wide variation in the angle of torpedo entry into the water, a result of the angle in which the torpedo was carried, rather than a defect in the torpedo. After further testing the only remedy was to reduce the nose-up attitude in which the aircraft carried the torpedo.[43] If 455 Squadron had come across the *Lützow* with its heavy shipboard anti-aircraft defences, it is possible that Jack and his comrades would have sustained more damage than a couple of leg wounds. Despite the incomplete formation training and possible problems with launching the torpedoes, Jack considered their 'formation flying throughout was outstanding', especially as the squadron had not yet practised formation flying during a fighter attack.[44]

The flap continued and Jack was on standby on 6 and 8 July 1942. On 9 July the detachment flew to Sumburgh. They refuelled and, armed with one torpedo each and accompanied by four bomb-loaded Hampdens from 415 Squadron RCAF, went in search of the *Lützow*, again reported off the Norwegian coast.[45] With Wing Commander Lindeman leading, the Hampden formation took off at 9.25 p.m. Accompanying them were six Beaufighters to carry out a diversionary attack on Trondheim, and a long-range Hudson on which the Hampdens would home. Jack, in P1287, was leading three of the second group of six. After about an hour, he hit a seagull and it crashed through the navigator's perspex window, 'making a hell of a mess and covering Alan with blood and entrails'. For a brief moment there was complete silence and then Jack heard Alan's 'string of abuse'.[46] Alan may have copped the blood and entrails, but Jack and his cockpit were covered in feathers. Conditions in the Hampden were far from comfortable. As well as the stink and the feathers and entrails which Alan picked off his maps and self for the rest of the trip[47], they had to contend with the almost unbearable cold. Alan spent most of his time on the floor with his charts to avoid the icy draft.[48] Jack 'was afraid we would have to turn back but we seemed to be able to keep up the speed and the aircraft seemed quite fair to manoeuvre so we stayed'.[49] They flew beyond Trondheim but, although the weather on the Norwegian coast was ideal, they did not see the *Lützow* so headed for home. Another fruitless search.

Jack did not mention it in his diary, but the large hole in the nose affected the Hampden's aerodynamics. He almost lost control and had difficulty on the return journey.[50] He touched down at Wick at 5.30 a.m., just as his starboard engine cut out. He climbed out of the cockpit, onto the wing and then fell off. He did not move. No-one took too much notice as he had made a name for himself as a clown and joker. A little time passed and Jack remained on the ground. Someone came up to him and prodded him. Still no movement. Then they saw he was so cold he could barely move.[51] He was helped up and taken to the briefing room. It may not have been too warm in there in those early morning hours but it was warmer than the cockpit.[52]

The Wick attachment returned to Leuchars on 14 July and, after taking some leave to Glasgow, Belfast and Dublin, Jack returned to more training. The rest of July and August was spent on training exercises and standbys but, other than a 'rotten trip' of a torpedo strike to southern Norway where nothing was sighted[53], there were no operations. There were, however, hints that something was up; repeated requests from Group headquarters for performance data, especially on the Hampden's range and fuel consumption both with and without torpedoes, was the first. The next was a note in the squadron's operations record book indicating that those who had not participated in the Wick flap were to continue training so they would be operationally fit by 14 August.

By early August it was well known something big was about to happen, and this was confirmed when a detachment of ground crew, led by Flight Lieutenant John Bilton, set sail for 'destination unknown on our secret excursion'.[54] As well as the ground crew, the American cruiser USS *Tuscaloosa* was carrying oil, stores and ammunition, equipment, 32 torpedoes, clothing and food for 134 men. Exact details of the 'secret excursion' still had not been revealed by 13 August. More information was forthcoming on 26 August during a conference with 144 Squadron but full details, including the destination, were still withheld. Nonetheless, preparations continued over the following days—including the issue of toilet paper, revolvers[55] and tropical kit. Jack laughingly recalled: 'Of course the moment we were issued with that kit we all knew we were off to the Arctic.'[56] Finally, on 31 August 1942, 455 and 144 squadrons were advised they would be deployed to Russia.[57]

8

Operation *Orator*

'a most frightening and hair-raising operation'

When Russia entered the war, there was great pressure on Britain and the United States to provide equipment and materiel to their northern ally and well-escorted merchant convoys regularly plied the Arctic waters with these vital supplies. In early July 1942, convoy PQ17 was well on its way to Russia when the Admiralty received intelligence from Sweden that the convoy would be attacked by German naval vessels. Believing a surface attack was imminent, the convoy was ordered to scatter. Ultimately, the German naval vessels did not attack but individual merchant ships were inviting targets. Twenty-two of the 33 merchant vessels were lost to U-boat and Luftwaffe attacks.

Russia desperately needed supplies and a large proportion of those promised by PQ17 was now on the ocean floor. Anglo–Russian relations were strained and Britain's reputation was seriously damaged as it appeared she could not adequately protect Allied convoys. The British Prime Minister, Winston Churchill, was determined to resurrect the situation and planning commenced for the next convoy. This time, every resource was provided to ensure PQ18's forty merchant vessels succeeded in ferrying their essential supplies to Russia. As well as a heavy naval escort that included 22 destroyers, two anti-aircraft ships, cruisers and a submarine group, the convoy would, for the first time, incorporate its own air cover with the inclusion of the aircraft carrier HMS *Avenger*. PQ18's naval escort and air support would have a good chance of protecting the convoy against air and U-boat attack but they would offer little resistance to the *Tirpitz*, *Admiral Sheer*, *Lützow*, *Prince Eugen*, *Hipper* and eleven

German destroyers which haunted the Arctic waters, ready to attack Allied convoys. Accordingly, the RAF was tasked to play its part in the defence of the convoy.

The RAF component, carried out by Coastal Command, was known as Operation *Orator*. It had three elements: anti-shipping; photo-reconnaissance; and long-range patrol and tracking. Operating from Vaenga, an aerodrome near Murmansk in Russia, 455 and 144 squadrons were to carry out anti-shipping attacks. They would be supported by four photo-reconnaissance Spitfires from 1 Photographic Reconnaissance Unit RAF which would report on any movements of the German naval force. The long-range Catalinas of 210 Squadron RAF could carry out 24-hour patrols to locate and then shadow vessels on the move.

There were some problems associated with the Russian deployment. Firstly, the crews had no experience in attacks against naval units. Secondly, even after refuelling in Sumburgh, the distance to Murmansk was beyond the Hampden's normal limit of endurance. There was not enough time to order and fit long-range tanks to maximise fuel carrying capacity. Without these and unburdened by torpedoes, the Hampden's 'safe' range was calculated to be no more than 1040 nautical miles. Flying at a steady 125 knots, without manoeuvring or climbing above high peaks, the range could be extended to 1360 nautical miles. Wing commanders Lindeman and James McLaughlin, of 144 Squadron, consulted Commander Finn Lambrechts, the Norwegian commanding officer of 210 Squadron, to determine their route. The safest, which would have taken the squadrons at least 60 miles from enemy territory at all times, assuming no deviation, would have been about 1314 nautical miles. The dangerous shoreline route was shorter, but still 1200 nautical miles and within constant range of enemy coastal defences. The shortest, most direct course of 1100 nautical miles was also dangerous as it involved flying over high mountains. This would require higher fuel usage and there would be no leeway for contingencies such as head winds, engine troubles, navigational errors or landing delays. That, however, was the route selected.[1]

After refuelling at Sumburgh, the squadrons would fly across the North Sea, northwards to a point off the Norwegian coast about halfway between Trondheim and Narvik. There they would turn eastward flying across Norway, neutral Sweden with its 6000 foot high mountains, and German-occupied Finland, with its fighter bases near Petsamo.[2] Although north of the proposed track, the fighter bases still posed a threat as the long northern days meant the Hampdens would most likely be within their range during daylight. The first Russian landing would be Afrikander and, after refuelling, it would be a short hop to Vaenga. As well as the threat from Petsamo, there would be other potential complications such as the usual early morning Russian fog that would make identification of their destination airfield difficult if not impossible, and the chance of being caught in a German bombing raid given Vaenga's proximity to the front.

Convoy PQ18 set sail on 2 September. That afternoon, 34 aircraft from 455 and 144 squadrons took off from Leuchars. The Hampdens had been cleaned and their fuselages rubbed down to reduce drag.[3] To minimise weight, the Hampdens were not carrying torpedoes but, in the eventuality that the USS *Tuscaloosa* was delayed or attacked, it was decided they would carry a core group of servicing crew. Accompanying Jack, Alan Bowman, Harry Harrison and Smithy in B-Beer was Leading Aircraftman W. McKay. Because of weight constraints, they had been told to take only enough gear for one week—little more than what they stood up in, their shaving kit, and a spare pair of socks and underpants—packed in a wooden box rigged in the empty bomb bays.[4]

Group headquarters wanted the squadrons ready to operate by 7 September but problems arose almost immediately. Sumburgh was a small aerodrome and, although it took only two hours to reach, the rest of the afternoon was taken up with landing and dispersing the aircraft. Then the Hampdens had to be refuelled carefully to ensure every possible drop filled the tanks, and by the time they had finished it was too late to resume their journey. The weather was against them the next day and, while Lindeman and McLaughlin tried to obtain up-to-date weather information, aircrew either wandered around the seashore, inspected the aircraft or, in Jack's case, slept in the afternoon.[5]

The weather improved somewhat by 4 September 1942 and the squadrons prepared to take off from 8.15 p.m. Two Hampdens had to return to Leuchars so only 32 made the long flight: sixteen from each squadron. As they waited to take off, the aircrew contemplated their forthcoming adventure. They well knew the dangers of the trip to Russia and any anti-shipping strike against German naval vessels: they had been briefed that, in all likelihood, at least a quarter of the

Hampdens would not arrive. Remembering that night many years later, Jack recalled that, as the engines roared in the soft dusk light, a contemplative quietness enveloped each aircrew.

> Everybody was very quiet indeed. In fact I think that they were quieter than when involved in a normal operation. We were going to fly over enemy territory for a considerable period of time and we were going to be doing it in weather that was not forecast to be very good. We would then have to fly very high indeed to [climb] over the mountains and the Hampden . . . was designed for low-level operations. I think the fact that we were taking one of the ground crew members in each aeroplane had a sobering effect on peoples' attitudes. They were obviously apprehensive.[6]

The weather improved enough to take off, but it was still not ideal. One by one, the Hampdens taxied to the end of the runway, their engines were shut down and a few final drops of fuel were added to top up the tanks.[7] Then, the Hampdens took to the sky at such a speed that Wing Commander Lindeman recorded they took off at the rate of about one a minute.[8] After reaching the northern-most point in their route, Jack turned over Norway at 9000 feet. Soon, it was so cold that 'icing became a severe problem'. First the starboard engine coughed, then the port. Leading Aircraftman McKay had never experienced this sort of thing and started to panic. Jack quickly put him to work with the de-icing equipment. 'We saw a classic example of a man pumping quickly.'[9]

The icing problem quickly abated and Jack continued through 'Sweden, Finland and the battle frontier after dawn had broken'. There was no peace during those first daylight hours. 'The Swedes objected to us crossing their border and put up some of the best and most accurate flak that we had experienced anywhere . . . the Finns were less accurate but equally enthusiastic.'[10] In the early morning light Jack saw 'desolate country, all lakes, forest, swamps and rocks'. There were no towns or identifiable landmarks[11] and, in the inhospitable landscape, 'there was nowhere anybody could force land an aeroplane with safety at all'.[12]

Alan Bowman did his best to maintain course during the long flight but by the time they entered Russian air space they were north of track and well within the Arctic Circle.[13] Their 1918-dated maps had not proved reliable but Jack felt something had interfered with their compasses: 'It's a disconcerting thing to look at your compass and see it go round in a complete circle'.[14] There is much iron ore in this part of the world and 'the feeling was some mineral deposits were sufficient to interfere with our compass activity'.[15] Perhaps not. Alan Bowman recalled the culprit was the metal torch Jack had tucked into his flying boot, next to his compass.[16]

Jack flew around for about twenty minutes while Alan tried to pinpoint their location over the great expanse of northern Russia which, at that early time of the morning, was covered by low cloud. As well as being off-track, they were low on fuel. Soon, they had a pair of Russian Hurricanes on their tail.[17] It seemed to Jack as if no-one had told these Hurricane pilots about the RAF and RAAF visitors and it looked like they meant business as they directed B-Beer down. The Hurricanes fired once and Harry Harrison called through the intercom: 'Let me have a go at them!'[18] Jack put the Hampden's manoeuvrability to the test as he tried to evade the Hurricane fire but still Harry wanted to shoot at them. Jack 'had a great deal of trouble restraining the rear gunner from having a go at them'.[19]

The Hurricanes directed Jack to Monchegorsk, a well-camouflaged airbase to the south-east of Murmansk and north of Afrikander. Jack lost no time climbing out of B-Beer because he 'was busting'.[20] He had been flying for 7 hours 25 minutes in stressful circumstances and there were limited facilities in the Hampden. Usually they used the bottom of a flame float which was shaped like a flower pot. It was held in place with a spike and, when full, the contents would be tossed through the flare chute to the sea below. It was not the most convenient 'convenience' because if it was filled above the holes, it leaked. As they were over land, they could not toss it out.[21] Jack was desperate, but, as he jumped from the aircraft, he discovered the Russians on the ground weren't very friendly.[22] Two bayonets were wielded and 'at least one drew blood', which probably wouldn't have helped with the bladder problem.

> I'll never forget Smithy . . . standing up on the top there and I'm saying to the Russians, 'English—English—English—Churchill—Stalin— English—English'. Nobody had any English at all. I'm saying this 'English' business, and 'RAF' and 'Churchill'. And Smithy said, 'Ah, you're a liar. Tell them you are a bloody Australian'.[23]

Appearances are everything. Jack may have thought the Russian pilots were forcing him down but, in reality, they were only guiding him to base. Despite their threatening behaviour, the Hurricane pilots would have known Jack and his crew were harmless because Squadron Leader Dennis Foster of 144 Squadron had already landed at Monchegorsk. Jack may have been 'attacked' by a bayonet-wielding local but soon afterwards 'the Russians were friendly and smiling'.[24] With hand gestures, the odd word of Russian and a great deal of smiling, it took an hour to sort things out. First opportunity, Jack gained some relief from his almost exploding bladder and then, tired and hungry, he and his crew followed the locals through the swamps to an old hut and sat down. There they met Squadron Leader Foster and his crew, who had already been greeted by the Hurricane pilots' commanding officer. The only Russian who could speak English was the engineering officer, who had worked for some time on a ship that had called regularly into English ports.[25]

It was not long before perhaps the strangest breakfast they had ever encountered was served: 'Radishes, goat's milk and above all vodka.'[26] The radishes and goat's milk might have been obvious to the visitors but the vodka was not: 'They poured us a mug, which we thought was water, but turned out to be vodka, and vodka on an empty stomach, and a pannikin full, is an over-rated pastime, and we were drinking "to victory, to victory".'[27]

Apparently, this was special army-issue vodka, made substantially from wood pulp and 'we had some queries about the poor quality of their timber'.[28] Regardless of its quality, the vodka continued to be poured—and drunk—as the local commissar made his speeches of welcome.[29] How much was understood by his visitors is not certain as 'we were very happy before breakfast was concluded'![30] In fact, their Russian hosts acclaimed their guests as 'genial, friendly, stimulating, laughing visitors, but of course, in short order, we were fairly inebriated'.[31]

Well—if strangely—fed, and in a very good mood, Jack and his companions were ready to complete their journey. The Hampdens did not have enough petrol for the short flight to Vaenga so the Russians set about refuelling them. This created some panic as the Russians referred to the fuel as 'kerosena, kerosena'. The phrase book was consulted and considerable comfort was found when they discovered kerosena was Russian for petrol.

Thirty-five minutes later Jack arrived at Vaenga to a great welcome. Because of their delay—well beyond the endurance of their Hampdens—he and Squadron Leader Foster had been reported missing. Only 23 of the 32 aircraft eventually arrived safely at Vaenga. 144 Squadron lost six aircraft and 455 Squadron lost three. P5323, piloted by Pilot Officer Rupert 'Jeep' Patrick, ran out of fuel and crashed at Kandalaksha. After some fraught moments with Russian soldiers who took some convincing that they were not from the Luftwaffe, Patrick and his crew were safely despatched to Vaenga.[32] 455 Squadron's other two non-arrivals were not so fortunate. Hampden P5304, piloted by Sergeant Edward Smart, was slightly north of track when it crashed into the side of a mountain at Arvestuottar, in northern Sweden.[33] Sergeant Smart, his navigator Sergeant Thomas Nicholls, his wireless operator/upper gunner Sergeant Louis Biggin, lower rear gunner Sergeant John Harris and passenger Corporal Donald Nelson, a ground crew fitter, were all killed.[34] At the time, no-one knew why the crash had occurred but Jack had his own theory. When he returned to the United Kingdom, he pasted into his diary a small, unattributed article headed 'Swedish A-A Threat Hits at RAF'. The article reported that the Swedish defence ministry had ordered their anti-aircraft guns to 'shoot to kill' night-time foreign air intruders and claimed a recently downed British aircraft.[35] In the margin next to the foreign plane claim, Jack penned 'Sgt Smart'. Jack maintained the belief that they were victims of Swedish anti-aircraft fire throughout his life.[36]

The last of 455 Squadron's Hampdens that failed to arrive was AT109, piloted by Squadron Leader Jimmy Catanach. AT109 had experienced a great deal of flak as it crossed the Norwegian coast in atrocious weather. Catanach realised they were quickly losing fuel. Rather than risk the engines cutting out, he took the first opportunity to land. He touched down safely on a strip of heather adjoining a beach near Vardo, in northern Norway. Catanach, his navigator Flying Officer George 'Bob' Anderson, wireless operator/upper gunner Flight Sergeant Cecil Cameron, lower rear gunner Sergeant John Hayes and their passenger Flight Sergeant John Davidson, a ground crew fitter, attempted to destroy their aircraft, but they were fired on by soldiers from one direction and a patrol boat from the coast. The five were taken prisoner. Catanach was one of the 50 escapees from Stalag Luft III at Sagan who was murdered in the post-escape reprisals.[37] Davidson died on a forced march in the last weeks of Germany's collapse and Anderson, Cameron and Hayes all attempted, unsuccessfully, to escape during their captivity. They survived and were released as the Allies advanced through Europe.[38]

The loss of two crews and three Hampdens was sobering news but the reunion with those crews who had survived the perilous journey, as well as Flight Lieutenant Bilton and the ground crew who had voyaged there on the *Tuscaloosa*, was a glad one. There was no time to celebrate in earnest, however, as the pressure was on to be available for an anticipated anti-shipping strike, and refuelling and servicing the Hampdens was top priority. As deputy flight commander for A Flight, Jack was the logical choice to fill Catanach's role as acting flight commander and he seriously and capably took up his new responsibilities.[39] Pilot Officer Aleck 'Hugh' Clarke took over as Jack's deputy flight commander.

The village of Vaenga is on the western side of Kola Inlet. It is a forbidding and icy part of the world and the living and working conditions were grim. It did not take the visitors long to realise their own uniforms were not warm enough and they were soon wearing the Soviet navy-issue fur caps with ear flaps, known as *ushanka*—literally, ear flaps hat—and waterproof, durable and warmish leather jerkins.[40] No matter how cold it was, however, they kept the ear flaps tied up to the crown as any Russian would, because it was considered unmanly to wear them down.

Vaenga's aerodrome was only a short distance from the front and was bombed frequently. Jack considered it to be very poor when measured against RAF standards. There was an earth surface and no runways as such.[41] Living accommodation was a shock after the comfort of well-established Leuchars. The two squadrons shared three long barrack blocks, with the officers in one and the other aircrew of each squadron in one block each. The rooms were small and bare, containing about three beds with thin mattresses and no other furniture. There were no indoor facilities. A tap in the open was 'where you went for your water. And it was pretty grim old water too.'[42] The octagonal rotunda-style toilet block was also outside. It had separate cubicles but was very primitive. There were steel bars to put their feet on while squatting over the open pit. It was none too clean and, despite good relations with the Russians, the visitors were not impressed by their hosts' tendency to leave the bars in a mess, especially considering they were only able to bathe once a week at the steam baths in a waterfront building at Vaenga village.[43] Despite the crude facilities, Jack and his friends initially thought they were lucky to be billeted in the barracks rather than in underground accommodation, but soon changed their minds:

> We . . . were grateful for them indeed until we had been there a day or two. We found that the Russians had all moved out and were living underground because the aerodrome was bombed most days. We were attacked by German bombers and fighters and we could lie on the ground and watch a great air show.[44]

The ground crew worked on the remaining Hampdens to ensure they were in peak condition as quickly as possible. The reconnaissance Spitfires went on regular patrols to determine if the German naval vessels had left their anchorage. The Hampdens were soon ready, but there was no sign of naval movement. The boys were ready to take off at a moment's notice, but with no news they were becoming restless.[45]

As Jack waited, PQ18 continued its journey. It had suffered loss from enemy aircraft and U–boats but its defences, for the main, had held. On 10 September 1942, the *Admiral Scheer*, *Hipper* and *Koln* moved north from Narvik to Alten Fiord. There was no movement from the *Tirpitz*. By 13 September the convoy was in range of the German warships but heavy cloud prevented the reconnaissance Spitfire from locating the *Tirpitz*. As it happened, she had simply moved to an adjacent fiord to carry out a training exercise, heavy cloud obscuring her position.[46] There was no way to tell if she was on the move so it was decided that all serviceable Hampdens would carry out a large scale pre–emptive search, known as a reconnaissance-in-force, on 14 September. Twenty-three Hampdens took off from about 8.30 a.m. The strike was led by Wing Commander McLaughlin and, as Wing Commander Lindeman had been recently injured by a small bomb, Squadron Leader Holmes led 455 Squadron's twelve aircraft.[47] 'It was one of these death or glory "dos". There was no chance of anybody sinking anything. There was no chance of us hitting anything but there was a very big chance of being hit.'[48]

85

Despite the difficult circumstances they patrolled the Barents Sea, flying to the furthest position the *Tirpitz* was likely to have reached, and then turned back on its probable track. They sighted nothing. Jack noted at the time that it was a 'rotten trip', with much of it flown at low level.[49] He later recalled it as 'a most frightening and hair-raising operation'.[50] It was bitterly cold and there was strong turbulence which made it even more dangerous. By the time they returned, most of the crews were suffering from air sickness.[51]

There was a sense of deflation when they returned as they felt cheated, that the whole Russian expedition had been a flop.[52] Jack and his friends 'were disgusted', but Churchill was not and he sent his Russian force a message of congratulation.[53] As far as he was concerned, he had proved to his allies that Britain could defend the vital Russian convoys. The RAF was well pleased too. Although thirteen merchantmen had been lost through aircraft and U-boat action, 27 had reached their destination safely. It did not matter that the Russian detachment had not engaged the *Tirpitz* or any other of the German naval force, as the RAF considered the success of its operation lay in its deterrent factor.

There was never any chance of the squadrons encountering the German surface vessels. After the war, they discovered their aircraft had been detected by German radar and Hitler had decided not to risk his heavy ships. All intended attacks were cancelled.[54] As well as radar detection, the Germans had received full details of the squadrons' role in the defence of the convoy from papers captured from one of the crews lost over Norway.[55] Frustrating as it was that their 'death or glory' operation had come to naught, perhaps it was just as well, as the crews had had no experience in attacks against naval units, and 23 Hampdens, each armed with only one Mark XII torpedo and the usual Browning and Vickers defences, would have had little hope against either the *Tirpitz* alone or a combined German naval force. Each and every crew member who took to the air that day knew: 'There would not have been one of us to survive.'[56]

The days grew shorter as the Arctic winter approached, but they appeared to be growing longer to Jack and his friends as boredom set in. Headquarters took its time arranging the return of 455 and

144 squadrons and it was eventually decided to hand over the Hampdens to the Russian navy.

In the interim, they filled in time as best they could. Jack and a few others fashioned hockey sticks out of some trees and played ice hockey: 'All we wore were our boots for the whole game . . . it's a wonder we didn't kill ourselves.'[57] Some went to Russian films and local theatrical productions at the Communal Club in Vaenga village; others played poker. They put on regular concert parties and everyone who could participated, including Jack who gave his baritone voice an airing. It was one more way of relieving the increasing monotony of their Russian existence.[58] There was a flurry of excitement the day a Russian Yak fighter crashed through the roof of the officers' barracks. No-one was injured but Alan Bowman, who had been doing his laundry at the time, later retrieved a flattened bucket and torn towel, and it was a close call for Flight Lieutenant John Bilton and some other die-hard poker players who had left the room to see what all the noise was about.[59] Everyone raced to the sole tap to form a bucket brigade and eventually quenched the flames.

On 18 October 1942, 455 and 144 squadrons finally received news that they would be returning home. A small party of ground crew would remain for a short time to assist in the Hampden handover, but the majority would be returning to the United Kingdom on HMS *Argonaut*. The visitors packed and farewelled their Russian friends, then went to the Murmansk wharf to await the arrival of their ship. Jack remembered that:

> It was snowing, it was a blizzard. The snow was thick on the ground. We pilots, aircrew, were in flying boots and they're not the sort of things you walk in and we walked all the way to the wharf at Murmansk. We stood there in this tin shed in which there was absolutely nothing and nowhere even to sit. And then the boat, a cruiser it was, didn't come in and we walked all the bloody way back.

The angry and disconsolate group hiked back through the snow, but the welcome back at their Russian quarters was not warm—they had used all their firewood the night before:

> So we then burnt whatever else we could find like bits and pieces of furniture and anything else so we're not freezing to death. *God it was*

cold. And then we walked down again the next night to the boat. So that was a very traumatic experience. And we boarded.[60]

The *Argonaut* left Russia on 22 October and Jack and his friends arrived at Leuchars on 29 October where they were 'heartily welcomed'.[61] They had been away for eight weeks. They were scruffy, unwashed, very rank and looked decidedly ruffianly but they were home, and it had never looked so good.[62] Their first priority was hot baths and after a good long soak they changed into clean uniforms.[63] A party was held that evening, 'such an orgy I have never seen'.[64] The Russian detachment was granted two weeks' leave, but before Jack left he was told he had been recommended to take over A Flight on a permanent basis. His work in Russia, 'in the most difficult circumstances', including how, 'by the force of his personality and example gained the confidence and respect of both flying and technical personnel', was later formally recognised in the recommendation for his Distinguished Flying Cross.[65]

The Russian detachment had shared some interesting experiences, and everyone who participated in the adventure talked about the great bond that had formed between the squadron members. In 1989 that bond was given a visual representation when the Presidium of the Supreme Soviet of the USSR awarded the commemorative 'Forty Years of Victory in the Great Patriotic War 1941–1945' medal to those who had come to the Soviet Union's assistance, including 455 Squadron. Jack was not the only member of the squadron to proudly wear this medal during Anzac Day marches and other appropriate formal occasions.

The squadrons may have been impressed by the friendliness, efficiency and sense of co-operation of their hosts[66] but, even so, the Russian experience was not one they wanted to repeat. Jack well recalled Wing Commander Grant Lindeman's BBC interview when they returned to London:

He was asked if he had enjoyed the visit to Russia and he replied 'if the opportunity comes for us to return to Russia again, we would gladly stand aside and allow someone else to go'.[67]

Jack did not contradict Lindeman.

9

Miss Sheila McDavid

'I've met the loveliest girl in Scotland'

From his return from Russia until early January 1943, Jack only carried out one operational flight, an uneventful patrol to Egersund on 18 December 1942. Frustrating as this period was from an operational perspective, there were two highlights for Jack. On 1 December 1942, he 'received notification of my promotion to squadron leader and was very pleased. Squadron leader at twenty-two.'[1] The celebrations started that night and continued the next. Just over eight months previously, Jack had been disciplined for 'Gross Carelessness' over his downwind landing. Much had happened since then and this promotion to acting squadron leader recognised his considerable leadership skills and flying ability.

Welcome as Jack's promotion was, it was eclipsed by another much more significant event a short time before. When the Russian contingent returned, a welcome-home party was thrown in the officers' mess. Jack, as president of the mess, was responsible for the arrangements. It was to be a large, festive occasion. They could always count on members of the Women's Auxiliary Air Force stationed at Leuchars for dance partners, but this time they sent invitations far and wide: 'We'd sent to Aberdeen and to Edinburgh, all over the place, to all the hospitals, with buses to collect girls.'[2] Jack later recorded it simply as 'a bit of a party'[3] but it proved to be much more. That was the night he met his future wife.

Sheila McDavid was not yet twenty. With her fair skin and raven hair, she was a Scottish beauty. She was the youngest child and only daughter of Dr James (Jim) Wallace McDavid and his wife, Jessie. Jim, who was awarded his Doctorate of Science from Edinburgh University, had worked for Imperial Chemical Industries Ltd (ICI) for over 30 years (and would later be awarded a CBE).[4] He was joint managing director of the Nobel Division, responsible for manufacturing, among other things, dynamite, gelignite, blasting powder and other military explosives. The main factory was located at Ardeer, a few miles from the family's home at Ardrossan, in Ayrshire, on Scotland's west coast, south-west of Glasgow. The McDavid's home, Crescent Park, a graceful Georgian house with large grounds, is situated on Ardrossen's North Shore with views of the ferry harbour, the rugged Isle of Arran and Horse Island.[5] Jim McDavid liked nothing better than to share a joke or tell a good story and he and Jessie were well known for playing pranks on family and friends. Sheila inherited her parents' great sense of fun as well as her mother's charm, elegance and social poise. Theirs was a close-knit family, comfortably off, with much shared laughter.

Sheila's elder brother Ian had joined the Royal Scots Fusiliers after receiving his Bachelor of Science from St Andrews University. Lieutenant McDavid had survived injuries from a bomb attack during operations in northern France but the ambulance taking him to the field hospital was strafed by a German fighter and he then sustained serious wounds to his right hand, part of which was subsequently amputated. He was invalided out of the army and went to work for ICI. The war prevented younger brother Stewart from going to university and he too joined ICI. He enlisted in the 'London Scottish' Territorial Army in 1939 and was selected for officer training at Sandhurst in 1941. On passing out, he joined the 4th/5th Battalion Royal Scots Fusiliers (52nd Lowland Division).[6]

Sheila was in the second year of her Master of Arts degree at St Andrews. She and her friend, Jean Turner, were walking past the notice board in University Hall when they saw an invitation to the dance at the officers' mess at Leuchars. Sheila turned to Jean and said: 'Well, I won't be going to that. It will be like a cattle market!' Jean thought about this for a minute and remarked that they would probably provide a good spread. Like all of the United Kingdom, Scotland was enduring severe rationing. With Coastal Command squadrons doing their best to ensure essential food items and material from Allied countries made it through, and thousands of people 'Digging for Victory' as they turned much of their arable land over to food production: 'Food was often upper-most in our thoughts'.

Everyone juggled ration cards and points to stretch the plain but stodgy fare as far as possible. The military, however, appeared to have an endless supply of decent food. For the sake of a 'really good feed', Sheila agreed to attend the dance.[7]

When they arrived at Leuchars, Sheila, Jean and a number of their friends were met by the president of the mess, 'a very good looking Australian . . . Jack Davenport'. Jack introduced the group to the rest of his squadron but Sheila was struck by Jack. To her dismay, he was not alone. He had on his arm a beautiful girl in a plum velvet dress with a matching muff. Sheila thought she looked 'very sophisticated and I suddenly felt totally naïve in my pale blue number. However, I had no lack of willing partners and decided Jack Davenport was a write-off with his gorgeous "popsy".'[8]

Sheila enjoyed her willing partners but one of them spilt a beer down the front of her frock. Jack took it upon himself to apologise and 'that's how it all started'.[9] He invited Sheila to dance an eightsome reel, a complicated round reel for four couples requiring skill as well as energy and enthusiasm. Sheila thought 'now this will be something . . . how will an Australian cope with an eightsome?' To Sheila, it seemed all Scottish girls and boys knew the traditional dances inherently: they were never taught, it was all something that 'seemed to happen . . . and Scottish boys took great pride in being light on their feet'. She inwardly cringed at the possibility that Jack might have been another 'great clodhopping' trier, but she politely accepted Jack's invitation to dance.[10]

It was not exactly love at first sight, but Jack was definitely interested in the beautiful young Scottish woman with the sparkling personality. After that first meeting he would phone her whenever he had a moment to spare, or they would meet for a meal or a film, or perhaps for a walk along the pier. Jack, however, was not the only one from his squadron who was interested in Sheila and she enjoyed many invitations from the boys over the following weeks. But as the old adage declares, 'All's fair in love and war', so Jack pulled rank. 'I was able to forestall the further operation that developed in the squadron to take this young girl out by increasing the incidence of night flying.'[11]

Jack occupied much of Sheila's time over the next few months and she found herself awaiting his calls with anticipation. Like many other women with boyfriends and husbands in the services, Sheila experienced the excitement of sharing brief moments snatched between operations, and the disappointment of cancelled plans when a last-minute op was staged. Like many, she waited in suspense for news of a safe return, and experienced relief when the news was good.[12] She was terrified of all that could go wrong for Jack and that fear never went away. If Jack could not phone after an operation, he arranged for someone else to call Sheila and let her know he was all right, and later, when they were married, 'the squadron were extremely good. If I was out operating there'd always be somebody to go home and talk to Sheila.' Despite her fear, Sheila tried to downplay it. She 'was very supportive; she'd say, casually, "take care" or something like that, but there was no great emotional upheavals ... she was quite remarkable'.[13]

January 1943 presented Sheila with a number of fearful moments. Generally speaking, it was a quiet month for Coastal Command; stormy conditions prevailed over much of its watch, no major operations were planned and there were few incidents of note.[14] 455 Squadron, however, experienced one of those few notable incidents. Intelligence about German shipping activity had been coming in from Norwegian operatives, resulting in a number of flaps. A detachment from 489 Squadron Royal New Zealand Air Force (RNZAF) had initially been sent to desolate RAF Wick and, in mid-January 1943, they were relieved by 455 Squadron's A Flight. Jack was in charge of this detachment which would carry out a series of attacks on German shipping.

Setting off in the early morning of 15 January, Jack led the detachment of six aircraft from Leuchars to Wick. He was flying AN148 and, like his fellows, was carrying two ground crew as well as Alan Bowman, Smithy and Harry Harrison. As 489 Squadron prepared to depart, the A Flight detachment settled in. The next day, a conference was called and it was decided to send a patrol to the Norwegian coast, where no sightings of enemy vessels were made. Jack did not participate in this and bad weather blighted any attempts to send out patrols on 17 January. It was a different matter on 18 January, however. Jack was awakened at 1.00 a.m. to arrange a first-light operation for five of his detachment. The briefing was at 7.30 a.m. and, with Jack leading, four of the aircraft took off from 9.10 a.m. Flight Sergeant Lincoln Lord had not taken off in time and was unable to catch up. The Hampden contingent rendezvoused successfully with their escort.

The target was the depot ship *Saar*. They did not locate it but a small destroyer was sighted at 12.30 p.m. As the formation approached, the destroyer opened up with tracer and Jack's tail plane was holed by light flak but did not suffer serious damage. There was insufficient time to position correctly for attack so Jack led the formation around Vigra Island, off the west coast of Norway. He then led the Hampdens into a low-level attack in the face of strong and accurate opposition. Jack, Pilot Officer Dick Humphrey and Sergeant 'Tango' Martin attacked low and Pilot Officer Colin Storry struck from 500 feet. Jack's bombs were seen to straddle the destroyer and Storry's were considered a near miss. All aircraft returned safely, landing at 4.20 p.m.[15]

Bad weather prevailed over the next few days and, other than training flights and air tests, it proved unsuitable for flying. The next operation, which was more successful than the previous one, occured on 22 January. Jack conducted the briefing but did not participate. Pilot Officer Colin Storry sighted and attacked a 2000-ton vessel in a snowstorm and the explosion was seen by his gunner, Flight Sergeant Roland Sheedy. Jack had his own success the next night when he dropped six bombs on an enemy vessel off Lervik, seeing at least three bursts.

Confirmation was received on 25 January that the German battleships, *Scharnhorst* and *Prinz Eugen*, were on the move. Joining forces with six aircraft from 489 Squadron, which was leading the strike, and six Beaufighters from 236 Squadron as escorts, Jack's detachment of five Hampdens took off at 1.05 p.m. Pilot Officer Dick Humphrey turned back with engine trouble and the others might as well have gone back too. The weather was bad and the strike force sighted only a couple of merchantmen and small flak ships. *Scharnhorst* and *Prinz Eugen* returned safely to port.

The Wick detachment carried out a number of patrols with little success. When it returned to Leuchars, the Wick station commander indicated he would be happy for it to return, 'but the feeling was not reciprocated'.[16] It had been a busy but frustrating period, with little to show for their efforts. For Jack it had been an opportunity to take on more responsibility and he acquitted himself well. His conduct during this period was later recognised in the recommendation for his Distinguished Flying Cross, and reiterated in its citation: 'This officer has displayed leadership, courage and administrative ability of a very high order'.[17]

Jack flew his final operations with Alan Bowman, Smithy and Harry Harrison during the Wick flap. After his promotion to Flying Officer, Alan was posted to 1 Torpedo Training Unit in Turnberry, Ayrshire, on 20 February, as was Smithy. Harry Harrison stayed with the squadron and continued to fly with Jack over the next few weeks. As far as the crew mates were concerned, new postings and distance may have separated them but they would maintain their connection during the war and beyond. Jack and Alan's talk about their Australian homeland had made such an impression on Harry he seriously contemplated migrating to Australia after the war.[18] They had grown close to each other and worked well together. Alan and Smithy corresponded for many years and Jack and Alan, especially, formed a deep bond that went beyond the usual trust shared by pilots and navigators. They would go on to enjoy over fifty years of friendship and professional relations during their work for the RAAF Association.[19]

The Wick flap had been an exhausting time and, much to Sheila McDavid's annoyance, Jack went on leave almost as soon as he returned to Leuchars without visiting her before he left or during his break. He spent some time in London and then visited his brother Phil at 461 Squadron at Hamworthy, Dorset, where he managed to hitch a ride in a Sunderland during a practice flight. He returned to Leuchars on 15 February and wasted no time in arranging to meet Sheila. They went to St Andrews for dinner and a film and, afterwards, took a walk along the pier. They had not seen each other for a month. Although Jack could not talk much about the operations from Wick, they still had plenty to discuss. They had a wonderful time together and Sheila almost missed her bus back to the university.[20]

Jack and Sheila had arranged to go out again a few nights later but, much to Sheila's disappointment, Jack had to cancel at the last minute. Sheila fully understood that Jack's first priority was the squadron but occasionally his absences and changed plans rankled. She hid her feelings from Jack but on this occasion hinted at her annoyance when she noted in her diary 'was to have gone out with Jack—but there's a war on'.[21] Four crews from 455 Squadron, including

Jack flying AD987, had been tasked with a rover patrol, or 'rover', where formations of two, four or six aircraft would fly together to the Norwegian coast then divide into two sections and patrol along the coast in opposite directions. For the first time, he was flying with an all-Australian crew—Jack's golf partner, Flying Officer Frank Dick was navigator and Pilot Officer John Murphy and Sergeant Cornelius McIntyre were the gunners. Taking off at 6.10 p.m., Jack was carrying four 500-pound bombs. At 8.10 p.m. he sighted Utsira Island and turned south to make certain of the pinpoint. Ten minutes later, he saw lights similar to a flare path near Haugesund and at 8.24 p.m. crossed the coast. He searched a fiord south-east of Stord Island without sighting anything and then returned to Lervik. He then saw two lights off shore in the south-west of the harbour, as well as a dark patch which could have been shipping. Dick dropped the bombs, which were seen to burst across the lights, but they could not see any damage. They returned to Leuchars shortly after midnight.[22]

Many changes occurred during February and March 1943. Wing Commander Grant Lindeman was posted to 1 Torpedo Training Unit, Turnberry, as Chief Flying Instructor and Flight Lieutenant John Bilton, who had been the squadron's medical officer since formation and was the one who had clearly seen Jack's operational exhaustion in April 1942, returned to Australia. Bob Holmes was promoted and succeeded Lindeman as squadron commander. Although extremely capable, and the logical choice to take over from Lindeman, Wing Commander Holmes was not able to place his stamp on the squadron for some time. He had suffered a serious shoulder injury after an accident in the mess and was to spend a great deal of time in hospital over the next few months.

During Holmes' absences, Jack took over the responsibilities of squadron commander. Consequently, although enemy cargo shipping was still active[23], Jack had only four operational flights during March 1943, his first being a shipping search on 2 March. Flying AN148, he took off at 7.35 a.m. along with seven other crews. This time, Flight Sergeant Pearson was his navigator, Harry Harrison took over as wireless operator/upper gunner and Flying Officer Bastian was lower rear gunner. Jack and his crew were the only ones to sight wreckage, including what looked like part of the superstructure. They then saw two lifeboats with survivors, and a third empty lifeboat. Jack's detachment had been escorted by a Beaufighter from

235 Squadron, but it departed soon after the first lifeboat had been spotted. Unprotected, Jack circled over the wreckage and survivors for some time before returning to Leuchars at 2.30 p.m.

The entire operation had taken seven hours and had been physically demanding. As well as being continually on the lookout for enemy aircraft, the high seas and large expanse of white caps on the water had made observation extremely difficult. It had been a long day, but Jack had made arrangements to see Sheila and, despite his tiredness, he did not cancel.[24]

Jack was afforded no chance to overcome his tiredness as the next afternoon, flying AT179, he led his squadron on a shipping reconnaissance to Stavanger. The eight Hampdens were escorted by seven Beaufighters from 235 Squadron, but no enemy vessels were sighted. The Beaufighter escort would prove a regular feature of operational work, providing top cover to divert the attention of enemy fighters and anti-aircraft defences while the Hampdens concentrated on the attack.

At the conclusion of the Russian sojourn, when Wing Commander Lindeman facetiously remarked that he would gladly stand aside and allow someone else the opportunity to have a Russian experience, no-one could have imagined that 455 Squadron would have another chance at an Arctic posting. Another was, however, being considered. Wing Commander Holmes was in hospital following his shoulder operation so, on 7 March 1943, Jack led all of 455's operational crews and accompanying ground crew on a detachment to Wick to carry out co-ordination exercises with 489 Squadron, which was also preparing for a Russian posting. They were there for five days, and Jack flew two strike operations. The first, on 10 March, was to Egero, in search of the *Lützow*, which had been reported on the move again. The second, the following day in vile weather, was in search of the *Tirpitz*. Neither vessel was sighted. Plans for the second Russian expedition soon fell in a heap and Jack led his detachment back to Leuchars on 12 March.

Much of the squadron's flying time on Jack's return from Wick was taken up training new crews and practice flights. Jack may not have been on operations, but he was busy with an increased administrative workload when Wing Commander Holmes was hospitalised for all but one week of March and again from 14 to 26 April 1943. He tried to arrange time with Sheila but often would have to cancel. By now, Sheila was accustomed to being placed second to Jack's squadron responsibilities. After all, as she had reminded herself on at least one occasion, there was a war on.[25] There was indeed, and Jack felt this very keenly when he heard that Harry Harrison, who had recently been promoted to flight sergeant, had been killed in a flying accident on 10 April 1943.[26]

As one of the squadron's most reliable and capable wireless operator/ air gunners, Harry had been selected for an advanced course for leaders at Central Gunnery School at RAF Sutton Bridge in Lincolnshire. He had joined the squadron in September 1941, soon after it had formed in the United Kingdom, and had been one of the longest serving aircrew. Harry was well liked and his loss was a great blow to the squadron and to Jack, who had last flown with him when the Wick detachment returned to Leuchars. Now Jack's last immediate connection with his close-knit crew was permanently gone.

As acting commanding officer, Jack had to write to Harry's father to inform him of his son's death. Despite his own grief, Jack tried to soften the blow as much as he could, telling him of his son's popularity and the standard of his work. Perhaps Jack did not think it appropriate to specifically refer to his own personal experiences with Harry as he carried out this sad duty, but it is clear he included himself as someone who knew Harry intimately, when he wrote that:

> His work was in keeping with his character and you may be sure that he worthily maintained the high standard of the Service. It is the more grievous that he should have lost his life whilst in training after having survived so much operational work, and believe me, his death is keenly felt by his squadron.

It was a difficult letter to write, but Jack hit upon the perfect combination of personal and official, and Harry's father particularly appreciated Jack's kind manner and was moved by the obvious sincerity of Jack's condolences. For him, it was a considerate touch that Jack mentioned Harry's character and the quality of his work. It was a fitting tribute for his son whose association with 455 Squadron had been one of the happiest from the very beginning, and who had hoped he would never be parted from it.[27]

•

Jack did not fly operationally again until 21 April 1943. Again escorted by Beaufighters from 235 Squadron, Jack, flying AN148, took off at 9.15 a.m., leading his Hampdens on a strike to Lister, Norway. He soon sighted a 5000 to 6000-ton merchant vessel, escorted by three trawler-type flak ships. Jack disliked these escort ships: 'They were terrible vessels, always underestimated' and their fire power was intense—'they could put up a hell of a fire screen'.[28] Operating at 'nought feet'—flying at almost wave tip so they would not be detected by radar—with their Beaufighter escorts trying to divert, with cannon fire, the attention of the anti-aircraft gunners on the flak ships, the Hampdens launched their torpedoes but no hits were observed. The anti-aircraft fire was plentiful and accurate throughout the operation and Jack sustained some damage to his cockpit cover. Despite the flak, the Hampdens and Beaufighters raked the ships with cannon and machine-gun fire. As Jack turned to strike, he saw one of the Beaufighters above him make a starboard attack on the merchant vessel with all guns blazing. Although no vessel was destroyed Jack and his fellows had acquitted themselves well against the determined work of the anti-aircraft gunners. It seemed that, from now on, they could expect nothing but fierce retaliation from flak escorts, aircraft, or the combined forces of both as the Germans made every effort to protect their merchantmen.[29]

Jack landed back at Leuchars at 2.10 p.m. but there was no rest for him after the post-operational briefing. That day, Flight Lieutenant Fred McKay, the Presbyterian padre, arrived to spend a few days with the squadron. Reverend McKay had been posted as one of the three chaplains to the Australian squadrons of the Western Desert Air Force in the Middle East. On his way there he stopped off in the United Kingdom and, before his arrival at Leuchars, had enjoyed a short pastoral visit to 460 Squadron RAAF, at Breighton.[30] Reverend McKay's time with 455 Squadron was similarly brief, but he and Jack formed a lifelong bond that survived despite only sporadic contact over the years.

Perhaps the recent death of Harry Harrison had turned Jack's mind to the loss of other friends during this war—school, militia, training and squadron friends—as well as the great sacrifice of lives throughout the world in a conflict that had expanded beyond the need to defeat the forces of Nazism and Fascism, and had now, with Japan's entry into the war, threatened Australia and the Pacific. Every man in his squadron had been touched by the war—the squadron itself had already lost 89 men since it had become operational in August 1941, and 38 since Jack had joined in March 1942.[31] Jack spoke with Reverend McKay about a way to honour the squadron's dead, as well as all who had fallen in this conflict. The timing was perfect.

To keep monies flowing into the war coffers, British cities organised great fundraising drives. There had been many scrap and aluminium collections and 'Banner Weeks' throughout the nation, and public monies had funded construction of Spitfires, Lancasters, warships and weapons. Dundee, the closest city to Leuchars and Scotland's third largest, had held a successful 'War Weapons Week' in 1941 and 'Warships Week' in 1942 and now planned a 'Wings for Victory Week' which was set to open on Easter Saturday, 24 April, with a forces' march past.[32] Led by the RAF Pipe Band, the parade would include detachments from the local Home Guard, the Women's Auxiliary Air Force, the Women's Royal Naval Service, the Army Cadets and the Women's Land Army, as well as police, air raid precaution wardens and children's groups, combined with representatives from the navy and air force. 455 Squadron had been invited to form part of the air force contingent.

Jack decided that, at the conclusion of the parade the squadron would march to the Dundee War Memorial for a wreath laying and commemoration ceremony. Jack put his idea to Reverend McKay, who gladly agreed to conduct a special pre-Anzac Day service. He well knew the sacrifices the Australian squadrons had already made in the war and suggested appropriate music and words to honour those men.[33]

The opening day of 'Wings for Victory Week' was blustery and overcast but the local populace came out in their thousands to cheer the parade. Those lining the streets were 'cheering and cheerful' as they gave the procession its warmest welcome.[34] After the parade, the squadron, along with the Leuchars Station WAAFs, was bussed part way up Law Hill and Jack took Reverend McKay in his staff car. Everybody alighted from the buses and regrouped. They marched the last few yards to the top of the hill to the strains of 'Oh! God our help in ages past'. There they gathered around the Cenotaph where they experienced a panoramic view which encompassed the

Firth of Tay and the city of Dundee. The grey skies were a fitting backdrop to the sombre occasion. It was a purely private ceremony; the public had not been invited to share in this personal commemoration. The pipers reprised 'Oh! God our help in ages past', with the boys now joining in, and Reverend McKay conducted a moving service. Jack read a lesson and then stepped forward to place a wreath on the Cenotaph, speaking a few words of remembrance as he did so. A lone piper then played a Scottish lament and the mournful bagpipe skirl filled the air.

This ceremony beautifully, soberly and sincerely honoured the contribution of their fallen comrades. It did much to reinforce the squadron bonds, and was remembered for many years afterwards.[35] The memory also remained in Jack's heart. In the early 1990s, shortly after he and Sheila had moved to their Mosman home, Jack hosted a reunion for his squadron ground crew. Recalling the pipers of that long ago ceremony, Jack's guests were piped into their meal by a lone bagpipe player. Not, this time, to the strains of a sombre hymn, but to the skirls of a traditional march. The years fell away, memories stirred as the past returned and the already strong bonds strengthened as wartime deeds, sacrifices and friends were remembered.[36]

Reverend McKay also remembered that long ago day, as well as Jack's involvement: 'He was a true-blooded Australian who wanted to show to the Scottish populace of Dundee that Australians really had a soul. And he did it all so properly.'[37] He recalled too, that, after a solemn period of contemplation, the bagpipers led the squadron back down to the buses which returned them to town. From there the boys dispersed, either to participate in Dundee's festivities or to one of the local hotels. After the service, Reverend McKay and Jack went for a quiet drink in the Tay Bridge Inn. There, Jack leaned across the table and confided his love for Sheila: 'Padre, I've met the loveliest girl in Scotland.'[38]

1 Torpedo Training Unit, Turnberry

'bloody lucky to have survived'

Reverend McKay was not the only Australian visitor to the squadron in April 1943. Jack's youngest brother, Keith, had recently arrived in the United Kingdom. While Jack and Phil had had to leave school early, Keith had stayed on. In 1940 he had been vice-captain of Sydney Boys High and took his leaving certificate. In 1941 he accepted a cadetship at *The Sun* newspaper and, like Jack, had enlisted with the 30th Battalion. He then enlisted in the RAAF on 12 September 1941 and went on the reserve list until he was called up. Like Phil, he had carried out his initial training at Somers, Victoria. After that, as did Jack, he had completed his elementary flying training at 5 Elementary Training School, Narromine but then received his wings at 8 Service Flying Training School, Bundaberg, Queensland. He was now marking time before his permanent posting came through. His posting to 461 Squadron would come in November, after completing advanced flying and beam approach training courses. Keith was the only brother not to have been commissioned off course.[1]

After he had been processed at the Bournemouth reception centre, Keith headed to Leuchars on his disembarkation leave, where he and Jack reunited. They spent as much time together as Jack's duties allowed but the visit was all too brief and, on 1 May, Jack and Sheila saw Keith off from Dundee station. Wing Commander Holmes had resumed command and as soon as Jack and Phil could manage to take leave at the same time the three brothers met in London. The three had last been together in March 1941, during Phil's embarkation leave. As well as seeing the sights of London and experiencing the latest on offer at the theatre, air force publicity had somehow caught onto the fact that the three brothers had met up again and staged a reunion for the BBC's *Anzacs Calling Home* program. After the broadcast, Jack, Phil and Keith stopped in on the Boomerang Club, a popular eating and meeting place for Australian airmen visiting London. While they were there, one of the club's helpers suggested they autograph the snack bar door. They obliged and started a tradition: soon, a 'Panel of Fame' was created as visiting airmen signed their names as well. Within a few weeks, the panel was so crowded with signatures the surrounding walls were threatened.[2]

By May 1943, enemy shipping movements were less frequent but the convoys were more heavily protected. As a consequence, Coastal Command placed greater emphasis on Beaufighter escorts as well as meticulous planning of strike operations.[3] Many new crews arrived at 455 Squadron and much of April and May was taken up training them. As commander of A Flight, Jack took this responsibility seriously and put in many hours training his new airmen. Although the squadron undertook a number of operational sorties during May 1943, Jack flew only three. His first was the most significant since the squadron's conversion to torpedo operations.

On 12 May 1943, escorted by two Beaufighters from 235 Squadron, Jack, flying AE384, led an evening rover to the Norwegian coast. Flight Lieutenant Leonard Jeffreys was navigator. His other crew members were Flight Lieutenant T.M. Cumberland and Flight Sergeant Harvey Rutledge. Flying Officer R.C. Barton returned shortly after take-off because of intercom failure but Jack and Flying Officer Byron Atkinson continued. By this stage, it was rare for enemy merchant vessels to set sail without an escort but they sighted an unaccompanied merchantman of approximately 2500 tons in the Naze area at the southern tip of Norway. The weather was bad with visibility only about 800 yards. Jack and Atkinson made three runs on the ship. Jack's torpedo struck home and he saw steam and smoke from the ship's funnel and, after the attack, circled for 8 minutes, observing a hole ahead of the ship's superstructure on the starboard side. The decks were awash with seawater as the ship listed to starboard and settled low into the water. As Jack and Atkinson returned to Leuchars, they saw the crew taking to their lifeboats.[4] This was Jack's first observed hit on an enemy vessel.

Flying L4105, Jack's next op was a night rover to the Naze–Skaw area on 20 May. This time, four Hampdens from 455 Squadron sighted and attacked two merchant vessels, one of 3500 tons and the other of 2500 tons. No torpedo damage to these was observed. His final operational sortie for the month was on 31 May, flying AE384, when he and three others carried out an afternoon rover patrol. Yet again, the weather was against them. Visibility was poor and the Hampdens lost contact. They searched independently but nothing was sighted.

The disappointing results of the late May operations were overshadowed by Jack's award of the Distinguished Flying Cross on 25 May 1943. It recognised his early operations in Bomber Command and his work as flight commander during the Russian posting. The Air Officer Commanding 18 Group sent him a personal signal offering his 'sincere congratulations'.[5] Jack was quietly pleased with his award. He did not skite or, to use RAF and RAAF parlance, 'shoot a line'. He modestly played it down and, apparently, when Sheila's mother asked him how he had won his award, he teased that it was for 'bringing home a dozen crates of eggs from Ireland to feed the starving people of England'.[6]

455 Squadron carried out a number of attacks on merchant shipping during June 1943 but Jack did not fly operationally: his tour had expired. Taking advantage of the quiet month, Jack took fourteen days' leave, spending most of it with Sheila, who was enjoying her long university break at home. Jack returned to Leuchars on 24 June but did not make his final farewell to Sheila until the next day when he extended the definition of 'local flying' to include Ardrossan and flew over the McDavids' large walled garden, waggling his Hampden's wings and having some fun.[7]

As Jack awaited news of his next posting, the final days of June were about as lazy as any on a RAF station in wartime—a little instruction work, the odd air test, ferrying aircrew to training in Tain and the inevitable tidying up of paperwork in the flight office. A little excitement—though hardly the excitement experienced while on operations—came on 30 June 1943 to brighten the twilight of Jack's first tour with 455 Squadron.

With its proximity to RAF and naval air stations, Dundee had not escaped enemy attention and had suffered a number of air raids. Its Home Guard was active and took seriously its remit to help defend vulnerable areas. In Dundee alone, the Home Guard manned 33 road blocks and frequently organised invasion and combined military and civil defence exercises.[8] 455 Squadron was called upon to assist in one such exercise on 30 June 1943.

Late that night, Jack, Wing Commander Holmes and Squadron Leader Brian 'Butch' O'Connor, the B Flight commander, and their crews were called to the ops room for a briefing. They were told they would be participating in an invasion exercise. As far as the local civil defence units were concerned, they would be German parachutists, landing in Scotland—they were not allowed to speak English at all. The twelve were told that, as separate crews, they would have to make their way back to Leuchars by 2.00 p.m. the next day, all the while evading Home Guard and police. They were then taken to a waiting truck where they arranged themselves on the benches and quietly speculated about their 'operation'.

They drove around for some time and had no idea where they were heading. It was only two days from the dark of the moon so there was little light but in the enclosed truck it was pitch black. They felt disorientated and lost track of how long they had been travelling. As it happened, they had only gone about 5 miles from Leuchars, but the circuitous route taken by their driver made it seem a much greater distance. The three crews were dropped off separately.[9] Using the stars as a guide, each group ascertained they were more or less south-west of Leuchars, so they set off in a north-easterly direction. It was slow going as they hiked through brambles and fields, leaving clear evidence of their path for anyone on the lookout.

Although Jack and his fellow 'German parachutists' knew they were participating in an exercise, the Home Guard was not aware of this. It was not like the large exercise held the month before, which had had its own carefully prepared blueprints for an all-night 'battle' consisting of 'blitz', seaborne and airborne attacks and an accompanying invasion, as well as publicity in the local press prior to the exercise.[10] Unbeknownst to Jack and his fellows, the local Home Guard had been advised of the possibility of German parachutists being in the area and they were on patrol. It was only a matter of time before the weary aircrew were captured. Without prior warning, Jack and his crew were surrounded by a group of Home Guard men, brandishing handguns. Eventually, Jack and his crew revealed themselves, and their identity was confirmed by a phone call to Leuchars.[11]

The mock invasion exercise was Jack's last 'operation' of his first tour with 455 Squadron. He had been a popular squadron member, flight commander and sometime squadron leader. He had managed to find an easy balance between friendship and leadership and still enjoyed himself as one of the boys while holding the respect of those whom he commanded. Before he left the squadron, the boys of A Flight took him to their favourite watering hole where they all relaxed into fond memories, good stories and a pint or two or six. As the hours passed, more than one became well and truly 'shickered'.

Someone sparked the bright idea of going for a walk, thinking perhaps the fresh air might clear a head or two. As they wandered, they found themselves on the boundary of a barley field. It was before harvest, and a bountiful crop was growing. The fresh air did more than sober the boys up, it set the blood flowing and stirred up the mischief-makers. As they passed a police guard post, the boys started to jump and wrestle. Limbs akimbo, a mass of boisterous bodies scrambled onwards. Jack managed to break free but, before he knew it, he was being chased through the field, followed closely and clumsily by his A Flight comrades. He may have acquitted himself well on squadron sports days, the squash court and football field but the thickly growing barley made for slow progress and he was soon tackled down. In the spirit of fun, it was not the traditional football tackle that pinned him to the ground. Despite a game struggle his trousers were soon around his ankles—he had been 'debagged'. Laughing, he picked himself up again, rearranged himself decently and, along with the boys who had flown with him, served with him and shared the exhilaration of successful operations and the grief of lost companions, he walked back to Leuchars.[12]

Tour-expired pilots were often posted to training stations to pass on their skills and Jack was no exception. These postings were considered rest periods, though an instructing stint was by no means a holiday. Jack's posting to 1 Torpedo Training Unit, Turnberry was effective from 1 July 1943. As an instructor, he maintained his acting rank of squadron leader and during this posting received notice of his substantive promotion to flight lieutenant on 26 August 1943.

Turnberry is near the Firth of Clyde, a day trip, or less, from Arran, Glasgow and Ardrossan. The training station was equipped with Oxfords, Wellingtons, Beauforts, Beaufighters and Hampdens. Jack was appointed flight commander of 1 Squadron, flying Hampdens and responsible for a mixed group of Canadians, New Zealanders, Australians and some RAF navigators.[13] As well as lectures, which in the warm summer days were often held outside, Jack would instruct on Oxfords and Hampdens, with much of the flying occurring over the Irish Sea. Jack's program included familiarisation flights, air tests and demonstration formation flights with his trainees, instructing them in emergency take-offs and landings, local and low flying, and dummy torpedo runs on an old naval vessel off Aisla Crag.[14]

1 Torpedo Training Unit had formed on 1 January 1943 and had 'a very, very high accident rate. It was alarming, and it did adversely affect morale.'[15] It was well known that the Hampden was not ideally suited to torpedo strikes but Jack considered 'the greatest problem was pilot problem. I think that people had not had enough training for the tasks that were required of them.'[16] Recognising that many of the pilots who had undertaken their operational training in Canada had not flown for some time before arriving at 1 Torpedo Training Unit, Jack ensured their flying skills were refreshed before they began specialised torpedo training. Over the next months, he trained many pilots who would eventually be posted to his squadron. That they survived is testament to their superb operational training as well as Jack's role in their torpedo training. Some, however, did not survive their month-long torpedo training course.[17]

On 16 August 1943, Sergeant Ron Warfield, an Australian navigator who had trained in Canada, was scheduled for a training exercise but his aircraft was unserviceable. Flight Sergeant John Maxwell, an Australian pilot, called him over. Maxwell's navigator was sick, so he asked Warfield to navigate for him on his exercise, which involved analysing the way torpedoes were released from the Hampden to determine if there were problems with the approach. Maxwell took off and when they were airborne Warfield slid into the Hampden's nose and laid out his charts. He had just settled into position when he looked out the window and saw the port engine on fire. They were flying over the Irish Sea and the Hampden dived into the water off Ayrshire. The seawater quenched the fire and Warfield was catapulted from the aircraft, the impact pushing him out through the hatch which had not been closed properly. If it had, Warfield would have drowned in the aircraft. The rear gunner, Flight Sergeant Doug Riordan, was killed on impact.[18] The wireless operator, Flight Sergeant Leslie Stenzel, suffered a broken nose and was shaken up. Stenzel and Maxwell, who was uninjured, climbed into the dinghy. Warfield, however, was unconscious. When he was thrown out, something sharp had hit him behind his left ear, knocking him out. The carbon dioxide bottle activated, his life jacket inflated and he floated face up in the water. They were in the water for about 45 minutes when a group of Scottish fishermen, who had seen the dinghy from a distance, picked them up and took them to the fishing port of Girvan.

The three survivors were taken by RAF ambulance to 74th British Army General Hospital. Warfield was in a bad way. The ligaments of his left leg were damaged and there was talk of amputation. He drifted in and out of consciousness over the course of many hours. Around midnight, a nurse asked if he could hear her, and he said 'yes'. The nurse then said: 'Your flight commander is here to see you, and he has been here for some time.'

As the Hampden flight commander, Jack had carried out familiarisation flying with Maxwell but he had not been involved in training Warfield, Stenzel or Riordan. Earlier, he had carried out a search for the crashed aircraft and now, despite not really knowing these injured men, he considered it his responsibility to ensure they were recovering. Jack had already seen Stenzel and Maxwell to find out what had happened. As they slept, he sat with Warfield. When he awoke Jack quietly told him that Riordan had died and that Maxwell and Stenzel were also in hospital, but resting comfortably. Warfield had not had any contact with Jack before this, but he had respected his abilities as a flight commander and instructor. He had seen that Jack was a caring person and felt that it was typical of him to show such consideration to the hospitalised aircrew.

Maxwell and Stenzel soon resumed their course and Maxwell would later be posted to 455 Squadron under Jack's command. Warfield stayed in hospital for a few weeks and then spent time in a convalescent depot before being posted to 461 Squadron. He did not meet Jack again during the war but did so years later, when working in the Queensland branch of the AMP. Soon after Jack had been elected to its board, MIM, one of AMP's biggest clients, held a board meeting in Brisbane. Some of the board members knew Warfield had met Jack during the war and invited him for drinks after the meeting. Warfield watched with admiration and respect as Jack mingled easily with everyone in the room. Warfield and Jack rekindled their acquaintance and talked over some of their war experiences, and about others with whom they shared a mutual acquaintance during the war.

As it usually did among those who had flown them, the conversation soon turned towards the Hampden, which for Warfield had almost lived up to its nickname of 'flying coffin'. They agreed the Hampden was not satisfactory for fighting Germans and was definitely worn out back then. They recalled Warfield's accident and their meeting in the hospital. Jack commented that Warfield was 'bloody lucky to have survived' and Warfield recalled his nurse, so many years before, telling him the situation was so bad the hospital had been on permanent standby for flying casualties and, although Riordan had died, he, Maxwell and Stenzel were the first to have survived such a training crash.[19]

Jack's days at Turnberry were full of instruction and training flights. Sheila's finals were imminent and she was busy too. As well as studying, she applied for jobs including the foreign office; the air ministry in Wales; an opportunity to go to Mauritius to learn Japanese; something of an extremely sensitive nature in Scottish Command; and something else of a highly secretive nature in the Auxiliary Territorial Service.[20] A degree would make her an attractive candidate for any job and on 20 September, after returning to Ardrossan, she heard she had passed all her exams and now had her Master of Arts. She phoned Jack, who came down from Turnberry to celebrate with her. The next day they shared a picnic on Fairlie Moor, high in the hills of North Ayrshire, exposed to the elements but protected from the cold wind by the warmth of their love and the happiness of being together.[21] Jack returned to Turnberry almost immediately to resume his duties but on 6 October 1943 phoned to say he was again on leave and would be arriving the next day.[22]

This would be no ordinary holiday. Jack had plans to spend as much time with Sheila as he could and hoped he would be spending it with his fiancée rather than his girlfriend. On 7 October 1943, the day he arrived, he proposed. They had known each other for almost a year. Sheila was not yet 21 and Jack was 23. Perhaps there was an element of the wartime whirlwind in the speed with which their closeness developed and the growing belief that their destinies were entwined. Jack did not record why he proposed when he did but perhaps Sheila's flurry of job applications, which would have meant a posting away from him and less time together, might have had much to do with it.

Sheila did not hesitate to answer. She accepted Jack's proposal and then endured a suspenseful few days as Jack travelled to London to speak with her father, who was there on business. In the time honoured tradition, Jack asked Jim McDavid for his daughter's hand in marriage. Jack had spent much time with Jim and Jessie McDavid over the last months and they had grown fond of him. They had discovered much in common and enjoyed many laughs and jokes together. Like Jack, Jim McDavid enjoyed sport—at Edinburgh University, he had secured blues for soccer and athletics and maintained his enthusiasm for football and other sports all his life.[23] And it was just as well Jack was becoming more proficient on the golfing green as Sheila and her parents were avid golfers. Despite the probability of separation at the end of the war, the McDavids approved Sheila's match with the young pilot who had made much of his air force career. Unlike many prospective bridegrooms, Jack did not have to elaborate on his intentions. Jim McDavid, who had already been tipped off by his excited daughter that Jack would be asking him an important question, merely stated that Jack's reputation preceded him[24] and gladly gave his permission for Jack and Sheila to wed. Jim and Jessie were confident Jack would care for and cherish their daughter but, even so, their delight at Sheila's joy was overshadowed by the knowledge that her future was in a country on the other side of the world. They hid their sadness from their beloved daughter, showed brave faces and celebrated her happiness.[25] All going well the young couple would be married on 8 January 1944, eight days after Sheila's 21st birthday.

PART 3
Second tour

11

Commanding Officer, 455 Squadron

'they were a remarkably fine bunch of people'

Even as Jack instructed the next generation of torpedo pilots, 455 Squadron appeared to be winding down its torpedo activities. It continued patrols and strikes from May 1943 but the day of the Hampden was all but over. It was too slow to work effectively with the faster Beaufighter and Spitfire escorts. Hampden operations continued only until squadrons could be re-equipped with the more manoeuvrable and dependable Beaufighter.[1]

The Bristol Beaufighter had already proven an effective night-fighter and had served admirably in the Middle East and Pacific theatres. In Coastal Command, it had been used successfully as a long-range fighter escort and formidable strike aircraft. The latest version, the Mark X, was a twin-engined, long-range aircraft with a cruising speed of 200 knots. It possessed super-charger technology, vital for low-altitude work as it allowed for increased power on take-off and during tight anti-shipping manoeuvres. It had two reliable 1770 horsepower Hercules XVIII engines that would continue operating after suffering considerable damage. It had a maximum speed of 303 miles per hour at 1300 feet, a range of 1470 miles, a service ceiling of 15,000 feet and a climb rate of 3.5 minutes to 5000 feet. The Mark VIF, which was superseded in March 1943, had been armed with four Hispano 20-millimetre cannon in the nose and four .303-inch machine guns in the wings. The Mark X still had the four nose cannon but, to reduce load on long-range operations, had only one .303 inch machine gun in the rear. Depending on modification, it could carry one torpedo or eight rockets plus two bombs under the wings. It would be nicknamed 'torbeau', 'bombbeau', 'rockbeau', or 'flakbeau', depending on task and weapons used.[2]

Coastal Command had a number of Beaufighter squadrons suited to strike tactics. The North Coates Wing had been successfully operating as a strike wing since April 1943; 489 Squadron RNZAF had started its conversion and, on 19 November, 455 Squadron was advised it would soon be converting to the Mark X. After conversion, the squadron would team with 489 Squadron, also at Leuchars, to operate as a strike wing. It would be known as the Leuchars Wing (and later the Langham Wing) but also, patriotically, the Anzac Wing. Aircrew welcomed the announcement as they were fed up with the lack of meaningful operations.[3]

About this time, Jack received word of his new posting. Wing Commander Holmes was repatriated to Australia on 5 December and Jack took over command of 455 Squadron just under 21 months after he first joined it. He was 23 years old and now an acting wing commander. It was a well deserved achievement. Despite his youth, age was never an issue for Jack or for his men, but some were surprised that he was so young. Flying Officer John Ayliffe, who was seven months older than Jack, thought his commanding officer was a much older man and was taken aback to find that this was not the case.[4] They may have been surprised at his age, but Warrant Officer Ivor Gordon, and all of the squadron for that matter, judged Jack by his results, not his years:

> He was a very efficient organiser, a man you could relate to without feeling under pressure. He wasn't an aggressive leader. He [was a] very human sort of fellow and had a good impressive stamp about him . . . he had more responsibility to carry, but he certainly carried it and he belonged as a leader and squadron commander.[5]

Jack certainly did not let age hinder good leadership: 'I didn't think about being a young man, and I didn't think about any of the squadron which I commanded thinking about me as a young man. They were all extremely co-operative of course. They were a remarkably fine bunch of people.'[6] Flying Officer David Whishaw, one of Jack's pupils at Turnberry who had been posted to 455 Squadron, was one of the many who quickly realised that Jack was an 'outstanding leader in every respect' and readily accepted Jack's challenge to do his 'very best as a member of his team'.[7]

Everything was falling into place for Jack. He was about to marry a beautiful, intelligent young woman and was now responsible for steering his beloved squadron through a period of great change and excitement as it entered a new phase in its operational career. The icing on the cake, so to speak, came two days later when, with Sheila and his brother Keith proudly looking on, he attended an investiture ceremony at Buckingham Palace to receive his Distinguished Flying Cross.

When Jack returned to command his old squadron he found it very different from the one he had left at the end of June 1943. Many of the familiar ground crew faces still remained but he recognised few aircrew as, at the end of August 1943, 38 of them had been declared tour-expired. Some were transferred to Bomber Command but 23 were posted back to Australia and new crews began to arrive. With the imminent conversion to Beaufighters, there would be another exodus of old hands and influx of new as the Beaufighter was a two-man aircraft. Along with the pilot, it required a specially trained navigator/wireless operator. There was not enough time to convert the Hampden navigators to the more specialised Beaufighter work but they would convert easily to other bomber types so, over the next few weeks, most were posted elsewhere, as were the now redundant wireless operator/air gunners. Specialist Beaufighter navigators soon joined the squadron to pair with converting pilots and, within time, already established Beaufighter pilot and navigator partnerships joined straight from operational training units.

Of the first influx, the few new faces Jack recognised were some of his pupils from Turnberry—flying officers David Whishaw, Bob McColl, Frank Proctor, Leo Kempson and Ted Watson, who soon became known amongst his squadron friends as 'Doc' because of his habit of carrying his large pilot's bag, similar to that carried by doctors, to briefings.[8] Over the next two months, more of Jack's former pupils from Turnberry joined the squadron, including Pilot Officer William Barbour, Flying Officer Lloyd Farr, Flight Lieutenant John Pilcher and Flight Sergeant John Maxwell, one of the first survivors of training crashes during Jack's tenure at Turnberry. The squadron may have looked different, but it was as skilled as ever. Jack had lost two flight commanders from the Hampden days who he knew well and trusted, but their replacements were two very capable pilots with considerable anti-shipping experience between them.

After training, Albert Lloyd Wiggins, known as Lloyd Wiggins, had ferried a Wellington to Egypt where he volunteered to join 38 Squadron RAF. In October 1942, then Flight Lieutenant Wiggins led an unescorted section of three Wellington bombers to Tobruk to attack one of Rommel's vital supply convoys. Despite heavy defence from escort destroyers and shore batteries, Wiggins destroyed a 6000-ton merchant vessel. One Wellington was shot down and his own was hit. He was awarded the Distinguished Service Order and his citation recognised he had 'displayed similar skill, courage and initiative on many occasions'.[9] He left the Middle East shortly afterwards and was posted to 455 Squadron on 19 October 1943 as A Flight commander.

Like Wiggins, Colin Milson had ferried an aircraft to Egypt, but his was a Beaufort. He joined 39 Squadron RAF, an anti-shipping torpedo strike unit based on Malta, operating against Rommel's supply column. Squadron Leader Milson was awarded a Distinguished Flying Cross on 20 April 1943, three days after his last operational flight. As well as recognising the part he had played in attacks on Mediterranean shipping and mine-laying operations off the North African coast, his award acknowledged two stunning actions against enemy shipping. In September 1942 he led an attack on a convoy of four merchant vessels escorted by eleven destroyers. Despite formidable opposition, one vessel was destroyed and another damaged. In March 1943 he attacked a tanker protected by three destroyers and fighters. Milson's force scored several hits on the tanker, destroying it. The citation noted that Milson had 'displayed great skill and leadership throughout the operation, contributing materially to the success achieved'. Throughout his career with 39 Squadron, Milson had 'invariably displayed courage and determination'.[10]

After returning to the United Kingdom, Milson joined an Air Ministry team that evaluated and reported on recent developments in the anti-shipping campaign. He then converted to Beaufighters and was to be posted as flight commander to 455 Squadron. Jack, however, had recently advised Flight Lieutenant Pilcher that he would be promoted. Recognising Pilcher's great work and confident in his ability to provide dedicated support as a flight commander, Jack did not want to see someone brought in over him so attempted to reverse Group's decision. He was unsuccessful. After a brief posting to 144 Squadron Milson took command of 455 Squadron's B Flight on 28 December 1943. Pilcher did not bear any resentment and Jack soon saw Milson's calibre.[11] All three recognised the dedication and talents of each other. They became good friends, and that friendship was maintained after the war.[12]

The courage, skills and experience of Jack's two new flight commanders were a perfect match for his own. Wiggins and Milson were individualists and independent thinkers who complemented Jack's leadership style of 'inspired example'.[13] They proved a formidable combination where 'each was able to inspire junior aircrew to train hard and perform well; they evoked a spirit of dedication in aircrew which ensured a fine temper to the spearhead of attack'.[14] That inspiration could not be underestimated. Flying Officer Ernest 'Blue' Bernau recalled that Jack always ensured he was leading any possible bad strikes.[15] Men will always follow those who demonstrate they are worthy of being followed. Jack, Milson and Wiggins did not take, or expect their men to take, unnecessary risks. They demanded nothing less than they were prepared to do themselves. They flew with commitment and competence on all occasions; they led by example and were respected.[16]

Jack, Milson and Wiggins quickly began to mould the new 455 Squadron into an effective strike force where discipline was paramount and unwavering.[17] Warrant Officer Noel Turner recalled the different personalities of this triumvirate: Jack was aloof and unbending; Milson was the ultimate martinet, the strict disciplinarian who hid too well his softer side; and Wiggins was laconic but ready to criticise when it was warranted. These seemingly negative qualities were demanded by circumstance and yet, Turner recalled, there was no resentment to their approaches to discipline and command. 'It was obviously a time of tension, virtually forming a new squadron and urgent operational work waiting—no time for pussy-footing around.'[18]

On 22 December, the squadron's operations record book announced 'Hampden flying to cease forthwith' and the first Beaufighters arrived. As commanding officer, it was Jack's responsibility to lead the conversion and training program. He had never flown a Beaufighter before but he was the first to fly Beaufighter T/455. His conversion was brief but effective. A test pilot from the Bristol company talked to the squadron about the aircraft and then took Jack up with him. Standing behind the pilot's seat, Jack carefully watched and listened as the test pilot-cum-instructor took the Beaufighter through its paces. When they landed, the test pilot started to climb out of the aircraft. Jack asked him where he was going. It was hardly a confidence-inspiring reply: 'You don't expect me to go up with you, do you?'[19] Despite his instructor's lack of confidence, Jack was an experienced pilot who had taken the opportunity to fly different aircraft whenever he had the chance.[20] He successfully completed a number of circuits and bumps and was thus, officially 'converted'. Jack had been fond of the Hampden, but 'the Beaufighter was very strong and we were thrilled with them'.[21] Jack considered that the:

> Bristol Beaufighters were a remarkable aeroplane and with 20-millimetre cannon and carrying rockets they were a formidable force. They showed their capabilities on a number of occasions. I can remember in Den Helder a pilot hitting the top of a mast of a ship and coming back with [it] still embedded in the nose of the aircraft, up against the rudder pedals.[22] The aeroplane landed perfectly safely. Others had the whole underside of the belly of the aircraft torn out on the masts of ships and still came back without any problem. You can throw them at the ground and walk away from them satisfactorily. It was a great comfort.[23]

Jack had been rated 'exceptional' at 1 Torpedo Training Unit and now successfully brought these skills to his own squadron as he converted his pilots to Beaufighters.[24] After standing behind Jack for about 45 minutes, they were then on their own, flying solo so they could familiarise themselves with their new aircraft, which had considerably more kick than the old Hampdens. They carried out the usual circuits and bumps, low-flying, steep turns and formation exercises. When they crewed up with their new navigators, they carried out navigational exercises and learned each other's little idiosyncrasies, developing the close working relationship upon which their lives would depend when flying operations. Warrant Officer Ivor Gordon recalled they each had at least a full month of training before their first operations.[25] Their training was not all in the air—they also sat through a number of important lectures on the squadron's new role and strike wing tactics.[26]

Jack met Sheila McDavid in late 1942, shortly after his return from Russia. (COURTESY BRUCE DAVENPORT)

Jack on HMS *Argonaut* in Iceland, returning from Russia. Sheila kept this photo in her 1943 pocket diary. (COURTESY BRUCE DAVENPORT)

Jack and his brothers Phil and Keith all joined Coastal Command squadrons. This photo was taken after Phil returned safely from captivity in May 1945. From left, Squadron Leader Phil Davenport, Wing Commander Jack Davenport and Flying Officer Keith Davenport. (COURTESY PHIL DAVENPORT)

8 January 1944. Jack and Sheila leaving
the Church of St Cuthbert, Saltcoats,
after a 'wonderful wedding in Scotland'.
(COURTESY JUNE ROSS)

Cutting the cake.
(COURTESY BRUCE DAVENPORT)

Taken during the minister's speech at Jack and Sheila's reception at the Eglington
Hotel. From left: Sheila, Jack, Brenda Worrall (bridesmaid), Phil Davenport (best man),
Mrs Jessie McDavid and Keith Davenport. (COURTESY BRUCE DAVENPORT)

Jack was proud of the squadron's crest and motto, 'strike and strike again', and kept a copy in the back of his flying log book. (COURTESY BRUCE DAVENPORT)

Beaufighters in formation. (COURTESY BILL HERBERT)

Jack Davenport (standing in foreground) briefing his crews for an operation in late June 1944. Standing from left: Flight Sergeant Albert Vigor (partly obscured), Flying Officer Ted Collaery. Seated, front row, from left: Flying Officer Steve Sykes (partly obscured), Flying Officer Ted 'Doc' Watson, Flying Officer Vic Smith, Flying Officer Lee Turner, Flying Officer Forbes Macintyre (map on knees), Flying Officer Jack Cox, Pilot Officer John Ayliffe, Flying Officer Neil Smith, Flight Sergeant Allan Ibbotson. Seated, back row, from left: Pilot Officer Vic Pearson, Flying Officer Fred Dodd, Flying Officer Bill Barbour, Flight Sergeant John Payne, Flying Officer Leo Kempson, Flying Officer Wally Kimpton, Flight Sergeant George Kerr. (COURTESY BRUCE DAVENPORT)

Jack and Group Captain Arthur Clouston DSO DFC AFC and Bar at Buckingham Palace at their investiture in October 1945. (COURTESY JUNE ROSS)

In Jack's office at Langham with his two flight commanders. From left, Squadron Leader Lloyd Wiggins, Jack and Squadron Leader Colin Milson. (COURTESY BRUCE DAVENPORT)

Jack and his Beaufighter navigator, Flying Officer Ralph Jones. (COURTESY BRUCE DAVENPORT)

Jack's protégé, Flying Officer Peter Ilbery (right) with his navigator, Flying Officer Bill Bawden, at Dallachy. (COURTESY IAN GORDON)

From left: Flight Lieutenant Wally Kimpton, Flying Officer Clive 'Tommy' Thompson, Jack, Squadron Leader Colin Milson and Flying Officer Colin Cock. They are enjoying Damon Runyon's *Take it Easy* and a spot of sunshine at Langham. 11 August 1944. (COURTESY SCOTT MILSON)

455 Squadron Beaufighters, in invasion stripes, line up at Langham.
(COURTESY BRUCE DAVENPORT)

This photo was captioned by Colin Milson: 'Leo Kempson, self and Jack Davenport saying cheerio to an aerodrome in Southern England' on 1 August 1944. Flying Officer Leo Kempson and his navigator Flying Officer Raymond Curzon died days later in a devastating strike on 10 August. (COURTESY SCOTT MILSON)

Crucial to the new tactics was skilled, steady formation flying at 50 feet or less to ensure they stayed under enemy radar. This was referred to as flying at 'nought feet'. Jack was stringent about this requirement and would determinedly hound his pilots about the importance of flying low. They also practised rapid take-off and formation. This would be essential when co-operating with 489 Squadron on a wing strike as both squadrons had to arrive at the target area at the same time. Another essential of strike wing tactics was to fly a 'vic' formation en route to the target, where, in groups of three, the lead aircraft formed the point of a 'V' with numbers two and three in tight formation beside it, and with nose to the lead aircraft's wing tips. This would provide the best form of defence against enemy fighters before breaking off into small attack sections as the target was approached. Other essentials were precise torpedo launching and accurate anti-flak attacks.[27] Jack would later describe a typical use of these tactics during a radio talk. Although he does not over-emphasise the hazardous role played by the anti-flak Beaufighters, it is clear it was dangerous:

> When the target is sighted, the leader gives the order to attack. This is the signal for the flak-busters to start and draw ahead, individual section leaders choosing their victim according to briefing. It is vital that every possible escort is effectively strafed in order that the torpedo aircraft may drop accurately without much interference from the flak. In other words, the anti-flak aircraft are there to firstly attract the enemy's fire and then to silence it. In practice, however, they achieve much more. Great devastation is caused by the terrific fire power of their cannon. Destroyer-like escort vessels have many times been quickly sunk, and almost without exception have been set on fire purely by cannon attack.[28]

The early stages of the training program progressed well and Jack confidently handed the running of it over to squadron leaders Milson and Wiggins, who were ably assisted by experienced pilots from 489 Squadron.[29] He had other things on his mind: he was about to be married.

Many weddings boast dramas galore before the bride and groom finally exchange vows, and Jack and Sheila's was no exception. After a pre-wedding party in the mess—noted for football in the anteroom, duels with pints of beer, a great deal of carousing and a presentation by Jack of mock service ribbons which had been ripped from Flying Officer Doc Watson's braces—a free-for-all broke out and Jack's braces where ripped off, just before everyone else lost theirs. Somehow in the scrum Jack's face was skinned and Doc Watson considered it 'bad luck for the wedding'.[30]

The bad luck continued. On the night before the wedding, Jack and the small RAAF contingent had booked into the Eglinton Hotel where the reception was to be held.[31] On the morning of 8 January 1944, Jack and his brother Phil, who was to be best man, were anxiously awaiting Keith's appearance. There had been no word from him until mid-morning when a telegram finally arrived explaining his delay. He had been on an anti-submarine patrol on the evening of 6 January and his Sunderland had returned to Pembroke Dock in south-west Wales just before midnight. What with debriefing, the wait for a train to Waterloo and the inevitable and seemingly interminable connections to Scotland, it was no wonder he was late but almost as soon as they opened his telegram, Keith appeared. Somehow, his uniform had been damaged so the other RAAF boys were measured and a tunic of approximate good fit was commandeered. While Keith showered, Jack wielded an iron and pressed his trousers; Squadron Leader Bob MacBeth, who had replaced Flight Lieutenant John Bilton as 455 Squadron's medical officer, put his needlework skills to good use and sewed pilot's wings onto the borrowed tunic while Phil cleaned Keith's shoes. The scratch valet service proved successful and Keith was rendered fit to carry out his usher's duties.[32] And there the bad luck ceased.

It is a long-held tradition that a rainy wedding day, although havoc for shoes and photos, heralds a long and happy marriage. Jack and Sheila eventually shared over 50 years of wedded contentment after exchanging vows on a bleak, snowy, cold, windy and very cloudy day. In fact, the cloud was so dense the squadron's planned beat-up, where they would fly low and fast over the church, had to be cancelled. Jack had been kept completely in the dark about the plans because, as a responsible commanding officer, he would have had to put his foot down. Even so, he admitted years later he felt a little disappointed that the weather had thwarted their plans.[33]

It was a 'wonderful wedding in Scotland',[34] celebrated at the Church of St Cuthbert, Saltcoats, a short distance from Sheila's family home at Ardrossan. As the muted afternoon light filtered through the stained-glass windows behind the altar, Jack and Sheila exchanged vows. Phil Davenport recalled the reception at the Eglinton as elegant and happy.[35] Somehow—Jack was never sure how—Sheila's father managed to acquire 'copious quantities of champagne'. There was never any doubt that this bounty was acquired legitimately, however. Jack shared the opinion of many: 'He was a meticulous person and he could have only done it in a proper fashion'.[36] The gift table was heavily laden. This far into the war there were few items available in shops, and certainly no luxury or gift items, so family and friends raided their own linen stores and collections of beautiful heirloom silver for the newlyweds.[37] Jack and Sheila were touched by these especially personal gifts, but there was one gift which was not so welcome. No doubt well meant, someone gave them a number of ration cards. Ration cards were individually allocated and these could only come from two sources—sacrificed from someone's own personal supply or from the blackmarket. If from the former, Jack and Sheila could not in all good conscience deprive someone of their own entitlement, no matter how kind the thought. If from the latter, they could not condone or profit from blackmarketeering. There was only one thing for it: they gratefully appreciated the gesture, but firmly returned the gift.[38]

There were two speeches on the day. Jim McDavid talked with much Scottish humour and tenderness about his only daughter. Even so, the spectre of a future with every prospect of an early widowhood—and the known certainty of emigration to a far country if her husband survived the war—entered the room as he spoke. But champagne flowed, voices rose in laughter and the spectre soon left. Jack stood on a chair to respond to his new father-in-law's speech. It was a riveting performance, and his speech was much more successful than his attempts to hide from witnesses and camera his mess-gained injuries. Phil read the telegrams, including one from the squadron complete with air force terminology and traditional wedding day innuendo: 'You are operational now and must keep your own end up. This sortie very tricky effort. No fighter cover available so take bags of evasive action. Report any operational failures immediately upon return to base'.[39] Understandably, Jack and Sheila did not let on about the success or otherwise of 'operations' but there was almost a failure in regards to operational secrecy. Jack had withheld the honeymoon destination, not wanting to risk unwelcome visitors, a barrage of air force signals or well-meaning beat-ups. As they would be travelling by train, however, Sheila had sensibly labelled their luggage. Jack spied the telltale tags and, exhorting Phil to keep their confidence, sent him to remove the tags. Phil and secrecy prevailed and soon it was time to cut the cake.

In the fifth year of war, rationing was stricter than ever. Eggs were almost an unimaginable delicacy amongst the civilian population and many wedding cakes were made without eggs unless the bride had access to farm eggs. Sheila was very touched when family and friends saved their rations and contributed fruit, sugar and eggs to her wedding cake. Icing had long been banned so, like other brides, her cake was adorned with a cardboard cover to give the appearance of royal icing for the photos.[40] The marzipan icing, which was usually laid under the royal icing, was replaced by an improvisation of haricot beans flavoured with almond essence. With a flourish, the cardboard cover was removed to reveal the two-tiered light fruit cake. As the guests looked on, Jack placed his hand over Sheila's and, laughingly, they cut the cake. 'It was a very good, happy day.'[41]

The happy days were to continue. Winter was not the perfect time to holiday in Scotland, and certainly not in the Scottish Highlands, with its moody weather where purple mists could descend and envelop with little notice and black rain clouds could mask the craggy heads of the mountains. But at any time of the year, the highlands and in particular its loch district, which included the Trossachs, were beautiful with its panorama of rich colours reflecting in the tranquil waters of the lochs scattered throughout the west of Perthshire. The isolated area was an ideal choice for a honeymoon and the Trossachs Hotel, overlooking Trossachs Pass on the banks of Loch Achray, and surrounded by heather-covered hills, was a perfectly romantic place to enjoy the solitude that many newlyweds crave.[42]

Solitude was all very well, but Jack and Sheila were sociable people and when Jack noticed that a young Australian airman had joined the hotel's company he invited him to share a drink. Sergeant Pilot Peter Ilbery, from Neutral Bay in Sydney, had recently arrived in the United Kingdom and was on leave while awaiting his posting. He had chosen the Trossachs, having long heard of its beauty from his family. The three hit it off and spent some time rambling about Loch Katrine before leaving the hotel together by car on 15 January and parting in Stirling.[43]

After a blissful week in the Scottish Highlands Jack and Sheila returned to the real world, where Jack resumed command of his squadron and Sheila set up their new home on a large and busy air station. They moved into solid brick, double-storey married quarters at Leuchars—just themselves and about 120 mice. One of the first tasks was to clear the place of the mice and, as Jack laughingly recalled, years later, 'it wasn't easy. They move! They provided a much more difficult target than a ship!'[44]

12

Beaufighter Leader

'he was competent and the sort of leader we wanted'

The battle of the mice continued for some time, but Jack had to turn his attention from the war against four-legged vermin to that against the two-legged type. Over the preceding months, the Allies had gained much ground. The Germans had collapsed in Sicily and mainland Italy, and in October 1943 Italy officially sided with the Allies, declaring war on Germany. Bomber Command's campaign had increased considerably since March 1943 and, along with the US Army Air Force, had brought about much devastation on German industrial towns. Although fierce fighting continued in New Guinea, Australians had successfully occupied Lae and Salamaua in September 1943 and by the end of the year Shaggy Ridge had been captured. Coastal Command had had its own successes. Its strike squadrons had sunk about 93,000 tons and another 23 ships (about 81,000 tons), had been damaged. By the end of 1943 its strike force was finally 'falling into the shape for which it had long been designed'.[1]

Jack returned to the squadron on 17 January 1944 to find the Beaufighter training program was progressing well. By that time there was only one navigator unattached to a pilot so he paired up with Flying Officer Ralph (pronounced Rafe) Jones, RAF Volunteer Reserve.[2] Jones may have been the last navigator available but he was by no means the rotten apple in the crate. He would eventually be awarded a Distinguished Flying Cross and Bar and his Bar citation tells it all: 'A navigator of outstanding ability who has contributed to the successful completion of many sorties . . . Throughout his operational career, this officer has displayed a fine fighting spirit and great devotion to duty.'[3] Nor, for Jones, was Jack the booby prize. Ralph had decided from the start he was going to fly with Jack and rigged things so he would end up with him.[4] It was a ploy Jack never regretted:

> That was one of the best things that happened to me. He was remarkable. He was called 'Gramps' because he, at that stage, was nearly thirty and he was the old man on the squadron among the aircrew. He was a meticulous navigator, extremely skilled, cool as a cucumber, the rougher things [were], the better his log turned out to be.[5]

The meticulous navigator and brilliant pilot forged a successful strike partnership. Jack found he owed much to Ralph Jones and always remembered his skill and great calm. Jack recalled that 'We had a great understanding', and from that understanding sprang friendship.[6] Although Jones resumed his employment with the British customs service after the war, he and Jack maintained a lifelong correspondence and whenever Jack flew to London on business the two would meet.[7]

Training progressed well during January and February but the burden of the program was ably continued by squadron leaders Milson and Wiggins, who had achieved good results while Jack was honeymooning. Even so, Jack ensured his trusted flight commanders followed a program that lived up to his own exacting standards and he became known as a strict disciplinarian. Flying Officer Wally Kimpton, who had joined the squadron in the Hampden days, recalled that during the conversion period Jack tried everything out himself beforehand, and there was the feeling that 'if it was good enough for him, it was good enough for the rest of us and it could be done'. Kimpton also recalled that Jack 'used to insist that we know the cockpit drill blindfolded . . . he'd already done it . . . He was very adamant'.[8]

455 Squadron was officially classed as operational on 1 March 1944 and its first Beaufighter operation was five days later. Jack did not have the honour of leading it as he was away from the squadron acting as president of a court martial. Led by Squadron Leader Milson, on his first operation with the squadron, eight Beaufighters from 455 Squadron provided an anti-flak escort to four torbeaus from 489 Squadron on a rover patrol off the Norwegian coast. A heavily escorted convoy was sighted and the torbeaus scored two

hits. 455 Squadron's Beaufighters raked the ships with cannon fire and numerous hits were seen on the decks and superstructures of both merchant vessels and their escorts. The strike force suffered no casualties, all aircraft returned and landed safely. The only damage to 455 Squadron was in one Beaufighter's tail.[9] Jack considered his squadron's first Beaufighter operation was well-timed and executed; it was 'an excellent attack showing that determined anti-flak escort is very effective'.[10]

Jack's first Beaufighter operation was on 10 March 1944. As the leader of the anti-flak contingent, it was his responsibility to brief his men on the strike strategy. For him, planning was all important: 'I always felt that to go on an operation without every detail being carefully worked out was inviting trouble.'[11] Ivor Gordon attested to Jack's planning and briefing skills:

> There was no question about that . . . When he was briefing us for an operation, he was clear and concise and decisive . . . We understood what he was saying and he knew what he was talking about . . . He was competent and the sort of leader we wanted. Nobody could have asked for more.[12]

Often, Jack would offer a telling opinion based on experience. John Ayliffe recalled that 'that's where he really showed out with his experience and [even if] he wasn't leading the operation, he would give whoever was going to lead it a fair idea of how to go about it.'[13] Knowing he had prepared his men as best he could, Jack led his anti-flak escort for four torbeaus from 489 Squadron, flying at 50 feet, along the Norwegian coast. Visibility was poor and no enemy shipping was sighted. Another patrol was carried out that afternoon, led by Squadron Leader Milson, but it too resulted in a nil sighting report.

On 16 March, fifteen Beaufighters from 455 Squadron, led by Jack and ten torbeaus from 489 Squadron, were detached to RAF Skitten, in the north of Scotland, close to Wick. A number of operations were carried out from Skitten, including an anti-shipping patrol along the Norwegian coast on 23 March where Jack led the 455 Squadron anti-flak escort for 489 Squadron's six torbeaus. The weather was bad and visibility was poor, which resulted in the formation breaking up and returning separately to base. The only success from the disappointing patrol came when one of the torbeaus sank a 700-ton merchant vessel after the formation scattered.

The Skitten detachment was not a success. Weather aside, it had become clear that Scotland, be it Skitten or even Leuchars, was too far north for the types of operations now needed. Intelligence reports indicated that shipping activity in the form of heavily escorted convoys was increasing along the German and Dutch coasts. On 26 March, 455 and 489 squadrons received signals advising them to transfer to RAF Langham, a newly established station in the county of Norfolk, under the control of 16 Group. It was the closest station to the Dutch coast, only about half an hour's flying time away.

RAF Langham was commanded by New Zealand-born Group Captain Arthur Clouston DFC AFC and Bar.[14] Clouston had had a distinguished flying career. In his early flying days he had broken Amy Johnson's London to the Cape record and lowered the round trip time by five days. He had broken the existing records for London to Australia and London to New Zealand flights and in 1935 had become one of the first two civilian test pilots appointed to the Royal Aircraft Establishment at Farnborough. Before taking command of RAF Langham, Clouston had commanded 224 Squadron RAF, which flew anti-submarine operations over the Bay of Biscay, often joining his crews on operations. Clouston was well known as a pilot and commander who knew what dangerous operations were all about. He was committed to establishing good relations with those in his squadrons and he was well respected by those whom he commanded. David Whishaw recalled the significant role Clouston would play as station commander: 'One could not imagine a more straightforward, cheerful, no-nonsense and positive man than Clouston to set the tone for the high morale which Davenport fostered to a pitch that was maintained for the whole of the Langham period'.[15]

455 Squadron had barely finished settling in to their new station when orders arrived that they were to 'engage in a bombing role against enemy shipping'.[16] Before an intensive program of practice bombing commenced, Clouston called his new squadrons together for a welcome briefing. He advised them the Langham Wing, as they were now officially known (though still patriotically, the Anzac Wing) would combine at times with the Strubby and North Coates wings. He assured them they would be kept busy. In addition to increased enemy shipping, German *Schnellbooten*, the fast motor torpedo boats

known to the Allies as E-boats, which carried out offensive operations, usually at night with torpedo or mine, were creating problems for Allied shipping in the English Channel. Their new objective was to clear the channel of enemy shipping. 455 Squadron carried out a number of reconnaissance patrols in the last days of April during which enemy ships were sighted, leading to some successful attacks by the Strubby Wing. Jack flew on two of these operations.

Despite high hopes after the conversion to Beaufighters, the squadron had seen little meaningful action. Many, including flying officers David Whishaw, Bob McColl, Neil Smith and Doc Watson, were starting to feel frustrated at the lack of results.[17] Bombing practice was still in train and when Jack led fifteen Beaufighters from the squadron, accompanied by fourteen from 489 Squadron, on an armed reconnaissance patrol off Cherbourg on 4 May 1944 the Beaufighters were armed with cannon, not bombs.

Jack recalled years later that they had been 'really looking for trouble that day'. With Jack leading in NE774, the Beaufighters took off from Langham at 4.45 a.m. They had been told 'to rub out any shipping south of a certain line and any shipping above that line that was not on a certain course'.[18] At 6.10 a.m. they received a signal stating there was a possibility of shipping 5 miles north of Cherbourg, one of the E-boats' main bases. They then set course from Beachy Head where their Spitfire escort joined them at 6.20 a.m. At 7.20 a.m., Jack saw three small vessels:[19]

> They seemed to be the size of German E-boats and I detached my right wing, under Flight Lieutenant Pilcher . . . to attack. I took the rest of the force on, reached the end of the patrol area, then headed towards the three ships we'd seen earlier.

From this point, the exact course of events is unclear. The squadron's operations record book states that the wing leader:

> . . . ordered two sections to attack. Vessels opened fire with light flak. Thirteen aircraft attacked and vessels took evasive action and increased speed. The vessels were then visually identified as friendly motor torpedo boats and the wing leader, who had just ordered his section to attack, ordered all aircraft to cease fire. The motor torpedo boats continued firing and then fired the colours of the day two or three times.

In his memoir, David Whishaw confirmed that the order came from Davenport for Pilcher's section, in which Whishaw was flying:

> To attack, whilst his [section] continued the patrol. In Beaufighter S, Jack [Belfield] and I were on the port extremity of our section, and a vessel lay directly in front on which I fired and scored several hits. The rest of our seven Beaus were now flying in line-ahead formation and spread out to allow for simultaneous attacks, which had actually commenced on both vessels.

Wishaw then identified Pilcher as the one who spotted the friendly vessels:

'Suddenly came Pilcher's urgent voice over the [radio]: "Look out—they're ours." I remember a feeling of incredulous shock as I flew on low over the water . . .'[20]

But in 1987, Jack recalled: 'I caught up with our right wing and was just about to attack when I saw the red ensign on one of the ships. I told our planes not to attack but three of our planes had already fired several rounds of cannon. These ships had also fired at us.'[21] There was much confusion that day and the accounts clearly diverge. As well as the discrepancy as to who initially identified the friendly vessels, Whishaw later recalled only two vessels (which agreed with the operations record book). But memory has a way of playing tricks over time. Immediately after firing on the enemy vessels, Whishaw turned his focus from the ships as he heard his port engine sputtering. He then left the target area and, shortly after, his engine stopped, until he remembered to spin his fuel control wheels to change from empty to full tanks. He was so worried about forgetting to change the tanks on his way down to Beachy Head and later potential repercussions that any recollection of the day's events were blurred. Acknowledging fallibility of memory, he admitted that 'official operations reports were occasionally inaccurate, relying as they did largely on the accounts of crews. I know that sometimes I misread the reality of events during operations.'[22] It may not be clear who fired first, but it is certain that the Royal Navy motor torpedo boats had not fired any recognition signals and even when Jack had ordered all aircraft to cease fire, they continued firing.[23]

The naval vessels had been involved in *Fabius*, the final D-day rehearsal exercise, and were returning after completing a patrol.[24] It seemed that Jack's reconnaissance patrol had strayed into a total bombing restriction area off St Catherine's Point on the southern tip of the Isle of Wight. Motor torpedo boats *708* and *720* had not initially fired off the colours of the day because, as far as they were concerned, there was no need.[25] Even so, the naval crews should have recognised that the sleek Beaufighters with their escort of distinctly elliptical-winged Spitfires were not enemy aircraft. As a consequence, *708* was full of cannon holes and had to be scuttled. *720* was damaged but made it to port. Seventeen officers and ratings were wounded, some seriously.[26] Jack stayed with the stricken vessel and its survivors to ensure a good fix on them for the air–sea rescue and sent the rest of his Beaufighters back to report the incident.[27]

It was a calamitous and potentially career destroying event. The next morning Jack recalled that, 'I was advised that I was under house arrest and there would be a court martial. Admiral Portsmouth was still screaming blue murder.'[28] The investigation continued over a number of days and 'my only defence was that we'd been told to destroy shipping south of a particular line, and that's where the ships were'.[29] Jack maintained that his patrol was not in a total bombing restriction area and the naval vessels were where they shouldn't have been but the Commander-in-Chief Portsmouth looked at it rather differently. He considered the principal cause of the incident was not that there happened to be Royal Navy ships in the area, but the Beaufighters' navigational error. Perhaps condescendingly—but it does come across sarcastically—he noted the Beaufighters were new to maritime operations and had not appreciated the high unlikelihood that German ships would be so close to the British coastline in daylight.[30] Despite this one-eyed assessment, Jack was exonerated. He received a telegram from Portsmouth congratulating the squadron on its 'most efficient attack', noting they could not believe the Royal Navy ships had been sunk by 42 rounds of cannon.[31]

For some, this incident gained a measure of notoriety and 4 May became the 'day we pranged the navy'.[32] Jack was thankful he had not been court-martialled but was 'sad as the navy's motor torpedo boats were our friends and we had worked together'.[33] Despite his compassion, he was relieved the incident had had no repercussions for himself and his squadron but was annoyed that some believed his aircraft had made the navigational error and not the naval vessels. He was adamant that the error had not been on the part of 455 Squadron.[34]

This was not 455 Squadron's only encounter with Royal Navy vessels. Soon after, on 10 June 1944, during an anti–E-boat patrol along the Cherbourg Peninsular led by Squadron Leader Lloyd Wiggins, Flying Officer Wally Kimpton sighted the wake of a vessel. He dropped two flares, circled the vessel which appeared to be an E-boat and then attacked with his two 500-pound bombs which burst 50 yards off the vessel's starboard quarter. Just as Kimpton circled to attack with cannon, the vessel fired the correct colours of the day. Wiggins and Kimpton, as well as Flying Officer Clive 'Tommy' Thompson, claimed the friendly vessel was in the free bombing area. John Ayliffe, who also flew that day, recalled that 455 Squadron was again exonerated when the Admiralty determined the naval forces were at fault.[35]

Jack never forgot the day his patrol fired on Allied vessels. His remorse was strong, but so also was his belief that the motor torpedo boats were off course. Following the war, Jack became friends with a former Royal Navy officer who had settled in Australia. Dick Mason and his wife Mary grew close to Jack and Sheila and spent many happy hours together throughout their long friendship. Along with another couple, they frequently holidayed at Lord Howe Island and at one time, when they were relaxing together with a few drinks, Jack started talking about the day they pranged the navy. He stressed to his friends that he did not agree with the Navy's verdict that his patrol had entered the restricted bombing area because of a navigational error. He blamed the naval vessels for failing to fire off the colours of the day and light-heartedly accused both the sailors and the Royal Navy of being stupid. He was laughing as he fired off another volley of 'stupids' when he suddenly stopped, realising Dick Mason was a former naval officer. Dick recalled that Jack 'almost burst into tears he was so distressed that he could have offended me'. Dick soon put Jack right and laughed along with him. Dick would never have made the mistakes of his fellows: he may have been Royal Navy, but he was a submariner![36]

For some time there had been speculation that the Allied invasion of Europe was imminent. The Commander-in-Chief Coastal Command had visited and advised the strike wings that they would be responsible for protecting the great invasion convoys from attack by enemy vessels.[37] No date was advised but by mid May 1944 it was obvious that D-day was imminent and suspicions and expectations were confirmed when the squadron's Beaufighters, along with every other aircraft in the invasion force, were painted in distinctive black-and-white striped invasion marking on fuselage and wings.[38]

Training exercises were carried out almost every day, with the squadron flying more training than operational hours during May, averaging about twenty hours per day.[39] It was tiring work but the practice was paying off. Towards the end of the month, Group Captain Clouston attended a conference at 16 Group headquarters, where errors in bombing practice were discussed. The Air Officer Commanding was particularly concerned and wanted those offending squadrons to improve immediately. The North Coates station commander asked him how they should do this as his squadrons felt they were doing their best. The Air Officer Commanding replied that the answer was '455 Squadron, Langham'. Clouston was proud of 455 Squadron's 'fine record' and now other squadrons had to aim for it. Congratulating Jack and the squadron he noted that 'it is through your high standard and exactitude in everything you undertake, which has placed you on this high level and it is a great credit to you all—good work—keep it up'. High praise, but Jack did not leave it there: 'There is still plenty of room for improvement. Let's keep on top. Assess each bomb you drop and let's have the figures.'[40]

It was not just the aircrew who were preparing for D-day—the ground crew had an important role to play as well. Flight Sergeant Jack 'Jeep' McKnight recalled that, shortly before D-day, Jack paraded the entire squadron and told them that he expected ground and aircrew to put in a maximum effort. He expected his ground crew to work non-stop to keep turnaround time to a minimum so an aircraft could be in the air again in as short a time as possible. He stressed that the more efficient they were, the better their contribution. Round-the-clock effort seemed a small sacrifice: they knew Jack had already told the aircrew that loss of lives would be heavy. Flight Sergeant McKnight and his fellow ground crew were all 'suitably impressed' with their commanding officer's exhortations, but they were deeply 'saddened at the increased prospect of losing some of our aircrew mates'.[41]

•

A convoy had been sighted along the main Dutch coastal convoy route and 455 and 489 squadrons were briefed for a large strike on 14 May 1944. Armed with 20-millimetre cannon, 455 Squadron's twelve Beaufighters were airborne between 11.29 and 11.40 a.m. These, along with six from 489 Squadron, provided the anti-flak escort for 489's six torbeaus. Jack led the anti-flak contingent in NE774.

Formation was effected on the way to Coltishall, where the Beaufighters rendezvoused with the Mustang fighters. 455 Squadron flew in two echelons, or parallel groups, as the torbeaus' starboard escort. 489's six anti-flak Beaufighters were on the torbeaus' port side. The strike force patrolled as far as Nordenay Island in the Frisian group but did not see any enemy vessels. Jack then turned the force on a reciprocal course. The weather throughout was terrible. Rain was heavy and non-stop, making a sighting difficult. But the rain, low cloud and sea haze were as much a boon as a hindrance. They effectively hid the strike force until the last moment: surprise was Jack's best weapon initially and he would make the most of it. An enemy convoy was sighted close to Ameland at 1.14 p.m. Four merchant ships were well defended by a ring of sixteen escorts, consisting of minesweepers and trawler-type auxiliaries. The merchantmen carried aerial rockets as well as balloons, which were designed to hamper attacking aircraft, the auxiliaries were armed as flak ships and the minesweepers were equipped with anti-aircraft armament. In addition, one vessel at the rear of the convoy was used as a flame thrower.

Almost as soon as the convoy was sighted, Jack radioed his pilots to 'prepare, prepare, prepare'. They climbed to their attack position and then, on his 'attack, attack, attack', each selected a target on which they would unload their cannon and dived towards the convoy. There was little room to manoeuvre and the intense flak from the enemy ships was well matched by flak from shore defences. Flying Officer Bob McColl unloaded 400 rounds of cannon into two of the leading minesweepers. As they dived, Jack and Flying Officer Ian Masson each shot an escort and attacked the merchantmen in their paths. McColl and other anti-flak pilots soon succeeded in dampening the severe flak to allow 489 Squadron's torbeaus a steady run-in. It was a stunningly successful attack. Six torpedoes were released. A 3000-ton merchantman was hit by torpedo and left blazing furiously, another was damaged and a thick column of smoke rose from it. One minesweeper was hit by cannon fire and was listing badly. In addition, hits were observed on a number of escort vessels.[42] Jack's force, however, was not unscathed. Flying Officer Ivan Pettitt and his navigator, Flying Officer Charles Lowcock of 489 Squadron, failed to return[43] and five Beaufighters from 455 Squadron and one from 489 were damaged.

Group Captain Clouston thought the attack excellent and well co-ordinated.[44] Jack considered his 'pilots made good attacks under difficult conditions and in the very little time available'.[45] Jack was particularly impressed with the work of Flying Officer Masson, one of his deputy flight commanders. The next day, he recommended the award of an immediate Distinguished Flying Cross for Masson. It is clear the qualities Jack recognised in Masson—the 'energetic determination in the face of very heavy opposition, and a keenness to meet the enemy' and the 'brilliant example and inspiration to all'—were traits he valued in himself and his aircrew.[46]

Jack's own work in the 14 May attack did not go unnoticed. Group Captain Clouston deemed Jack's role to be of a high order and recommended him for the Distinguished Service Order:

> In spite of fierce opposing fire a most determined and successful attack was made . . . In this well escorted operation this officer displayed high powers of leadership, great skill and determination which contributed materially to the results obtained. This officer has rendered great service and his sterling qualities have impressed all.[47]

Jack's immediate Distinguished Service Order was promulgated in the London *Gazette* on 9 June 1944, his 24th birthday. Although delighted to receive the award, Jack was not convinced that he alone deserved this accolade: 'I felt that it was a reward for the squadron as much as for me'.[48] The RAAF media unit was intent on publicising its own so was having none of Jack's natural diffidence; it wanted to promote Jack as one of Australia's high-calibre leaders in Britain. When his award was announced to the Australian media it was noted that Jack was the third RAAF commanding officer in Britain to receive this decoration. Highlighting its young commanding officers' talents, the RAAF also commented on Jack's age with the release headed: 'Young Australian "Flakbeau" CO Wins DSO', including Jack in a 'quartet of youthful RAAF commanding officers' in Britain.[49]

•

Jack participated in Exercise *Sunk* on 31 May 1944, a bombing practice where the Langham and North Coates wings combined. Jack considered that the formation and rendezvous with North Coates Wing as well as the ensuing attack had gone well. However, he observed that the ways in which the Langham and North Coates wings had carried out their attack were not totally harmonious, and could result in less than satisfactory results. While the Langham Wing approached its target flying at 'nought feet' the North Coates Wing anti-flak aircraft flew at about 2000 feet, with the torbeaus slightly lower and behind. Such a height meant they were susceptible to radar detection. In addition, the lag between North Coates' torbeaus and anti-flak aircraft meant it was more difficult for the following Langham formation to move into position quickly and effectively.

After the exercise, Jack suggested to Group Captain Clouston that it would be better for the Langham Wing to lead the formation when working with the North Coates Wing because the element of surprise would not be lost. Following the anti-flak Beaufighters closely into the attack, the torbeaus would enable the second wave to follow even closer behind, thus flooding the defences. North Coates would not be handicapped by a pre-warning of their attack because, as the higher formation, even though flying behind, it would certainly be sighted first.[50] Clouston agreed with Jack's suggestions and they were implemented successfully.

Jack found potential to improve even more and recommended further refinements to their joint tactics. A significant delaying factor in mounting an operation came about because North Coates personnel had to fly to Langham for the pre-operational briefing and took off from there to rendezvous with the Langham contingent, which was already in the air. Jack recommended that, before a reconnaissance, crews be briefed at their own stations and provided with all call signs and details of rendezvous points of the torpedo aircraft and fighter escort. When Langham received the sighting report it would contact North Coates and watches would be synchronised at what would be called 'zero hour'. At zero plus 30 minutes, all aircraft would start; at zero plus 50, take-off would commence; at zero plus 70, North Coates would set course for Langham; and at zero plus 90, Langham would set course with North Coates in formation. If the fighter escort was rendezvousing at Langham, it would also set course at zero plus 90 and would rendezvous with the strike force at zero plus 96.[51]

455 Squadron was declared fully operational on 2 June 1944 and on 5 June its crews were put on standby, on six-hourly shifts, for operations throughout the day. Despite the squadron's estimation that 'over 4000 ships are running a shuttle service across the English Channel, and that over 11,000 Allied planes are standing by', 455 Squadron's D-day effort was limited to an armed reconnaissance of the Boulogne area, with only minimum success; a small shipping reconnaissance in the Dunkirk area, with no sighting; and a shipping reconnaissance off the Dutch coast, with no sighting. Jack did not fly on D-day at all.[52]

Coastal Command's part in the June offensive increased soon after and was impressive: just under 2000 anti-shipping sorties during June 1944, where over 400 aircraft delivered attacks, and Jack was one of the many who contributed to these totals.[53] Jack's first post-D-day operation, four days after his 24th birthday, was an anti-E-boat patrol off the French, Belgian and Dutch coasts, ranging from Gravelines, near Calais on the French coast, to the Hook of Holland, where they would join the North Coates Wing.[54]

Leading eleven other Beaufighters from 455 Squadron, Jack, flying NE774, took off at 3.40 a.m., just before first light on 13 June 1944. The Beaufighters, each armed with four 20-millimetre cannon and two 500-pound bombs, flew in two formations (except Flying Officer Doc Watson, who failed to gain formation and proceeded alone to the patrol area). The patrol was uneventful until they reached the island of Schouven off the Dutch coast, near the Hook of Holland, and their expected rendezvous with North Coates.

There were no E-boats in the area but, at 4.53 a.m., in near perfect conditions, Jack and Warrant Officer Noel Turner sighted an armed trawler-type auxiliary and two smaller vessels. Jack called the attack and he and Turner dived. The enemy vessels and shore batteries lost no time in protecting themselves, with tracer fired vertically, and a thick ring of anti-aircraft fire. Turner did not think any aircraft could possibly fly through it, and skirted along the fringe until he was able to take advantage of a possible gap by turning sideways and flying in. Despite the seeming safety of the gap, Turner's starboard wing was clipped and his Beaufighter started vibrating seriously. He did not feel his aircraft could sustain the pressure of a high-speed dive so he dropped his bombs on the most convenient target and scored a direct hit on one of the vessels. Jack also managed to evade the intense anti-aircraft fire but recorded only a near miss on another vessel.[55]

Turner's aircraft vibration grew worse and, fearing his wing would fall off, he flew out of the convoy area after dropping his bombs. 455 Squadron was still to rendezvous with North Coates and Jack led his remaining force on to the Hook of Holland. At about 5.00 a.m. Jack sighted four vessels in vic formation, all flying balloons, and then shortly afterwards three more ahead. As with the earlier sighting, these were trawler-type auxiliaries. The Langham Wing were yet to join the North Coates Wing and Jack decided to attack the trawlers with cannon fire after their rendezvous. Accordingly, he ordered bombs to be jettisoned to ensure maximum manoeuvrability. Jack then turned out to sea to meet with the North Coates Wing. Rendezvous was effected between 5.17 and 5.34 a.m. and the combined force spotted the seven trawlers at 5.45 a.m.

Plunging from 2000 feet to mast height, Jack led his squadron into attack, and Wing Commander Tony Gadd led the North Coates Wing. They encountered accurate flak from the ships, which was so intense it was later recorded that one of the vessels might have been a small *Sperrbrecher,* a specialist minesweeper heavily armed with 88-, 37- and 20-millimetre guns as well as machine guns. Squadron Leader Colin Milson, Jack's number two on this operation, noted that 'the wing commander and I have met some flak, but never before like that'.[56] Despite the heavy defences, five enemy vessels were damaged severely and were on fire, and two were claimed as damaged.

The morning's effort resulted in damage to five aircraft from 455 Squadron, including damage to Jack's starboard tail plane and port main plane, and one missing crew. Flying Officer Douglas 'Keith' Carmody radioed to advise his engine was damaged and he would have to ditch. Despite circling the area, the downed Beaufighter was not located. Carmody and his navigator, Flying Officer Gilbert Docking, were picked up by the Germans and spent the rest of the war in Stalag Luft III. Notwithstanding the loss of Carmody and Docking, and the damaged Beaufighters, the two attacks were considered successes and formed part of Coastal Command's boast of 'widespread attacks on shipping' that day, with over 30 separate attacks.[57]

Warrant Officer Turner had landed safely at Langham. He may have been out of the line of enemy fire, but he soon found himself in the face of friendly fire. At the debriefing, Jack asked Turner which ship he was aiming at. Knowing full well he had dropped his bombs on the most convenient target, he fudged, 'Er, number three'. Jack was not pleased. 'You hit number two. Typical of you, Turner, aim at one ship and hit another.'[58] Turner bore warranted criticism well and learned from it. He matured into one of the most experienced pilots of the squadron and was awarded a Distinguished Flying Cross on 26 June 1945.

Despite its success, Jack's 13 June 1944 operation was not the one to receive the most kudos. Two days later, Squadron Leader Milson led the 455 Squadron contingent in a strike on a convoy in the Ameland area of the West Frisian islands. It was a combined operation consisting of cannon-firing Beaufighters from 455 Squadron and 489 Squadron, and torpedo- and rocket-armed Beaufighters from the North Coates Wing. In all, 41 Beaufighters were escorted by Mustangs from Coltishall. The result was a 'crushing blow'[59] to the enemy convoy with a 4000-ton naval auxiliary sunk, an 8000-ton merchantman run aground with its stern blown off, one minesweeper sunk, another four minesweepers left burning and the remaining escort vessels severely damaged. This was Coastal Command's largest and most successful strike and all squadrons well deserved the messages of congratulations from the Air Officer Commanding Coastal Command, the Commander-in-Chief Nore and the Air Officer Commanding 16 Group.[60]

Jack considered Milson's part in this operation was of a high order and his opinion of Milson never wavered. He thought Milson was 'a mighty bloke' and 'an outstanding pilot'.[61] Milson was not a comfortable mixer like Jack and could come across as gruff[62], but Jack saw through the façade, knowing he was 'shy and by nature retiring, and overcame these things by doing everything with his whole heart and abilities'. Above all, Jack saw Milson as 'a dashing leader, who was every bit as scared as any of us, but whose courage and guts always won the day'.[63] With little delay, Jack sat down and wrote his recommendations for awards for Milson and Flying Officer Matthew Southgate, Milson's navigator. (A Bar for the Distinguished Flying Cross and Distinguished Flying Cross respectively). Milson's immediate award was granted soon after.[64]

Early in his command, Jack had recognised the importance of giving credit when it was warranted. He had been fortunate that his flight commanders were extremely skilled fighters and leaders. Within a few weeks, he was recommending a Distinguished Flying Cross for Squadron Leader Wiggins who had, by that stage, 'participated in numerous sorties, including several successful attacks on enemy shipping'. In particular, he had pressed home an attack on a convoy of ten enemy ships despite considerable anti-aircraft fire. 'By his gallant and skilful leadership, [he] played a prominent part in the success of a well executed operation'.[65]

Wiggins' and Milson's awards were just two of those received by members of 455 Squadron. Excluding Jack's own awards, 38 George Medals, Distinguished Service Orders, Distinguished Flying Crosses and Bars and Distinguished Flying Medals were received between January 1944 and May 1945. Of these, Jack had a direct hand in at least eighteen and, following Jack's example of recognising impressive work, Milson was responsible for the rest.[66] Sometime after the squadron had transferred to Dallachy, Jack, who was then at 18 Group headquarters, paid a visit to the Mess. Doc Watson had recently been awarded a Distinguished Flying Cross and voiced the opinion, shared by some of his friends including David Whishaw, that some of the decorations awarded to the squadron had been won too easily. Jack would have none of this attitude. He knew the worth of every one of them—not only were they courageous men, they were superb pilots. He told them they could believe they were not brave if they wanted, but they should realise that to have survived so long they had demonstrated some 'distinguished flying' which was represented by the Distinguished Flying Cross award. Whishaw remembered that 'that comment made us all feel a bit better'.[67]

13

Dangerous work

'we shall all miss him very much indeed'

Jack flew two more operations during June 1944, both large-scale joint reconnaissance patrols; the one on 19 June in company with 489 Squadron and 236 Squadron RAF, and the one on 27 June with the North Coates Wing. Other than a small group of ships on 19 June, which was not attacked, no sightings were made. July 1944 was a dismal month weather-wise and operational and flying hours were lost. Even so, Coastal Command's offensive against enemy shipping continued to grow in intensity. While the number of aircraft sent on anti-shipping duties was slightly less than in June, the number of aircraft attacking enemy vessels set a new record. A total of 1897 aircraft were tasked with anti-shipping duties and, of these, more than 500 delivered attacks. Coastal Command operations covered a great area and attacks were carried out off the Dutch and Belgian coasts, in the English Channel, in the Bay of Biscay and off the coast of Norway. As well as a new record in attacks, Coastal Command now boasted a record for claims, with eleven enemy ships believed to have been sunk and 69 more damaged. The waggish scribe of the July 1944 edition of *Coastal Command Review* speculated: 'It must be disconcerting for the German sailor to find that in the same month he is liable to be got at practically anywhere on the coast of western Europe.'[1] 455 Squadron contributed to the consternation of those German sailors by flying 30 operations, increasing their attack and claim tallies.

Jack carried out three fruitless operations during July but his one successful strike more than made up for the other lack of results.[2] On 15 July, flying NT958, Jack made his first return to the Norwegian

140

coast since the squadron's transfer to Langham. *Coastal Command Review*'s humorous scribe reminded his readers that 'the northern shipping routes had been unmolested by our strike aircraft for a considerable time and it seems that the enemy were caught unprepared'.[3] The result of Coastal Command's 'surprise visit' by Langham and North Coates wings was an attack where every single ship was either on fire or sunk.

Forty-four Beaufighters from Langham and North Coates combined on a shipping reconnaissance-in-force. Their destination was the Mandel area of south Norway. Despite their intensive rocket training, 455 Squadron's twelve Beaufighters were armed only with cannon. Those from 404 Squadron RCAF were armed with rockets. Joining them were twelve torbeaus from 489 Squadron and anti-flak Beaufighters from 144 Squadron which, like 455 Squadron, were armed with cannon. The Beaufighter force was accompanied by a Mustang escort.

The aircraft took off between 3.25 and 3.50 p.m. Jack led with 404 and 144 squadrons on the flanks and 489 Squadron at the rear. Jack recalled: 'The weather on the way up was appalling, but even though visibility was sometimes less than 1000 yards in heavy rain, we managed to keep formation and make our landfall exactly on time.'[4] 404 Squadron, however, lost contact with the others.

The weather improved when the main force reached Lister; the cloud base lifted and the aircraft climbed to 400 feet in the patrol area. Off Mandel, about a mile from the coast, Flight Sergeant William Jones sighted an enemy convoy comprising four merchant vessels and five escort ships. Being so close to the shore, the convoy was also under the cover of land battery. Jack:

> Gave the order to attack and the flak-busters climbed up to about 1500 feet and drew ahead of the torpedo aircraft which remained close to the water. Just before we dived to attack, the trawlers opened fire. The flak was quite heavy to begin with but that was soon silenced. We dived down to deck-level firing as we went and even before we pulled away the largest merchant vessel had already been set on fire by our cannon. During our attack the German gunners were in many cases literally blown off the ships. As a last resort they fired off some rockets at us, but without effect. In a matter of seconds the torpedo carrying aircraft struck.[5]

The anti-flak aircraft were so effective the 'torbeaus were able to drop their "fish" with little opposition'[6] and with such ease it was as if they were on a regular, everyday approach and landing test:[7]

> What a sight it was! The whole convoy which a moment before had been sailing peacefully down the coast was now covered by a pall of smoke. Ships were on fire and sinking. Everywhere, dozens of aircraft were diving, firing and turning in all directions. As I broke away, I saw the largest vessel in the convoy with a mass of flames from stem to stern. Just in front of it there came a terrific explosion and steam and water spouted up to 300 or 400 feet. When it subsided, the ship that had been there was there no longer. She blew up without leaving a single trace.[8]

The final result was outstanding. A 3000-ton tanker was ablaze from bridge to bow; the 3000-ton merchantman Jack saw was probably destroyed by its own exploding ammunition; another 3000-ton merchantman and a 5000-ton cargo liner were struck by torpedoes; a ship of between 1000 and 2000 tons and three trawler-type auxiliaries were all on fire; and a gun-coaster burned as it sunk.[9] It was 'one of the largest and most successful operations ever undertaken by Coastal Command. And we didn't lose a single aircraft.'[10] After this successful attack, Air Ministry and RAAF news bulletins dubbed Jack an 'ace ship-buster'.[11] It was not a nickname he welcomed and, although it gained some currency during the war, it was not remembered afterwards.

Jack's *nom de guerre* was soon given a new shade of meaning. Coastal Command had been looking at the effective use of rocket projectiles, usually referred to as 'rockets', for some time. There had been some use of them during 1943 but results had not been entirely satisfactory so more research was carried out. During the early months of 1944, 455 Squadron did some rocket training and by 1 April 1944 Jack had completed twelve trial rocket attacks over three sessions. Jack considered the rocket was 'a fantastic weapon' and recalled that at that time, the squadron had 'welcomed [the rockets] with open arms. We found the rocket to be a remarkable weapon; it would go into the side of a ship, through the cargo, and out the other side.'[12] With the transfer from 18 Group to 16 Group, the squadron had ceased rocket training but Jack and the squadron continued to follow Coastal Command's use of rockets with interest. They had been impressed with the possibilities offered by rockets in their earlier practice sessions, but they were also concerned at the potential for reduced aircraft manoeuvrability, especially when flying at 'nought feet'. An opportunity to again become involved presented itself and on 4 July, Jack carried out four practice runs with rockets, especially focussing on manoeuvrability. Jack performed many acrobatic moves and was happy with the way the Beaufighter handled. Coastal Command headquarters was notified immediately.

Coastal Command followed up Jack's test flight by asking the squadron to carry out specific tests to determine the best firing techniques, operational tactics and weapons settings, and to evaluate the effectiveness of the various types of rockets. The best way to do this was to create as real a situation as possible and Coastal Command arranged for the Air Ministry to provide a large cargo ship for target practice. It was anchored off The Wash, the low-lying coastline of Norfolk. The target ship was:

> painted checkerboard fashion, black-and-white. We were required to take off experimentally and fire different types of rockets into different parts of the ship which was loaded with all sorts of different cargoes. We would sink it. It would go to the bottom, the tide would go out, it would be patched up and re-floated and we'd attack it again. It was in this fashion that it was discovered that the solid 25-pound head rocket was much more effective than the 60-pound explosive rocket. This rocket would go into one side of a ship, through a cargo of coal and out the other side leaving a hole three or four feet in diameter.[13]

The experiments were carried out over a period of about six weeks. The practice runs were carefully observed in the air and on the ground by 'the boffins', who measured and tallied results, changed this, adjusted that, plugged holes, rearranged cargo and did everything to ensure the best results. Standing behind Jack's seat, one of the boffins watched the rocket attacks from the air. It was a serious affair but Jack could not resist a leg-pull. The painted squares were about 3 feet across and appeared to offer perfect targets. Deadpan, Jack asked which square he should hit. The boffin told him, so Jack asked which part of the square. The leg-pull had to end sometime and Jack finally told the boffin: 'We'd be bloody lucky to hit the ship at all, much less any part of it.'[14]

As it happened Jack did hit the ship, then and several times over the next six weeks. Perhaps the most spectacular strike was on 17 August. The intention was to hit the ship's engine room. Despite his earlier scepticism regarding shooting to order, Jack struck with his first pair of rockets, creating a huge gaping underwater hole through which water poured in a great gush. The display was observed by crews in a nearby launch, as well as by Major Horton-Smith, an armament expert who watched from the air. All witnesses thought Jack had carried off a magnificent shot. Although the first pair of rockets had successfully found their target, the next three pairs were affected by a strong following wind and overshot the mark. Even so, the 'results of the trials have been so astonishing that [Major Horton-Smith] took his departure and was more than satisfied that the 25-pound ['J' type] rocket projectile is a truly damaging weapon'.[15]

Jack's role in the successful testing program ceased the next day. Overall, he thought he 'must have sunk that ship 24 times.'[16] He was, indeed, a ship-buster. Thirty-five attacks were made, of which 31 successfully sunk the ship; the only failures were when different types of rockets, which were later abandoned, were used.[17] It was eventually determined that hits in two holds would be required to sink a 3000-ton vessel. From this, it was calculated the optimum number of aircraft per attack would be six. Soon, cannon and rocket harmonisation was perfected: 'We would start firing cannon on our approach until the cannon was hitting the enemy ship just on the waterline. Then we would press the button and fire the rockets.'[18] It was dangerous work.

Despite Coastal Command's successes, German torpedo boats had been creating havoc as they continued to harass Allied shipping with its precious invasion supplies. Jack recalled that the E-boats would:

> Stand off from our convoy protection boats at night and taunt them until one would break from the line and attack them. That was all they needed. The E-boats would wheel around and ambush the invasion force flank. That would leave a hole in the line of protection and the E-boats would torpedo our convoy ships.[19]

The Air Ministry made quashing this damaging E-boat activity a top priority and handed the responsibility to the Langham Wing. The ministry briefed Jack and 489 Squadron's commanding officer, Wing Commander Dinsdale, and ordered them 'to do something about it'. Not such an impossible demand, except for the fact that by this stage the E-boats were operating at night and all of the Langham Wing's strikes—at least from the moment when they attacked enemy shipping—were in daylight. 'The stardard tactic was to dive, usually ending up very close to the water.' It would have been too dangerous to even contemplate using this tactic at night. Jack and Dinsdale thought it would be possible to develop tactics suitable for night attacks, but that it would probably take several weeks. The situation was too urgent for that, however: 'They gave us forty-eight hours.'[20]

At that time, the navy was responsible for protecting the invasion supply line and refused to withdraw unless they were guaranteed airborne attacks would be successful.[21] With the Air Ministry, Coastal Command and the navy all eagerly expecting success, Jack and Dinsdale set to work. The main problem to overcome was gauging height at night. In normal circumstances, a radio altimeter was used, but in the dark the pilot wouldn't be able to see it when he was in a dive. That meant the navigator would have to tell the pilot what his height was so they experimented with the time it took for the navigator to pass that information to the pilot. Another significant problem was formation flying at night. For Jack, there would be no problem because, as leader, he did not have to formate on anyone but even so he had to fly meticulously so the others could formate on him: 'We finally worked out that if we got close enough we could see the glow of the exhaust of the plane in front . . . In fact, we had to tuck right behind the wing of the plane in front. This type of flying was a very over-rated pastime.'[22]

It was dicey. There was no moonlight, and no lights at all were allowed. On the first trial, two crews lost contact and the formation was broken.[23] The new techniques were soon perfected however, and a night-time anti-E-boat operation was planned. 455 and 489 squadrons sent six crews each to Thorney Island near Portsmouth and the Isle of Wight on the south coast of England. It was expected the operation would be dangerous and a high level of skill was required. Accordingly, Jack selected five of his most experienced crews: Squadron Leader

Colin Milson and his navigator, Flying Officer Matthew Southgate; Flying Officer Colin Cock and navigator Flight Sergeant Alan Lyneham; Flying Officer Tommy Thompson and Warrant Officer Ivor Gordon; flying officers David Whishaw and Jack Belfield; and flying officers Leo Kempson and Raymond Curzon.

The detachments from 455 and 489 squadrons arrived at Thorney Island on 1 August 1944 and were put on immediate standby. The weather, however, let them down. They stayed on standby over the next few nights but the weather would not oblige. They were all keyed up and had had little sleep and one miserable night, as they waited in the mess, Jack nodded off in his chair. He felt someone put his hat on his head and kick his foot. He ignored it and his tormentor continued to kick him. Eventually Jack was sick of it and lashed out. As he did so, an enormous, lanky figure loomed over him:

> I opened my eyes and saw a uniform sleeve with a thick blue stripe and four thin stripes. I said 'Jesus Christ!' The sleeve's owner answered 'No, but I'd like you to get a new hat'. It was Marshal of the Air Force, Lord Trenchard.[24]

Jack had been caught out putting up one of the blackest 'blacks' possible; while a civilian gentleman never wore a hat inside, servicemen never wore hats in the mess. To make matters worse from Trenchard's perspective, Jack's hat was not in the best condition. Even so, old and ratty hats were clear signals their wearers had much operational experience. No-one liked wearing new hats.[25]

Jack survived his encounter with Trenchard and by 4 August 1944 the weather improved. Targeting the Le Havre coastline, Operation *Purblind* commenced in darkness at 10.45 p.m. when, flying NT958, Jack led the force. The Beaufighters were accompanied by a Wellington from 524 Squadron, which would drop flares to illuminate the enemy vessels. Jack's aircraft were each armed with cannon and two 500- and 250-pound bombs. The force was under control of the French-based invasion force radar. As usual, precise flying at low level, perfect navigation and split-second timing were required so the pilots could fly exact courses and change direction at predetermined times and positions. Crews were issued with chronometer watches to ensure total timing accuracy, and setting course from Selsey Bill they flew in a large box shape, slowly moving towards Le Havre.[26]

When the formation reached Cap D'Antifer, it circled until the Wellington dropped its twelve flares. Faulty wiring resulted in only six illuminating but enemy vessels were identified: three were probably *Raumbooten*, small motor minesweepers, similar to E-boats but slower. Known to the Allies as R-boats, they were leading a trawler-type auxiliary in a vic formation. Behind them were what looked like three more R-boats. The Normandy-based controller directed Jack's force towards the enemy vessels. Jack then positioned the formation to strike but, before they could do so, Jack ordered individual attacks. By now the moon had risen, providing some light.

The strike force surprised the enemy vessels. Flying Officer Thompson later reported the enemy anti flak vessels did not even seem to fire on them until the torbeaus had screamed down in their bombing dive. 489 Squadron's torbeaus dropped their bombs and some near misses were observed. Jack saw 'two nice explosions' in the target area.[27] There had been considerable anti-aircraft fire but the flak from one vessel ceased after a bomb burst. Jack, Thompson and Flying Officer Whishaw then attacked with cannon. Jack concentrated on the leading vessels and four strikes on the trawler-type auxiliary were observed. Then Squadron Leader Milson noted two large 'Christmas tree' explosions, as if ammunition had gone off. The Wellington noticed a bomb burst in the target area but thick cloud began to move in from the north-east, obscuring vision. They were ordered to return to base. On the way back, the Wellington observed a group of E-boats. The Beaufighters were instructed to shadow the group, but it was soon lost in cloud. The aircraft returned to Thorney Island between 2.15 and 2.43 a.m.

Naval headquarters in Normandy later reported the trawler-type auxiliary had been set on fire and subsequently sunk by British motor gun-boats, and that only three of the other vessels had been seen returning to their base.[28] Jack's strike force proved that, regardless of the name of the operation, it was not dimly sighted—it was a success and opened a 'spectacular' month of anti-shipping operations for Coastal Command, with almost nightly harassment of the E-boats in the English Channel.[29]

Triumphantly, Jack led the detachment back to Langham and heard the news that he had been awarded his second Distinguished Flying Cross and that DFCs had also been awarded to Squadron Leader Wiggins and flying officers Ralph Jones and Matthew Southgate.[30]

•

Many significant land victories had been made in July and August 1944. In the north, the new Russian offensive had been going well, beginning with a renewed assault on Finland and advancing towards the Baltic states. July saw the fall of Vilna, and one after another, Pinsk, Volkovsk, Narva and Lublin were captured from the Germans. In France, Bayeau, Cherboug and Caen had been captured in the first weeks and, at the end of July, the American Third Army had broken through German lines to capture Granville and Avranches. Rennes was liberated on 3 August and three days later the Americans had cut off the Brittany peninsular. The Allied air forces had provided significant support to the invasion forces and Coastal Command had carried out its part with success. Despite much fog and generally adverse weather conditions, Coastal Command had sunk 49,281 tons of enemy merchant shipping and a further 22,120 tons from June to the end of August.[31] Prime Minister Churchill sent a message congratulating Coastal Command on the 'splendid work' of the last three months.[32] One consequence of this success was that the Swedish government decided it would no longer insure Swedish ships travelling to or from German ports as the risks were too great. If Germany wanted Swedish ore, it would have to use ships from its own sorely depleted merchant navy.

As well as success, August 1944 brought 'the heaviest loss that [455 Squadron] has sustained in any one attack' since the Beaufighter conversion.[33] A shipping convoy had been reported in the Heligoland area of the German Bight, in the south-eastern corner of the North Sea, and a maximum effort was ordered on 10 August 1944. The Langham Wing, led by Squadron Leader Milson, comprised thirteen Beaufighters from 455 Squadron and twelve torbeaus from 489 Squadron. Fifteen Beaufighters from North Coates' 254 Squadron had also been briefed but they did not make the rendezvous, resulting in a significant decrease in the strike force's capabilities. The convoy of five merchant vessels and ten escort vessels was sighted. Milson called the attack and, as expected, flak was intensive. 455 Squadron gamely countered the flak and the torbeaus landed three hits on two of the merchant vessels. Two escort minesweepers were on fire, another burned fiercely, another was seen to be burning as it sunk, and yet another escort vessel was blown up by rockets. Such success came at a great cost: three aircraft from 455 Squadron and one from 489 were shot down. Eight men were killed.[34] It was a devastating loss.

Two days later, after the official telegrams had been sent, Jack sat down to write to his men's next of kin. It was a task he had carried out too many times before. His very first confirmation letter, to the father of his friend and crew member, Harry Harrison, had been written while he acted in the place of a hospitalised Wing Commander Holmes, eight months before this tour commenced. Since returning to the squadron in December 1943, 23 men had died: eighteen on operations, four in air accidents and one accidentally. More would die before the end of Jack's command.

This was perhaps the hardest duty for any commanding officer but, ever efficient, the air force had a form letter. Jack, however, was too compassionate to simply fill in the blanks—after all, he would be penning the very letter his own wife and mother feared to receive. Even so, there were some standards. All operations were important, and all attacks were courageous and determined. Jack could not devalue the dead men's contributions by saying anything less; their deaths had to be seen to be as significant as they really were, and they had to appear meaningful. So too was the standing of the men in the squadron. They all played important roles in the life of the squadron and, although the phrase was stock, Jack always managed to convey heartfelt sentiment when he wrote of each of his men, that 'we shall all miss him very much indeed'.[35] To those standard but important phrases, Jack added details of their loved one's contribution to the war effort; in this he was able to offer dignity to their grief and sense to the tragedy of their loss. Above all, he gave the next of kin the opportunity to gain comfort from the knowledge that the sacrifice had been true and valiant. When Jack informed Flight Sergeant Jack Costello's father that his son was missing after a forced landing in the sea during operations on 6 July 1944[36], despite the distress he and his wife felt over the news, Mr Costello was able to tell Jack that 'it is a great comfort for us to know that the work by our lad has been done by keenness and ability and that [it] has been appreciated by you' and thanked Jack not only for his kind letter, but for 'the interest taken by you in the welfare of our son'.[37]

When Jack's men died on operations, the sacrifice was clear: they had been participating in an enemy action. But sometimes, as in the case of an accident, Jack would have struggled to impart meaning to a grieving family. Although Flying Officer John Billing had been with the squadron just a few short days when he was killed taking a familiarisation flight on 1 July 1944, Jack was able to inform his father that 'his keenness was evident even in the short time he was with us'.[38] The squadron was unable to contact Mr Billing in time to discuss his wishes for burial so Jack arranged it himself. He told Mr Billing that his son had been accorded full service honours with the Union Jack covering the coffin. Wreaths had been sent from Group Captain Clouston and all ranks of Langham Station and from Jack and 455 Squadron. Jack enclosed photographs of the service and informed Mr Billing that his son's grave would be cared for by the Imperial Graves Commission.[39] Jack might not have been able to offer a grieving father a meaningful context for this death, but he was able to offer the comfort of knowing that Billing had had a dignified and honourable burial.

In what would be his hallmark, Jack made his next-of-kin letters as personal as possible and his letters to the families of Warrant Officer William Jones, Warrant Officer Harold Brock, Flying Officer Leo Kempson, Flying Officer Raymond Curzon, Pilot Officer Geoffrey Batchelor and Pilot Officer Harold Morris, who had all died during that devastating 10 August strike, were no exceptions. Jack told Jones's father that his son's 'ability and determination were of a very high order, and, backed by keenness, he was a very valuable member of the squadron'.[40] Mrs Brock read that her son had been very busy since joining the squadron in April that year and 'had completed outstanding work, both training and on operations. His ability and keenness were always evident, backed by determination and sound commonsense.'[41] Mr Curzon was told that his son had 'carried out every job given to him with ability and his keenness and efficiency made him a valuable member of the squadron'.[42] Kempson's father, himself an airman and one of the RAAF's first 1000 enlistees, would have been proud to read that his son had been 'very keen and, with his capability, made a very good pilot and he has done a great deal of work on operations. His consistency has won everybody's admiration.'[43]

As well as the comfort of personal comment, Jack tried to offer the comfort of reality. He did not fudge the news, nor offer false hope that the airman may have survived. He firmly, but kindly, advised the facts. This in itself could be reassuring. When Flying Officer Colin Cock died on 25 September 1944, Jack told Mrs Cock that her husband would have died instantly and she was 'thankful for the knowledge that he would at least be saved any agonising pain'.[44] Some, like Mr Harrison, would not allow their grief to turn to despondency as this would devalue the sacrifice of someone who knew 'that his life might be forfeit on any day'.[45] Others, like the wife of Flying Officer Edward Collaery, who was lost in action on 29 June 1944[46], found acceptance difficult and wrote to Jack a number of times, as well as to the Red Cross and the Vatican, hoping to hear that her husband had survived. Over the course of a number of letters Jack, with patience and consideration, provided more details of the circumstances of her husband's death than was usual. From his initial 'he was not seen [despite an intensive search] and is believed to have lost his life when the aircraft ditched', he next advised that 'it is believed that Ted lost his life when the aircraft first hit the sea'. His final letter to Mrs Collaery was stronger in tone and, though apparently harsh, was meant to convey that there was no hope that her husband could have survived: 'There is very little doubt that Ted was knocked unconscious when the aircraft first struck the sea.' Sometimes one must be brutal to be kind, and perhaps Jack had erred too much towards cruelty with this final letter to Mrs Collaery, but he knew he could not foster any false optimism. Mrs Collaery admitted that it was 'difficult not to hope' and she never gave up.[47] She remarried, but always wondered if her Ted would turn up some day.[48]

Jack had witnessed death and lost many friends during this war and although he tried to protect himself from the effects of loss—'you kind of built a mechanism to cope with it'—it was always difficult, a great strain[49], and sometimes cracks formed in the mechanism. When he wrote his first next-of-kin letter to Harry Harrison's father, Jack did not mention their friendship. Perhaps, only acting briefly in Wing Commander Holmes' stead, he did not think it appropriate to mingle the personal and the official. He had no qualms, however, when he wrote to Flying Officer Colin Cock's wife. Mixing his tenses, Jack told Mrs Cock that 'it is my privilege to consider [Colin] a close friend . . . At work, he was invaluable and took a great deal of the training worries from off my shoulders.' In mixing the past and present tenses—and this was not an isolated incidence—Jack seems to have indicated that perhaps he had not yet fully come to grips with the death of his friend. Continuing his letter, he told Mrs Cock that 'I was delighted when [Colin] recently received a

well-deserved Distinguished Flying Cross'[50], but he did not tell her
that it was he who had recommended it. Mrs Cock later wrote to
Jack and told him that 'it is comforting to know that he was held in
high esteem by the members of the squadron and I am very proud
to learn from his commanding officer that his recent decoration was
well merited'.[51]

Jack was never able to fully shore up the cracks in his protective
mechanism. He never forgot his friends and squadron members who
died during the war. He 'always considered one of my saddest episodes
during the war was the death of young Barbour'.[52] Flying Officer
William Barbour's aircraft crashed into the sea on 6 July 1944, the
same day Costello had died.[53] Like Kempson, Barbour had been one
of those trained by Jack at Turnberry. Just shy of his 22nd birthday,
Barbour, with his popularity, fresh-faced youth, ability and keenness[54]
seemed so much younger than Jack. Jack remembered Barbour, but
the names of others who had died invariably faded. The memory of
their sacrifices, however, never dimmed. In 1995, to commemorate
the 50th anniversary of the end of the Second World War, the
Commonwealth Department of Veterans' Affairs launched the
'Australia Remembers' campaign. Many ex-service men and women
were asked to share brief reminiscences of the war. These were
broadcast so younger generations could gain a deeper appreciation of
the sacrifice made by their fathers and grandfathers, mothers and
grandmothers. Jack was one of those asked to share a striking memory
of that long ago conflict:

> The thing I always remember most, particularly on occasions when
> there are commemorative services, is flying alongside a young pilot
> who was on his first or second trip. He'd been badly hit. His plane was
> on fire and he couldn't cope with the situation of putting it out and
> there was nothing he could do. And gradually he was getting closer
> and closer to the water, which was fairly rough. I was flying 30 feet
> away from him and I could see this young man with very little chance
> of survival. It always made a great impression on me.[55]

That unnamed but ultimately courageous pilot who silently dived to
his death represented all of Jack's men who died. Jack never forgot
them nor their sacrifice. He did, indeed, miss all of them.

14

George Medal

'I am particularly pleased to be awarding my medal'

Other than leading a reconnaissance-in-force on 16 August 1944 where no enemy activity was sighted, Jack did not fly operationally again until 25 August. The Langham Wing and 144 and 254 squadrons were briefed for a reconnaissance-in-force to the Heligoland area. At 7.00 p.m., flying NT954, Jack led thirteen Beaufighters equipped with rockets and cannon from 455 Squadron, twelve from 489, six torbeaus from 144 and fifteen Beaufighters from 254 Squadron, escorted by six Mustangs. Visibility was bad and Jack ordered the patrol back to base at 8.09 p.m. At 8.34 p.m., a Mustang pilot reported two ships to port, with a number of other vessels in their wake.

Thoughts of return were quickly abandoned and Jack ordered the formation to make a wide starboard turn to intercept the ships. Within ten minutes the convoy, including merchant vessels, minesweepers, an armed trawler and escorts flying balloons attached to steel wires, was sighted off the coast of Borkum. Jack ordered the attack. The balloons hindered the Beaufighters, visibility was bad and room to manoeuvre was so limited some aircraft were crowded out. There was much heavy and light flak from the escorts, and heavy, inaccurate flak from the Borkum defences. Five Beaufighters from 455 Squadron, including Jack, whose rockets were not working, attacked the leading minesweeper with cannon. Others from 455 Squadron struck at the leading escort vessel, which appeared to be an Artevelde-type—an incomplete Belgian fisheries protection vessel (which also doubled as a Royal yacht) captured by the Germans in 1940 and now used as a convoy escort—as well as one in the port column. 489 Squadron fired with cannon and scored hits but the torpedoes dropped by the torbeaus missed. Although Jack was not able to use rockets, the techniques he had experimented with over the previous weeks had been successfully implemented on this strike. Later, Jack reported the 'Beaufighters were almost queuing up to attack'.[1] Seven pairs of rockets were fired and results could not have been better. The Artevelde-type was hit by three complete rocket salvos as well as by cannon fire. Heavy explosions were seen and it blazed brilliantly. The leading minesweeper had been hit by cannon as well as two underwater and one waterline rocket salvos—heavy plumes of smoke engulfed it. An unidentified vessel on the port column appeared to have sustained underwater rocket hits and many cannon strikes, leaving it on fire.[2] All Langham aircraft landed safely at base by 11.08 p.m.

9 September 1944 was a busy day for the squadron. Flight Lieutenant Pilcher led an early morning reconnaissance-in-force to the Heligoland Bight in conjunction with 489 Squadron. They sighted and reported a convoy, but did not attack. During the course of the day, six other solo reconnaissance patrols were carried out. Much valuable information was gathered and all flights but one went smoothly.

Flying Officer William 'Bill' Stanley and his navigator Flying Officer Kenneth Dempsey flew to the Dutch coast on the day's last reconnaissance. They took off at 4.59 p.m. and at 6.20 p.m. radioed requesting that air–sea rescue be alerted as their port engine had failed. Langham station immediately went on standby. The fire tenders and ambulance rushed to the landing area and Stanley and Dempsey's friends gathered to await their return. Whenever he could, Jack would be in the control tower waiting for his crews to return and this occasion was no exception.[3]

Flying on one engine, Stanley nursed his Beaufighter back to Langham. As he approached, the flying control officer ordered Stanley to make a glide approach for landing. This is a steep and difficult manoeuvre in a Beaufighter so Stanley elected to make a single-engine approach, correcting with his rudder. This failed and the Beaufighter ground-looped.[4] Flying Officer William 'Bill' Herbert, who had participated in Pilcher's early morning reconnaissance, saw Stanley make 'a mess of it'.[5] The undercarriage collapsed and the aircraft burst into flames. Dempsey was able to open his hatch and escape by jumping through the fire, but the pilot's cockpit was completely surrounded by flames. Stanley could not escape. The force of the impact had pushed the instrument panel back and it completely pinned him down, his long flying boots catching so he could not wriggle out.

The fuel tanks burst and cannon shells and ammunition exploded. Dempsey ran to the front of the aircraft but was held back by the furious petrol-fed inferno.[6] It was so intense Warrant Officer Ivor Gordon and his pilot Flying Officer Tommy Thompson, who were approaching Langham at the conclusion of their own patrol, could see the tall plume of smoke coming up from the middle of the airfield.[7] Langham was well dispersed and when Jack dashed down from the tower he flung himself into his car and sped to the furiously burning aircraft. Ammunition started exploding and Jack yelled to everyone to keep away. Ignoring his own orders, he immediately rushed forward, climbed onto the wing and, astride the canopy, struggled with the pilot's hatch. Then, hanging down head first[8], he 'grabbed hold of him and pulled, and he wouldn't come'.[9] During the struggle, the burning main plane collapsed under Jack's weight[10], but still he wrestled with the rigidly trapped Stanley. 'With a great heave, with strength that I probably didn't have, I pulled him out of his boots.'[11] He dragged Stanley to the waiting ambulance. The flying control officer considered Jack's rescue efforts the 'most amazing thing I have seen in this war'.[12] He was not alone. Putting it down to 'the presence of mind and courageous action of Wing Commander Davenport', the squadron scribe had no doubt Jack had saved Stanley's life.[13] Nor had Flying Officer Bill Herbert: 'If it hadn't been for Jack Davenport going out there, it'd be the fire crew and other people standing around, watching the aircraft on fire.' Warrant Officer Noel Turner was much more graphic: 'Anyone who saw the extent of Bill's scars later would know the crash truck would have arrived in time to remove nothing more than a well-cooked crisp.' Insensitively explicit maybe, but Turner spoke for all of the squadron when he went on to say: 'Makes you proud of your CO.'[14]

Stanley was badly burned but, ignoring his own injuries, insisted on seeing Jack before he went to hospital as 'he thought that I had been badly burned but I was able to assure him that mine were only slight burns and of no consequence'.[15] Jack rode in the ambulance with Stanley and satisfied Stanley that he was not harmed. But even then Stanley would not rest and Jack could not stop him from reporting the results of his reconnaissance. Commending Stanley's 'guts', Jack later commented with intermingled pride and amazement that 'although burned about the face, hands and body and in pain, he sat up in the ambulance and said "there's a convoy moving down the coast" and gave us the bearing and number of ships involved'.[16]

Although Jack had sustained shock, with burns to his own face, hair and hands, and further burns to his legs when the main plane collapsed, he was in much better condition than Stanley. Typically, he underplayed his injuries—when Warrant Officer Noel Turner later asked about them, Jack said that only his battle jacket had been singed.[17] Stanley's injuries, although extensive, were not life threatening. After time in the local hospital he was sent to a rehabilitation centre in Devon and, after a number of operations, made an eventual recovery.

Jack may have made light of his injuries to his men, but his wife was not fooled. After he had been attended by medical staff, he returned to his little cottage in a nearby village. Sheila had been out that day and Jack arrived home before her. He was sitting in the lounge when he heard her open the door. He tried to stave off any comments about his appearance by hiding his face behind a broadsheet newspaper. Lowering the paper, he started to say: 'Take it easy, I'm not as bad as I look.' By now perfectly attuned to Jack and any attempts to dissemble, Sheila was fully alert that something was wrong: he had been 'reading' the paper upside down.[18] Jack's burns healed quickly, leaving only an 'interesting' scar on his forehead.[19]

A perfect media opportunity presented itself. The day after Jack rescued Stanley, the Air Ministry news service released a bulletin and the story was carried by British and Australian papers with headlines and captions such as, 'Hung head in fire to get out pilot'; 'Pilot's chief pulled him from flames'; 'Upside down rescue from blazing plane'; 'Pulled pilot out of boots'; and 'Blazing plane rescue'. The parochial 'Sydney hero rescues pilot from fiery death' from *The Sun* had as its lead sentence 'An heroic rescue of a pilot from a blazing plane was performed single-handed by Wing Commander J.N. Davenport DSO DFC of Sydney'. It was reminiscent of the much earlier article that considered Jack's rescue of Alan Bowman from their yawing Hampden as one of the 'stories of heroism' of the war.[20]

Jack's brother Phil acknowledges that Jack would have been the last to think of himself as a hero and would certainly not have promoted himself as one.[21] Even so, the news of his heroic rescue was soon widespread.[22] The papers brought Jack's actions to the attention of the public and the RAAF grapevine did as much within the air force. Like Warrant Office Turner, Jack's men were proud of their commanding officer and told their friends in other squadrons. Full of pride at the exploits of a fellow Australian, they then told their friends. Soon, most of the Australians in the United Kingdom were aware of Jack's actions.[23]

Group Captain Clouston soon submitted a recommendation for the George Medal, a non-operational decoration which, like the George Cross, recognises acts of great bravery. The Victoria Cross, George Cross, George Medal and all gallantry and bravery medals recognise valour—courage and self-sacrifice of the highest order. From the earliest days of his air force career, Jack took responsibility for the lives of his crew. In saving Bill Stanley, he proved again that he would honour this commitment, even at the expense of his own life. In his study of Victoria Cross winners, General Sir Peter de la Billiere lists the fundamental qualities shared by the bravest of the brave: determination, coolness in the face of danger, outstanding leadership, modesty, compassion, loyalty, sense of duty and selflessness. De la Billiere comments that 'it is not surprising that many [Victoria Cross] winners have similar characteristics, of which courage is the common denominator . . . Selflessness is another predominant factor.'[24] His assessment holds true for the George Medal.

During the Second World War, 46 awards of the George Medal were made to members of the Australian services, of which twenty were to members of the RAAF.[25] The British and Australian public discovered Jack's worth when it was announced that 'one of the most daring of RAF Coastal Command's ace ship-busters', had become 'the only pilot in the RAAF to win the George Medal as well as the DSO, DFC and Bar in this war'.[26] King George VI, too, would have no doubt that he was giving his award to an outstanding pilot and leader.

Accompanied by Sheila, Jack attended his investiture ceremony at Buckingham Palace on 16 October 1945:

> It was quite an event. The Palace, of course, is absolutely grand, the decorations and the curtains . . . and the carpeting; everything is absolutely grand, including the artwork. The King stood on a small podium, and one by one the recipients moved forward, presented to the King, and he then took your medal from a cushion placed in front of him, and pinned it on.

The King spoke to each award recipient and to Jack, who had already been awarded the Distinguished Service Order and Distinguished Flying Cross and Bar, said, 'I am particularly pleased to be awarding my medal'.[27]

As enemy-occupied Channel ports continued to fall, anti-shipping actions moved eastward to Dutch waters. The combined wing tactics of July and August proved so successful that by September only one enemy merchant convoy sailed during daylight hours off the Frisian Islands. The reluctance to present themselves as targets of devastating air stikes meant enemy convoys hugged the coast more and anti-shipping squadrons found they had to attack well-protected enemy harbours. During September, Coastal Command's Beaufighter squadrons carried out five strikes, and 455 Squadron played an important part in ensuring enemy shipping remained vulnerable even in well-defended anchorages.[28]

455 Squadron opened September 1944 with an armed reconnaissance of the Dutch shipping lanes between Ijmuiden and Ameland, followed by a rover on 2 September of the waters between Den Helder, a heavily defended garrison town on the northern tip of Holland, and Gravelines, on France's northern coast. Enemy ships were not sighted on either of these operations. A number of other patrols and strikes were carried out over the next few days. Jack had little success on 8 and 17 September as he experienced trouble with his port engine on both occasions. His third operation for September, to the Heligoland Bight, also brought 'no joy'.[29] His next strike, on 23 September, achieved some enemy damage, but not quite what had been anticipated.

Coastal Command committed considerable resources to its third attack on Den Helder harbour. It had already sent a Mosquito from the photographic reconnaissance unit as well as a Mustang fighter to photograph shipping in the harbour. Then, in the early afternoon, Flying Officer David Whishaw and his new navigator Flight Sergeant Bert Iggulden, were tasked with a detailed solo reconnaissance. They sighted what appeared to be four or six E- or R-boats, three minesweepers, four armed trawlers and two larger enemy vessels.[30] Hours later, sixteen Beaufighters, led by Jack and armed with rockets and cannon, were airborne for a strike on Den Helder. Accompanying them were nine anti-flak Beaufighters and six torbeaus from 489 Squadron, sixteen anti-flak Beaufighters from 254 Squadron, thirteen anti-flak Beaufighters from 143 Squadron and fourteen anti-flak Beaufighters from 236 Squadron. Wing Commander Cartridge from 254 Squadron led the formidable formation.

The large force soon started to straggle, including Jack's contingent. Mustangs from RAF Coltishall, tasked with dive-bombing shore based anti-aircraft defences, were late and by the time they arrived the Beaufighters had spread out so much Cartridge decided it was impossible to launch a co-ordinated attack. He called it off and led the formation on a south-westerly course over Den Helder peninsular and towards the open sea. At this point, a number of aircraft attacked land installations as targets of opportunity. Jack, flying NT947, and Warrant Officer R. Walker attacked a flak position on top of a house at Bergen Aan Zee. Jack then attacked a wooden flak tower near a mine and a motor transport vehicle. All of his Beaufighters, as well as those from 489 Squadron, scored cannon strikes on various targets including a radar station, wireless masts and gun positions. Some Langham aircraft received minor damage but all returned safely.[31] Given the intention of this major strike force had been to sink enemy shipping, it was disappointing that they had failed to destroy anything on the water.[32]

Another massive Beaufighter force was assembled for 25 September 1944. There were no doubts that this strike on enemy shipping in Den Helder harbour would be a risky venture. At his briefing, Jack conveyed the complete 'impression of confidence' but he knew this would be a dangerous operation and did not tell his crews of the anticipated loss rate of 75 per cent.[33] As had been seen two days earlier, the sheer size of a multi-wing strike force would result in problems if disciplined flying and precision timing were not maintained. Earlier experiences over Den Helder indicated the harbour and surrounds were heavily defended, and the land batteries were strongly reinforced by flak ships in the canal. They would not be able to rely upon the element of surprise as the force was too large but they could confound the enemy somewhat by attacking from the land side, rather than seaward.[34]

Squadron Leader Derek Hammond of 489 Squadron led the formation, which included: twelve Beaufighters from 455 Squadron, led by Jack in NT947 and armed with rockets and cannon; ten Beaufighters and four torbeaus from 489 Squadron; and twelve Beaufighters from 236 Squadron, fourteen from 143 Squadron and thirteen from 254 Squadron, all in the anti-flak role. Accompanied by a Tempest escort and Mustang dive-bombers, the Beaufighter strike force left Langham at 3.38 p.m. Flying at about 30 feet, to remain under enemy radar for as long as possible, Hammond led his force between Vlieland and Terschelling at 4.26 p.m. and experienced accurate heavy flak. The Mustangs bombed the flak installation three minutes later and then, flying over Holland, the Beaufighters wheeled round for the harbour and climbed to 2000 feet. Then, between 4.32 and 4.38 p.m., they attacked shipping and flak positions. Twenty-three vessels were anchored in the Marsdeip and a convoy stretched between Den Helder and Texel Island. When Jack ordered the attack, eight squadron Beaufighters attacked from shallow dives. Hindered by flak from Den Helder and Texel as well as balloon cables, Jack's contingent gamely and determinedly picked off their targets. Jack unloaded his eight rockets and cannon into the hull of a merchant vessel. Then, along with Flying Officer Steve Sykes, he attacked two armed trawlers with cannon, assailed a tug with Flight Sergeant Norman Steer, and fired at a gun position on the western side of Den Helder with Pilot Officer Charles 'Chick' Smith. Flying Officer Tommy Thompson dived on a minesweeper; Squadron Leader Colin Milson and Pilot Officer Thomas Higgins struck at another minesweeper. Then Higgins attacked an armed trawler, and Sykes two more. Steer attacked another tug; Pilot Officer Neil Smith fired on a minesweeper and an armed trawler; and Chick Smith unloaded all his rockets and some cannon into another vessel.

Jack's last operation was a great success. In total, 61 rocket hits and many cannon strikes against the enemy vessels were claimed. Not for nothing had they become known as the Australian ship-busting squadron and Jack an ace ship-buster. Jack's contingent was not the only one to claim a great success that day. Hammond led a supremely successful wing strike. As well as explosions seen on the hull of a 3000-ton merchant ship, and many rocket and cannon strikes on minesweepers, tugs and trawlers, the tally included one destroyed minesweeper and one left fiercely burning; four trawlers, three tugs and a barge all aflame; and a floating crane and a number of land targets out of commission.[35] The next day, the squadrons received a signal of appreciation from the Captain Coastal Forces, Nore. Group Captain Clouston replied on behalf of Langham station saying the boys had been 'proud to assist you in the great work'.[36]

Proud they were, but their work had come at a heavy cost. Five squadron aircraft, including Jack's Beaufighter which had been hit in the port elevator and starboard engine, had been 'fairly heavily damaged by flak'.[37] Even worse, one crew from 455 Squadron and two from other squadrons had not returned. Flying Officer Colin Cock, who had been with the squadron since the Hampden days and who had recently received a well-deserved Distinguished Flying Cross, and his navigator Warrant Officer Alan Lyneham, who had been with the squadron for over a year, were fatally struck by flak and their blazing aircraft plunged into the sea.[38] For Jack, the loss of this crew was a double tragedy. With Cock, he had lost another friend.

The loss of friends and comrades was something Jack had long been acquainted with and, like every other man on the squadron, he had long ago learned to put aside his grief. But the loss of Cock and Lyneham was something more to Jack: they were the only crew to die on any operation where Jack had led the squadron since taking command. It is to his credit that his meticulous care in training, his detailed planning and briefing, his strict exhortations to maintain precise timing and precision formation flying, which had stood him in good stead in every previous operation, still prevailed to the extent that no more of his crews had been lost on this dangerous strike.

15

Veteran Commanding Officer

'I was fortunate to have served with some wonderful people'

As the year progressed, the Norwegian coast—the thoroughfare for Germany's import traffic, including vital supplies of Swedish iron ore—became the focus of anti-shipping operations.[1] While convenient for Channel and Dutch strikes, RAF Langham was too far south to be a comfortable base for Norwegian strikes so Coastal Command decided a move north was inevitable. Five Beaufighter and Mosquito strike squadrons had already transferred to Banff in Scotland and on 20 October 1944 455 and 489 squadrons received notice to transfer to RAF Dallachy, in Morayshire, Scotland. The Langham Wing, 144 Squadron RAF and 404 Squadron RCAF would now be known as the Dallachy Wing, under the control of 18 Group.

Coastal Command required the transfer to be completed by 24 October 1944 and the main party and first group of aircrew arrived by this time but, because of the distance and unreliable train transport, the last of the ground crew did not arrive until 28 October. Jack did not oversee this transfer. His second tour with 455 Squadron had expired and on 23 October he received news of his new posting to 18 Group headquarters in charge of operational planning for the strike wings.[2]

The head of Coastal Command, Air Chief Marshal Sir Sholto Douglas, wanted Jack to stop enemy shipping travelling from Norway to the Baltic, but also to be the voice of reason in operational planning; with his considerable knowledge of their inherent difficulties he would be able to temper some of the navy's enthusiasm for large and dangerous operations.[3] Working in Pitreavie Castle, 18 Group's vast underground headquarters near St Andrews, Jack would be in charge of planning for all the group's strike squadrons and their fighter escort—the recently formed Dallachy Wing and Banff's Mosquito squadrons (235, 248 and 333 squadrons) air–sea rescue and other ancillary squadrons. In addition, he was to co-ordinate planning and co-operation with the long-range anti-submarine squadrons.[4] As well as continuing a close association with 455 Squadron, he would also be directly responsible for operations flown by his brother Phil, who would join 235 Squadron on 15 November 1944.

The move to 18 Group headquarters was an important step in Jack's career but it meant the end of operational flying—the risk of being captured and interrogated was too great.[5] This was welcomed by Sheila, who had recently discovered she was pregnant with their first child. As did any young couple, she and Jack shared the unalloyed joy of knowing they would soon be parents but for Sheila, her happiness was now free of concern. Jack would soon find operational planning was an almost continuous activity[6] and Sheila would endure the irregular hours and frequent absences necessitated by her husband's new duties, but never again would she fear that he would fail to return home.

Jack, however, was not as pleased with his new posting. He was reluctant to leave 455 Squadron and resented Sholto Douglas' invitation. Initially, he refused it:

> I tried very hard to stay with the squadron because we had a wonderful outfit, doing a remarkable job . . . The squadron was doing famously, we were a very tight-knit group, we all respected and had confidence in one another and that is so very important; I felt that my place was there. To have to go off on what was a planning and administrative job was something that I found very hard to take and resisted as much as I possibly could.[7]

Jack knew full well how much his ground crew, navigators and pilots had contributed during his months of command. His men were 'young and enthusiastic and able'. His ground crew had 'achieved the highest level of serviceability in conditions which were frequently appalling'. He had 'great admiration' for his navigators, the 'unsung heroes'. His pilots, carefully moulded by his own fine example, 'were of a very high calibre, aggressive and daring'. The squadron, as a whole, 'was a series of remarkable groups of people whose dedication and determination [were] constant'. He had no doubt: 'I was fortunate to have served with some wonderful people.'[8]

Jack had grown considerably since joining the squadron in March 1942. From those early days when his flying log had been endorsed for 'Gross Carelessness' he had evolved into a disciplined and skilled pilot: 'Downwind Davenport' was now regarded as an 'exceptional pilot'.[9] Jack's commitment to others, demonstrated in the first days of his air force career when he embraced the responsibilities of a multi-engine aircraft pilot, was seen time and time again and exemplified no better than when he stayed with his yawing Hampden to save Alan Bowman's life and when he plunged through the blazing petrol-fed flames of a burning Beaufighter to rescue Bill Stanley. His inherent compassion underpinned his relationship with all his air and ground crew and he had moulded them into an expert fighting squadron by encouraging their progress and building on their skills.

When Jack had taken up his command, the squadron had received a great influx of new members and one of Jack's first priorities had been to develop squadron unity. This was essential because it translated directly to high performance on operations. Jack proved his commitment to a cohesive squadron soon after the arrival of the first new pilots with the traditional Christmas party in the officers' mess, where officers served and entertained the sergeants, and the following informal dance and free-for-all. Next was the New Year's Eve dance and then his own pre-wedding party.

Jack well knew that parties in the mess—and 'without a doubt, oh, yes, we had some very wild parties'—were vital in releasing stress:

> I can recall at one station we had battled very hard to get a piano, and one had been donated to us by somebody. Obviously nobody else was prepared to have it—it was a terrible piano—and the station commander decided that he would get a piano from group funds or bust. So he took—fairly late in the evening, I must admit—an axe and he charged across the room and threw the axe into the top of the piano, and it kept going ping! ping! Ping-ping-ping! for quite some time. He then complained to Group that the piano was out of order and we needed a replacement; we'd provided the previous one, Group had to provide the next one.[10]

Riots in the mess were one way to ensure squadron unity, but even better was Jack's commitment to making 455 Squadron an entirely Australian squadron. The ties of nationality are strong, and a shared patriotism does much to engender morale. Most of the pilots were Australian, but in the early Beaufighter days most of the navigators were English. Even though RAAF navigators began to replace those from the RAF, the wholly Australian goal was never attained but the RAF navigators, such as Flying Officer (later Flight Lieutenant) Ralph Jones and Flight Sergeant Bert Iggulden, a survivor from the Hampden days, never felt out of place. Jack ensured they were included in mess activities and he made it clear they were valued members of the squadron.[11] His endeavours—as well as the genuine friendliness of the Australians—certainly worked. Iggulden never wanted a posting elsewhere as he had a great deal of affection for his Australian companions. He felt he belonged and even when he was offered a posting to a Mosquito squadron after his pilot left he declined and teamed up with another 455 pilot.[12]

Shared nationality, good squadron training and parties were clear ways to develop a close-knit squadron but friendly competition was another. Sports days and interservice or squadron matches always featured on 455 Squadron's social calendar, but Jack came up with another way to tap into the competitive spirit of his men. Soon after he took command, he announced a one guinea prize would be awarded to whoever submitted the winning design for a squadron crest.[13] Imaginations fired and bright sparks flared, resulting in a number of designs being forwarded to the adjutant before the 31 January 1944 deadline.

Bureaucracy moves slowly, and RAAF overseas headquarters was no exception. June 1944 arrived and a decision had not been made about the squadron crest. Six days after D-day, the public relations officer wrote to Jack to advise him of the recent suggestion that all Australian squadrons be dubbed with a peculiarly Australian nickname. He asked Jack to suggest three names, in order of preference, so headquarters could then select, record and hand out details in publicity material. In the mind of the public relations officer, this nickname, perhaps drawn from a native bird or animal, or some other significant Australian name, would 'help to stimulate enthusiasm among the personnel of the squadrons themselves'.[14]

As if Jack did not have better things to think about in the days immediately following D-day and almost five months after the close of the competition. Even so, he and the boys discussed the matter. In as polite language as the obnoxious suggestions deserved, Jack replied that while the crews 'unanimously agree that it is an excellent and valuable idea, great difficulty was experienced in deciding on names which were not hackneyed or which did not revolt on Australian minds'. Any suggestion of this ilk had been 'ridiculed by one and all' and Jack forwarded only one name—'The Australian Viking Squadron':

> This name associates itself with the role of the squadron, namely, swift sharp raids over the sea against enemy shipping, and is typical, I feel, of the free spirit of the Australians. In addition, the squadron crest, which is being submitted for approval, is built around the Vikings' helmet with the motto 'strike and strike swiftly'.[15]

30 Squadron RAAF had already claimed 'strike swiftly' so, when the squadron crest was duly approved, 455's motto became 'strike and strike again'. By the end of the war, it was obvious that nothing better could have summed up the continuing work of 455 Squadron.

Jack no doubt saw the incongruity of a Viking emblem associated with a kangaroo, emu or possum but it seemed as if the public relations boys had their hearts set on some animal-type name. Whether it liked it or not, 455 was touted as the Kangaroo Squadron in press releases. Despite the occasional media mention and reference in Coastal Command's published account of its role in the war, *Coastal Command Leads the Invasion*[16], it did not gain currency and, when RAAF public relations officer Ken Llewelyn asked Jack in a 1993 interview when the squadron became known as the Kangaroos, Jack laughingly stated: 'I've not heard of them being called the Kangaroos.'[17] As far as Jack and his squadron were concerned, 'The Australian Viking Squadron' had become the 'Viking Boys', and that is how the squadron members saw themselves:

> The type of work carried out by this squadron is akin to that of the Viking—short sharp swoops across the sea by a compact, well armed force . . . The spirit of the Australians is like that of the Vikings, adventurous and free.[18]

For the last Christmas of a long war, squadron members sent out cards wishing 'a merry Christmas from the Viking Boys'.[19] But what of the winner? As the boys sent their Viking Boys Christmas greetings, Wing Commander Colin Milson, who had taken command of 455 Squadron, sent Jack a facsimile of the squadron crest, crediting it to Jack as his brainchild: 'I hope you spent the guinea prize wisely!'

Jack had been committed to fostering high morale among his men. One of the most significant aspects of this was a continued desire by all to fly on operations. Over the months of his command, Jack ensured leave was taken when due to help alleviate operational stress and he provided plenty of personal challenges to his pilots. Squadron leaders Milson and Wiggins led 455 Squadron on operations; deputy flight commander Flight Lieutenant John Pilcher had similar opportunities, as did recently promoted Flight Lieutenant Wally Kimpton; and Pilcher's leadership abilities were further developed through inclusion on a junior commanders' course. Flying Officer David Whishaw's flying skills were constantly stretched when he notched up six solo patrols during his service with 455 Squadron. Not everyone had the skill and courage to carry out these operations. It was one thing to enter enemy territory supported by a fighter escort and the strength in numbers of the Beaufighter strike force. It was quite another to fly there solo.[20] Jack's men responded to his challenges and good leadership as he melded them into a top-class squadron.[21]

Despite his efforts to create an environment where his aircrew wanted to fly on every operation, he failed on one occasion. The Air Ministry had long recognised that aircrew could experience operational fatigue and had set in place steps for medical officers to diagnose and address the situation. In most cases, rest was all that was needed. In some instances, operational fatigue became more serious and, even though the airman attempted to carry out his duties, his commanding officer might lose confidence in his abilities. If there was a medical reason for this, careful handling would usually lead to a swift return to operational effectiveness. Unfortunately, however, there were times when an airman openly admitted that—usually through sheer terror built up through the unrelenting pace, but more rarely through genuine cowardice—he did not intend to fly again.

Men in these situations were considered to be Lacking in Moral Fibre, or 'gone LMF'.

The Air Ministry had provided guidelines on how to deal with men in this situation. If there was no medical aspect to the case, they were to be quietly, and with little fuss (because there was a certain belief that LMF was contagious, or could at least affect other personnel) sent to a disposal centre for processing. Many men were treated harshly and often unfairly at these centres and suffered greatly from the stigma of being classified LMF. Rather than subject their men to this callous procedure, many commanding officers chose to deal with the situation sensitively and unofficially, quietly organising a non-operational posting elsewhere, to perhaps Ferry Command or a training unit. Jack was one of these more sensitive commanding officers.

Jack had been fortunate early in his career that, when he had been suffering the effects of operational fatigue Flight Lieutenant Bilton, the squadron's medical officer, had stepped in and taken him off ops. With timely intervention, Jack was able to move beyond a temporary fatigue. Like many, Jack rarely spoke of incidences of LMF or how they were handled. He did admit, however, that he only had one airman who became too terrified to climb into an aircraft again. Jack mentioned that he 'quietly eased him out, and he went on his way and returned to Australia'. Jack did not 'feel disgust in such a case . . . It was a rare and isolated case'.[22] It is testament to his leadership skills that Jack's men, on the whole, experienced high morale: 'There was an eagerness, when you are allocating crews to go out on operations, there was always an eagerness to go, there were no instances of holding back.'[23]

Jack became known as even-handed in discipline and precise and exacting in his standards. Ground and aircrew alike knew they could expect his support, encouragement and praise when it was warranted, and they knew they would receive a blast if they were careless. But it did not always happen that way. Flying Officer David Whishaw was carrying out an air test one day and, as he came in to land, his aircraft, without warning, dropped from about 20 feet and there was 'an almighty bump'. The undercarriage was fine, but the tail wheel assembly was badly damaged and had partly crushed into the fuselage. At that time the squadron was short of its full complement of Beaufighters and this meant they would be lacking yet another during the all-important training period, and they were on a deadline. Although he had no control over events, Whishaw knew the accident had been his responsibility and anticipated Jack's ire. Sure enough, he was called to Jack's office but, perhaps remembering his 'downwind' accident, Jack was not interested in laying blame:

> I then had my own experience of Davenport's consideration of his crews' reactions when he said at once in dismissing me that he was not in the least concerned how it had happened, and that I should forget about it. Great relief for one pilot![24]

Whishaw's case was not an isolated example. It was raining heavily one day and Flying Officer John Ayliffe made a heavy landing, still with bombs loaded, breaking his aircraft's tail wheel. Jack called him up to explain himself. Ayliffe expected censure but 'oh! He was really good about it. Don't worry about it.'[25] Another relieved pilot.

Jack's equanimity was not always as apparent, however. He had good ground crew, and well recognised their 'remarkable skill and dedication'. He credited his men with achieving miracles and considered 'Australian ground crew were a race apart'.[26] Even so, he did not simply leave his ground crew to it; he always kept a close eye on the situation. At one time, there was a shortage of serviceable aircraft and Jack placed great pressure on his ground crew to ensure a rapid turnaround for replacements. Flight Sergeant Jack 'Jeep' McKnight, B Flight's senior ground crew non-commissioned officer, recalled it was a bitterly cold night and there were delays de-icing the leading edges and tail planes. Jack was becoming impatient and strode out to the dispersal area to hurry things along and told the boys he could 'piss on the ice and get it off quicker' himself.[27] It seems a harsh attitude, but 455 Squadron had a good reputation for keeping aircraft available and it was Jack's responsibility to maintain it.

Flying Officer Jack Cox was another who at one time failed to meet Jack's high standards and caught the sharp edge of his tongue. Part of 455 Squadron's strength was its ability to fly low to escape detection by enemy radar. Flying at 'nought feet' over water was part of the standard training program. On one occasion, Cox was carrying out a low-flying formation exercise with three other aircraft. He thought he was flying low and was, no doubt, pleased with his efforts. But Jack wasn't. When Cox landed, Jack came over to him and declared: 'If you ever fly that high again, I'll shoot you down myself'.[28] Neither Cox nor McKnight resented Jack's stance, but they might have smiled on at least one occasion when Jack fell victim to his own high standards.

During a period of target training with rockets, a number of engines and airframes were affected by flying debris. Jack threatened 'dire consequences' to any pilot who managed to damage his aircraft during or after target practice. Flying debris continued to make its mark on the Beaufighters, but no 'dire consequences' were ever experienced. Suddenly, all was silent on the matter—around the time Jack returned from target practice with minor damage to his own aircraft![29]

Rockets were Jack's downfall on another occasion. Jack touched down after an operation and all eight of his rockets went off. They flew straight up over the station headquarters—a practical demonstration of what could go wrong if you forgot to put the safety switch on. But this was not a demonstration. Forgetting the safety switch was a common failing and Jack had previously threatened 'dire consequences' to anyone who failed to safeguard against wilful rockets. Once again all was silent, except for the good-natured chuckles from the boys who had fallen victim to castigation for exactly the same thing.[30] Once again, Jack had learned at his own expense that high standards and reality were not necessarily compatible but, rather than providing grounds for accusations of double standards, Jack's fallibility endeared him even more to his squadron.

Jack's concern and interest in his men were two of the hallmarks of his command. 132 Operational Training Unit, East Fortune became the main anti-shipping training school and many of its graduates were posted to 455 Squadron. Jack kept a weather eye on the training unit and on at least one occasion suggested changes to the training syllabus.[31] In addition, he often visited the hotels frequented by the trainees and make himself known to them.

Navigator Flying Officer Ernest 'Blue' Bernau and his pilot Flying Officer Wallace B. Rowse Jr had all but completed their operational training and were relaxing in a hotel in nearby Edinburgh. While they were having a drink, Jack and Sheila walked over to them. Jack introduced themselves and said: 'I guess you boys are from East

Fortune.' 'Yes, sir', they replied. 'Well, I'm your new commanding officer. When are you coming over to see me?' He stayed and chatted with the boys about their training and how they had enjoyed it, and then left them to it. It was a brief encounter but Bernau was impressed Jack had gone out of his way to speak with them. Later, after joining the squadron, he said Jack would always stop and chat whenever they met on the station.[32]

Jack's welcome was not limited to pub introductions. When new crews arrived at the station, he called them to his office. Flying Officer Bill Herbert joined the squadron on 14 August 1944, after completing his operational training at East Fortune. He and the other new boys reported one by one and 'Jack was very interested in knowing just what your background was and where you'd done your training'. Herbert also recalled Jack often came into the officers' mess to have a drink and chat with his boys. Herbert was impressed by Jack's approachable nature.[33] He did not realise it but there was more to Jack's general enquiries about training and background. He interviewed all new crews to gain a sense of how they would fit in and how they would perform on operations. He followed up his preliminary assessments over the following weeks as he kept a close eye on their training progress but deferred his final judgement until he had watched them on their first operational flight.[34]

Perhaps the earliest example of Jack's interest in his crew can be seen in the relationship he fostered with Peter Ilbery, dating from their meeting at the Trossachs Hotel in January 1944. In the wartime dining room, Ilbery, dressed in his RAAF sergeant pilot's uniform, was the only one for dinner until Jack and Sheila were seated in a far corner. Jack sent the waiter over to Ilbery to invite him to share a drink with them. Over coffee, Jack asked how Ilbery came to be there. Ilbery told him how relatives had recommended the area and had spoken highly of its beauty. Then, a little reluctantly, he confided that he was from a holding unit outside Birmingham and had been separated from his friend, Bill Mitchell, who was at Brighton.[35] They were disappointed that, although trained on fighters, it appeared inevitable they would be going on to bombers.

When Jack met Ilbery the next day, his mufti was replaced by his RAAF uniform. Somewhat to his consternation, Ilbery discovered he had confided his hopes to a wing commander who happened to command a Beaufighter squadron. One of Jack's talents was that he could quickly gain the measure of someone and assess his commitment and ability. He put Ilbery at his ease and asked if he would like to join 455 Squadron. Ilbery immediately said 'yes', and asked if there would also be a place for Bill Mitchell. Ilbery was excited and wrote home shortly after. 'Here's hoping. This is what I came over here wanting to fly so it was lucky he was here. But it sounds too good to be true and I will not count too much on it.'[36] Ilbery underestimated Jack, and it was the last time he ever did.

Once he made a commitment, Jack did not shirk it. Shortly after returning to the squadron he wrote to tell Ilbery he had arranged for him and Mitchell to commence training at an advanced fighter unit, where they would be paired up with a couple of navigators, and then to a Beaufighter operational training unit, ahead of an expected arrival at Leuchars at the end of March 1944.[37] Unfortunately, despite Jack's efforts things did not run smoothly for Ilbery and Mitchell. Jack wrote to (now) Flight Sergeant Ilbery a few weeks later to advise the training protocols had changed and it had been decreed that 'all pilots on this type of squadron will have done a general reconnaissance course. This has upset my calculations completely.' Jack advised Ilbery to contact him again before the end of the course and he would try to arrange for him and Mitchell to be paired with navigators destined for the squadron so they could carry out their operational training together: 'Remember—Nil Desperandum!'[38]

Ilbery did not despair and, despite the delay in making his way to 455 Squadron and its Beaufighters, enjoyed his general reconnaissance training. A further hitch in the process came when, by June 1944, the squadron had no spare navigators. Jack advised them to crew up if they could, as this might expedite things. Ilbery had been corresponding with Jack steadily over the months, letting him know his progress and decided to seek his advice on commissioning. Jack advised him that, although it was more difficult to put in a request for a commission before he had completed his training, there would be no harm in making the written application now. Jack also reminded Ilbery it would have to be backed by good reports and above average results. As well as advice, he offered encouragement: 'Keep plugging away and keep me informed of your activities. We have been very busy and are really achieving results so we shall have plenty for you to do.'[39]

Ilbery and Mitchell progressed to East Fortune, thanks to Jack's encouragement and their own determination but credited by Ilbery as 'magic. Strings were pulled'. They were posted to 455 Squadron on 18 October 1944, just before Jack left, so Jack never led his protégés in a strike.[40] Jack and Ilbery became friends after the war and Jack never regretted the intervention in Ilbery's wartime career that set them on the path to friendship:

> It seems odd to say it after so many years, but the considerable effort involved in your appointment to 455 was based on the great impression I formed of you all those years ago. Of course it was a good assessment as has been clearly substantiated.[41]

Peter Ilbery had nothing but praise for Jack but he was one of the few who experienced a rare miscalculation on Jack's part.[42] After Jack left 455 Squadron to take up his operational planning position in 18 Group headquarters, he would occasionally visit the squadron to attend the post-op briefing of a strike he had planned. One such occasion was after a 'particularly dicey do'.[43] On 24 March 1945, eight Beaufighters from 455 Squadron armed with rockets and cannon joined a combined wing strike on shipping in Egersund Harbour. Nine days earlier, Ilbery had learned that his great friend Bill Mitchell was missing, presumed killed on operations.[44] His grief was still raw.[45] Although this was his third operation since hearing of Mitchell's loss, the previous two were without incident. This one was different: there was considerable anti-aircraft fire and Ilbery recalled that 'a wall of flak bursts barred the approaches into the harbour as each aircraft sought a target beyond the shrapnel curtain'.[46] Ilbery was in a vic of three and on his right were Warrant Officer George Longland and Flight Sergeant Errol Nayda. He saw their Beaufighter hit by flak and watched as it fell away; those behind saw it crash and explode.[47] While in his cockpit, Ilbery's mind closed to the tragedy of that death which could so easily have been his own. Along with Flying Officer William Edwards, the pilot of the other Beaufighter in Ilbery's vic, he attacked a 2000-ton merchantman which was later seen to be smoking.[48]

It was not until he returned to base that Ilbery felt the full impact of the strike. The memories of Mitchell and his recent death came flooding back. Jack sat behind Ilbery at the post-op briefing. He leant forward and said, 'it's just like shooting ducks, isn't it?' It was a light-hearted comment, meant to lift the group's mood, but it went wide of the mark.[49] Battle-hardened Jack had uncharacteristically misread the situation but Ilbery later recognised it was an atypical insensitivity on Jack's part: 'he would have known perfectly that it wasn't like that. Yes, that was an unfortunate remark; out of context. Very unlike Jack, really.'[50]

Career-wise, Jack had achieved much in a relatively short period of time. He had been made deputy flight commander of A Flight within two months of joining 455 Squadron. He had been promoted to acting squadron leader in November 1942 and acting wing commander and commanding officer of 455 Squadron in December 1943. He had been awarded the Distinguished Flying Cross during his first tour and during this second tour the Distinguished Service Order, a Bar to his DFC and recommended for the George Medal. All of this had been achieved before his 25th birthday. Group Captain Clouston's esteem was reiterated every time he took pen to another award recommendation. Others saw Jack as 'a mature man and a keen judge of human nature' and he was valued as a 'strict disciplinarian . . . [whose] squadron had been trained to form up into perfect flying formation when going out on strikes'. He was well known to have an 'extremely high' flying standard, insisting all his pilots be 'at least as good'. His absolute fearlessness on a strike was commended, as was the ultimate consideration of his men that led him to stay in the air after an operation to escort home those whose aircraft had been damaged in battle.[51]

455 Squadron's opinion of Jack was also high and his men were sorry to lose him.[52] To them, it was clear their leader was part of their success as an effective strike squadron. David Whishaw considered that 'under Davenport's coercive and inspiring example, and the whole wing presided over by Clouston's strong and positive presence, 455 had come of age as a truly effective fighting force'.[53] John Ayliffe recognised Jack's human qualities, his compassion and approachability, as well as his great leadership abilities.[54] Ayliffe and Whishaw were not alone in recognising Jack's talents: the two men who along with Jack were considered 'three of the most pugnacious and inspiring tacticians' of Coastal Command's shipping campaign, both recognised Jack's leadership talents.[55] Lloyd Wiggins thought 'Jack Davenport was a very nice man; a capable officer who made a

very good squadron commander'. He had known many high-calibre commanders and to him, Jack was on a par with these: 'As a squadron commander he did his job in much the same way, neither better nor worse than the manner in which other good squadron commanders that I had the privilege of knowing, had done theirs.'[56] Colin Milson, writing to his father in October 1944, just before Jack's departure, firmly credited the squadron's recent success to Jack: 'All is going very well with us here—have been very busy for the last six months and the squadron has been very successful, thanks to our CO, who is an outstanding chap.'[57]

Recognition of Jack's talents extended beyond the squadron, and beyond the war. The squadron's historians both praised Jack's contribution to the war effort. John Lawson, the squadron's adjutant during Jack's early days with 455 and well placed to view Jack's growth as a pilot and junior commander, believed Jack 'had combined exceptional operational success with real leadership, considerable administrative ability and a genius for initiating and perfecting new tactics and devices'.[58] Ian Gordon, at the time a colonel in the Australian Army with a distinguished career that would eventually see him as Deputy Chief of Army, judged Jack 'a great leader'.[59] These assessments could be considered biased; perhaps a one-time squadron adjutant and the son of a squadron navigator are not the most disinterested commentators but their evaluations follow clearly that of John Herington, official historian of the RAAF's activities during the war in Europe. He believed 455 Squadron was lucky to have Jack, a veteran in his field, as its commanding officer during the post D-day phase of the war. Speaking equally of Jack, Milson and Wiggins, he noted that their 'personal courage, audacity to attack and care in planning' did much to inspire their junior aircrew and create a spirit of dedication within the squadron. He considered that, by emulating these fine leaders, other squadron pilots also became fearless leaders.[60]

The squadron's feeling of loss was mitigated by the belief that they were fortunate that one of their own, someone who had had first-hand operational experience, would now be watching out for them. Wally Kimpton believed Jack was the 'right one to go [to headquarters]. He was clued up, he knew all about it. He'd been there and done

175

that. The right man to go up there.'[61] Ivor Gordon agreed: 'We were fortunate to have somebody there who knew something about the process . . . to stabilise things and [keep] them on track a bit.'[62] John Ayliffe felt Jack's aversion to risk and his reputation as a careful planner would work in their favour:

> When we were in 16 Group we used to think that some operations that they put on were really pointless . . . but when we heard that Jack was going to 18 Group and we were moving up there, I thought we would perhaps have better deals.[63]

The squadron was confident Jack would do his best for them and, despite his initial reluctance, Jack too, 'was comforted in that he would be doing the planning of operations for the strike wings including 455 Squadron'.[64] As he went to Pitreavie Castle, he had no sense of abandoning his beloved squadron as he had recommended that Colin Milson take command and could not have been more pleased when Milson was appointed.[65]

Jack and Milson 'always had a great rapport, right from the time he arrived on the squadron in 1943 and our lives together at that time imposed tests and strains of unusual types on people'. Jack considered Milson was 'an outstanding pilot—one of the few who was able to realise what an aeroplane could really do and used its capabilities to the full'. Jack was in no doubt that Milson's leadership skills were of a high order: 'His consideration for people on the squadron was very real, even though he would at times attempt to conceal it with a gruff approach.' Milson, so much a part of the squadron's proud tradition, was the right man to lead it during the final months of the war: 'We were a proud lot when it came to 455 Squadron. We felt its achievements made a legend and Colin was a real part of it.'[66]

Jack would not have admitted it, but he too was part of 455 Squadron's legend. His contribution is even more significant given that Coastal Command worked as a team. By largely performing anti-flak work, Jack was rarely solely responsible for destroying an enemy vessel. Coastal Command stood apart from Fighter and Bomber commands as it was the only command to seek out its targets, whether U-boats in the Bay of Biscay, harassing E-boats in the English Channel or merchant convoys plying Dutch and Norwegian coastal routes.[67] It may not have been able to boast the same level of success as Fighter and Bomber commands, but its attacks on German merchant shipping—with the resultant destruction of vessels and vital war and civilian supplies—contributed much to the war effort. At the end of Jack's tenure, 455 Squadron boasted a sound record. It had flown 2103 operational sorties in total, with 941 since the Beaufighter conversion. It had sunk nine merchant vessels, one U-boat, four minesweepers and three escort vessels; and damaged 26 merchant vessels, one destroyer, one U-boat, 32 minesweepers, two large gun boats, 59 escort vessels, four R-boats and one E-boat.[68]

Jack had made a formidable contribution to 455 Squadron and Coastal Command and was known in the media as an ace ship-buster for good reason. The commitment he made to his crew when he first decided he would prefer to pilot multi-engine aircraft was extended to a dedication to his squadron. That commitment to others would continue as 18 Group's operational planner. Now he would hold many more lives in his hands. Although initially reluctant to leave his squadron he did not eschew that new responsibility and would do his utmost to maximise success while all the time minimising the risk.

16

War's end

'the successful conclusion of the European war'

Jack's new position did not bring a promotion but he played an important role in 18 Group's operational structure. Groups were commanded by an Air Vice Marshal, with an Air Commodore as deputy. Underneath him, on an equal level, came the planning officers responsible for intelligence and operations. As operational planner, Jack worked closely with the intelligence section, staffed by RAF and Royal Navy staff, which fed information obtained as a direct consequence of breaking German codes.[1]

Jack encountered a number of problems. One was the great pressure to ensure the Germans remained unaware that their codes had been broken and Jack was careful to protect this information. In normal circumstances, he regularly sent reconnaissance flights to gather detailed information on the make-up of enemy convoys, their escorts, position and speed but, to protect information of German origin, he would initiate reconnaissance flights even when he knew what they would find. Despite the care with which it was treated, German information came in handy: 'At times, recces would report no sighting when it was known that a target was in fact there.'[2]

Another problem was the time lag between acquiring useful information about enemy shipping movements and launching a strike. Although reconnaissance aircraft were used constantly and reports acted upon expeditiously, there were many occasions when shipping bolted for a safe harbour or sought shelter in protected fiord waters underneath sheer cliffs. To counter this, strike forces were kept on standby for long periods so they could act quickly. In addition, the practice of reconnaissances-in-force, where the squadron or wing went looking for targets on spec, was continued.[3]

Jack also worked with Coastal Command to develop new methods which would take into account the command's 'changing objectives which came with the continual flow of intelligence and the increasing knowledge of the enemy's plans'.[4] With changing objectives came new tactics to take into account the special dangers inherent in operating within the confines of Norway's narrow fiords. Often, the fiords were a mere 200 to 300 yards wide, with overhanging cliffs rising 2000 feet or more which protected the German vessels as they hugged the coast until reaching their destination. When they were not on the move, enemy shipping would shelter deeper in the fiords. This made it difficult to detect enemy convoys. As well as their natural defensive features, the fiords were well and heavily fortified with anti-aircraft protection—mobile light defensive positions were built into the cliff faces to add to enemy firepower. In addition, there was no room to effectively manoeuvre for a torpedo attack so torpedoes were virtually abandoned and rockets and cannon became the weapons of circumstance. Despite the narrowness of the fiords, the large force was not abandoned, remaining an essential component of strike tactics. Use of a larger force was more complicated and full of inherent dangers such as firing on its own aircraft as individual pilots jockeyed for position in the narrow fiords, but Coastal Command persevered as it believed it made it harder for the enemy anti-aircraft gunner to pick on a specific target with so many aircraft dashing about all at once.[5]

Jack played an important role in the ongoing development and refinement of strike tactics. One of his first innovations ensured detailed shipping information, while minimising the risk involved in obtaining it. Initially one, then two, aircraft would reconnoitre the patrol route some distance ahead of the main force. They would fly inland, following the general line of the coast, skirting across fiord after fiord, keeping a close eye out for vessels nestled under the steep cliffs. These outriders would then radio the leader, giving the location and numbers of enemy shipping before returning to the wing to lead it to the target. The outriders were usually Norwegian Mosquito pilots of 333 Squadron who drew on their own personal experience of Norway's rugged coastline but the squadrons would often use their own pilots, who had received comprehensive briefing on specific landmark points from the Norwegians. After the strike leader received the outrider reports, he would decide which target to attack. As he approached the target area, he would veer his formation inland and bring his attack over the cliffs from the land, towards the sea.

One of the first strikes where outriders were successfully used was on 8 November 1944 when Wing Commander Tony Gadd led the Dallachy Wing. The Norwegian outriders flew to the entrance of Norway's Sogne Fiord. They scouted through the string of islands known as the Inner Leads and, finding nothing, continued north to Midtgulen Fiord where they sighted two merchant ships. They flew up the fiord and came across one coaster-type vessel in the fiord entrance and two closer to the coast. They radioed Gadd the number and positions, details of the natural defences and how they could escape once the attack was completed. One of the outriders then returned to the main formation to lead it to the target area. The remaining outrider reported five more merchant vessels—the fiord was proving a bountiful hunting ground. This was the first time 455 Squadron had faced enemy vessels sheltering deep under the protection of the coastline and they took the ships completely by surprise. There was some flak and damage to the Beaufighters but the cost to the enemy was greater. 455 Squadron reported black smoke rising to 500 feet from one 2500 to 3000-ton merchant vessel before an explosion; another was smoking heavily; and a coaster-type vessel belched smoke and possibly flames from its superstructure.[6] Coastal Command headquarters considered it the 'outstanding operation of the month'.[7]

Jack's outrider initiative proved sound and he soon gained a reputation as a skilled and detailed planner. Despite his care, however, he did not always enjoy success. One such operation took place on 9 February 1945 and became known as 'Black Friday'.[8] Coastal Command was under the operational control of the Admiralty. Although Coastal Command mounted its own operations and deployed its own air resources, it had to follow the Admiralty's general policy for the conduct of the war, adhering to its predetermined priorities. One key target, and Coastal Command's primary commitment, was major enemy naval vessels. Further down the list of favoured targets was merchant shipping.[9] At this stage of the war there were few naval targets. The *Tirpitz* had been destroyed on 12 November 1944 and

Germany had few warships left on the loose, but the Admiralty was keen to despatch those remaining. Early on 9 February, reconnaissance patrols were sent from Banff and Dallachy, and the Dallachy Wing was put on standby. Two crews from 489 Squadron reported sighting a merchant vessel of about 1500 tons in Stong Fiord and a Narvik-class destroyer of 2300 tons with its minesweeper and flak-ship escorts within the protective depths of Forde Fiord; five merchant vessels, including one of about 5000 tons, in Nord Gulen; and further north, two minesweepers and another anti-flak ship near Bremanger. On the face of it, the easiest and potentially more damaging target would have been the merchant convoy but the Admiralty's priority was clear. Although the Narvik-class destroyer was well protected and in a difficult position, it was to be the target.

Thirty-two Beaufighters took off from Dallachy later that day. They rendezvoused with twelve Mustangs from 65 Squadron RAF at Peterhead and set course. Wing Commander Colin Milson led 455 Squadron with 404 Squadron on his left and 144 Squadron on his right. The Mustangs followed. The outriders could not see the target as it was hidden deeply in Forde Fiord, but it was clear something was there when shore batteries opened up as the strike force approached. Milson led the force over the fiord and then turned starboard, about to lead the Beaufighters in an attack towards the sea. This proved impossible as the destroyer was too well protected under a cliff on the southern side. The attack had to be straight down the narrow fiord into the face of the destroyer and its escorts and the continuously blazing shore batteries. The flak barrage was intense. In addition, because of the time taken to move the force into an attack position, twelve Focke-Wulf FW 190 fighter aircraft of Jagdgeschwader 5 arrived on the scene. With little room to manoeuvre and with aircraft seeming to jostle constantly with their fellows, Milson's strike force made a 'very gallant attack'. A number of damaging hits were scored on the destroyer and five FW 190s were lost. Three pilots survived, but two were killed, including fighter ace Leutnant Rudi Linz.[10]

'Black Friday' was the most costly anti-shipping strike of the war.[11] The force limped home with varying degrees of flak damage. One Mustang pilot was shot down by the German fighters. 404 Squadron, which had taken the main flak onslaught at the entrance of the fiord, lost six Beaufighters and there was only one survivor. 144 Squadron lost one Beaufighter but both crew survived and 455

Squadron lost two Beaufighters, with two survivors.[12] All became prisoners of war.[13]

In taking up the planning position in 18 Group, Jack had hoped to reduce the risk pilots took when participating in strike operations but those on 'Black Friday' were too high and could not be reduced. The natural geography of the fiords meant the element of surprise was not with them. Jack's sense of personal loss after this operation was very real. He admitted years later that 'I planned this whole operation and was indeed upset with the losses'.[14] He had not known Warrant Officer Donald Mutimer, who had joined 455 Squadron in December 1944, nor Mutimer's navigator, Flight Sergeant John Blackshaw, who had joined in October 1944, a few short days before he had handed over his command to Wing Commander Milson. But they were members of the squadron he had commanded and for which he had been responsible for many months. He may not have known Mutimer and Blackshaw but he had, however, known the pilot of the second Beaufighter, which had been hit by a shore-based battery. In the days immediately following the strike, Flight Lieutenant Bob McColl, one of Jack's former pupils from Turnberry, had been assumed killed and it was sometime before it was known that he and his navigator, Warrant Officer Leslie MacDonald had been taken prisoner of war. Jack was moved by the loss of so many men whom he considered 'a great group of blokes'[15] Even so, it was not in his nature to dwell on failure; he would learn from mistakes and, if possible, ensure that they did not happen again.

Jack never forgot the disastrous human cost of 'Black Friday'. Nor did the people of Norway. As well as the 40th anniversary of VE Day, 8 May 1985 was the 40th anniversary of Norway's independence from the long years of German occupation. It was a sunny spring day and the people of Forde unveiled a monument to those who had died in the 'Black Friday' battle of 9 February 1945. The sacrifices were recalled as, too, were the kindness of the Norwegians who had provided succour to the wounded who were later taken as prisoners of war. The memorial was later repositioned outside the newly completed Bergen Airport.

In June 1987, Jack visited Norway. One of the places he most wanted to visit was Forde, now a prosperous town with a shipbuilding industry and reputation as a salmon-fishing resort. But he was not visiting Forde for the fishing: his destination was the memorial obelisk.

He had turned 67 a few days before and now, remembering those fourteen men from Australia, Britain and Canada and, recalling all airmen, many of whom were friends, who remained forever young, he laid a wreath at the foot of the obelisk.

Jack did not let the failure of 'Black Friday' deter him from his attempts to plan risk-averse operations but, despite some modest success, Coastal Command's claims for February 1945 of two ships sunk and sixteen damaged were low.[16] More success, however, was enjoyed by 18 Group throughout March and April 1945. On 2 April, the Banff Wing attacked a concentration of shipping in Sandefiord with 39 aircraft, sinking two merchant vessels of 8500 tons and damaging a further 22,000 tons of merchant shipping. Jack followed this with an 'excellent attack' on a number of small ships in Porsgrunn Harbour on 11 April, where three merchant vessels and a tug were sunk and three other merchant vessels were damaged.[17] As with many other strikes, those early April Banff Wing attacks came at a cost— two aircraft were lost on the Sandefiord strike and two on the Porsgrunn strike.

Jack had long ago accepted that close friends, squadron colleagues and crews who relied on his briefing skills could be lost on operations he either led or planned. With the Porsgrunn strike that loss became more personal than ever before. Phil Davenport was flying with 235 Squadron that day. It was his 89th sortie, and his thirteenth with 235 Squadron.[18] For some, thirteen is an unlucky number and so it proved for Phil; this would be his last operation. Phil's regular navigator was unfit for flying duties so he was paired for the first time with Flying Officer Ron Day. They were in the first wave of a formation of 40 Mosquitos. The Mosquitos' course took them off track and, as they approached, they were north of Porsgrunn. As they approached, the harbour was abeam so the formation wheeled right into a southerly heading, tightly turned west and then flew north to position themselves for a diving attack. As they dived, enemy fighters pounced. Phil's Mosquito was hit. He had difficulty controlling the aircraft and he realised the control surfaces and fuselage had been badly damaged. Streaming black smoke, Phil flew away from the harbour with a fighter on his tail.[19]

Even if the mountainous ridges, tightly covered with tall conifers, had proved a hospitable surface for a parachuting airman or two, they did not have enough height to bale out. Phil saw a possible landing area. As he dived, levelled off and extended flaps, Day prepared to release the cockpit hatch cover. The aircraft crashed onto the ice and bounced sideways, then plunged into the icy water and sank. The two airmen were wearing their Mae West life jackets. Day released the hatch and floated to the surface but Phil was trapped. He struggled to free himself and, when his leg came free, paddled to the surface where he was relieved to see the bloody-faced Day afloat. The submerged Mosquito's life raft burst from its stowage compartment and sprung to the surface. Phil and Day, who was concussed, clambered aboard. They were shivering, injured and, for some time afterwards, both passed in and out of consciousness, but they were alive.

Jack followed the progress of the raid closely. He received the radio reports as they came in, and verbal reports were phoned through after the returning crews had been debriefed. He heard with dismay that two crews had not returned: a Norwegian crew from 333 Squadron and his brother Phil and his navigator. Both aircraft had crashed, one in flames[20], the other, 3 miles from the first crash, into the icy waters of Langen Lake. Jack did everything he could to find out whether Phil had survived but no news was available. If he had survived, however, and been taken prisoner, he would find out via Red Cross channels in the usual manner. All he could do was wait.

Phil and Ron Day had almost reached the shore when they saw a man making signs for them to come to him. Gudmund Hegland, his brother Fohannes and friend Per Grini watched as Phil attempted to paddle the life raft towards them. They saw Phil pass out again so they took to the waters in a leaky row boat. Phil awoke to see the row boat gliding towards them. A man reached out, grabbed his wrist, and pulled the bright yellow dinghy to the shore.[21] Phil recalled that 'There was vast comfort in the warm, strong shoulders of the men that lifted us from the liferaft.'[22] Phil and Day were taken to a cottage where they enjoyed warmth and safety. Phil had been badly bruised, Day was still concussed, and both suffered the effects of immersion. Their frozen limbs were massaged and they huddled under piles of blankets as the kindly Norwegians dried their clothes in front of the fire. Day's head injuries were dressed but he was far from well. Soon, the Germans arrived: Phil and Day were now prisoners of war.

The war may have been over for Phil, but for Jack it had to be business as usual. Coastal Command was still mounting operations against enemy shipping because, although it was popularly expected the war would end soon, 18 Group believed the Germans intended to prolong it in Norway. Accordingly, it continued to maintain pressure on German shipping and enjoyed success upon success. On 23 April 1944, the Dallachy Wing sighted and attacked a merchant ship and two escort vessels in Risnes Fiord. The merchantman was left listing and many cannon strikes were made on the escorts. The Banff Wing opened May 1945 by damaging a minesweeper in the Kattegat and on 3 May the Dallachy Wing topped Banff's success by sinking a minesweeper and damaging a tanker in the Great Belt. The next day, again in the Kattegat, the Banff Wing sank yet another merchantman, damaged another and sank three escorts. It was a good way to end the war and Coastal Command was proud of its record: 'The work of the anti-shipping squadrons during the final week of the war is consistent with their previous fine record . . . they have contributed in no small measure to the successful conclusion of the European war.'[23]

Jack had much to celebrate on VE Day, 8 May 1945. Hostilities were over and he could soon return to Australia and establish a new life with Sheila and his soon-to-be born child. He shared in the relief the McDavids felt, knowing that Sheila's brother, Major Stewart McDavid who had entered the war in October 1944, playing his part in Operation *Vitality*, the third major phase of the Battle of the Scheldt, would soon be home. Even so, the worry Jack felt for his brother's fate was uppermost in his mind. He spoke to Commander Haakon Jorgenson, who was piloting the official delegation to take the German surrender in Norway, asking if Jorgenson would try to find out if Phil had survived.

Jack was not the only one trying to discover Phil's fate. Their youngest brother, Keith, had flown with 461 Squadron for over a year but was now posted to a public relations position with RAAF overseas headquarters in London. As soon as the war ended, he headed to Dallachy to negotiate an aircraft to fly to Norway to find Phil.

As Keith tried to convince someone to let him fly to Norway, Phil was enjoying more success with his own persuasion skills. A RAF Dakota had landed at Fornebu, apparently country-hopping to be 'first' in the newly liberated Scandinavia, pipping the official delegations for the honours. Phil asked the senior officer to take him and two fellow prisoners to the United Kingdom. As the Dakota headed towards Copenhagen, it passed Commander Jorgensen's Catalina and the official surrender delegation.

It was a long trip home, via Copenhagen and Brussels. When the Dakota landed at RAF Northolt, Phil made every effort to contact Jack and Keith. Despite all he had gone through since crashing in Norway, he could think only of his brothers. He had been possessed by nightmares, dreaming that something was terribly wrong. All he wanted to do was telephone them and assure himself they were safe. He argued with an officious admin-type but was not allowed to phone from Northolt. Apparently, he could only do this at the Brighton reception centre. Tired, unwell and feeling the effects of his leg injury, Phil was determined to go straight to Brighton, via London, where he stayed overnight with friends.

Phil was not sure where Jack would be in those post-VE days but he finally tracked him down at Sheila's family home in Ardrossan. Jack had only just arrived when he took the phone and heard a voice he readily recognised say 'good day'. It was the best phone call of his life. He recalled 50 years later that Phil's phone call was 'a great memory'.[24] The relief was immense and was soon surpassed by elation. Sheila shared Jack's excitement. The brothers agreed to meet at Brighton and, when Phil had rung off, Jack contacted Keith to tell him of Phil's safe arrival. The reunion in Brighton was a great day for all three of them. They had survived the war relatively unscathed.

Memory plays funny tricks and, over the years, the joy and relief Jack and Sheila experienced when they heard of Phil's safe return brought about a telescoping of events. When their son passed on his parents' memories of that time, he told of how Sheila had been so overwhelmed when she heard Phil had survived that she immediately went into labour. Bruce's birth was not that rapid, and it was not until the morning of 19 May 1945 that Jack and Sheila's first child was born in Sheila's bedroom in her childhood home.[25] As was common then, Jack was not with his wife during her labour but it was not something Sheila regretted. Years later, she would laugh with friends that she was glad Jack had not been present. She knew her perfectionist husband with his penchant for doing things in the most efficient manner too well. She could hear him saying, 'There has to be a better way of doing this'.[26]

John Bruce Stewart Davenport's birth was a joyous occasion for Jack and Sheila and their pride in and love for their first-born was clearly evident in the many photos taken soon after his birth. But much as Jack wanted to stay with Sheila and his son, the air force decreed otherwise: Coastal Command wanted Jack to go to Norway in charge of an investigation into the effectiveness of its aerial attack on German sea communications and the extent of Norwegian sabotage.[27] Despite the inconvenience of the timing, this trip was not simply about fulfilling his duty: Jack had a very personal reason for wanting to make the uncomfortable voyage to Norway in a 110-foot air–sea rescue boat. He wanted to visit those who had assisted Phil and give them his personal thanks.[28]

Jack saw considerable war damage in Norway and heard disturbing accounts of German reprisals against the resistance. His interpreter and guide, an active member of the resistance, showed him his back, crisscrossed with lash marks suffered at the hands of the Gestapo.[29] Jack saw first-hand the 'extraordinary work that the Norwegian underground had carried out during the war; they did a wonderful job'.[30] During the last months of the war, the Norwegian population had experienced much privation as food had been diverted from civilians to the German military and the entire Norwegian fish catch of 1944 was sent to Germany.[31] Jack recognised the sacrifice of the Norwegian men who had assisted his brother and his navigator. He sought out Gudmund and Fohannes Hegland and Per Grini and discovered their circumstances were dire. He spent all the money he had with him buying food and clothing for their families.[32]

After Jack visited Phil's rescuers, he continued his investigations. He sailed to some of the ports in southern Norway, liberating most of them on the way. He returned to Scotland briefly and was then sent on a similar investigation through Northern France, Holland, Germany and Denmark.[33] These investigations resulted in the first of the major reports into Coastal Command's anti-shipping campaign. Among other things, they determined that, although mines caused the most widespread damage, the next most effective weapon, and the best for its size, was the 'J' type rocket, which had been tested by Jack and later used so successfully by him and 455 Squadron. Interviews with former ships' crews also indicated an adverse effect on enemy morale from high explosive 20-millimetre cannon fire, also used to great advantage by Jack.[34]

Phil Davenport was repatriated to Australia in August 1945 on SS *Orion*, along with many other former prisoners of war. Keith Davenport continued his work with the public relations unit for a time and then took extended leave from the RAAF, turning his hand to a variety of occupations, such as van driver, salesman, decorator and journalist with the Newcastle *Herald* until he embarked for Australia in June 1946.[35] It was many years before the three brothers were together again. For the rest of their lives they spent much time apart: business commitments on separate continents and travel and family life intervened so reunions for many years were few. But their strong sibling bond never weakened. Looking back, towards the end of his life, Jack recorded that 'I was very proud of my brothers ... They were two great blokes.'[36]

When the reports had been written after his second investigation, Jack was briefly posted to command RAF Banff in September–October 1945 and was then sent to RAAF overseas headquarters in London in late October while Air Vice Marshal Henry Wrigley CBE DFC was in hospital. During Wrigley's absence, Jack acted as the senior air staff officer taking responsibility for the affairs of Australian airmen. Since the end of the war in the Pacific, their repatriation to Australia was of the utmost priority and Jack played a considerable part in this process.[37] Jack rarely spoke of these days; there was nothing exciting about his administrative duties, especially compared with his experiences on operations. One event, relating to the overcrowding of the SS *Orion*, stood out but of this Jack spoke only obliquely and with no elaboration: 'I was sent to Kodak House London to look after things—another story, including revolt'.[38]

Orion had recently returned to the United Kingdom to collect its next military contingent for repatriation. It could carry 5235 troops, but this was reduced to 4676 for voyages east of Suez.[39] Even so, it was still hopelessly overcrowded. It was anticipated that, when the *Orion* crossed the equator into the southern hemisphere's summer, the increasing heat would make the voyage even more intolerable so the number of repatriates was further reduced to 3441 with many officers and warrant officers to be accommodated on the troop deck.[40]

After inspecting their quarters and seeing that 300 men would be crammed into spaces just 50 by 30 feet in area, and that they would be expected to sleep in hammocks slung elbow to elbow[41], a number of men decided not to suffer a long voyage in hugger-mugger conditions. Over 300 men walked off.[42] The accommodation had been approved by the Board of Inspection, and considered satisfactory in all respects[43] so, disregarding the mutinous intentions of the men, the draft commander ordered them to reboard. The men would have none of it so he contacted RAAF overseas headquarters. Jack, along with wing commanders Bill McFadden DFM and Anthony Willis DFC DFM, the Australian liaisons for Flying Training and Bomber commands respectively, drove to RAF Gamston in Nottingham, where the men had been sent to cool their heels.

Jack, McFadden and Willis were shown into an icy hangar where the rebellious aircrew awaited them. Jack took the lead in the negotiations and adopted a firm line with the assembled throng. When he could not immediately sway the men by reason, he stated that their refusal to obey orders could be considered mutinous and they could be court-martialled. The men finally saw sense and agreed to reboard. Jack then dismissed the men and arranged for them to take a few days' leave. As their pay books had been confiscated, overseas headquarters distributed funds for those who needed them.[44] The walk-off had been mentioned in the papers and, because of a demand for an enquiry into 'cattle truck' conditions, would even be referred to in parliament.[45]

As the *Orion*'s passengers finally sailed towards Australia, contemplating their postwar futures, Jack's thoughts, too, turned in that direction. Air Vice Marshal Wrigley returned to duty and Jack was no longer required at Kodak House. His immediate superior, Air Commodore S. Webster, considered he had 'plenty of tact and commonsense, coupled with a good sense of humour', was 'of outstanding ability' and had done 'excellent work whilst at this headquarters'. Webster's superior, Air Vice Marshal S.P. Simpson, was just as effusive in his praise. He thought Jack was 'an outstanding officer with great drive and initiative. Although new to staff duties he rapidly adapted himself and made a great success of his duties.' Simpson had seen Jack's 'exceptional powers of leadership', considered him tactful with a 'delightful personality' and had 'no hesitation in recommending him most strongly for a permanent commission'.[46] Jack's sterling service with overseas headquarters was recognised formally and publicly by a Mentioned in Despatches.[47]

PART 4

Postwar

17

Concrete Industries (Monier)

'it had to involve working with people'

Air Vice Marshal Simpson had no hesitation in recommending Jack for a permanent commission but Jack had no intention of accepting one. Sheila was now pregnant with their second child and 'I wanted to come back to Australia first and foremost'.[1] The repatriation of Australians was now at an advanced stage and Jack did not have to wait long for transport. Most married Australians travelled ahead, with their wives and children on designated 'war bride ships', but Jack arranged for his family to travel together. Three days before his second wedding anniversary, Jack, Sheila and baby Bruce boarded the Blue Funnel Line's SS *Sarpedon* and travelled first-class to Australia via South Africa. They disembarked at Sydney on 12 March 1946.[2] Jack brought his family to 51 Kyle Parade and their neighbour Pat Curnow recalled how Jack, still in uniform, proudly introduced his wife and new son to their neighbours.[3]

Jack returned to many changes. Before the war, he and his two brothers were still living at home with their parents, grandmother and Uncle Bob. Now, Keith was still in the United Kingdom and within a month Phil would be on his way to China with the United Nations Relief and Rehabilitation Administration. Their grandmother had died in 1941 and Uncle Bob was now living in the Masonic homes at Glenfield. Soon, Grace and Roy moved up the hill to number 87, with Jack and Sheila remaining at number 51: their first real home as a family.

Jack knew the close relationship with his mother would not change but the tensions between Jack and his father before the war were still apparent and would never be resolved.[4] Grace Davenport became an important part of the lives of Jack and Sheila and their children. She was a good grandmother and mother-in-law and was much loved by Jack's family. She welcomed Sheila with open arms and proved a strong support to her over the following months and years as Sheila acclimatised to a very different life. As well as emotional support, Sheila relied upon Grace for practical assistance. Reminiscent of when Jack took his young bride to their first home in the middle of a mice plague, Jack and Sheila found they had arrived amidst a flea infestation.[5] Sheila was allergic to flea bites and her first encounter with Australian 'wildlife' was distressing. With Grace's assistance, that irritating problem was soon solved. Grace also helped with the practicalities that Sheila had not had to deal with as the child of affluent parents with staff. She taught her daughter-in-law how to heat and use the copper and other household tasks. Jack soon engaged a nurse to assist with Bruce and baby June, who was born in June 1946, but in those first years in Australia Sheila experienced much isolation as Jack worked long hours. For some time, the highlights of her week were the regular visits from vendors bringing groceries, eggs, ice and bread.[6]

Despite Sheila's loneliness in those first years, the strength with which she endured Jack's absences on dangerous operations during the war did not desert her and she never contemplated returning to Scotland. She grew close to her mother-in-law and gradually became friends with her neighbours and, later, with the wives of Jack's work colleagues.[7]

When Jack arrived back in Australia, there was great pressure to find a job. Some of his friends had decided to stay in the RAAF but he didn't think a career in the permanent air force in peacetime was for him and he was demobilised on 3 May 1946.[8]

Laws, with generous conditions, had been passed to give servicemen the right of reinstatement to their former occupations. They would be entitled to any pay increases that had occurred in their absence and all of their original rights of employment such as pension entitlement were safeguarded.[9] Jack had not resigned from the Commonwealth Bank before he embarked for overseas service but had been placed on extended military leave. If he decided to return to the bank, he would be in a junior position and his annual gross salary would be only £360.[10] The security of the bank might have appealed still and, as a much decorated, high-ranking airman, the bank would have considered him an asset if he had decided to take up a position there[11], but Jack knew the bank would not offer the same challenges he had enjoyed during his war service:

> The responsibility that one had thrust upon one, the requirements and stresses of the time, the fact that you could work for many, many hours, covering several days, without sleep if necessary, it stretched one and made one appreciate the potentials that perhaps existed.[12]

Jack had no firm ideas about what he wanted to do, but 'I felt that it had to involve working with people'.[13]

Throughout the war Jack had exchanged letters with his friend and mentor, Clem Shaddock. Clem's company, Cement Linings Limited, had expanded considerably over the last years, operating in a number of states. Its core business was still the patented system of cement linings that tripled the life of water mains but, in 1941, its merger with two companies meant its area of operations now extended to making concrete pipes and other products for industrial and domestic use. The company had been declared a protected industry during the war and had turned its energies towards defence work and essential services.

At the end of the war, Australia faced a severe housing shortage. Thousands of houses were required to satisfy demand, but materials and skilled labour were scarce. The company saw a way to take advantage of this situation. It obtained the patent for a concrete building unit called 'Monocrete'. These cored concrete slabs, which slotted easily into each other, did not require plastering and service pipes and electrical wires could be laid with little trouble within the wall cavities. Four men could erect the walls of a house on a prepared foundation in one day and it would be ready for occupancy within a few weeks.[14] Importantly, skilled labour to manufacture the slabs was not required. Before the company could gear up to manufacture the Monocrete slabs it had to obtain ministerial sanction, and this was given in May 1946. Around about this time, the company changed its name to Concrete Industries (Australia).[15]

Soon after he returned to Australia, Jack took Sheila and baby Bruce to visit Clem Shaddock. Clem had followed Jack's air force career with interest and had suggested he come to work for him after the war. Clem valued his friendship with Jack and believed Jack would be an asset to his company. His progress through the ranks and his high-level operational planning abilities indicated Jack was not only a proven leader but a man of talent. Clem's offer was more than just personally motivated: he knew the board of directors, as well as company clients, would be impressed by Jack's war service record.[16]

Clem reiterated his offer of employment to Jack, telling him about the Monocrete patent and his plans for expansion into postwar housing and public building construction. Monocrete Pty Ltd, a separate company within the Concrete Industries portfolio, would be responsible for these operations and Clem wanted Jack to manage it. He also wanted Jack to be his personal assistant so he could learn about all of Concrete Industries' operations. With this knowledge, combined with hands-on management experience, Jack would be in a prime position to succeed Clem when he retired. Jack could see that, with this small but aggressively growing company, he would have all the challenges he could want. He accepted on a starting salary of £650 and resigned from the bank shortly after.[17]

Jack may have landed the dream job but he had to prove he was worthy of the faith Clem Shaddock had placed in him and that he was capable of managing a new and dynamically growing company. It was clear Jack was being groomed for the future and there was some resentment from long-term employees. It was a real test of Jack's interpersonal skills to negotiate his way through this potential minefield of antagonism and jealousy. He set about charming those who doubted or mistrusted his abilities, but he did not rely on his charm alone.[18] He worked hard at building relationships, putting the company first in all his actions. He had much to learn and he accepted guidance from Clem and other experienced managers. From the start, he displayed his loyalty to Clem Shaddock and Concrete Industries. He set his own personal standard of responsibility—which he soon made clear that he expected all to adopt: 'Responsibility in business is when you place the affairs of the company above your own.'[19]

Jack complemented Clem in all respects. Their personalities may have been dissimilar—Jack more outgoing, Clem quieter and more reserved—but they shared similar traits. They believed in people and making the most of them and were committed to health and safety issues on the factory floor. Clem was an accountant, but Jack thought like an accountant and they both looked carefully at the bottom line. They shared a straight-laced integrity. Clem's son Lyn recalled how, when he took some pencils home from the technical college where he was doing a mechanical drawing course, his father accused him of stealing. When Jack discovered one of his executives had replaced his company car's hardly worn tyres and then sold the used ones, he was furious that someone could have been so dishonest. That executive did not last much longer on the payroll.[20] As Clem showed faith in Jack, even though untested in the business world, so too did Jack display faith in his employees' abilities. He firmly believed 'the organisation depends on its people. All should have the opportunity and responsibility of contributing what they can.' It made sound business sense: 'any company which does not involve its people is only getting a fraction of the value it pays for.'[21] Frank Thomas, who worked for Jack for 27 years as the company's insurance manager, had wide-ranging access to all areas of the company. Frank saw and admired how Jack loved his employees and how well he treated them. He recognised that Jack valued his staff and developed their talents. If Jack thought they could handle a matter he would allow them to do so, giving them free reign but supporting them if they needed it.[22] Kevin Parnell, who ran the Monocrete operations in Canberra, felt the same. He too considered that Jack knew how to elicit the best from people: he never scolded or blamed anyone if things inadvertently went wrong. Kevin thought Jack was a good manager and he trusted him implicitly.[23] When Lyn Shaddock, who wasn't even yet twenty, joined the company some years later, Jack gave him responsibility for multimillion-dollar building contracts and the opportunity to engage in money-making ventures for the company: 'I was given a lot of freedom as a kid that I don't think too many kids at that age ever have.'[24] Jack, who had commanded a squadron at 23, well recognised that age was not necessarily everything.

Clem Shaddock fostered a family atmosphere in his company, with social gatherings, sports days and a general sense of togetherness.[25] Long hours were common and the company's history tells how those working late in the small Erskineville office on winter's nights would heat frankfurts and chips for tea on the upturned radiator.[26] Although a manager, Jack did not hold himself aloof from his staff. He stopped his car and offered lifts to other workers.[27] He played at the works' sporting days and, along with Sheila, other staff and their wives, rushed to the Villawood plant to help save records and clean up when a drain flooded into the building.[28] He believed in making himself accessible and visited the plants as often as he could. He was a well-known figure on site in the early days but, as the company grew and his responsibilities turned more to the board than the factory, it became difficult to maintain this sort of presence.[29] Regardless of the frequency of his visits Jack developed a reputation for eagle-eyed inspections so, if a plant manager wanted to hide something from Jack, he tried to distract him with a dirty milk or Coke bottle. He would place the bottle where Jack would be sure to see it. The rationale was that it was better to risk Jack's wrath over a small oversight than endure an interrogation about more serious problems. It didn't often succeed as Jack was known to run a tight operation and knew full well what was going on in his factories.[30]

As Jack became a part of company life, so too did Sheila: wives were expected to play their part in their husbands' careers. At that time, it was rare to conduct business in restaurants. Clients were entertained in the home, often at short notice and out of the family budget. More and more, Sheila was called upon to cater for clients and other company managers and their wives. She was warm, genuinely interested in her guests and had the ability to make them feel at ease. She was a good and innovative cook and enjoyed preparing meals for special occasions. Despite little notice, and often three or four nights a week, she soon proved a competent and charming hostess and an invaluable asset to her husband's career.[31]

In his eulogy at Jack's memorial service, Reverend McKay credited Sheila with being the 'secret behind Jack Davenport's adventuring greatness; he had someone at his side who was going to stick with him through the thick and thin of war and through the thick and thin of life'.[32] But Sheila was more than her husband's helpmate; she was also Jack's close friend and companion and theirs was a true partnership of equal intellect based on love. She was a keen reader with broad tastes. She enjoyed challenging discussions on a wide range of current social issues or philosophy, and was firm in her opinions and caring in her outlook. She was a loving mother, a good homemaker and a patient wife who never complained when her husband was constantly working late hours or away for weeks on a business trip. She also enjoyed golf and gardening and, later, was a devoted grandmother. She became involved in charity work and gained much satisfaction from teaching English to migrant women and enjoyment and stimulation from a discussion group started under the auspices of WEA but which continued for many years.

Although hers was a fulfilled life, Sheila did experience frustration and, to some extent, was overshadowed by Jack's career and success. Despite being awarded a Master of Arts from St Andrews University and her obvious intelligence, Jack would not allow her to go to work as, at that time, this was taken to mean that the husband, the main breadwinner, could not support his wife and family.[33] It was many years before she found an outlet for her inquisitive mind outside the family home. Although Jack and Sheila travelled extensively, Jack's business responsibilities meant their holidays were usually short and extended stays in Scotland were always promised for Jack's retirement years. Her sense of frustration aside, her love and commitment to Jack were wholehearted and lifelong.[34]

As for so many, Jack's time with the air force was a great influence on his life.[35] He believed the skills he had learned there had provided him with a good platform to stand on in his postwar life and he was certainly never averse to blatantly using tried and true techniques.[36] On one occasion he was driving past a building site and saw some vandals. He told his companion he was going to treat this as a military operation. He jumped out of the car, marched up to the louts, tore strips off them, shook them up a bit, and then sent them away with a metaphorical boot up their backsides. He was not going to press charges, but he would not tolerate such behaviour.[37] On another occasion, he was in Canberra to sort out a problem with a public housing contract to build Monocrete houses in the new suburb of Narrabundah. Jack went into a meeting knowing he was at a disadvantage but came out the victor: 'They had all the guns, but they did not know how to fire them!'[38]

Jack's expectation of military precision and punctuality soon became well known. He regularly held senior staff meetings on Friday evenings, starting at 5.00 p.m. As the time approached, he would start glancing at his watch. At 5.00 exactly, he would call for the door to be locked and anyone who had not arrived had to provide an explanatory note the next day.[39] Just as he expected his squadron to constantly do better, so too did he expect high standards from his staff. His constant catch-cry to his long-term secretary, Hope Gibb, was: 'It just isn't good enough, is it, Hope?' Jack often asked for the impossible, and Hope discovered, time and time again, 'just how often the impossible can be achieved and Mr Davenport knew it could all along'.[40]

Under Jack's management, Monocrete Pty Ltd grew from strength to strength. Shortly after he joined the company, a Monocrete Victory Home was built to publicise the new construction method. It was promoted by radio station 2KY and raffled off, dismantled and re-erected for the winner in Chatswood. It was the first of many Monocrete houses. Jack won hundreds of thousands of pounds worth of construction projects from the New South Wales Housing Commission as well as many other public projects. The New South Wales Department of Public Works also succumbed to Jack's drive and charm as he convinced them of the appropriateness of Monocrete buildings in its rapid expansion of educational facilities in the postwar years. Costing less than conventional structures, their durability and ease of construction made them attractive and the department commissioned about twelve a year, over a ten-year period.[41]

Monocrete was in great demand. More factories were built and the company expanded interstate. Monocrete was even chosen for the meteorological station at Macquarie Island in 1949. By 1950, with the rapid postwar baby boom, there was an estimated need for 90,000 new homes annually. Monocrete had come into its own.[42] As well as being the construction material of choice for many families, so too did Jack use it for his new home. He had faith in his company's product and was proud of it but there was also an element of pragmatism. Realistically, Monocrete was still the quickest, most cost-effective building material available. He had purchased a large block of land in Blakehurst and in the early 1950s the Davenport's three-bedroom Monocrete house was constructed. Monocrete was not the only company product used for Jack's new home; he laid down crazy paving from broken Monier slabs.[43]

Concrete Industries also grew considerably in the immediate postwar years. By 1950, at least 80 per cent of the total value of building materials of a standard family home could be supplied by

Concrete Industries. In 1951, the Villawood factory increased its capacity to 11 million tiles per year[44] and many houses around Australia were soon topped with Concrete Industries' tiles. Jack was as proud of those tiles as he was of Monocrete. Often when driving around Sydney he would point to a roof and say 'That's one of ours'.[45]

Under Clem Shaddock's guidance, combined with his own capacity to learn quickly, work hard and build effective working relationships, Jack developed into a more than competent manager. In August 1955, Clem died suddenly in Zurich while on an extended business trip. His death was a great shock to his family and company, and to Jack. Despite his long working hours, Jack had spent much of his free time with Clem. He would take Sheila and the children to visit and while the adults chatted the children gambolled in the Shaddocks' pool. The bond formed before the war, when Clem became both friend and surrogate father, had strengthened over the years.

After the immediate shock of Clem's death had subsided, Jack fully expected the board to appoint him managing director. Even Clem's family thought this would be the case.[46] Despite his drive and business dynamism, Jack was still only 35 and, in a company that prided itself on the loyalty of long-serving employees[47], it was understandable that the board offered the position, and an invitation to join the board, to Keith Milburn. Milburn was a much-loved man who had been with one of Concrete Industries' predecessor companies since 1934, working his way up from pipe layer to general manager. He was known as a people person, had wide-ranging experience throughout the company and a long history of producing excellent profits.[48]

Jack was greatly disappointed. He thought carefully about his future and seriously considered resigning. Initially there was some competitive tension between Jack and Milburn but, in the end, Jack decided he would stay with the company and offered his full support to Milburn. Once he had made his decision, there was no white-anting—he gave Milburn his total loyalty. Lyn Shaddock was working for Jack at the time and sensed no friction. He saw everyone pull together to ensure the company overcame the hurdle of losing its founding managing director. He had seen Jack's disappointment, but had also seen him put it aside. It was character building.[49]

Shortly after Clem Shaddock's death, Jack was appointed general manager. His talents and dynamic dedication to the company were further recognised in 1961 when he was promoted to senior general manager and then chief general manager in 1963, where he worked closely with Keith Milburn. Jack and Milburn were visionary men. In 1962 they sponsored a name change to Concrete Industries (Monier) Ltd, as a clear sign that there was more to the company than concrete and related products. The company continued to expand and Jack played an important part in this expansion. He was not shy of looking at different ways to improve business, taking paths that were not necessarily the safest, or looking creatively at the future.[50] Nor was he shy of exploring current management practices and adopting modern techniques to manage performance—for instance, Jack's long-term secretary Hope Gibb, as well as other staff, undertook a number of psychological evaluation tests before they were employed and before he retired, Jack initiated a large-scale staff survey.[51] The time Jack and senior management fought a hostile takeover from a foreign company became legend. Jack was devastated when the English company, Redland PLC acquired 49.9 per cent of Monier. Jack and the senior managers phoned shareholders and requested they not sell out. Jack took it further, and exhorted his faithful employees to also make calls.[52] He was proud of the company and his part in it and did not want it to fall into foreign hands.[53]

In 1993, Jack reflected on his air force career and what perhaps he could have changed about it. Typically, he did not relive operations or think about how he could have benefitted from the gift of hindsight. 'I think I'd have devoted more time to the people around me. One was very busy and sometimes didn't spend enough time in that context.'[54] His squadron and company perhaps would have disagreed: devotion to the needs of his staff was one of Jack's management hallmarks.

He never forgot that people were Concrete Industries' greatest assets. As the company expanded in the immediate postwar years, it required more and more skilled workers which Australia could not produce. Jack went to the Bathurst migrant camp to canvass workers. He selected a number who proved to be excellent and loyal employees and, like Jack, stayed with the company until retirement.[55] When Hope Gibb joined the company in the mid 1960s, it was not common for women to join superannuation schemes. Jack encouraged her to sign up, and she did. It was not a decision she ever regretted. Although Jack was a perfectionist who expected the most and more that a person could give, Hope never found him a difficult boss. She recognised the gentle side of his nature and never saw him lose his temper. She admired the cool manner he displayed and took to heart the invaluable lessons he taught her—tenets that he himself held dear: always keep your dignity, have pride in what you do, remain confidential in all your dealings and have confidence in your own abilities.[56]

Jack showed by his words and example that the company and its people were all-important. In everything he did, he maintained his personal standards of loyalty, integrity and commitment to staff. He preferred to promote from within where he could; the majority of his senior managers had many years of company experience. If someone needed help, he would offer it. When Hope was hospitalised, Jack and Sheila visited her. When one of his interstate general managers fell ill, Jack arranged for him to visit a top specialist at short notice. When another of his general managers had problems with the interest payments on a land purchase, Jack had the company pay them in recognition of dedicated service. There were many examples where he helped his staff, but it was all very quietly done as the essence of Jack's charity was that he would not draw attention to it.[57]

Jack's dedication and entrepreneurial talents continued to be recognised by his board of directors. He was invited to join the board in 1968 and in 1970 he was appointed managing director when Milburn retired. Under Jack's direct stewardship, Concrete Industries (Monier) Ltd continued to grow and strengthen. In 1974, *The Sun* published a snapshot of the business careers of Jack and his brother Keith. At that time, Keith was chief executive of the Australian operations of Reed Consolidated, a large international publishing house. The article made much of both businesses' multimillion-dollar annual profits, noting that 1974 would likely see them chalk up almost $300 million in sales. A stickler for accuracy, Jack quipped privately that the combined sales total would be more in the order of $600 million.[58]

By 1977, although still formally known as Concrete Industries (Monier) Ltd, the company was known more familiarly as Monier. It was aggressively expanding into new markets and much of its growth came from product diversification. This proved successful in many instances, but not always. The acquisition of Chesney Industries, a caravan production company, was a failure because of a rapidly changing market. Jack pushed for the acquisition, but when sales dramatically declined he promptly made the decision to withdraw from the market. He considered the initial decision to purchase Chesney was sound, the operation efficient and the product good, but when the market changed he had to pragmatically walk away.[59] The Chesney venture proved one of only a few failings in Jack's stewardship but his part in Monier's overseas expansion far outweighed his failures. The importance of Monier's offshore growth cannot be underestimated. From the early 1960s, the company extended its operations to the Philippines, Papua New Guinea, Thailand, Indonesia, New Zealand, Germany and Japan. It was one of the few Australian businesses at the time to successfully venture offshore and its American operations, including roofing, metal building products and fly-ash, proved very profitable.[60]

The Chesney failure showed that, although an exceptional businessman, Jack did have faults. Interestingly, his management weaknesses were exaggerations of some of his particular strengths. Jack was a careful financial manager; he treated the company finances almost as if they were his own and he could not abide extravagance. Although he always drove a big car himself, for years, without a concern for company image, his salesmen drove small cars and he ensured that mileage was carefully recorded. If someone was not strictly entitled to a company car, Jack would not set a precedent, even in the case of his own secretary. Jack was always mindful that he had to report to the shareholders and any excess, or perceived excess, would be queried. Even so, Jack's careful attention to company expenses did appear to be more parsimonious than frugal.[61] As with anyone, Jack had his fair share of faults but his obvious leadership and management talents and great concern for people overshadowed these negatives and they are barely remembered—and then with difficulty or reluctance—when Jack Davenport's achievements are recalled.[62]

The Australian building industry experienced a downturn in the late 1970s but Jack continued to steer Monier through a period of high profits. In 1977, recognising Jack's part in boosting Monier's profit from $7.9 million to $10.1 million despite difficult conditions in the building and construction industries, he was named as one of The Australian's top ten businessmen of the year. Nominations came from the newspaper's readership (and in that year 250 executives from mainly large public companies were proposed). The final selection was made by the editor of *The Australian* and the News Limited finance editors.[63] Jack was also one of *The Australian*'s top ten of 1978, this time in recognition of his leadership of Monier to a 19.9 per cent profit rise and an expansion into a tough US market in addition to the company's general move into Asia, Papua New Guinea and New Zealand.[64] Although prestigious, *The Australian*'s top ten was not quite peer recognition—even though many of the business section readers would have been peers. This came in 1982 when the Australian Institute of Management awarded Jack the Storey Medal which recognised significant contributions to management. In Jack's case, it applauded his innovative management style while leading Monier through a time of considerable overseas expansion.[65]

Jack was also recognised by clients and business partners as a man of high talents. Devon Minchin owned Metropolitan Security Services which Jack contracted to manage the security and surveillance on Monier's sites. Devon enjoyed excellent relations with Jack and considered him highly regarded throughout the business world.[66] Dick Mason joined Ampol as an industrial representative tasked with drumming up business from large companies. It was his practice to pitch Ampol's services and prices to key managers but, until he asked to speak to Concrete Industries' general manager in charge of purchasing, he had rarely managed to wedge a foot in the executive door. Dick was immediately impressed that he should be given an audience by someone as high placed in the organisation as Jack. Dick succeeded in obtaining all of Monier's business. It was a big account and he received much kudos as a consequence. What amazed him more than obtaining the account, though, was that Jack had taken the time to talk with a sales representative. That fortuitous meeting was the beginning of a close business and personal relationship that lasted until Jack's death.[67] Wilfred Jarvis, a behavioural scientist and authority on the theories and practices of effective leadership, consulted to Jack's companies for many years. He considered Jack shared many of the rare attributes of great leaders such as Churchill, Nelson Mandela, Gandhi and Martin Luther King: committed to their cause or belief; able to attract followers through persuasion rather than domination; strong; striving for high achievements; demanding, expecting and receiving excellence from employees and colleagues; and providing those employees and colleagues with the autonomy to act, and supporting wholeheartedly any decisions they made. He believed Jack consistently lived by those rare standards.[68]

Those who worked with Jack would have enjoyed many more years of fruitful business relations but Monier had a strict policy of retirement at 62. When Jack reached retirement age in 1982, he had led Monier for twelve years and had been an important part of the company for 36 years. He had become a much-loved leader and many felt genuine regret when he retired. For Frank Thomas, Jack was an idol, someone to look up to as a real leader. When Jack retired, Frank felt a part of himself was lost and, shortly after, decided to retire as well.[69] At his farewell, Jack was recognised as 'an integral and vital part of Monier'. Hope Gibb spoke of how proud she had been to be Jack's secretary and how much she would miss him. Ron Duncan, the Group General Manager, Concrete and Steel, spoke of the pleasure it had been to serve as a general manager under Jack for fifteen years and how, during that time, he could never remember not wanting to come to work.[70]

Early in Jack's career with Monier, one of the board members told him he was too straight; he would never succeed in the business world.[71] Jack's personal integrity, with the associated strength to always stand up for what was right, and in such a way that would not alienate others, proved that man wrong. Integrity became as much a part of Monier as it was of Jack. Stan Owens, the company chairman, had no doubt about this:

> We are very proud of the company that Jack has left us with. His integrity is reflected in the standing of Monier, renowned in all spheres of operation as honest and trustworthy and a good corporate citizen . . . His understanding of people and deep concern for people is reflected in the people of our office today . . . His leadership from the horrific days of World War II until today has been a model for all who follow.[72]

Monier was proud of Jack and his contribution and Jack was 'proud of Monier as an organisation'. He would not look back with any sense of regret on the years he had dedicated to the company.[73]

18

Integrity and humanity

'his personal and business ethics are of the highest order'

Jack was not content to simply retire after many years of productive contribution to Monier. For some time he had been sounded out about accepting directorships to the boards of top Australian entities. He was much in demand at the time but he considered invitations carefully: he would not lend his name to just anything—he had to be prepared to give his all to that company.[1] In the two decades before his death he devoted time and expertise to many boards, including the Australian Aircraft Consortium, Colinta Holdings, Dalgety Farmers, Note Printing Australia, TMOC Resources and Volvo Australia. His years of dedicated and distinguished service began in 1974, when AGL's new chairman, David Anderson, canvassed him about joining his board. David convinced him of AGL's merits and Jack accepted his first directorship.[2]

Jack served on AGL's board for eighteen years, the last seven as chairman. Throughout that time he became known as a man of imagination, planning skills and leadership, who would share his successes with his team, giving them generous credit. He managed from a basis of firm objectives and would orchestrate the board with consummate skill, solicit the opinions of each director, and reach decisions with speed and decisiveness.[3]

Jack displayed self-confidence, firmly founded on experience and achievement, which, for many, is the essence of leadership. Dick Mason, friend and fellow AGL board member, recognised the negative side to such self-assurance. Jack usually brought the board round to his way of thinking with skilful negotiating and silky persuasion. But, if he failed, he would become stubborn:

I did see that glint when those lovely blue eyes would become very steely if he was being crossed or someone was not doing what he wanted them to do. He could turn very quickly from the genial, charming person and he was really tough.[4]

There is not much of a stretch from self-confidence to stubbornness. Both involve courage of conviction but one risks bad feeling and disaster. Fortunately, the stubborn side to Jack elicited little ill-will but it did result in an occasional bad decision being taken by the board. As with the failure of Chesney caravans, Jack would face the unsound decision, admit fault and concentrate on making good the situation. Stubbornness moved to expediency.[5]

Nowhere was Jack's pragmatism seen more clearly than when AGL was breached by a corporate raider. Jack resisted the moves by the raider, including public requests for shareholders not to sell their AGL investments.[6] Despite this, the raider acquired 42 per cent of the shares. With such a huge tranche, he demanded representation on the board and Jack had to cede two places. He did not like it but was pragmatic enough to accept the situation and carry on with building a better AGL for the minority shareholders.[7]

As at Monier, Jack's talents outweighed his faults and he was forgiven those rare displays as he steered AGL to ever-growing success. When he retired as chairman, he handed over a healthy company with excellent management and a confident profit future and outlook.[8] At his final shareholders' meeting, anxious to give everyone his or her fair say regarding company management, Jack endured many a pregnant pause and waited for the usual barrage. An elderly gentleman walked slowly from the back of the room. He was mobbed by two microphone-waving attendants. The man struggled to free himself from the microphone wielders and, exclaiming that he only wanted to sit down, slumped into a front row seat. All was then silent, and Jack continued to wait for the traditional grilling. He soon found that almost the only thoughts to which loquacious shareholders were prepared to give voice were tributes to their outgoing chairman.[9]

Jack's next board appointment was perhaps his most prestigious. At his farewell to Monier, Stan Owens had spoken of Jack's great integrity. With his appointment by the Liberal government to the board of the Reserve Bank of Australia in 1977, that great integrity received the highest political and public acknowledgement.[10] Jack proved a valuable asset. One of his strengths was that in his business dealings, he was apolitical. When he retired, he was the only Fraser government appointee still on the board.[11] Bernie Fraser, governor of the Reserve Bank and chairman of its board from 1989 to 1996, considered Jack a decent man whose values constantly shone through. He found Jack conscientious in exercising his responsibilities as a board member and a 'genuine person' who always conducted himself in a gentlemanly way. He believed that Jack was, without doubt, a man of integrity.[12]

That integrity extended to a reputation of incorruptibility. Jack was proud that he had never been offered a bribe and had never laid himself open to even the suspicion that he could be corrupted.[13] The Independent Commission Against Corruption (ICAC) had been established in 1988 to promote the integrity and accountability of public administration and to investigate, expose and prevent public corruption. Jack's unimpeachable character would be an asset and he was invited to be a foundation member of its Operations Review Committee, established in 1989 as an important discipline and check in the work of the Commission.[14]

Years after the war, Bluey Collins asked Jack at a 455 Squadron reunion if he had ever regretted not staying in the air force, or continuing to fly in some way. Jack told him no. He had moved on.[15] Jack may not have taken the controls of an aircraft again—he left that to his brother Phil, who was a Qantas pilot for many years—but he renewed his contacts with aviation in a more tangible way in 1980 when he was invited to join the Qantas board. As with the Reserve Bank, he was appointed by a Liberal government, with reappointments by Labor. He served on the board for ten years, including as vice chairman. He was also chairman of the Qantas subsidiary, Qantas Holidays, from 1987 to 1989.

During Jack's tenure, Qantas continued to upgrade its aircraft. In 1987, it committed to the 747-400, which had a new wing design and improved avionics that allowed a two-pilot operation. Most importantly, it had a very long range, which meant Qantas could operate Sydney to Los Angeles services with minimal payload penalties as well as one-stop flights from Sydney to London. As a publicity measure, Qantas decided to set a long-distance record with the delivery flight of its first Boeing 747-400, and Jack and Sheila were two of the few passengers on that record breaking flight.[16]

As with his other directorships, Jack proved an asset to the Qantas board. His catch-cry became 'no surprises'; he demanded full knowledge of what would be discussed at a meeting and would prepare thoroughly. No matter how bad the information or news, he had to know about it beforehand.[17] Jack contributed his professionalism to the Qantas board and that of Qantas Holidays and, as ever, he demonstrated his high degree of integrity at all times. A Qantas directorship came with ample travel perks, but Jack would never abuse them. He enjoyed them but, true to his principles of careful management of corporate funds, was never excessive.[18] His position was that the company could not afford indiscriminate abuse of privilege, so as others were frequently upgraded to business class his family travelled down the back.[19]

During his time with AGL, Jack had experienced some frustration managing a company constrained by government legislation. He and fellow board member and succeeding chairman Dick Mason fought to liberate AGL from government strictures. Jack experienced similar frustration with Qantas as it moved along the path of corporatisation towards privatisation. Despite this, he carefully worked within the existing framework, offering his expertise drawn from experience in a commercial world with more freedoms.[20]

Steve Heesh was Qantas' assistant company secretary as well as the company secretary for Qantas Holidays and he had many dealings with Jack. Jack's professionalism impressed him, as did his core tenets: his undoubted integrity, honesty, clarity and concern for others. Dealing as he did with so many board members and executives who had such different experiences, values and ways of dealing with people, Steve discovered that those, like Jack, who had been through the war, were better able to relate to everyone in the organisation. It did not matter if that person was the chairman or a mechanic, Jack had the common touch. For Marion Hare, long-time secretary to chairman Jim Leslie, this common touch was translated to 'old world charming'. Jack was always polite and endearing to Marion and other administrative staff and often sent large arrangements of flowers in appreciation of their hard work. Marion saw how seriously Jack took his responsibilities as a director, fulfilling his duties with the highest moral principles. Many people experienced regret when Jack left their company or board, and Steve and Marion were two of these.[21]

Jack's accolade as one of *The Australian*'s top-ten businessmen of 1978 recognised the work he had done in leading Monier's expansion into the extremely lucrative but notoriously tough US market. This achievement was also recognised by American business interests. Alcoa of Australia Ltd was the world's largest producer and exporter of alumina at the time, and its board comprised representatives from a number of Australian companies and one from its American shareholder, Aluminum Company of America (ACOA). By agreement, some of the non-executive directors were nominated and represented by ACOA, and some by the Australian companies. A board vacancy occurred in 1986 and Jack was nominated by the ACOA representative. The board accepted his nomination and, soon afterwards, Sir Arvi Parbo, the board's chairman, invited Jack to join Alcoa's board.

Alcoa was a good fit as far as Jack's personal business commitments were concerned. It was an efficient, cost effective and well-managed company. It cared for its employees and valued their achievements, and was committed to investing in the future through better equipment and technology.[22] Sir Arvi had a high opinion of Jack: 'His integrity was obvious—there were never any hidden agendas with Jack.' Sir Arvi and Jack worked well together and Sir Arvi, who was also the chairman of the Munich Reinsurance Company of Australia, invited Jack to join that board in 1987.[23]

Jack's time with Alcoa covered the whole range of industry conditions: from economic recovery in the late 1980s from the recession brought about by high oil prices, through to the 1991 collapse of the Soviet Union, where large quantities of metals, including aluminium, suddenly became surplus and flooded western markets. Alcoa was an efficient and low-cost producer and weathered this roller-coaster of market crises. When Jack retired profits were low, but still good. Jack made a major contribution to Alcoa and Paul O'Neill, the chairman and CEO of ACOA, wrote to Jack on his retirement to tell him how much the company valued his 'stewardship while serving as director. The company which you have helped to shape is a world leading example of what human enterprise

211

can accomplish. It will be a lasting legacy of your own contribution.'[24] In his speech at Jack's retirement dinner, Sir Arvi reiterated the accolades that other boards had heaped on Jack and noted that businessmen of Jack's calibre were a dying breed: 'His personal and business ethics are of the highest order. He is the kind of person one is hoping to attract as an external director, and who are regrettably in very short supply.'[25]

Jack's childhood provided him with an acute awareness of how the innocent victims of economic downturn struggled daily against poverty. Throughout his adult life, Jack displayed a quiet, personal philanthropy which saw him help out friends and others in need. He simply, but deeply, cared about other people, and went out of his way to lend a hand over and over again.[26] Dick Mason recognised that this selflessness was an 'integral part of his character. He had sympathy for all people less fortunate . . . he cared for those who could not care for themselves. Great humanity.'[27]

When Jack left the RAAF he maintained a strong link with it and his air force friends. Shortly after demobilisation, he joined the New South Wales division of the Royal Australian Air Force Association. He was appointed life member of that division in 1960; made a life vice-president in 1965; and was appointed a national vice-president in the 1970s.[28] He was especially sensitive to the fact that he had returned from the war whereas many had not. His daughter June remembers him time and again showing her photos of those from his training schools and squadron who had died so young. He wanted more than just his family to appreciate the great losses wreaked by war, especially on those wives and children left behind. He was determined to help ameliorate some of the war's great toll and so he dedicated many years to lobbying for veterans' entitlements and assistance to their families. He had developed great persuasive skills during his war years and he now turned these towards benefitting others. If someone said no to him, he would try another way because he could not bear any suggestion that someone could not have the best medical care, or that they would be financially distressed. He lobbied continually to ensure any returned soldier, or the families of those who had not returned, received the best attention.[29] He never stopped and his work with the association ensured those who had sacrificed their futures for others were never forgotten. Jack's dedication to committee work was as great. He carried out many official functions in the absence of the New South Wales president. His advice and considered opinions during meetings and conferences were sound and 'he was always regarded as the rock that had the right answer'.[30]

Shortly after he returned to Australia in 1946, Jack was elected the first president of 455 Squadron Association and held that position for almost 50 years. In 1956, Bluey Collins spoke for all when he wrote that '455 Squadron would not be an association without [Davo's] superb leadership'.[31] Neither Bluey nor any other squadron member resiled from this belief. The bonds formed during the war endured and Sydneysider members met monthly and visitors from interstate and overseas dropped in whenever they were in town.

Wartime friendships continued to grow and the care Jack had displayed as a commanding officer never ceased. If his old comrades needed help, and he could help, he did. When 'Tango' Martin, a fellow pilot from the Hampden days, needed assistance picking his peach crop, Jack, Sheila and their children were there.[32] When Mal McArthur, one of the squadron's stalwart ground crew engineers, had difficulty obtaining bricks for his new home in the postwar shortages Jack told him he would organise a Monocrete home for him and it was only a matter of time before the vast concrete slab walls were being craned into position.[33] When the daughter of one of the squadron pilots wanted to find out about her father who had died when she was only a baby, Jack was able to help. He had been killed when the Hampden he was piloting crashed into the sea while on patrol and Jack was able to tell her something of her father's life on the squadron and how to obtain her father's records. But Jack did not leave it there. He also put the family in touch with Legacy, who helped with her education.[34] When Noel Turner and his brother bought a service station after the war, which they eventually built up into a successful car dealership, Jack proved a valued customer in the early years and sent much of his firm's business to the Turner brothers' repair shop.[35]

Jack's propensity to help did not extend just to his squadron friends. Many of his friends and business associates benefitted from Jack's assistance over the years and Michael O'Dea, one of Jack's solicitors, was one. In 1986, Michael and his wife Marianne took their nine children on an extended overseas holiday. They had spent eight weeks over the long December–January school holiday period travelling through India and Europe and had finished up skiing in Austria. Their last destination was Lech, and from there they would return to Australia, in time for the new school year. They were due to fly out on the Saturday morning, but it had been snowing steadily throughout the night. When they awoke, they found they were snowed in. They missed their flight home and, at this time of the year and at short notice, it was impossible to book eleven seats on the same aircraft. Michael tried every carrier, but with no success. He was very anxious and decided to phone Jack, who had been on the Qantas board since 1980. Jack said to leave it with him. Within a few hours, Michael received a call from Qantas at Heathrow. His family was booked onto a flight leaving from Rome the next day, 24 hours after their original flight.[36]

By the late 1970s, Jack's children had grown up, left home and established lives of their own. His own career with Monier was nearing its end. His quieter, more personal charity work then took a public face[37] as the business world realised he would easily and gladly turn his considerable commitment and organisational abilities to fundraising. This led to his appointment to the Australian War Memorial Council. In the early 1980s, Noel Flanagan, the director of the Australian War Memorial from 1975 to 1983, decided that, as well as someone with a distinguished service career, the council needed a good fundraiser and expert on practical finance. He and General Sir Thomas Daly, who was the council's chairman, decided Jack held all these qualities. Jack was happy to put his talents at the service of the council but he had another agenda for accepting Flanagan's invitation. To Jack, the memories of the Second World War had not dimmed but he had noticed a general unawareness in Australia's younger generation of what that war had been about and an increasing tendency to criticise the fighting of that war. He believed that 'as individuals we have within ourselves abilities and capacities well above the levels we ourselves had even contemplated. If we can apply ourselves just halfway within those capacities and abilities to the service of this country—particularly in helping the young, this will be a better country for all.'[38] Directing his abilities to a well-funded Australian War Memorial would be one way of ensuring that

On 15 July, flying NT958, Jack made his first return to the Norwegian coast since the squadron's transfer to Langham. The result of the combined Langham and North Coates strike was an attack where every single ship was either on fire or sunk. After this successful attack, Jack was dubbed an 'ace ship-buster'.
(COURTESY SCOTT MILSON, VIA IAN GORDON)

Rockets from 455 Squadron Beaufighters speeding towards an enemy vessel escorting a convoy off the Norwegian coast.
(COURTESY MARK LAX)

On 25 August 1944, Jack led an attack on a heavily defended convoy off the Borkum coast. This photo well illustrates the seeming confusion of this and any attack at close quarters.
(COURTESY MARK LAX)

One of Jack's favourite holiday spots was Lord Howe Island. His friend Dick Mason recalls that those days were some of the most carefree of Jack's life. This photo was captioned on the back 'The Pirate'! (COURTESY JUNE ROSS)

Jack and Sheila Davenport. (COURTESY BRUCE DAVENPORT)

an appreciation of the sacrifice of Australia's service men and women would extend into the wider community.

Jack's 'retirement years', were certainly not idle. In fact, he never, ever really retired. Rosemary Duncan, the wife of Ron Duncan, one of Monier's general managers and a good friend of Jack and Sheila, recalled bumping into him at Brisbane airport and, although they had not seen each other for some time, Jack could not stop and chat as he was rushing for a flight. Rosemary felt saddened by this: he looked tired and, in his supposed retirement had not appeared to slow down at all.[39] Maybe so, but Jack enjoyed a full and energetic public life. Part of his success as a fundraiser was his friendly but persuasive ability to draw on his broad network of friends and business acquaintances.[40] The Salvation Army was one of the many charities which benefitted from Jack's assistance. Ted Sly, who had flown Kittyhawks and Spitfires during the war, was one of Jack's successful businessman friends who helped out with a Salvo door knock when Jack asked him to take over the Newport–Palm Beach area in Sydney's north.[41] As well as encouraging his friends and business associates to wear out their shoe leather, Jack displayed great skill in twisting their arms to write cheques and empty their wallets. Dick Mason recalled 'Jack was tremendous at fundraising. It was very difficult to refuse and people knew when Jack came into their office . . . [he] wouldn't leave unless he had a substantial cheque'.[42]

Dick may have had his arm twisted on numerous occasions in the name of friendship and good causes but he soon made sure his own causes benefitted from Jack's skill at parting fat cheques from cheque books. At one stage, the Royal Australian Navy called upon Dick to assist in raising funds for the Naval Memorial Chapel of St George the Martyr at HMAS *Watson*. Dick press-ganged Jack into service and they quickly raised what was needed. The commitment to the naval chapel was not just Dick and Jack's. As they raised the money, their wives, Mary and Sheila, did the tapestry work for the chapel kneelers.[43] In the early 1980s, Dick called on Jack's services again. He was chairman of the *Krait* Appeal Fund, which had set a target of $250,000 to restore and maintain the vessel that had travelled over 5000 miles to Japanese-controlled Singapore Harbour so its crewmembers could carry out the daring and successful Operation

Jaywick. Jack told Dick to leave the prime minister and New South Wales premier to him and before Dick knew it, a sizeable amount of public funds had been committed to the appeal: 'Jack was very good with government . . . He was a very hard man to refuse.'[44]

Politicians were not the only ones unable to refuse Jack. He was called upon to assist with the fundraising for the Australian War Memorial's commemorations for the 50th anniversary of the end of the war. His path had often crossed Max Roberts' over the years. As president of the Royal Blind Society from 1987 to 1992, Max had been a dedicated and successful fundraiser for the society and, knowing this, Jack persuaded Max to assist the efforts for the commemoration activities. As a former serviceman, he was glad to join his talents to Jack's. He considered Jack a skilled organiser, with a clear ability to target the appropriate people.[45]

One organisation that benefitted most from Jack's ability to target the right people was The Heart Research Institute. For some time, the National Heart Foundation and the AMP Society had dreamed of an institute dedicated to cardiovascular disease research. Dr David Richmond introduced Jack to the project and had little difficulty in gaining his support. Jack was involved in the early planning for The Heart Research Institute from 1986, and when the Board of Governors and the Development Council were formed in early 1987 he took on the role of deputy chairman of the board and chairman of the development council. Jack worked tirelessly for the institute, calling on friends, commercial organisations and government for donations— even the Reserve Bank of Australia was a regular donor thanks to Jack's encouragement.[46] In 1995, in recognition of his record of consistent and continuing effort and support, Jack was accepted as Fellow of The Heart Research Institute. After almost a decade of operations, Jack was only the institute's second fellow.[47]

In addition to his many directorships and fundraising activities, he was a foundation councillor of the Institute of Urban Studies, a governor of the National Institute of Labour Studies, a councillor of the Chamber of Manufacturers of New South Wales, and for many years the vice president of the Commercial Law Association of Australia. He developed a great interest in science and research and, as well as his work with The Heart Research Institute, devoted time to the Industry Forum of the Australian Academy of Science, was a councillor of the Australian Science and Technology Council, and a governor of the Ian Clunies Ross Memorial Foundation. In 1995, he accepted Macquarie University's offer to confer the award of an honorary Doctor of Science, in recognition of his assistance to scientific research.[48]

Jack's threefold commitment to business, industry and community was first recognised publicly in 1981 when he was made an Officer of the Order of Australia (General Division) (AO). The AO recognises distinguished service of a high degree to Australia or to humanity at large. There is a quota; excluding honorary appointments, not more than one hundred officers are appointed in a calendar year.[49] His service was further recognised in 1991 when he was appointed a Companion in the General Division of the Order of Australia. The AC is Australia's highest civilian honour and companions are appointed for eminent achievement and merit of the highest degree in service to Australia or to humanity at large. Like the AO, the AC has a quota and, excluding honorary appointments, no more than 25 companions are appointed in any calendar year.[50] Jack Davenport had contributed much in his public life and the full range of his awards and honours were testimony of his great service during both war and peace.

19

Family and friends

'he was a very genuine, warm and conscientious person'

Jack worked hard in the immediate postwar years. His long hours, with little time off during his career with Concrete Industries, were as much about overcoming opposition from those who resented him walking in over employees of many years' standing, as ensuring comfort and security for his family. He had suffered as a child through the Depression because of his father's lack of permanent, stable employment and he determined that his own family would not endure the effects of financial hardship.[1]

Jack's intentions might have been sound, but there were inevitable consequences—he had little time to spend with his family. When June Davenport was born on 6 June 1946, shortly after he commenced with Concrete Industries, Jack was only able to visit Sheila and his new daughter in hospital late at night.[2] He had to travel often in those early years, sometimes for weeks on end, and Sheila was left at home with her two young children, increasing the isolation she was experiencing in a new country.[3] Of course, there was family time: picnics, days spent with the Shaddocks, gardening blitzes and morning swims at Cronulla beach, where Bruce and June would excitedly compete to be the first to glimpse the water from the back seat of the Holden.[4] Even so, family time and holidays were limited in those early years. On one occasion, after his mother had moved to the northern beaches area, the family moved into Grace's house for a few weeks. While Sheila and the children enjoyed the sea change, Jack drove to and from work every day.[5] For him, the most important thing he could offer his family was the security, comfort and stability he had not had as a child and this drive was stronger than his desire to be with them.

In the mid 1950s, Jack purchased a double block of land in Beecroft in Sydney's northern suburbs. Sheila, by this stage, had developed a circle of her own friends and many of these lived northside, and so it was she who had suggested a move across the bridge. Jack commissioned a large family home and he and Sheila established a beautiful garden over many years, that became renowned for its camellias and exotic plants. Jack loved building things, especially from recycled materials, and his backyard was his workshop.[6] Although creative, his constructions were not always known for their beauty or practicality, and his family would be the first to comment on their lack of quality. There was the fountain, with multiple tiers, spouts and falls, and the 'cathedral', the hot house in which he struck camellia cuttings. There was the barbeque with its unique chimney arrangement, which came into its own when Jack and Sheila hosted parties or squadron reunions which featured a swim and tour of the rare and beautiful shrubs, softly lit by tiki lights.[7]

Jack may have been an absent father for much of the time but he cherished his wife and children. There was never any doubt that his love of Sheila was absolute. He loved his children and was proud of their achievements.[8] He was generous and tolerant of their 'crazes'. When young June succumbed to a horse phase, pleading to have a horse of her own, Jack built a stable in the bush behind the house, sought out a horse suitable for an eleven-year-old and presented it to her for Christmas. As well as a loved friend, Trooper became a good source of income for June as Jack good naturedly paid for the manure she delivered to the garden.[9] When it was important, he was there. Bruce knew that if he needed his father he could turn to him. One of the first things Jack told Hope Gibb when she started work for him was that if Sheila phoned, no matter what he was doing, Hope was to put her through.[10]

One of the few regrets Jack had in later life was that he hadn't spent more time with his children, but it was not something he dwelt on. In some ways, he made up for this in the next generation. He adored his grandchildren and showed great interest in their lives. He would often offer advice when he thought it necessary (but they did not!) and relished the opportunity to take his country grandchildren to Sydney or Canberra to introduce them to what he perceived to be the broader world.[11]

As Jack's business career consolidated and he acquired the financial security that was so important to him he was able to fulfil a dream he had nurtured since childhood. Ever since Coonamble, he had developed a strong love of the land. In 1966 he purchased his first property, 'Drumadoon', a cattle property at Wollomombi, near Armidale, New South Wales. It was not a glamorous property—only a few hundred acres of cleared but unimproved land—but for Jack it was his own bit of dirt[12], a way to connect to the land and to experience the freedom and romance of the bush that had touched him as a child.

Jack was not one to let his land lie fallow. He had spent much time in France on business and had come across Charolais cattle, a popular beef breed. On one occasion, when Jack and Sheila were holidaying in France with Dick and Mary Mason, they were travelling through Charolais country—not by accident, as Jack had planned this part of their itinerary—and stopped at an inn for dinner. Jack asked Madame if she had any Charolais steaks and she said 'of course'. Out came the biggest steaks you could ever imagine, equal in size only to the smile on Jack's face as he tucked in.[13] From knowing little about the Charolais, and a simple gut feeling they would do well in Australia, arose a new passion. Jack talked to the right people, did some research and, with his first order of semen in 1969, embarked on a breeding program. When first-cross New Zealand heifers were available, he imported these and years later, embryo transfer provided a more rapid way of building up his 'Drumadoon' stud.

Work commitments meant Jack could not be as hands-on at 'Drumadoon' as he would have liked but he had a more than capable manager, June's husband, Malcolm Ross. As well as running their own property, Malcolm managed the Charolais stud and Jack's commercial herd. Jack and Malcolm enjoyed success at the Sydney Royal Easter Show, including showing a junior champion bull. Jack's practice of allowing his managers at Monier the freedom to do their jobs without interference flowed through to the running of 'Drumadoon' and he and Malcolm enjoyed a fruitful partnership for almost 30 years.[14] Jack later purchased 'Daisy Hill', a neighbouring property to which he and Sheila would visit alone or invite friends such as the Masons, who would tease Jack about his near infatuation with his cattle, joking that he knew each cow by name. As far as Dick Mason could see, Jack was never happier than when he was on the back of a horse, riding around 'Daisy Hill', admiring his herd.[15]

Friendship was important to Jack and some of his closest friendships were with his old squadron friends. Like Jack, Johnny Pilcher, who had been there the day they 'pranged the navy', loved the land. This shared passion, as well as their squadron connection, proved a strong basis for friendship. John and Barbara Pilcher would take their family to visit the Davenports in Sydney for holidays, and the Davenports would later holiday on the Pilchers' farm at Inverell. Sheila and Barbara were also close and corresponded often over the years, and young June Davenport attended pony camp at Inverell.[16] The Davenports also stayed with Bob McColl's family at Young and with Tommy Thompson at Orange.

While still in Sydney, Doc Watson and his wife and children enjoyed barbeques with the Davenports and, when they moved away, maintained their close friendship, as did Grant Lindeman and his family. Les Oliver was the Davenport family dentist for many years and, long after he was obliged to keep an eye on the Davenport teeth, he continued to pay close attention to his old squadron friend's career. Les told his son he had bought shares in Jack's companies. In every one he did well but, he added wryly, he was not as successful in the companies in which he invested of his own accord![17] The Pilchers, Watsons, McColls, Thompsons, Lindemans, Olivers and many others, all became honorary uncles and aunts to Bruce and June Davenport and, in many cases, the friendship of their parents extended into the second generation.[18]

Neighbours and work colleagues also became friends. Jack and Sheila spent more than 30 happy years at Beecroft. They were good neighbours: the children of the area were allowed free access to their pool (as long as they were supervised) and their neighbours Laurie and Doreen Taylor recalled the picnics, dinners and cocktail parties they shared. Jack and Sheila were fun-loving people and all of their neighbours loved them.[19] Vivienne Dart recalled the laughter shared between friends on one memorable evening when Jack and Sheila hosted a dinner party for Vivienne, her husband John and her brother Stan Taylor (who worked with Jack at Monier) and his wife Edith.

There was much mirth that night as Jack, John and Stan tossed quips off each other. Sheila also joined in with her wry sense of humour. This mad night was typical of all of their get-togethers—laughter was the basis of their 'wonderful friendship'.[20] Jack and Sheila enjoyed entertaining their friends and their New Year's Eve parties, which marked Sheila's birthday as well as the Scottish Hogmanay, were festive, boisterous affairs with much Scottish dancing and hilarity.[21]

No matter how often work intruded on Jack's free time, he still managed to find time to play golf. He and Sheila were keen golfers and were members of Pennant Hills Golf Club for many years before they joined Elanora Country Club.[22] Jack enjoyed the challenge of golf; that each round presented a new test of his skills. He played regularly, enthusiastically and competitively, always praising the good shots of his partners, and was never guilty of gamesmanship. His short game was superb. Dick Mason recalled Jack's concentration, then the smooth chip, right into the hole: 'He's done it again.'[23] After a successful day on the green, whisky in hand, Jack liked nothing more than talking his game over with Sheila.[24]

Later in life, Jack and Sheila spent more and more time with Dick and Mary Mason. They would holiday together each year and, every second year, along with Keith and Hillary Daymond, Lord Howe Island was their destination.[25] Those days were some of the most carefree of Jack's life. Dick Mason can still see Jack sitting on the verandah of their guest house, surrounded by hooks, lines, sinkers, all the fishing paraphernalia you could imagine, in his old smelly clothes that looked as if they had never seen the inside of a washing machine, whistling away, happy as a sand lark as he fixed hooks to his lines. When he was all set, he would head out on the water in a little dinghy and had much success hauling in his catch.[26]

Those relaxed days in the holiday dinghy were a far cry from another sailing episode over 40 years earlier. One of Phil Davenport's great dreams was to undertake a long sea voyage in his own boat. He had messed about on the water from an early age and the dream had stayed with him since boyhood. After his stint in China with the United Nations Relief and Rehabilitation Administration Phil joined Qantas Empire Airways as a long-haul pilot. He continued to cherish his dream and, in 1948, asked Jack to scout around for the best boat-builder. Jack met Jock Muir of Hobart and commissioned him to build a sturdy 46-foot cutter. Because of his frequent absences from Australia, Phil relied on Jack to liaise with Muir.[27] *Waltzing Matilda* was launched in July 1949 and Phil, together with his brother Keith, embarked on an ambitious plan to sail from Australia to England. Before voyaging to England, however, Phil entered *Waltzing Matilda* in the 1949 Sydney–Hobart yacht race.

Phil and Keith were the real sailors in the family but, even so, it was important for Phil that Jack be a part of his crew. Despite his work commitments, and knowing he would be in Hobart for Sheila's New Year's Eve birthday, Jack agreed. Jack's presence on board *Waltzing Matilda* may have been for more personal than practical reasons, but Phil intended to set him to work and Jack was designated the boat's official timekeeper. Phil knew Jack would be absolutely spot-on; none of the other crew members would have been as accurate.[28]

A large crowd massed on the shores of Sydney Harbour and on the water in an estimated 1000 small craft to await the starter's pistol. In brilliant sunshine, the fifteen competing yachts crossed the line almost together at 11.00 a.m. Five days, ten hours, 33 minutes and ten seconds later, at 9.33 p.m. on 31 December 1949, in what was the second slowest time on record, *Waltzing Matilda* was the first to cross the finishing line at Constitution Dock in Hobart. With *Margaret Rintoul* only two minutes behind, the *Sunday Herald* reported *Waltzing Matilda*'s race for the line as 'the most exciting finish in the history of the event'. Phil and his crew may have had the satisfaction of line honours, but *Trade Winds*, which had been third over the line, won on corrected time. After the race, Phil told the assembled media it had been a fairly good trip, with no unusual incidents.[29] He did not let on that his time keeper was so exhausted from the five-day voyage that he was curled up on a pile of rope in *Waltzing Matilda*'s doghouse.[30]

Jack's post-Monier years were full of love, friendship, community work and continued dedication to his boards and industry groups. He expected to have many happy and fulfilled years ahead of him but fate had other ideas. The first inkling that something was wrong was in 1995, on holiday with the Masons, when he noticed his golf swing was off. There was a twinge, a niggle that would not go away.[31] Sheila had recovered from bowel cancer some time before but had not been well recently so each arranged specialist appointments. On the same 'black Wednesday' in May[32], they were told they had cancer: Sheila in the breast and Jack in the oesophagus. It was devastating but each took some strength from the fact they were facing illness together.

It is never easy to tell someone you care about that you are ill and when Jack told Dick and Mary Mason, he did so while driving them home from dinner. It was as if the blow was softened by the distraction of driving, and with Jack and Sheila not having to physically face their friends as they told them.[33] Soon, more of their friends knew. Devon Minchin was dumb struck. Hope Gibb called to offer sympathy. Marion Hare sent a note of support and sympathy and Jack McKnight quietly told their 455 Squadron Association friends. Letters, cards and phone calls flooded in.[34]

Jack experienced anger at his illness, and the sense of 'Why me?' when he had so much left to do.[35] He was just short of his 75th birthday and Sheila was only 71. They both should still have many years ahead of them. But having to face an operation that had limited chance of long-term success, and with Sheila ill again, it was difficult for Jack to feel positive or optimistic for the future. This was one of the few times he let people see a glimpse of despair about what the future would bring.[36] But Jack was never one to dwell on what he could not change and he did not give in to those initial glimmers of despondency. Drawing on each other's strength, as well as the love and support of their family and friends, Jack and Sheila battled against their illnesses: 'We both have had a rough time . . . but we are progressing well and we hope that soon it will all be behind us.'[37] Jack told Phil: 'All of our friends have been kind and supportive and their messages do help.'[38] For Jack, it was business as usual. He continued with his few remaining directorships, he honoured commitments to the 'Australia Remembers' tribute and spoke of his war experiences at Elanora Country Club.

In late November 1995, Ron and Rosemary Duncan hosted a dinner party at their home. It was a reunion of former Monier executives and their American legal advisers. It was a magical night. Candles flickered on the table and, cocktails in hand, guests moved about the room or stood on the balcony overlooking Sydney Harbour. Conversation flowed back and forth over shared memories. Sheila was frail and Jack was not well either but they had not even contemplated missing the evening. They were the guests of honour, and when Rosemary Duncan seated her guests, Jack and Sheila were in the centre of the table so everyone could speak with them easily. It was a memorable night, made more so by the fact that it proved to be the last time the Duncans saw Jack, and Sheila herself would succumb to her cancer on 7 January 1997, just over twelve months after Jack's death, on the day before what would have been their 53rd wedding anniversary. That final dinner was a wonderful climax to a special friendship.[39]

Jack and Sheila spent a happy and relaxed Christmas with family and friends. Sheila's nephew, Graeme McDavid and his wife and children, who had recently arrived in Australia, came for a Christmas morning drink. June and her family came for dinner and much laughter and joy were shared at the extended family gathering.[40] On New Year's Eve, as had been their happy habit for a number of years, Jack and Sheila drove down to Dick and Mary Mason's property at Berry to celebrate Sheila's birthday and New Year. They spent the evening with their closest friends but Jack was not feeling well so they left for home early the next morning. He was not improving so Sheila called an ambulance. Some hours later, he died quietly in Royal Prince Alfred Hospital on 1 January 1996.[41]

Jack was cremated in a private family ceremony but his family knew his air force colleagues, his friends and business associates, industry and community contacts, and the many whose lives he had touched in some way, would want to say farewell. On 22 January 1996, close to a thousand filled St Stephen's Uniting Church in Macquarie Street in Sydney to pay tribute to Jack at his thanksgiving memorial service.[42] Bruce Daymond, who had trained as a pilot with Jack so many years ago, was there. Steve Heesh and Marion Hare, who had not seen Jack since he had left the Qantas board, felt moved to attend. Hope Gibb, who had so admired Jack as a good man and a good boss was among the mourners. Laurie and Doreen Taylor, friends and neighbours from the Beecroft days, also bid their final farewell. Ted Peacock, whose relationship with Jack extended back to the early Monocrete days, was there. Bluey Collins, who had participated in the 1943 'German parachutist' exercise with Jack came down from the Central

Coast to say goodbye to his old squadron friend. Even Cyril Johnson, who had not known Jack during the war and had met Jack only once in his life, came to honour the man he had long admired as an outstanding pilot and leader. Representatives from the RAAF Association, along with former school friends from Sydney Boys High School and colleagues from The Heart Research Institute, sat in the pews with former state governors, state and federal members of parliament, high-ranking public servants, representatives from Jack's charities, and business colleagues and employees of Monier, AGL and the many other companies with which Jack had worked. Prime Minister Paul Keating sent a message via his representative, Michael Lee: 'As you mourn your loss, I hope you will be comforted by the knowledge that Jack's contribution was always most appreciated by those associated with the institutions and companies he served. He was a very genuine, warm and conscientious person.'

Reverend Dr Fred McKay, who was officiating, recalled the time Jack told him 'I've met the loveliest girl in Scotland'. He spoke of Jack's great contribution to Australian life, of his part in the vital life of our community, and asked that the sense of loss experienced by those who knew and loved Jack be 'tempered by feelings of true thanksgiving that this man has passed our way'. Dick Mason gave a moving eulogy, reminding all of Jack's wartime heroism and peacetime accomplishments, and counterpointing the life of achievement with vignettes of a man content with the simple pleasures of life. Paraphrasing Edgar Guest's 'Myself', Dick spoke the words that had meant so much to Jack as his personal credo—the tenets which he had held dear all his life:

> I have to live with myself and so I have to be able myself to know.
> I have to be able as days go by always to look myself in the eye.
> I don't want to stand in the setting sun and hate myself for things I've done.
> I want to stand with my head erect. I want to deserve all men's respect.
> And so this struggle for life and self I want to be able to like myself.
> I don't want to look at myself and know that I'm bluster and bluff and empty show.
> I see what others can never see, I know what others can never know.

So whatever happens, I want to be self respecting and conscience free.

Dick had witnessed how Jack had successfully lived up to these ideals. For him, Jack was the 'finest son that Australia has produced to date'.

At the conclusion of the service, Sheila asked Dick to speak on her behalf, and her words resounded and held true for everyone in the church: 'His physical courage speaks for itself and perhaps I more than anyone know his great moral courage . . . Jack was a chivalrous gentleman in the true sense of the word . . . He was a good man.' Reverend McKay took Sheila's personal accolade even further and affirmed that Jack was 'a great man'. He called Jack's friends, colleagues and family to prayer, but it was not to mourn, it was to give thanks to Jack's life and achievements:

We give thanks that the man Jack Davenport came among us
We give thanks for the utter integrity of the man in everything he did
His daring leadership
His great family devotion
His helpfulness to needy people
His loyal friendship
His children
His own inner faith and strong compassion
We give thanks for Jack Napier Davenport.

Epilogue

'achievement, integrity and compassion'

Many who returned from the war found it difficult to adjust to their new lives. Some were disturbed by their experiences. They suffered nightmares, turned to alcohol, became lost in a depressive spiral. Jack was not one of these. He did not regret his part in the war and never philosophised about the rights and wrongs of warfare. As far as he was concerned it was merely a matter of what he did, he did. It was a part of his concept of duty. There was no weighing up of the consequences.[1] If anything, Jack regretted that, in the dying years of the twentieth century we had not learned anything from the Great War, the Second World War or any conflict since. He especially considered that 'the young people of today need to know of the terrors of those years. They also need to have pointed out to them the dangers of pacifism, of complacency, and of their country being militarily unprepared against a would-be aggressor'.[2] And as far as he was concerned, Australia was unprepared: he 'deplored the inadequacy of Australia's defences' and, in particular, the reduction in size and funding of the air force. 'I think that strength is a wonderful thing in defence and a frightening thing in attack.'[3] Looking back on his business career and the way management practice had changed over the years, he often felt disappointed by the behaviour of senior executives who were primarily rewarded for managing things and not for leading people, and lamented that 'I observed more leadership in the RAAF during a month than I have seen in commercial organisations during the last decade'.[4]

Jack admitted there were negative consequences of war but rather than dwell on any impact on himself, he recalled the good experiences of wartime, the companionship of squadron life and the friendships that endured. He incorporated much of what he learned as a squadron commander into his postwar management style. In the true spirit of compassion and the great love for humanity which were perhaps his most admirable and memorable qualities[5], Jack dedicated himself to honouring those of his confrères who had died in battle and accident. His work with the RAAF Association, the Australian War Memorial, the 'Australia Remembers' tribute, his personal pilgrimages to memorial sites such as the 'Black Friday' obelisk at Forde in Norway, and his support of Peter Ilbery's move to establish the Commonwealth Air Memorial at Dallachy exemplified this lifelong commitment.[6]

Two years before he died, Jack was in the surf at one of Sydney's northern beaches. He saw a body that moved only with the waves. He was no longer a strong swimmer but, almost without thinking, he swam to the bobbing body. He struggled to hold the unconscious man's head above water. No-one answered his calls for help and he was exhausted by the time he dragged the man onto the beach. Lifesavers appeared and carried the man to the clubhouse, ignoring an exhausted Jack who had collapsed onto the sand. Jack eventually recovered and walked away.[7]

The selflessness honoured so long ago by the George Medal still existed. Jack had proved that that award was well deserved. He never lost his great courage nor any of the qualities that made him so deserving of that or any of his other war and peacetime accolades. Jack was the quintessential, understated hero: a man of true valour and humanity. Throughout his life, Jack had carried out many actions and deeds of great value. His only regret at death was that he still had more to do and would not be afforded the time to do it.[8] As Phil Davenport had recognised, Jack's life was 'remarkable for achievement, integrity and compassion'.[9] He was undeniably a man we can look up to and emulate.[10]

APPENDIX A

Award citations

Distinguished Flying Cross

Squadron Leader Davenport has participated in attacks on some of the enemy's most heavily defended targets, including Hamburg, Essen and Dortmund, and has also taken part in mine-laying operations. Early in September 1942, he was captain of an aircraft which flew to a North Russian base and participated in patrols over the Barents Sea. While in Russia Squadron Leader Davenport acted as flight commander and by his example obtained the confidence and respect of all personnel. This officer has displayed leadership, courage and administrative ability of a high order.

London Gazette, 25 May 1943, p. 2321

Distinguished Service Order

Wing Commander Davenport has taken part in a large number of sorties, including many attacks on shipping, during which much loss has been inflicted on the enemy. Recently he led a formation of aircraft in an attack on an enemy convoy which was escorted by armed ships. In spite of fierce opposing fire a most determined and successful attack was made. Two medium sized merchant vessels and one of the escorting vessels were very severely damaged. In this well executed operation this officer displayed high powers of leadership, great skill and determination which contributed materially to the results obtained. This officer has rendered great service and his sterling qualities have impressed all.

London Gazette, 9 June 1944, p. 2753

Bar to Distinguished Flying Cross

Since being awarded the Distinguished Service Order, Wing Commander Davenport has taken part in numerous attacks on enemy shipping. Much of the success obtained can be attributed to this officer's brilliant and courageous leadership. His outstanding ability and personal example have impressed all.

London Gazette, 19 September 1944, p. 4325

George Medal

One night in September 1944, a Beaufighter aircraft, returning from operations with damaged engines, crashed on a runway. The petrol tanks burst and the aircraft became a mass of flames, with bursting cannon shells and ammunition. Wing Commander Davenport, having witnessed the crash, hastened to the scene in his car, leading the ambulance and fire tender. While attempting to subdue the flames with their hoses, the fire crew were forced back by the heat and exploding ammunition. The [navigator] in the aircraft was able to open his hatch and escape by jumping through the fire, but the pilot's cockpit was completely surrounded by flames. His cockpit hatch was seen to open partially and fall shut again. Wing Commander Davenport immediately dashed forward, opened the pilot's top hatch and struggled to free him. The pilot was severely burned and his feet were jammed. Wing Commander Davenport pulled him out of his flying boots and lifted him bodily through the blazing inferno. Wing Commander Davenport sustained shock, with burns to his face, hair and hands, but by his prompt and most courageous action, he saved the pilot's life.

London Gazette, 5 January 1945, p. 225

APPENDIX B

Anzac Day speech 1960

On a number of occasions during the 1950s, Jack Davenport provided radio commentary when the air force contingent marched past on Anzac Day. On Anzac Day 1960, he spoke about the meaning of 'Anzac' and the importance of remembering the actions of those who fought during Australia's twentieth-century wars. Through this speech, below, we can see how much it meant to him to remember the sacrifices of his friends and comrades. We can clearly understand his personal commitment and dedication to honouring their memories and deeds.[1]

Anzac

. . . What is Anzac and what has it come to mean? We not only recognise and remember the sacrifice and achievements of the dead, we remember all those who fought and all those who contributed. The concocted word 'Anzac' has come to mean a great deal more now than originally was the case. Sacrifice, heroism and uncounted odds, excitement and battle, monotony, dirt, tiredness, sweat, fear and comradeship—somehow too—discipline and swy[2]: being in the line and out of the line also get mixed up in it somehow. It is good that from time to time we set ourselves to remember those that were kicked, and those that came back, and probably most of all, the reasons why.

On this occasion I think it is well to remember the stark reality of the many scenes which to me mean Anzac. Without the memory and appreciation of these things and a conscious effort even in our everyday life, in recognition and consideration of our fellow man, these things can and will recur—if we remember all the horror and the sacrifice it perhaps can be worthwhile.

It all began on the beaches of Gallipoli, the bleak hills, the bare beach, the murderous fire from the Turks, the lugging of stores from the transports to the trenches, sudden death and slaughter. An ill-conceived operation, typical of War. Australian and New Zealand guts making up for the incompetence of the planners or manipulators of War.

It goes further in that era—to the trenches of France, the cold, the mud, the rain, and the sheer misery day in day out, bayonets and patrols, prisoners and fear and always at hand sudden death and slaughter. For those that did not experience that era, to me, it is hard to visualise such stark, purposeless misery of static trench warfare.

At sea in the rough and calm, in temperatures way over the hundred, in freezing, with the enemy lurking everywhere; the terrible sight of an oil tanker on fire. I think of the engine room crew in those days in a ship in action. No eyes to see what went on outside, really hard work, but working harder and harder, hoping to lose the fear in exertion. Slightly dry mouths and always a great expectancy. Visualise the spirit of the men who flew the box kites of the First World War. As far as death was concerned, they were their own worst enemy.

And eventually came the end of the war to end all wars, the war that eventually proved to be a great dress rehearsal for the slaughter and destruction and the new horrors developed in the Second World War. We have the more murderous weapons, the mighty guns, the submarines, the aircraft, the bombs, the rockets. The allies hopelessly unprepared have, as an aftermath of the political bungling, the fantastic scenes of Dunkirk and the incredible heroism and contribution not only of the soldiers and sailors, but of the ordinary man. A small group of pilots outclassed in equipment and numbers fighting a back to the wall, do or die battle. They did and they died. Blenheims, Fairey Battles and Hurricanes. Perhaps these three aircraft against three squadrons three times a day.

We go to the heat of the desert, sand and heat and heat and sand, aircraft in the sky looking lazy and peaceful but suddenly so deadly. The land mines, the mad frantic dashes from position to position, the discomfort. Can the supplies arrive in time? Can we unload the ships before the Luftwaffe sinks them? The wounded, the prisoners, against the heat and the sand. The waiting.

The aircraft over Europe, the incredible Guy Fawkes display [of] flak making the peacetime displays cheap unspectacular comparisons; the grasping, needling fingers of searchlights, their tenacity and refusal to let go when they [caught] an aircraft in their beams. Glaring blindness. The warning shout of a rear gunner as the enemy night-fighter comes in for the kill—diving and weaving—contortions borne of some panic. The glorious darkness as the cone of lights is shaken off. The cold, the freezing of the sweat of fear, the smell of flak, the blazing wrecks hurtling, apparently quite remotely, downwards. Fire and destruction.

The clash of the German battleships in the Channel—the death and glory. Attacks by 100 miles per hour Swordfish, by Hampdens with bombs. Men doing a vital job with practically no chance, but asking no questions. In London where death stalked everyone at all hours with the wicked V1 and V2. The hushed expectancy as the motor puttered overhead—the waiting for it to stop. Or the sudden explosion from nowhere. The fires and the amazing calm.

In the jungle of New Guinea, the swamp, the mud, the rain, the waiting. Sudden death in the jungle where so often disease too took sides with the enemy.[3] The navy in the Pacific. The terrible fires, the fanatical enemy with human shells. The beaches and more fanatical inhuman enemies. So often I think of those fantastic convoys through the North Sea to northern Russia. Seas in which a human being could not survive for more than two minutes.[4] Ships with their superstructure so thick in ice that they were in danger of capsizing, where the human hand could not touch any metal. Where living was almost impossible and fighting was frightful. Convoys proceeding, for many parts of their journey, unescorted, because of the decision of somebody sitting in a warm office in London.

Visualise the frame of mind of the lone Hurricane pilot sitting and waiting, day in and day out, in the most appalling conditions, to be rocketed off a rig in front of some merchant ship, pitching and tossing in the sea, to meet a greatly superior numerically enemy force. The convoy must get through. This is the David and Goliath operation. If he is shot down, two minutes in the sea and he is dead. When the battle is over, if he survives what does he do? He cannot get back to friendly territory. If he has enough petrol he can fly and bale out over the snows of enemy territory. If he has not enough petrol he can bale out near the convoy hoping to be picked up in less than two minutes. Men volunteered for this work, truly brave men—I think of the Malta convoys—

Let us remember the fortitude and sheer guts at the prison camps, where only the Anzac spirit and heritage enabled survival at times. Let us too think of those left at home—for some of these the sacrifice was indeed great. And again more recently we have had the bleak, frightening fighting and cold of Korea. To me, all these things are the backdrop of Anzac. From these scenes come what today we call Anzac. It was there and it is the reason why we can and should now tell of these things. Some of them are great and brave—others are horrible but they all have a reason, they must have a reason.

Particularly at times like this we recognise all these achievements and the manner of these achievements [and] we remember the background—let us also remember the reason. Let us try and carry some of these qualities, even characteristics, self-sacrifice in particular, not only in war but into our daily life. And in remembering try and construct our way of life, our attitude to our friends and our neighbours and to other peoples so that the scenes cannot again recur. For day by day the means of destruction grow greater and greater.

APPENDIX C

Boards and associations

The following is a list of boards and associations to which Jack Davenport belonged.

Alcoa of Australia Ltd
Australian Aircraft Consortium
Australian Gas Light Co Ltd
Australian Science and Technology Council
Australian War Memorial
Colinta Holdings Pty Ltd
Dalgety Farmers Ltd
The Heart Research Institute
Ian Clunies Ross Foundation
Independent Commission Against Corruption Board of Review
Institute of Directors, NSW Division
MIM Holdings Ltd (Mount Isa Mines)
Monier Ltd
Munich Reinsurance Company Australia Ltd
National Institute of Labour Studies
Note Printing Australia
Qantas Ltd
QH Tours Pty Ltd
Reserve Bank of Australia
Royal Australian Air Force Association (including president of 455 Squadron Association)
TMOC Resources Ltd
Volvo Australia Pty Ltd

Bibliography

Primary resources

National Archives of Australia (NAA)

SERVICE RECORDS

SERIES A9300:
Allan Fletcher Ada
Jack Napier Davenport
Keith Hand Davenport
Philip Roy Davenport

SERIES A12372:
Bruce Cunynghame Daymond

SERIES B4747:
Jack Napier Davenport

SERIES B2455:
Leslie Norman Davenport
Cyril Robert Hutton
Clement Horace Shaddock

SERIES B883:
Anthony Arthur Banks Nugent
Anthony Felix Booth

ACCIDENT AND CASUALTY FILES

SERIES A705:
166/9/597 Flight Lieutenant Philip Davenport 403216–Casualty–Repatriation Aircraft–Mosquito RS505–Norway 11 April 1945
166/26/553 Flying Office Duncan George Fletcher MacRae 403364–Casualty–Repatriation
166/5/604 455 Bomber Squadron–Loss of Beaufighter NE348–F/455–Flying Officer Barbour and Flying Officer Dodd
163/23/121 411115 Pilot Officer Roy Stuart Beveridge

SERIES A11271:

140/43/P1 455 Bomber Squadron accident to Hampden AE135 25 March 1942 Pilot Officer Davenport

140/74/P1 455 Bomber Squadron–Flying accident to 1000251 Sergeant Clifford Harrison

140/101/P1 455 Bomber Squadron–Loss of Beaufighter LZ194–U/455 on 6/7/44–Flight Sergeant Costello and Flight Sergeant Taylor

140/99/P1 455 Bomber Squadron–Loss of Beaufighter NE733–C/455 Flying Officer Billing and Flying Officer Edwards

140/105/P1 455 Bomber Squadron–Loss of Beaufighter NE340–L/455–Warrant Officer W.T. Jones and Flight Sergeant Brock

140/104/P1 455 Bomber Squadron–Loss of Beaufighter KW277–D/455 Flying Officer Kempson and Flying Officer Curzon

140/98/P1 455 Bomber Squadron–Loss of Beaufighter–LZ 192 Flying Officer Collaery

140/107/P1 455 Bomber Squadron–Loss of Beaufighter NT987–W/455 Flying Officer Cock, DFC and Warrant Officer Lyneham

4/1/AIR 455 Bomber Squadron Mobility Scheme

OTHER FILES

SERIES A11271:

36/6/Air Training at Crail

136/P1 No. 455 Bomber Squadron Crest and Designs

11/2/AIR Surfat Reports

146/P1 Messages of Congratulations April 1943–October 1944

36/1/AIR 455 Bomber Squadron–Squadron Training Syllabus

9/AIR 455 Bomber Squadron–Air tactics

107/P1 455 Bomber Squadron–Recommendations for Honours and Awards

104/P1 455 Bomber Squadron–Discipline

SERIES A907:

1946/3/11 *Sarpedon* passenger list, arriving Sydney 12 March 1946

Office of Air Force History

455 Squadron Operations Record Book (ORB)
461 Squadron ORB

Australian War Memorial (AWM)

AWM 64:

2 Embarkation Depot Bradfield Park ORB

5 Elementary Flying School Narromine ORB

455 Squadron Picturesque Patter [Line Book] (February 1942–June 1945)

126/1 Operations of 455 Squadron December 1942 to December 1943 and May 1944. History of Squadron.

RAAF Formation and unit records. Operation Records 455 Squadron 1.3.44–20.5.45

AWM 65, DAVENPORT, JACK NAPIER 403403, CONTROL SYMBOL 965 INCLUDING:

RAAF release 535, no. 113 8 June 1944

Air Ministry bulletin, no. 14345, 14 June 1944

Air Ministry bulletin, no. 14728, 16 July 1944

Radio talk, host Ian Wilson, recorded 26–30 July 1944, broadcast 4 August 1944

Air Ministry bulletin, no. 15411, 26 August 1944

RAAF release, no. 724, August 1944

Air Ministry bulletin, no. 15584, 10 September 1944

RAAF release, no. 776, 19 September 1944

Air Ministry bulletin, no. 15753, 26 September 1944

Air Ministry bulletin, no. 16950, 5 January 1945

SOUND RECORDS:

S00197: 'Coastal Command Attack a Convoy off Norway', by Wing Commander Jack Davenport 455 Squadron RAAF, 16 July 1944

S01651: Jack Napier Davenport/Ken Llewelyn Oral History Recording, 24 March 1993

Australian Defence Force Academy library

Headquarters, Coastal Command, Royal Air Force, *Coastal Command Review (CCR)*

Reserve Bank of Australia (RBA)

Records relating to Jack Davenport's appointments to the Reserve Bank of Australia and Note Printing Australia including Statement by the Acting Treasurer, Senator the Hon. John Button. Reserve Bank Board: Retirement of Mr J.N. Davenport, 28 September 1992.

Annotation on extract from The Heart Research Institute's 1995 annual report held by the RBA archives.

Commonwealth Bank of Australia

Staff card, Jack Davenport.

Bank Notes: Quarterly staff magazine of the Commonwealth Bank of Australia, September 1940, March 1941, September 1944, March 1945, March 1946, June 1946.

Honours and Awards Secretariat, Government House

Media notes for Jack Davenport's Officer in the General Division of the Order of Australia and Companion in the General Division of the Order of Australia.

Royal Australian Air Force Association

Jack Davenport's membership record.

Sydney Boys High School archives (SBHS)

Individual school record and record of admission: Jack Davenport.
Sydney Boys High School Jubilee 1883–1933 Record, 1933.
The Record: The magazine of the Sydney Boys High School, vol. XXIV, no. I, June
1932; vol. XXV, no. I, June 1933; vol. XXVI, no. II, December 1934;
vol. XXVII, no. II, December 1935; vol. XXX, no. II, November 1943;
vol. XXXVI, no. II, November 1944; vol. XXXVIII, no. II, November
1946; vol. XLIII, no. II, November 1951.

National Archives, United Kingdom

Air 27/544 58 Squadron RAF ORB.
Air 29/702 320121 1 Torpedo Training Unit Turnberry ORB.

Author's records (AR)

Edward Amaral letter 7 July 2007.
John Ayliffe interview 27 June 2006; conversation 8 July 2008.
Ernest 'Blue' Bernau interview 20 September 2006.
Alan Bowman conversation 6 and 7 July 2007 and 18 October 2007; notes
on early drafts 15 November 2007 and January 2008.
Barry Brooke interview 23 March 2007.
Mark Butler conversation 2 July 2007.
Jack 'Bluey' Collins interview 21 August 2006; conversations 9 and 15 November
2006 and 15 April 2008; additional written comments May 2007.
Pat Curnow conversation 20 December 2006.
Vivienne Dart conversation 17 May 2007.
Bruce Davenport interviews 14 June 2006, 19 October 2006 and 14 March
2007; emails 30 March 2006, 1 November 2006, 8 May 2008, 28 June
2008; conversations 14 May 2008 and 9 July 2008; undated comments
on draft manuscript June 2008.
Phil Davenport interview 20 June 2006; conversations 10 March 2007, 5 May
2007, 11 May 2007, 24 May 2007, 7 June 2007, 16 June 2007, 5 October
2007, 31 October 2007, 2 November 2007; undated comments on draft
manuscript June 2008.
Bruce Daymond interviews 15 June 2006 and 20 October 2006; conversation
4 July 2007.
Ron and Rosemary Duncan interview 14 March 2007.
Ron Duncan conversation and notes on draft 18 June 2008.
Noel Flanagan conversation 3 July 2007.
Bernie Fraser conversation 26 March 2007; fax 1 April 2007.
Hope Gibb interviews 14 October 2006 and 20 March 2007.
Ivor Gordon and Wally Kimpton interview, 5 September 2006.
Tim Griffiths email 6 July 2007.
Marion Hare email 11 December 2006; interview 12 March 2007.

Steve Heesh emails 13 January 2007 and 14 May 2008; conversation 25 January 2007; interview 13 March 2007.

Bob Holmes interview 5 September 2006; conversation with Ivor Gordon on behalf of Alexander, 22 June 2007.

Dick Humphrey conversation 30 April 2008.

Peter Ilbery interviews 18 November 2005 and 25 January 2006; emails 29 March 2008, including 'Egersund recollection' written shortly after the event, and 16 April 2008.

Wilfred Jarvis letter 3 July 2007; emails 10 August 2007 and 8 July 2008.

Cyril Johnson conversation 2 February 2007.

Gordon Johnstone email 21 April 2008.

Fred Kaad conversation 30 October 2007.

John Kingsmill letter 24 November 2006.

Jim Lumsdaine conversation 7 August 2007.

Doris McArthur letter 27 February 2007.

Alastair and Keith McDavid email 8 March 2008.

Graeme McDavid email 13 February 2008; letter 22 February 2008.

Virginia Macdonald email 28 June 2007.

Bill McFadden interview 21 March 2007; letter 31 August 2007; conversation 21 May 2008.

Jack 'Jeep' McKnight conversation 3 June 2006.

Frank McTighe email 3 August 2007.

Dick Mason interview 17 October 2006; letters 16 March 2007 and 4 April 2007.

Dick and Mary Mason interview 16 March 2007.

Devon Minchin conversation 4 July 2007.

Ross Moyle conversation 7 February 2007.

Michael O'Dea conversation 20 April 2007.

Sir Arvi Parbo letter 15 October 2006.

Kevin Parnell conversation 4 July 2007.

Lindsay Patience conversation 10 August 2006.

Ted Peacock conversation 5 July 2007.

John Pearson conversation 1 October 2007.

John Pilcher conversation 2 July 2007.

David Price conversation 4 July 2007.

Geoff Raebel interview 18 October 2006.

Alan Righetti email 29 February 2008.

Max Roberts conversation January 2007.

June Ross interview 24 October 2006; emails 13 May 2008 and 9 July 2008; letter 15 June 2008.

Robin Sen email 25 November 2007.

Lyn Shaddock and Tony Carroll interview 15 March 2007.

Lyn Shaddock email 7 June 2008.

Ted Sly conversation 13 December 2006.

Marina Stanley emails 13 and 14 May 2008.

Laurie and Doreen Taylor conversation 6 July 2007.

Frank Tomasich (Thomas) conversation 3 July 2007; letter 13 July 2007.

Ron Warfield conversation August 2006; additional written comments 30 April 2007.

Geoff Watson emails 6 December 2006, 23 February 2007, 9 May 2007 and 3 July 2008.

Pam Watson interview 24 October 2006.

Lloyd Wiggins emails 11 December 2005 and 28 June 2007.

Richard Youden conversation 23 June 2006.

Private records (PR)

PHIL DAVENPORT

Davenport, P., 'Things are Seldom What they Seem (Eighty Years of Memories)', unpublished memoir.

Letter Jack Davenport/Phil Davenport July 1995.

Photos.

BRUCE DAVENPORT

Jack Davenport, service diary, 18 May 1941–7 December 1942.

Sheila McDavid diary, 1943.

Sydney Boys High School order of service, dedication and unveiling of the Roll of Honour in commemoration of the old boys of this school who gave their lives in the Second World War, 1939–1945, 4 November 1951.

Jack Davenport, Anzac Day speech 1960.

Jack Davenport, RAAF Europe dinner speech, September 1978.

Jack Davenport, RAAF Association archives interview, 'A Wing and a Prayer', 2 April 1981.

Recording of speeches from Jack Davenport's farewell dinner from Monier, 7 April 1982.

Jack Davenport, speech, opening of the Gallipoli Gallery, Australian War Memorial, 20 August 1984.

Letter Jack Davenport/Captain G.G. Cooper 31 October 1984.

Jack Davenport, annual Services dinner speech 1 June 1990.

Letter Dick Mason/Sheila Davenport 13 November 1992.

Jack Davenport, speech notes, Bomber Command dinner, 13 November 1993.

Recording of Jack Davenport: 'Australia Remembers. 50th anniversary of the end of the Second World War', produced for the Commonwealth Department of Veterans' Affairs.

Jack Davenport, 'Australia Remembers' speech at Elanora Country Club annual dinner, 1995 (draft).

Jack Davenport, undated and untitled speech at Elanora Country Club.

Sheila Davenport, handwritten note describing how she and Jack met, 1996.

Photos.

JUNE ROSS
Sheila and Jack Davenport's 'My Wedding Book'.
Photos.

JOHN AYLIFFE
Ayliffe, 'RAAF Experiences of John Colin Ayliffe', unpublished memoir.

BRUCE DAYMOND
RAAF call-up papers 18 December 1940.
Service diary.
Photo collection.

IAN GORDON
Interview Jack Davenport 4 November 1987.
Letter Noel Turner 3 April 1991.
Letter Jack Davenport 24 July 1992.
Letter Noel Turner 12 August 1992.
Letter Madge Watson 11 June 1993.
Letter Noel Turner 18 August 1993.
Undated note and letters Bert Iggulden 10 and 30 August 1993.
Letter Scott Milson 16 September 1993.
Letter Noel Turner 1 November 1993.
Letter Jack Davenport 4 April 1994.
Jack Davenport, comment on draft of *Strike and Strike Again*, and additional comments 4 April 1994.
Letter Grant Lindeman 15 July 1994.
Jack Davenport, comment on draft of *Strike and Strike Again*, 26 September 1994.
The Viking Boys Christmas card.
Recommendation for Honours and Awards, Flying Officer Ian Hamilton Masson.

PETER ILBERY
Letters Sergeant Pilot Peter Ilbery to his aunt Miss M.A. Ilbery 13–14, 18 January 1944 and 15 March 1945.
Letter Jack Davenport 25 January 1944.
Letter Jack Davenport 28 February 1944.
Letter Jack Davenport Ilbery 26 June 1944.
Letter Jack 'Jeep' McKnight 5 March 1992.
Letter Jack 'Jeep' McKnight 23 July 1995.
Letter Jack Davenport August 1995.

DICK MASON
Recording of the thanksgiving memorial service Jack Napier Davenport 22 January 1996, St Stephens Uniting Church, 197 Macquarie Street, Sydney. Officiating minister, Reverend Dr Fred McKay; Eulogy by Dick Mason (thanksgiving service).

Recording of Dick Mason's speech in honour of Jack at Jack's farewell from AGL 6 November 1992.

SCOTT MILSON
Letter Jack Davenport/Arthur Milson (on the death of Colin Milson) 20 July 1975.
Photos.

SIR ARVI PARBO
Speaking notes at retirement dinner for Jack Davenport 3 March 1993.
J.N. Davenport—notes, Alcoa of Australia Ltd retirement dinner 3 March 1993.
Correspondence Davenport/Parbo relating to Alcoa directorship and service
Letter Paul O'Neill/Jack Davenport 14 April 1993.

GEOFF RAEBEL
Conversation Jack Davenport/Geoff Raebel (undated) relating to early draft of Geoff Raebel's *The RAAF in Russia–1942*, Australian Military History Press, Loftus, 1997.
Interview John Bilton/Geoff Raebel (undated) for Geoff Raebel's *The RAAF in Russia–1942*.

FRANK TOMASICH (THOMAS)
Letter Jack Davenport 17 October 1977.
Monier. Concrete Industries (Monier) Limited annual reports to stockholders and employees.
Company newsletters, variously known as *Concrete Industries News*, *Monier Memo*, *Monier Staff News*, *News Line*.

GEOFF WATSON
Ted Watson service diary.

Secondary resources

Newspapers and journals/magazines

AIM News, October 1982, undated 1982.
Ardossan and Saltcoats Herald, (undated) May 1964.
Armidale Express, 12 March 1971.
The Argus, 11 November 1945, 12 November 1945, 14 November 1945.
The Australasian, 17 May 1941, 8 April 1944.
The Australian, 8 December 1977, 31 December 1977–1 January 1978, 7 December 1978, 30–31 December 1978, 5 January 1978.
Australian Women's Weekly, 1 December 1945.
British Australian and New Zealander, 17 June 1944.
Daily Mail, 11 September 1944.
Daily Mirror, 27 January 1942, 11 September 1944.

Daily Telegraph, 11 September 1944, 1 January 1950.

Davenport, J.N., 'These are the ship-busters', *John Bull*, 20 January 1945.

Dundee Courier and Advertiser, 21 April 1943, 26 April 1943, 27 May 1943, 31 May 1943, 9 October 1943.

The Highlander: Monthly magazine of the 30th Battalion, NSW Scottish Regiment, August 1939, September 1939.

Journal of Comparative Legislation and International Law, series 3. Vol. 12, 1930.

Lethbridge Herald, 2 September 1941.

Manchester Guardian, 12 September 1944.

News Chronicle, 11 September 1944.

The Sun, 11 September 1944, 23 April 1974.

Sunday Herald, 1 January 1950.

Sunday Telegraph, 7 April 1946.

Sydney Morning Herald, 3–4 April 1931, 25 January 1936, 20 May 1941, 2 January 1950, 29 September 1992, 6 November 1992.

The Times, 20 November 1945.

Wings: Official magazine of the Australian Flying Corps and Royal Australian Air Force Association, 1 December 1947, vol. 8 no. 9, June 1956, vol. 8 no. 19, December 1956, vol. 16 no. 1, December–February 1964, vol. 20 no. 3, August 1968, vol. 33 no. 2, June 1981.

Books and articles

Australian War Memorial Council, *Annual Reports 1981–1986*.

Baskerville, R. and Warfield, R. (editors), *'Ditched'. Saved from the Sea: Sea rescue stories from 'The Goldfish' Brisbane*, the editors, Kenmore, 2002.

Bean, C.E.W., *The Australian Imperial Force in France 1917. Volume IV: The official history of Australia in the war of 1914–1918,* Angus & Robertson, Sydney, 1937.

Bird, A., *A Separate Little War: The Banff Coastal Command Strike Wing versus the Kriegsmarine and Luftwaffe 1944–1945*, Grub Street, London, 2003.

Bishop, P., *Bomber Boys Fighting Back 1940–1945*, HarperPress, London, 2007.

Brown, E., *Skylarks: The lighter side of life in the RAAF in World War II*, Air Power Centre, Fairbairn, 1998.

Cannon, M., *The Human Face of the Depression*, the author, Mornington, 1996

Chorley, W.R., *Royal Air Force Bomber Command Losses of the Second World War. Volume 3: Aircraft and crew losses 1942*, Midland Publishing, Hinckley, 2006

Clouston, A.E., *The Dangerous Skies*, Cassell, London 1954.

Clune, F., *Land of Hope and Glory: An Australian traveller's impressions of post-war Britain and Eire*, Angus and Robertson, Sydney, 1949.

Commonwealth Bank of Australia in the Second World War: An outline of the bank's principal wartime activities from the outbreak of war in September 1939 to the termination of hostilities in September 1945, John Sands, Sydney, 1947.

Dawson, B., *Strength in Concrete: A history of the formation and early years of the company, now known as AMATEK 1936–1959*, the author, Weetangera, 1989.

de la Billiere, *Supreme Courage: Heroic stories from 150 years of the Victoria Cross*, Abacus, London, 2005.

Docherty, T., *Training for Triumph: A history of RAF aircrew training in World War II*, Woodfield Publishing, Bognor Regis, 2000.

Eschel, D., *Bravery in Battle: Stories from the front line*, Arms and Armour Press, London, 1977.

Fruits of the Shaddock Tree: Memoirs of the descendants in Australia of John and Ann Shaddock, privately published, 1987.

Gibbs, P., *Torpedo Leader*, Wrens Park, Barton-Under-Needwood, 2002.

Gibson, G., *Enemy Coast Ahead—Uncensored: The real Guy Gibson*, Crecy Publishing, Manchester, 2005.

Gordon, I., *Strike and Strike Again: 455 Squadron RAAF 1944–45*, Banner Books, Belconnen, 1995.

Goulter, C., *A Forgotten Offensive: Royal Air Force Coastal Command's anti-shipping campaign, 1940–1945*, Frank Cass & Co, London, 1995.

The Heart Research Institute, *Annual Report 1995*.

Hendrie, J., *The Cinderella Service RAF Coastal Command 1939–1945*, Pen & Sword Books, Barnsley, 2006.

Herington, J., *Australia in the War of 1939–1945: Air power over Europe 1944–1945*, Australian War Memorial, Canberra, 1963.

ICAC Independent Commission Against Corruption, *Annual Report to 30 June 1991*.

Ilbery, P., *Empire Airmen Strike Back: The Empire Air Training Scheme and 5SFTS, Uranquinty*, Banner Books, Maryborough, 1999.

Jackson, R., *Before the Storm: The story of Bomber Command*, Cassell, London, 2001.

Jeffrey, A., *This Dangerous Menace: Dundee and the River Tay at war, 1939 to 1945*, Mainstream Publishing, Edinburgh, 1991.

Kemp, P., *Friend or Foe: Friendly fire at sea 1939–1945*, Leo Cooper, London, 1995.

Kingsmill, J., *The Innocent. Growing up in Bondi in the 1920s and 1930s*, Angus and Robertson, North Ryde, 1990.

Lark, C., *A Lark on the Wing: Memoirs, World War II and 460 Squadron*, privately published [no date].

Lawrence, W. J., *No. 5 Bomber Group RAF (1939–1945)*, Faber and Faber, London, 1952.

Lawson, J. H. W., *Four Five Five: The story of 455 (RAAF) Squadron*, Wilke & Co, Melbourne, 1951.

Lindeman, Group Captain G.M., 'Some Memories', private publication [no date].

McCarthy, J., *A Last Call of Empire: Australian Aircrew, Britain and the Empire Air Training Scheme*, Australian War Memorial, Canberra, 1988.

McGinlay, P., *A History of Tigh Mor Trossachs (The Trossachs Hotel)*, Trossachs Publications, Scotland [c2000].

McKenzie, M., *Fred McKay*, Boolarong Publications, Brisbane, 1990.

Maton, M., *Gallantry and Distinguished Service Awards to the Royal Australian Air Force in the Second World War*, the author, NSW, 2002.

Middlebrook, M. and Everitt, C., *The Bomber Command War Diaries: An operational reference book, 1939–1945*, Viking Penguin, Harmondsworth, 1985.

Milson, S., *The Earth Brought Forth: The Milsons of Milsons Point 1806–1973*, 4SQ Books, Bondi Beach, 2006.

Moyle, H., *The Hampden File*, Air-Britain (Historians) Tonbridge, 1989.

Nesbit, R Conyers., *The Strike Wings: Special anti-shipping squadrons 1942–1945*, William Kimber, London, 1984.

Order of Australia brochure, Governor-General's Officer, Government House, Canberra [undated].

Partridge, E., *A Dictionary of RAF Slang*, Michael Joseph, London, 1945.

RAAF Historical Section, *Units of the Royal Australian Air Force—A Concise History Volumes 1 to 10,* Australian Government Publishing Service, Canberra, 1995.

Raebel, G., *The RAAF in Russia—1942*, Australian Military History Press, Loftus, 1997.

Schofield, E. and Conyers, N.R., *Arctic Airmen: The RAF in Spitsbergen and North Russia 1942*, William Kimber, London, 1987.

Southall, I, *They Shall Not Pass Unseen*, Angus & Robertson, Sydney, 1956.

Stone, G., *1932: A hell of a year,* Pan Macmillan Australia, Sydney, 2005.

Tunnicliffe, D., *From Bunnies to Beaufighters: The autobiography of Donald McKenzie Tunnicliffe DFC incorporating a history of 489 Squadron RNZAF, November 1943–May 1945*, Alan Tunnicliffe, Christchurch, 1990.

Thetford, O., *Aircraft of the Royal Air Force since 1918*, Putnam & Co, London, 1971.

Wade-Ferrell, T.F., *In All Things Faithful: A history and album of the 30th Battalion and New South Wales Scottish Regiment 1885–1985*, Fine Arts Press, Sydney, 1985.

Wells, M.K., *Courage and Air Warfare: The allied aircrew experience in the Second World War*, Frank Cass, London, 1995.

Wilson, Squadron Leader M.C.D. and Robinson, Flight Lieutenant A.S.L., *Coastal Command Leads the Invasion*, Jarrolds Publishers, London [c1945].

Whishaw, D., *That Airman! Last of the Seven*, Libra Books, Sandy Bay, 1997.

Woodman, R., *The Arctic Convoys 1941–1945*, John Murray, London, 1984.

Websites

http://www.australiansatwarfilmarchive.gov.au: Australians at war film archive

www.awm.org.au: Australian War Memorial WWI embarkation and nominal roll records and 1st Division war diary

http://www.awm.gov.au/units/: Australian War Memorial's Australian military units http://www.bbc.co.uk/ww2peopleswar: the BBC's World War II People's War archive

http://www.cwgc.org: Commonwealth War Graves Commission (CWGC register)

http://www.gazette-online.co.uk: *London Gazette* citations

http://home.no.net/thsord/mosquito.htm

http://www.itsanhonour.gov.au: the Australian Government's Honours and Symbols website

http://www.nzmaritimeindex.org.nz: New Zealand maritime index: *Aorangi*

http://www.ww2roll.gov.au: World War II nominal roll

Endnotes

Prologue

1 AR, Pam Watson, 24 October 2006.
2 PR, Ian Gordon, Madge Watson, 11 June 1993.
3 AR, Geoff Watson, 6 December 2006 and 9 May 2007; Pam Watson, 24 October 2006; June Ross, 15 June 2008.
4 AR, Pam Watson, 24 October 2006.
5 PR, Bruce Davenport, speech notes, Bomber Command dinner, 13 November 1993.
6 AR, Wilfred Jarvis, 10 August 2007 and 8 July 2008.
7 PR, Dick Mason, thanksgiving memorial service Jack Napier Davenport 22 January 1996 (thanksgiving service) and Phil Davenport, 'Things are Seldom What they Seem (Eighty Years of Memories)', unpublished memoir (Phil Davenport, unpublished memoir).
8 PR, Sir Arvi Parbo, speaking notes at retirement dinner for Jack Davenport and Dick Mason, thanksgiving service.

Chapter 1   Depression era childhood

1 Unless cited from elsewhere, the family chronology in this chapter comes from PR, Phil Davenport, unpublished memoir.
2 Marriage certificate, Roy Davenport and Grace Hutton.
3 Jack had only scant knowledge of the Adelaide Davenports. When his father died in 1957, Jack was the informant and he recalled for the registrar that his Davenport grandfather had been a hotel keeper, but he did not know the name of either of his grandparents.
4 383 George Street, Sydney.
5 Roy's father was not the first Davenport hotel keeper. Family lore had it that a Davenport had been a publican in Staffordshire, England.
6 AWM embarkation and nominal roll records for Cyril Robert Hutton.
7 'Napier' was always pronounced 'Na-peer' in the family.
8 *Sydney Morning Herald*, 10 June 1920.

9   PR, Phil Davenport, unpublished memoir.

10   AR, June Ross, 24 October 2006.

11   AR, Phil Davenport, 7 June 2007.

12   AR, Bruce Davenport, 14 June 2006.

13   *Journal of Comparative Legislation and International Law,* series 3, vol. 12, 1930.

14   AR, Phil Davenport, 7 June 2007. Jack's son, Bruce, recalled that Jack rarely spoke of his childhood, but he was aware that the family often wondered from where the next meal would come. AR, Bruce Davenport, 14 June 2006.

15   AR, Phil Davenport, June 2008.

16   Quoted in PR, Phil Davenport, unpublished memoir.

17   *ibid.*

18   AR, Phil Davenport, 16 June 2007.

19   *ibid.*

20   *Sydney Morning Herald,* 3–4 April 1931.

21   Sydney Boys High School (SBHS).

22   *The Record: The magazine of the Sydney Boys High School*, vol. XXIV no. I, June 1932.

23   AR, Phil Davenport, 7 June 2007; Kingsmill, *The Innocent: Growing up in Bondi in the 1920s and 1930s*; and AR, John Kingsmill, 24 November 2006.

24   AR, Phil Davenport, 11 May 2007, and PR, Phil Davenport, unpublished memoir. In the attachment to his Form 1369, Confidential Report, completed in 1945, Jack listed the whole gamut of his athletic and sporting interests over the years: 'Athletics, running, jumping, cricket, rugby, golf, sailing, swimming, baseball (NSW junior team), tennis, squash.' NAA A9300, Jack Napier Davenport.

25   SBHS, *Sydney Boys High School Jubilee 1883–1933 Record*; *The Record,* vol. XXVI, no. II, December 1934, and vol. XXVII, no. II, December 1935; AR, Jim Lumsdaine, 7 August 2007.

26   AR, Fred Kaad, 30 October 2007.

27   AR, Phil Davenport, 11 May 2007; PR, Phil Davenport, unpublished memoir. Phil is unsure of when exactly they moved to 51 Kyle Parade, Kyle Bay, and is not sure whether Louise Hutton purchased the cottage or whether Roy Davenport did with some of the profits from the wool business. AR, Phil Davenport, 31 October 2007.

28   AR, Jim Lumsdaine, 7 August 2007.

29   *ibid.*

30   SBHS and *Sydney Morning Herald,* 25 January 1936. There was no mention of a Latin pass when the *Sydney Morning Herald* published the results of the intermediate. Jack had only received seventeen marks in his school Latin assessment and if he had sat that paper in the intermediate, he did not pass as only A and B passes were recorded in the *Herald*'s results list. Like Jack, his wife Sheila was none too strong in Latin: she detested it

and ended up failing a Latin exam. She noted later that, when she told Jack about failing, he was 'sweet about Latin'. PR, Bruce Davenport, Sheila McDavid's diary, 17 June 1943. She eventually passed a make-up exam.

31 AR, Bruce Davenport, 14 June 2006; Phil Davenport, 20 June 2006 and 2 November 2007. Keith would be the only Davenport boy to gain his leaving certificate.

32 SBHS, *The Record,* vol. XXX, no. II, November 1943, and vol. XXXVI, no. II, November 1944.

33 Commonwealth War Graves Commission (CWGC) register: Elder, Sub-Lieutenant Bruce Alfred, HMAS *Sydney*, Royal Australian Naval Reserve. 20 November 1941, age 21. Panel 60, Column 2, Plymouth Naval Memorial. Charlton, Pilot Officer William Roy Kenneth, 411121, RAAF. 17 April 1943, age 25. 8. A. 9, Durnbach War Cemetery.

34 SBHS, *The Record,* vol. XXXVIII, no. II, November 1946; AR, Bruce Davenport, 19 October 2006.

35 Lieutenant-General Gordon Bennett unveiled the roll, followed by the sounding of the Last Post and two minutes' silence. The names of the fallen were then read out by Lieutenant-Commander A.R. Callaway RANR, Lieutenant-Colonel D.J. Duffy MC ED and Jack. Jack's connection with High lasted all his life. In 1933, for the school's jubilee, he was one of the boys assembled for the school photograph. In 1958, for the school's 75th anniversary, he was an invited guest. Jack attended many school functions over the years, including the poignant 1990 commemoration of the 75th anniversary of the Gallipoli landings. Shortly before I visited their archives in October 2006, the school had put on display a portrait of Jack in its entrance foyer. It is mounted alongside portraits of fellow old boys Sir Roden Cutler VC and Lionel H. Taprell. SBHS, *The Record*, vol. XLIII, no. II, November 1951; PR, Bruce Davenport, Sydney Boys High School Order of Service, dedication and unveiling of the roll of honour in commemoration of the old boys of this school who gave their lives in the Second World War, 1939–1945, 4 November 1951; and AR, Tim Griffiths, 6 July 2007.

Chapter 2   30th Battalion

1 PR, Phil Davenport, unpublished memoir.
2 SBHS.
3 CBA.
4 AR, Bruce Davenport, 14 June 2006.
5 AR, Phil Davenport, 7 June 2007.
6 Details of career from CBA.
7 CBA; Cyril Johnson, 2 February 2007.
8 AR, June Ross, 24 October 2006.

9   *Commonwealth Bank of Australia in the Second World War*, 1947, p. 267. In addition, after 5 September 1939 the bank decided to make up the difference between its staff members' pay and military pay for those serving in the Australian armed forces.

10 The *Highlander*, September 1939; NAA B4747 Davenport, Jack Napier Army Number N18593. Wade-Ferrell, *In All Things Faithful*, p. 54, notes that Jack joined the battalion in late 1937, however his militia attestation form on NAA B4747 clearly states his joining date as 5 July 1939.

11 AR, Richard Youden, 23 June 2006.

12 Neither Phil Davenport nor Lyn Shaddock are sure of when Phil first met Clem Shaddock. However, Clem first appeared on the electoral roll for Bowden Cresent, Connells Point, in 1936.

13 AR, Phil Davenport, 20 June 2006 and 10 March 2007; Lyn Shaddock, 15 March 2007.

14 AR, Lyn Shaddock, 15 March 2007.

15 AR, June Ross, 24 October 2006.

16 AR, Lyn Shaddock, 15 March 2007; *Fruits of the Shaddock Tree*, p. 49.

17 The Commonwealth Bank announced this new phase in Jack's career in the September 1940 issue of *Bank Notes*: 'Mr Jack Davenport of Black Watch fame is busily employed "trainin' 'em" at Walgrove, but has been accepted by the RAAF and has hopes of discarding the skirt for trousers very shortly.'

18 PR, Bruce Davenport, 'Australia Remembers' speech at Elanora Country Club annual dinner, 1995 (draft). When recalling this story at the annual dinner, Jack elicited a great roar of laughter as he humorously recalled a 'problem' he encountered with his recruits when they attempted to form the required razor-sharp line before they started drill: 'Should I dress them from their fronts, or [sh]ould I dress them from their behinds?'

19 AR, Richard Youden, 23 June 2006.

20 AR, Edward Amaral, 7 July 2007.

21 AWM S01651 Jack Napier Davenport/Ken Llewelyn Oral History Recording, 24 March 1993.

22 *ibid*.

23 McCarthy, *A Last Call of Empire*, p. 35.

24 Jack was just one of many who were influenced by their older male friends and relatives. *ibid*., p. 34. Given the almost geographic estrangement from the Adelaide Davenports, however it is not likely Jack knew too many details of his Davenport uncles' war experience and, in particular, his Uncle Leslie's death on 16 February 1917 when the 32nd Battalion was located in Switch and Needle Trenches in front of Trones Wood. NAA B2455 Leslie Norman Davenport.

25 C.E.W. Bean records that the heaviest loss was borne by the 4th Brigade during First Bullecourt: it suffered 2339 casualties from the 3000 who engaged in battle. Bean, *The Australian Imperial Force in France 1917, volume IV*, p. 343.

26 *Fruits of the Shaddock Tree,* p. 49; NAA B2455 Clement Horace Shaddock; Australian War Memorial's Australian Military Units: 13th Battalion: http://www.awm.gov.au/units/unit_11200.asp

27 NAA B2455 Cyril Robert Hutton.

28 *ibid.*; 1st Division War Diary, AWM website. My thanks to Jim Underwood for his assistance interpreting these records as they relate to Bob Hutton's injury on 22–23 July 1916.

29 PR, Bruce Davenport, Jack Davenport, Anzac Day speech 1960.

30 PR, Bruce Davenport, Jack's diary; AWM S01651.

31 Ilbery, *Empire Airmen Strike Back*, p. 29.

32 McCarthy, *A Last Call of Empire,* p. 37.

33 NAA B883 Anthony Arthur Banks Nugent. CWGC register: Nugent, Lieutenant Anthony Arthur Banks, NX14767, AIF 2/13 Battalion, 29 November 1941, age 26. 8.H.4. Tobruk War Cemetery.

34 NAA A705 163/23/121 411115 Pilot Officer Roy Stuart Beveridge. CWGC register: Beveridge, Pilot Officer Roy Stuart, 411115, RAAF. 1 May 1942, age 20. Gen. Select Sec. 21. Grave 4500, Sydney (Waverley) General Cemetery. Smith, Sergeant Bruce Henry, 8603, RAAF. 1 May 1942, age 22. Panel 5, NSW Cremation Memorial, Sydney.

35 NAA B883 NX17385 Anthony Felix Booth. CWGC register: Booth, Corporal Anthony Felix, NX17385, Australian Infantry, AIF 9 Division Carrier Company. 9 February 1944, age 24. B2. F. 2, Port Moresby (Bomana) War Cemetery. My thanks to Brigadier Tony Gill and Professor Dennis Shanks for assistance in interpreting Booth's medical records.

36 NAA A705 166/26/553. CWGC register: MacRae, Flying Officer Duncan George Fletcher, 403364, RAAF. 118 Squadron. 23 August 1944, age 24. Panel 257, Runnymede Memorial.

37 *Commonwealth Bank of Australia in the Second World War,* pp. 264–5 and 316–24. Over 2700 of the Commonwealth Bank's clerical staff enlisted and, as much as possible, their progress was recorded in *Bank Notes*, the bank's staff journal. As with so many others, Jack's enlistment was recorded—he was mentioned in the 'Awards and Distinctions' column when he was awarded his Distinguished Flying Cross and Bar, Distinguished Service Order and George Medal (including a separate article detailing the rescue of the pilot from a burning aircraft that led to the award of George Medal). Although not specifically named, Jack's brave rescue was also described in the bank's Second World War history, and he was considered 'outstanding among these gallant men'. *Bank Notes*, March 1941, September 1944 and March 1945.

Chapter 3   Bradfield Park, Narromine and Macleod

1 Jack's call-up papers are no longer extant but his were identical to those received by Bruce Daymond who was also asked to report to 2 Recruitment Centre, Woolloomooloo, on 6 January 1941. PR, Bruce Daymond.

2   Lark, *A Lark on the Wing*.

3   AR, Bruce Daymond, 20 October 2006.

4   PR, Ian Gordon, Jack Davenport, 4 November 1987.

5   *ibid*.

6   Jack wrote and spoke little about his RAAF training in Australia. Unless
    credited elsewhere, narrative of Jack's Bradfield Park and Narromine
    experience is drawn from my conversations with Bruce Daymond as well
    as Bruce's interview for the Australians at War film archive, www.
    australiansatwarfilmarchive.gov.au/aawfa/ interview reference 0039.

7   NAA A9300, Allan Fletcher Ada.

8   Bruce Daymond could not recall if Allan Ada was also in A Flight.

9   PR, Bruce Davenport, Jack's diary, 18 May 1941.

10 *ibid*.

11 *ibid*. He was ranked third on the course.

12 *ibid*.

13 *ibid*.

14 AWM S01651.

15 PR, Bruce Davenport, 'Australia Remembers' speech at Elanora Country
    Club annual dinner.

16 General narrative of Elanora jaunt from AR, Bruce Daymond, 4 July
    2007.

17 PR, Bruce Davenport, 'Australia Remembers' speech and undated and
    untitled speech at Elanora Country Club.

18 PR, Bruce Davenport, Jack Davenport, undated and untitled speech at
    Elanora Country Club. Jack and Bruce both became members of Elanora:
    Bruce in the 1940s and Jack in the late 1960s.

19 Consisting of 214 Empire Air Trainees, nine Royal Air Force, twelve
    Royal New Zealand Air Force, six escorting party and three officers to
    the United Kingdom.

20 PR, Bruce Davenport, Jack's diary, 20 May 1941.

21 AR, Bruce Daymond, 20 October 2006.

22 AWM S01651. Unless otherwise credited, the general chronology of Jack's
    voyage is from PR, Bruce Davenport, Jack's diary.

23 PR, Bruce Davenport, Jack's diary, 28 May 1941.

24 *ibid*., 12 June 1941. Bruce Daymond recorded that 'Jack, who was pretty
    well in with the commanding officer, managed to get us changed back
    to bombers, our original recommendation from Narromine.' PR, Bruce
    Daymond, Diary, 13 June 1941.

25 See Ilbery, *Empire Airmen Strike Back*, Appendix 1, for the full text of the
    agreement between the governments of the United Kingdom, Canada,
    Australia and New Zealand relating to training aircrew in Canada.

26 PR, Bruce Davenport, Jack's diary, 14 June 1941.

27 *ibid*.

28 AR, Bruce Daymond, 15 June 2006.

29 PR, Bruce Davenport, Jack's diary, 16 June 1941.

30 AR, Bruce Daymond, 15 June 2006.

31 PR, Bruce Davenport, Jack's diary, 24 June 1941.

32 AWM S01651. It sounds strange that the furnace would be on during the summer months but the climate varies greatly in Fort Macleod and district so it is not uncommon to have the central heating on in June or early July and then a few weeks later to be sweltering both day and night. AR, McTighe, 3 August 2007.

33 PR, Bruce Davenport, Jack's diary, 15 June 1941.

34 *ibid.*, 24 June 1941.

35 AR, Bruce Daymond, 15 June 2006.

36 Jack totalled twenty hours on the Link trainer at Macleod. PR, Bruce Davenport, flying log.

37 PR, Bruce Davenport, Jack's diary, 15 July 1941.

38 *ibid.*, 19 July, 22 and 23 July 1941 and flying log.

39 'The training is 100 per cent on that of Narromine and seems a little easier.' PR, Bruce Davenport, Jack's diary, 19 June 1941.

40 *ibid.*, 26 June 1941.

41 PR, Bruce Daymond's diary, 26 June 1941.

42 PR, Bruce Davenport, Jack's diary 17 June 1941.

43 *ibid.*, 21 August 1941.

44 *Lethbridge Herald*, undated, in *ibid.*, 29 August 1941. Frank McTighe, editor and publisher of the *Macleod Gazette*, commented that Jack and his fellow trainees made a big impact on the Fort Macleod community, with many of them participating in community events. AR, McTighe, 3 August 2007.

45 PR, Bruce Davenport, Jack's Diary, 30 August 1941.

46 AWM S01651.

47 PR, Bruce Davenport, Jack's diary, 1 September 1941.

48 AR, Bruce Daymond 15 June 2006.

49 PR, Bruce Daymond, Jack's diary, 12 September 1941.

50 PR, Bruce Davenport, Jack's diary, 13 September 1941.

51 AR, Bruce Daymond, 15 June 2006. Of the 50 who completed their elementary training at Narromine, 22 died during the course of the war. Of those 22, five were members of the Narromine Choir. Allan Ada died on operations with 58 Squadron. CWGC register: Ada, Sergeant Allan Fletcher, 403297, RAAF. 6 May 1942, age 28. Panel 111, Runnymede Memorial. John Martin died on operations with 12 Squadron. CWGC register: Martin, Flight Sergeant John Edward Freese, 403060, RAAF. 15 October 1942, age 31. 3.D.12, Heverlee War Cemetery, Belgium. Rex Marre was serving with 3 Squadron RAF. CWGC register: Marre, Sergeant Rex Joseph, 403355, RAAF. 15 March 1942, age 23. Plot O. Row 2. Grave 54, Hawkinge Cemetery. Gordon 'Stumpy' Lee died on operations with 460 Squadron. CWGC register: Lee, Pilot Officer John Gordon, 403363, RAAF. 4 April 1943, age 21. 1. E. 13, Kiel War Cemetery. Ian Thomson died accidentally while serving with 92 Squadron RAF in the middle east. CWGC register: Colquhoun–Thomson, Pilot Officer Ian

Douglas, 403177, RAAF. 26 August 1942, age 21. AIV. G. 3.e1 Alamein War Cemetery.

Chapter 4   Operational training

1   PR, Bruce Davenport, Jack's diary, 30 September 1941. Unless credited elsewhere, general chronology of this chapter is drawn from Jack's diary.

2   Jack and his brothers would enjoy the hospitality of a number of British families, most organised under the auspices of Lady Ryder's scheme.

3   PR, Bruce Davenport, Jack's diary, 20 October 1941.

4   AR, Alan Bowman, 15 November 2007.

5   AR, Alan Bowman, 6–7 July and 15 November 2007.

6   PR, Bruce Davenport, Jack's diary, 23 October 1941.

7   PR, Ian Gordon, Jack Davenport, 4 November 1987. In this interview, Jack states that his friend was Seth Manners. This is a slip of memory as Seth was posted to 455 Squadron on 25 March 1942, ten days after Jack arrived at the squadron, and killed in action on 11 April 1942. Jack does not mention the swap in his diary.

8   PR, Bruce Davenport, Jack's diary, 18 November 1941.

9   *ibid.*, 18 November 1941.

10   AR, John Pearson, 1 October 2007. Jack did not refer to his crewing up process in his diary.

11   AR, Alan Bowman, 6–7 July 2007; PR, Bruce Davenport, Jack's diary, 25 November 1941. Jack did not record when he and Alan made the decision to fly together, and Alan does not recall the exact moment it came about. What he does remember, however, are the effects of the good choice they made.

12   *ibid.*, 27 November 1941.

13   Moyle, *The Hampden File*, pp. 7–12.

14   AWM S01651.

15   PR, Ian Gordon, Jack Davenport, 4 November 1987; Bruce Davenport, Jack's diary, 9 December 1941.

16   AWM S01651.

17   *ibid.*; AR, Ron Warfield August 2006 and 30 April 2007.

18   Wells, *Courage and Air Warfare*, p. 115.

19   The term 'stabilised yaw' was not in common use until the middle of 1941—see Moyle, *The Hampden File,* p. 167—and Jack does not use it in his diary; he notes that the 'plane yawed'. PR, Bruce Davenport, Jack's diary, 13 December 1941.

20   AR, Jack 'Bluey' Collins, 9 November 2006 and Grant Lindeman, quoted in Moyle, *The Hampden File,* p. 167.

21   AR, Jack 'Bluey' Collins, 9 November 2006.

22   CWGC register: Webb, Pilot Officer Anthony Philip, 108140, RAF Volunteer Reserve. 13 December 1941, Compt. 7. Grave 37, Cottesmore

(St Nicholas) Churchyard extension. Thornton, Sergeant Kenneth Frederick, 402623, RAAF. 9 [*sic*] December 1941. Age 25. Compt. 7. Grave 36, Cottesmore (St Nicholas) Churchyard extension.

Note: Both CWGC and Australian WWII nominal roll indicate that Thornton died on 9 December 1941 at Cottesmore, but Moyle indicates he died with Webb.

23 PR, Bruce Davenport, Jack's diary, 13 December 1941.
24 *ibid.*, 14 December 1941.
25 *ibid.*, 16 December 1941.
26 They had all flown together on 10 January on a bombing exercise. PR, Bruce Davenport, flying log.
27 AR, Alan Bowman, 6–7 July 2007.
28 PR, Bruce Davenport, Jack's diary, 28 January 1942.
29 AR, Alan Bowman, 15 November 2007.
30 AR, Alan Bowman, 6–7 July and 15 November 2007.
31 PR, Bruce Davenport, Jack's diary, 28 January 1942.
32 AR, Alan Bowman, 6–7 July and 15 November 2007.
33 PR, Bruce Davenport, Jack's diary, 28 January 1942.
34 *ibid.*
35 AR, Jack 'Bluey' Collins, 9 November 2006 and PR, Bruce Davenport, Jack's diary, 29 January 1942. Although a little shaky Jonas recovered quickly. Like Jack, he would eventually be posted to 455 Squadron (9 April 1942) but he did not fly with Jack again. 455 Squadron ORB.
36 PR, Bruce Davenport, Jack's diary, 28 January 1942.
37 AR, Alan Bowman, 6–7 July 2007.
38 Wells, *Courage and Air Warfare*, p. 119.
39 PR, Bruce Davenport, Jack's diary, 28 January 1942.
40 *Daily Mirror*, undated article pasted into PR, Bruce Davenport, Jack's diary.

Chapter 5   Fresher Pilot, 455 Squadron, Bomber Command

1 PR, Bruce Davenport, Jack flying log and diary, 1 March 1942.
2 PR, Bruce Davenport, Jack's diary, 25 February 1942.
3 *ibid.*, 2–4 March 1942.
4 PR, Phil Davenport, unpublished memoir; NAA A9300 Philip Roy Davenport.
5 PR, Phil Davenport, unpublished memoir.
6 PR, Bruce Davenport, Jack's diary, 4 March 1942.
7 RAAF Historical Section, *Units of the Royal Australian Air Force. A Concise History. Volume 3. Bomber Units*, pp. 112–13 and http://www.awm.gov.au/units/unit_11153.asp
8 Lawson, *Four Five Five*, p. 51.
9 PR, Bruce Davenport, Jack's diary, 15 March 1942.
10 AWM S01651.

11 Jack's diary records that the first flights with this crew, a night flying test and cross-country exercise, occurred on 16 March but his log book indicates that they took place on 17 March. Alan Bowman's log book indicates this crew's first flight was on 17 March 1942. AR, Alan Bowman, 18 October 2007.

12 PR, Bruce Davenport, Jack's diary, 17 March 1942.

13 AR, Alan Bowman, 6–7 July 2007.

14 *ibid.*

15 Narrative of 'downwind' incident from NAA A11271 140/43/P1.

16 AR, Alan Bowman, 15 November 2007.

17 NAA A11271 140/43/P1.

18 *ibid.* In his history of 455 Squadron, Lawson, who was the squadron's adjutant, wrote that 'whether the indicators on the ground, which should have shown Davenport the change of wind, were, or were not changed, was, at the time—and remains—a matter of argument'. Lawson, *Four Five Five,* p. 55.

19 Partridge, *A Dictionary of RAF Slang*, pp. 8–9.

20 NAA A11271 140/43/P1. As is the way of all good stories, this one was subject to some exaggeration as time went by. When Lawson wrote his history of the squadron in the early 1950s, he recorded that the promotion bar was for at least eighteen months. Lawson, *Four Five Five,* p. 56.

21 PR, Bruce Davenport, Jack's diary, 5 April 1942.

22 AR, Alan Bowman, 15 November 2007.

23 AWM S01651.

24 455 Squadron ORB.

25 PR, Bruce Davenport, 'A Wing and a Prayer'.

26 AR, Alan Bowman, 6–7 July 2007; AWM S01651.

27 PR, Bruce Davenport, 'A Wing and a Prayer'; AWM S01651.

28 PR, Bruce Davenport, 'A Wing and a Prayer'.

29 In early 1937, Prime Minister Neville Chamberlain announced to the House that only military objectives would be bombed, and every measure would be taken to avoid civilians. On the first bombing raid of the war, Guy Gibson's squadron was specifically forbidden to bomb civilian establishments, including houses. Bishop, *Bomber Boys Fighting Back 1940–1945*, p. 11; Gibson, *Enemy Coast Ahead—Uncensored*, p. 34.

30 Middlebrook and Everitt, *The Bomber Command War Diaries,* p. 240.

31 Lawrence, *No. 5 Bomber Group RAF (1939–1945)*, pp. 56–9.

32 Before it transferred from Bomber Command in April 1942, 455 Squadron carried out 29 mine-laying operations. *ibid.*, p. 62; Middlebrook and Everitt, *The Bomber Command War Diaries,* p. 771.

33 Middlebrook and Everitt, *The Bomber Command War Diaries,* p 253 and 455 Squadron ORB.

34 PR, Bruce Davenport, Jack's diary, 1 April 1942.

35 455 Squadron ORB; AR, Alan Bowman, 15 November 2007.

36 PR, Bruce Davenport, Jack's diary, 1 April 1942.

37 AWM S01651; AR, Alan Bowman, 15 November 2007.

38 Chorley, *Royal Air Force Bomber Command Losses of the Second World War. Volume 3*, p. 60. CWGC register: Maloney, Pilot Officer John Edward, 402376, RAAF. 2 April 1942, age 29. Panel 111, Runnymede Memorial. Woodburn, Sergeant Calder Fenton, 400301, RAAF. 2 April 1942, age 25. Panel 113, Runnymede Memorial. Rowley, Sergeant Horace Edward, 402611, RAAF. 2 April 1942, age 28. Australia. Panel 113, Runnymede Memorial. Young, Flying Officer Harry Neville, 402629, RAAF. 2 April 1942, age 21. Panel 111, Runnymede Memorial.

39 PR, Bruce Davenport, Jack's diary, 3 April 1942.

40 *ibid.*, 5 April 1942.

41 As it happened, only three crews proceeded to Essen and of those, one crew was lost. CWGC register: Wincott, Sergeant Arthur Henry, 1283559, RAF Volunteer Reserve. 7 April 1942, age 26. Plot 13. Row 2. Grave 28, Amersfoort (Oud Leusden) General Cemetery. Roberts, Flying Officer Trevor Emlyn, 400105, RAAF. 7 April 1942, age 26. Plot 13. Row 2. Grave 27, Amersfoort (Oud Leusden) General Cemetery. Gammie, Sergeant Colin, 402829, RAAF. 7 April 1942, age 22. Plot 13. Row 2. Grave 25, Amersfoort (Oud Leusden) General Cemetery. McIlrath, Sergeant Kenneth William, 400282, RAAF. 7 April 1942, age 26. Plot 13. Row 2. Grave 26, Amersfoort (Oud Leusden) General Cemetery.

42 PR, Bruce Davenport, Jack's diary, 8 April 1942.

43 AWM S01651.

44 PR, Bruce Davenport, Jack's diary, 8 April 1942; AR, Alan Bowman, 15 November 2007.

45 AWM S01651.

46 PR, Bruce Davenport, Jack's diary, 4 April 1942; 455 Squadron ORB.

47 AWM S01651. In January 1945, Jack wrote about the Bomber Command barrage against Hamm: 'Every time they bombed Hamm (and how often did they bomb Hamm!) they forced Jerry to try and get his supplies to the occupied lands by merchantmen sneaking along the coasts.' He did not respond to his rhetorical exclamation but, if the 8 April 1942 incident is anything to go by, the answer is at least one more than they had planned! 'These are the ship-busters', *John Bull*, 20 January 1945.

48 Bishop, *Bomber Boys Fighting Back 1940–1945*, p. 78.

Chapter 6   Ruhr operations

1 PR, Bruce Davenport, Jack's diary, 10 April 1942.

2 AWM S01651.

3 Middlebrook and Everitt, *The Bomber Command War Diaries*, p. 241.

4 PR, Bruce Davenport, Jack's diary, 10 April 1942.

5 AWM S01651. The 455 Squadron ORB clearly states Jack missed the primary target and hit the alternative one, and yet, in his DFC

recommendation, Bob Holmes states that the primary target was attacked. Alan Bowman's log book records the primary target was attacked. NAA A11271 107/P1; AR Alan Bowman, 15 November 2007.

6   Alan Bowman recalled that he counted 50 cones that night, and there were obviously more as he could not see anything behind him from his position in the Hampden's nose. AR, Alan Bowman, 6–7 July 2007.

7   AR, Alan Bowman, January 2008.

8   PR, Bruce Davenport, Jack's diary, 10 April 1942.

9   AWM S01651.

10 AR, Alan Bowman, 6–7 July 2007.

11 Gordon, *Strike and Strike Again*, p. vii.

12 AR, Alan Bowman, 6–7 July 2007.

13 AWM S01651.

14 *ibid.* This night, however, they missed out on the Wigsley welcome. Rather than risk flying to Wigsley on the dodgy engine as they had a few nights before, Alan Bowman plotted a course to Coningsby, where they landed about 4.00 a.m. 455 Squadron ORB; PR, Bruce Davenport, Jack's diary, 10 April 1942.

15 CWGC register: Manners, Flying Officer Seth Tilstone, 403142, RAAF. 11 April 1942, age 26 1.C.17, Rheinberg War Cemetery. Harland, Flying Officer Charles Antony, 404790, RAAF. 11 April 1942, age 27. 1.C.20, Rheinberg War Cemetery. Larkin, Sergeant Joseph Anthony, 1310060, RAF Volunteer Reserve. 11 April 1942, age 26. 1.C.19, Rheinberg War Cemetery. Ormston, Sergeant Charles Kay, 1355088, RAF Volunteer Reserve. 11 April 1942, age 26. 1.C.18, Rheinberg War Cemetery. Roberts, Flying Officer Robert Charles, 3200, RAAF. 11 April 1942, age 29. 6.C.10, Rheinberg War Cemetery. Keck, Flight Lieutenant Frederick Abbey, 400623, RAAF. 11 April 1942, age 27. 6.C.11, Rheinberg War Cemetery. Wright, Sergeant John Ripley, 1057411, RAF Volunteer Reserve. 11 April 1942, age 21. 6.C.8, Rheinberg War Cemetery. Canning, Sergeant Frank Hill, 408045, RAAF. 11 April 1942, age 21. 6.C.9, Rheinberg War Cemetery.

16 AWM S01651.

17 PR, Bruce Davenport, Jack Davenport, Anzac Day speech 1960.

18 Eschel, *Bravery in Battle*, p. 8.

19 PR, Bruce Davenport, Jack's diary, 12 April 1942.

20 455 Squadron ORB; PR, Bruce Davenport, Jack's diary, 12 April 1942

21 Middlebrook and Everitt, *The Bomber Command War Diaries*, p. 256; Jackson, *Before the Storm*, p. 187.

22 PR, Bruce Davenport, Jack's diary, 14 April 1942. The shot-down aircraft was not from 455 Squadron as all crews returned safely. It was one of five Wellingtons and four Hampdens that were lost that night. 455 Squadron ORB; Middlebrook and Everitt, *The Bomber Command War Diaries*, p. 257.

23 PR, Bruce Davenport, Jack's diary, 14 April 1942; 455 Squadron ORB.

24 AWM S01651.
25 *ibid.*
26 PR, Bruce Davenport, Jack's diary, 15 April 1942.
27 AWM S01651.
28 Air Ministry Pamphlet 100, May 1939 outlined causes and symptoms of psychological problems in aircrew and provided a framework for dealing with them. Wells, *Courage and Air Warfare*, pp. 188–90.
29 AWM S01651.
30 PR, Bruce Davenport, Jack's diary, 15 April 1942; AR, Alan Bowman, 15 November 2007. Lawson notes that about this time Bilton grounded three pilots until they had a full night's rest. Apparently Group headquarters was both critical and angry at Bilton's actions, which Lawson termed 'courageous'. Lawson does not give the names of the pilots but states all three took part in further operations and survived the war. Lawson, *Four Five Five*, p. 31.
31 NAA A12372 Bruce Cunynghame Daymond; PR, Phil Davenport, unpublished memoir.
32 PR, Bruce Davenport, Jack's diary, 16 April 1942.
33 *ibid.*
34 PR, Bruce Daymond caption on photo of Bruce, Jack, Phil, Allan and Dave at Waterloo Station as they farewelled Jack 17 April 1942.
35 58 Squadron RAF Operations Record Book.
36 Southall, *They Shall Not Pass Unseen*, pp. 24–30; AR, Bruce Daymond, 15 June 2006; Alan Righetti, 29 February 2008. CWGC register: Ada, Sergeant Allan Fletcher, 403297, Royal Australian Air Force. 6 May 1942, age 28. Panel 111, Runnymede Memorial. Stobie, Sergeant Thomas Craig, 1174907, Royal Air Force Volunteer Reserve. 6 May 2942. Panel 94, Runnymede Memorial. Barfield, Sergeant Eric William, 1376341, Royal Air Force Volunteer Reserve. 6 May 1942, age 22. Panel 77, Runnymede Memorial. Savage, Sergeant Keith Edward, 1198507, Royal Air Force Volunteer Reserve. 6 May 1942, age 20. Panel 93, Runnymede Memorial. Schofield, Sergeant Murray Alfred, R/76039, Royal Canadian Air Force. 6 May 1942. Panel 106, Runnymede Memorial. Moore, Sergeant John, 1252152, Royal Air Force Volunteer Reserve. 6 May 1942, age 22. Panel 89, Runnymede Memorial. Laurenti, Flying Officer David, 407749, Royal Australian Air Force. 12 August 1942, age 25. Panel 110, Runnymede Memorial.
37 Gibson, *Enemy Coast Ahead—Uncensored*, p. 10.
38 AWM S01651.
39 Chorley, *Royal Air Force Bomber Command Losses of the Second World War. Volume 3*, p. 65.
40 AWM S01651.
41 *ibid.*
42 *ibid.*
43 *ibid.*

44 *ibid.*
45 PR, Bruce Davenport, RAAF Europe dinner speech.
46 AWM S01651.
47 AR, Sir Arvi Parbo, 15 October 2006.
48 PR, Bruce Davenport, Jack's diary, 14 April 1942.
49 AR, David Price, 4 July 2007.

Chapter 7   Costal Command

1 PR, Bruce Davenport, Jack's diary, 22 April 1942. The 455 Squadron ORB notes that instructions from 5 Group to cease operations as a bomber squadron were received on 17 April 1942.
2 Lawson, *Four Five Five*, p. 58; Gordon, *Strike and Strike Again*, pp. 9–10.
3 See Goulter, *A Forgotten Offensive* and Hendrie, *The Cinderella Service RAF Coastal Command 1939–1945*. Because of the greater publicity emphasis on, and recognition of, the operations of Fighter and Bomber commands during the war, Coastal Command considered itself the 'Silent Service' of the Royal Air Force. See authors' note, Wilson and Robinson, *Coastal Command Leads the Invasion*, p. 9. Unlike Fighter and Bomber commands, Coastal Command was not honoured with a national memorial until 2004, when the Queen unveiled its tribute in the south cloister of Westminster Abbey.
4 As claimed by Squadron Leader John Lawson in *Four Five Five,* p. 60.
5 Or, as Lawson puts it, 'retained by judicious special pleading'. *Four Five Five,* pp. 58–9. It seems Jack did not attempt to persuade Lindeman to argue that he stay with the squadron: there is no mention of these negotiations in his diary. But, as noted by Alan Bowman, 'we were not consulted. Did as we were told!' AR, Alan Bowman, 15 November 2007.
6 AR, Phil Davenport, 7 June 2007.
7 AR, Jack 'Bluey' Collins, 21 August 2006.
8 PR, Bruce Davenport, Jack's diary, 7 May 1942.
9 AR, Bob Holmes, 5 September 2006.
10 PR, Bruce Davenport, 'Australia Remembers' speech at Elanora Country Club annual dinner, 1995 (draft).
11 Lawson, *Four Five Five,* p. 59. Although, no doubt, an exaggeration, there is a germ of wry truth in this anecdote: Patrick Gibbs recalled that when he left 22 Squadron in the autumn of 1941, he was one of the very few pilots to have survived a tour of operations. Gibbs, *Torpedo Leader,* p. 13.
12 PR, Ian Gordon, Grant Lindeman, 15 July 1994.
13 NAA A11271, Item 36/6/Air.
14 PR, Ian Gordon, Grant Lindeman, 15 July 1994.
15 PR, Ian Gordon, Jack Davenport, 4 November 1987.

16 Lindeman, *Some Memories*, p. 13.

17 As far as John Lawson was concerned, there did not seem to be any reason for this operational work other than to 'keep interest alive'. Lawson, *Four Five Five,* p. 64.

18 PR, Bruce Davenport, Jack's diary, 3 May 1942.

19 455 Squadron ORB.

20 PR, Bruce Davenport, Jack's diary, 3 May 1942.

21 AR, Dick Humphrey, 30 April 2008.

22 AR, Alan Bowman, 6–7 July 2007.

23 PR, Bruce Davenport Jack's diary, 12 May 1942.

24 *ibid.*

25 Raebel, *The RAAF in Russia–1942*, p. 46. Drawing on Grant Lindeman's Russian diary in Lawson, *Four Five Five,* p. 163, Raebel also attributes the artwork on Jack's Hampden to Leading Aircraftman Lamb RAF, the squadron artist, just before the squadron's move to Russia.

26 AR, Phil Davenport, 20 June 2006.

27 PR, Bruce Davenport, Jack's diary, 9 June 1942.

28 *ibid.*, 10 June 1942.

29 455 Squadron ORB.

30 PR, Bruce Davenport, Jack's diary 1 July 1942.

31 Because of the delay in take-off, the second formation had no chance of success.

32 *ibid.*, 5 July 1942.

33 Lindeman, *Some Memories*, p. 13.

34 AR, Alan Bowman, January 2008.

35 AR, Alan Bowman, 15 November 2007.

36 As was common at the time, Jack's diary entry referred to ME 109s. PR, Bruce Davenport, Jack's diary, 5 July 1942. Alan Bowman advised that they were 109Es. AR, Alan Bowman, January 2008.

37 PR, Bruce Davenport, Jack's diary, 5 July 1942.

38 PR, Bruce Davenport, Jack's diary, 5–6 July 1942; AR, Alan Bowman, 15 November 2007.

39 PR, Bruce Davenport, Jack's diary, 5 July 1942.

40 455 Squadron ORB.

41 PR, Bruce Davenport, Jack's diary, 5 July 1942.

42 455 Squadron ORB.

43 NAA A11271, Item 36/6/Air.

44 PR, Bruce Davenport, Jack's diary, 5 July 1942.

45 455 Squadron's ORB claimed that they were searching for the *Tirpitz* but Jack noted in his diary that it was the *Lützow*. PR, Bruce Davenport, Jack's diary, 9 July 1942. Lawson noted they were again in search of the *Lützow. Four Five Five,* p. 69.

46 PR, Bruce Davenport, Jack's diary, 9 July 1942.

47 AR, Alan Bowman, January 2008; Lindeman, *Some Memories*, p. 13.

48 AR, Alan Bowman, January 2008.

49 PR, Bruce Davenport, Jack's diary, 9 July 1942.

50 Lindeman, *Some Memories*, p. 13.

51 AR, Kevin Parnell, 4 July 2007. Kevin did not witness Jack's collapse from the cold. He was told the story by Bill O'Donnell, 455 Squadron's engineering officer who was there at the time.

52 Sometime later, Jack reread his diary account and recalling the bitter conditions annotated it with 'FROZEN!' PR, Bruce Davenport, Jack's diary, 9 July 1942.

53 PR, Bruce Davenport, flying log, 4 August 1942.

54 PR, Bruce Davenport, Jack's diary, 11 August 1942.

55 *ibid.*, 28 August 1942. Although they would be posted close to the front, the revolvers were not for self protection. Apparently, as far as the Russians were concerned, if a serviceman did not wear a side arm, he was not considered a fighting man nor deserving of respect. AR, Jack 'Bluey' Collins, 21 August 2006; Alan Bowman, January 2008.

56 PR, Ian Gordon, Jack Davenport, 4 November 1987. Jack mentioned no such speculation in his diary and Alan Bowman recalled that the kit issued was in fact warm weather gear. But tropical kit does make for a much better story! AR, Alan Bowman, January 2008.

57 455 Squadron ORB; PR, Bruce Davenport, Jack's diary, 31 August 1942.

Chapter 8   Operation *Orator*

1   Schofield and Nesbit, *Arctic Airmen*, pp. 191–2.

2   Moyle, *The Hampden File*, p. 44.

3   PR, Bruce Davenport, RAAF Europe dinner speech.

4   PR, Ian Gordon, Jack Davenport, 4 November 1987; AR, Alan Bowman, January 2008 and Jack 'Bluey' Collins, 21 August 2006.

5   Lindeman's Russian diary in Lawson, *Four Five Five*, p. 168; PR, Bruce Davenport, Jack's diary, 3 September 1942.

6   PR, Geoff Raebel, Jack Davenport's comments.

7   PR, Bruce Davenport, RAAF Europe dinner speech.

8   Lindeman's Russian diary in Lawson, *Four Five Five,* pp. 168–9.

9   AWM S01651.

10 PR, Bruce Davenport, RAAF Europe dinner speech.

11 PR, Bruce Davenport, Jack's diary, 4 September 1942; PR, Ian Gordon, Jack Davenport, 4 November 1987.

12 PR, Geoff Raebel, Jack Davenport comments.

13 AR, Alan Bowman, January 2008.

14 AWM S01651.

15 PR, Geoff Raebel, Jack Davenport comments.

16 AR, Alan Bowman, January 2008.

17 PR, Bruce Davenport, Jack's diary, 4 September 1942.
18 AWM S01651.
19 PR, Bruce Davenport, 'A Wing and a Prayer'.
20 AWM S01651.
21 AR, Alan Bowman, January 2008.
22 AWM S01651.
23 *ibid.*
24 PR, Bruce Davenport, Jack's diary, 4 September 1942.
25 AR, Alan Bowman, January 2008.
26 PR, Bruce Davenport, 'A Wing and a Prayer'. Alan Bowman recalled that those radishes caused considerable burping. AR, Alan Bowman, 15 November 2007.
27 AWM S01651.
28 PR, Bruce Davenport, RAAF Europe dinner speech.
29 PR, Bruce Davenport, Jack's diary, 4 September 1942. Jack's brief notes of the happenings of 4–5 September are the only diary record of his Russian trip. Jack and his compatriots were forbidden to take their diaries owing to the danger of falling into enemy hands. Jack paperclipped his notes to the pages of his diary on his return but they managed to unclip themselves and are no longer extant.
30 PR, Bruce Davenport, 'A Wing and a Prayer'.
31 PR, Bruce Davenport, RAAF Europe dinner speech.
32 Moyle, *The Hampden File*, p. 45.
33 *ibid.*, p. 46.
34 CWGC register: Smart, Sergeant Edward John, 400842, RAAF. 4–5 September 1942, age 25. 4. A. Coll. grave 1–5, Kviberg Cemetery. Nicholls, Flight Sergeant Thomas Graham, 400331, RAAF. 5 September 1942, age 22. 4. A. Coll. grave 1–5, Kviberg Cemetery. Biggin, Flight Sergeant Louis Arthur, 1358006, RAF Volunteer Reserve. 5 September 1942, age 27. 4. A. Coll. grave 1–5, Kviberg Cemetery. Harris, Sergeant John Mackenzie Oberlin, 408129, RAAF. 5 September 1942, age 20. 4. A. Coll. grave 1–5, Kviberg Cemetery. Nelson, Corporal Donald Henry, 6707, RAAF. 5 September 1942, age 21. 4. A. Coll. grave 1–5, Kviberg Cemetery.
35 Undated, unattributed news clipping captioned 'Swedish A-A Threat Hits at RAF' in Jack's PR, Bruce Davenport, Jack's diary, pasted over his entry for 4 September 1942.
36 Jack stated this opinion publicly on at least two occasions. During his 1978 RAAF Europe dinner speech, when referring to the accurate Swedish flak, he noted that the Swedes had 'in fact shot down two of our aircraft'. In a 1993 interview, Jack stated that 'The Swedes shot down, I think, two—they were neutral, but we were flying over their territory'. PR, Bruce Davenport and AWM S01651. Moyle, *The Hampden File*, pp. 46 and 140 notes the second Hampden to crash into a Swedish mountain was 144 Squadron's AE436. It flew into Tsatsa Mountain, Kvikkjokk after

losing height because of icing. Its pilot, Pilot Officer D.I. Evans, and ground crew passenger Corporal B.J. Sowerby survived and were repatriated by the Swedish authorities. Its three other crew members were killed. Given that AE436 had problems with icing, Moyle speculated that P5304 had also succumbed to icing.

CWGC reigster: Bowler, Flying Officer William Henry, J/7210, RCAF. 4 September 1942, age 31. 2. C. 1c, Kviberg Cemetery. Jewett, Flight Sergeant James Steven, R/56296, RCAF. 4 September 1942, age 21. 2. C. 1a, Kviberg Cemetery. Campbell, Flight Sergeant John Parker, R/69686, RCAF. 4 September 1942, age 27. 2. C. 1b, Kviberg Cemetery.

37   CWGC register: Catanach, Squadron Leader James, 400364, RAAF. 29 March 1944, age 22. Panel 284, Runnymede Memorial. Davidson, Flight Sergeant John Donald, 5372, RAAF. 17 March 1945, age 36. Coll. grave 9. A, Poznan Old Garrison Cemetery.

38   Details of AT109's flight and Catanach's fate from Bob Anderson's recollection in Moyle, *The Hampden File*, p. 46. Details of the fate of other members of AT109's crew from Lawson, *Four Five Five,* p. 72.

39   AR, Jack 'Bluey' Collins, 21 August 2006.

40   Jack's jerkin survived the war and became a favourite item of clothing, especially when he was doing the gardening. AR, June Ross, 24 October 2006.

41   PR, Geoff Raebel, Jack Davenport comments.

42   *ibid.*

43   AR, Jack 'Bluey' Collins, 21 August 2006; Raebel, *The RAAF in Russia– 1942*, p. 66

44   PR, Bruce Davenport, 'A Wing and a Prayer'.

45   Grant Lindeman's Russian diary in Lawson, *Four Five Five,* p. 186.

46   Woodman, *The Arctic Convoys 1941-1945*, p. 276.

47   In 1990, Jack was the guest of honour for the annual Services dinner (PR, Bruce Davenport). He opened his speech with the words 'It is all so long ago. Almost 50 years and memory plays such terrible tricks'. Indeed it does. In his 1978 speech at the RAAF Europe dinner (PR, Bruce Davenport), Jack mentioned the squadron made two attempts to locate the *Tirpitz* whilst in Russia. This recollection is contradicted by both Jack's flying log and the 455 Squadron ORB. Reinforcing that memory can indeed be unsound, in a 1987 interview Jack told Ian Gordon that he led the operation. Ian included this recollection in his *Strike and Strike Again*, p. 15. As acting A Flight commander, Jack may have led the aircraft in a smaller formation, but he did not lead 455 Squadron. The squadron's ORB states that Squadron Leader Holmes led the formation. Given Jack's recollection and Phil Davenport's considered belief that Jack had led the squadron on its only Russian strike, I decided to check this further. I was not able to fly to Perth again to speak with Bob Holmes so I asked Perth resident Ivor Gordon, Ian Gordon's father and a member

of the squadron in the Beaufighter period, if he could ask Bob Holmes who had led the strike. Without hesitation, Bob advised Ivor that he had. Bob Holmes/Ivor Gordon 22 June 2007. Finally putting the matter to rest, Alan Bowman, who navigated with Jack that day, stated emphatically that Holmes led the strike. AR, Alan Bowman, 15 November 2007 and January 2008.

48 PR, Bruce Davenport, 'A Wing and a Prayer'.
49 PR, Bruce Davenport, flying log.
50 PR, Ian Gordon, Jack Davenport, 4 November 1987.
51 AR, Alan Bowman, 7 July 2007 and January 2008.
52 Grant Lindeman's Russian diary in Lawson, *Four Five Five*, p. 187.
53 AWM S01651. The *Tirpitz* finally succumbed to the effects of 76 'Tall Boy' deep-penetration bombs, dropped in three separate attacks by 9 and 617 squadrons, on 12 November 1944.
54 Lawson, *Four Five Five*, p. 73; Gordon, *Strike and Strike Again*, p. 15.
55 Woodman, *The Arctic Convoys 1941*, p. 259.
56 AWM S01651.
57 Or freeze, if we take this recollection literally! PR, Geoff Raebel, Jack Davenport comments.
58 AR, Jack 'Bluey' Collins, 21 August 2006.
59 PR, Geoff Raebel, John Bilton; AR, Alan Bowman, January 2008.
60 PR, Geoff Raebel, Jack Davenport comments.
61 PR, Bruce Davenport, Jack's diary, 29 October 1942.
62 Grant Lindeman's Russian diary in Lawson, *Four Five Five*, pp. 194–5; AR, Alan Bowman, January 2008.
63 AR, Alan Bowman, January 2008.
64 PR, Bruce Davenport, Jack's diary, 29 October 1942.
65 NAA A11271 107/P1.
66 Grant Lindeman *With the Australian Forces in Britain*, 4 November 1942 in Raebel, *The RAAF in Russia*, p. 108.
67 PR, Bruce Davenport, 'A Wing and a Prayer'. Jack also referred to Lindeman's comments in AWM S01651. See *With the Australian Forces in Britain*, in Raebel, *The RAAF in Russia*, p. 109 for Lindeman's comments. This comment was broadcast live to air and apparently did not impress the RAF.

Chapter 9   Miss Sheila McDavid

1 PR, Bruce Davenport, Jack's diary, 1–2 December 1942. Jack was made acting squadron leader with effect from 16 November 1942.
2 AWM S01651.
3 PR, Bruce Davenport, Jack's diary, 13 November 1942. In 1996, after Jack's death, Sheila wrote that she had met him in November 1942 at a party at the officers' mess at Leuchars, but did not specify the date. Jack

only kept up his diary until 7 December 1942 and did not mention Sheila in it. He recorded many social activities in his last diary entries but, other than a couple of parties in the WAAF mess, this is the only party in November that he noted. Given this, it is likely that the night Jack met his future wife was Friday 13 November 1942. PR, Bruce Davenport, Sheila Davenport, undated handwritten note.

4　Jim McDavid's war work was recognised when he was awarded the CBE in June 1945, http://www.gazette-online.co.uk: *London Gazette*, supplement 14 June 1945, p. 2953. Years later, Sheila's brother Stewart was also awarded the CBE for services to British Industry in Spain, after retiring as president of ICI Spain.

5　Crescent Park is now a bed and breakfast: see http://www.crescentparkhouse. co.uk for photos of the house and surrounds.

6　AR, June Ross, 15 June 2008; Graeme McDavid, 13 and 22 February 2008 and Alastair and Keith McDavid, 8 March 2008.

7　PR, Bruce Davenport, Sheila Davenport, undated handwritten note.

8　*ibid*.

9　AWM S01651.

10　Sheila did not record whether Jack proved to be a clodhopper, but, many years later, Reverend Fred McKay recounted that Jack was just as expert in dancing the Scottish reels at that dance as he was at flying Hampdens. Even so, Jack must have felt he needed some expert assistance as two nights later he took some instruction in Scottish dances from some WAAF officers. PR, Bruce Davenport, Sheila Davenport, undated handwritten note; Dick Mason, thanksgiving service; Bruce Davenport, Jack's diary, 15 November 1942.

11　AWM S01651.

12　PR, Bruce Davenport, Sheila McDavid's diary, 11–12 January 1943.

13　AWM S01651.

14　Headquarters, Coastal Command, Royal Air Force, *Coastal Command Review* no. 9, January 1943. *Coastal Command Review (CCR)* was an in-house RAF publication which first appeared in February 1942 and provided a detailed summary of Coastal Command operations for the preceding month. It included analysis of operations and even feedback from crew members.

15　Details of this strike were included in Jack's Distinguished Flying Cross citation. Wing Commander Holmes included it 'not so much for its own interest, but as demonstrating the leadership, enthusiasm and determination which Squadron Leader Davenport has displayed in all his operational work'. NAA A11271 107/P1. While at Wick, Jack kept a diary of operations, with supplements from his deputy, Flight Lieutenant Hugh Clarke. This, as well as the 455 Squadron ORB and PR, Bruce Davenport, flying log, forms the basis of the 'Wick flap' narrative. Lawson, *Four Five Five*, Appendix C, pp. 153–60.

16   Lawson, *Four Five Five,* p. 160.

17   NAA A11271 107/P1.

18   NAA A11271, 140/74/P1.

19   AR, Alan Bowman, 6–7 July 2007.

20   PR, Bruce Davenport, flying log and Sheila McDavid's diary, 15 February 1943.

21   Sheila may have been disappointed by the cancelled date but all was soon forgiven when Jack took her to the 455 Squadron dance the next night. It was the 'happiest evening I have ever spent'. PR, Bruce Davenport, Sheila McDavid's diary, 18 and 19 February 1943.

22   455 Squadron ORB. The chronology of these last few days is uncertain. Jack's flying log (PR, Bruce Davenport) mentions that the rover patrol took place on 19 February. Sheila noted that 'there's a war on' on 18 February, and that she attended the 455 Squadron dance on 19 February. The ORB notes the operation on 20 February.

23   *CCR* no. 10, February 1943.

24   PR, Bruce Davenport, Sheila McDavid's diary, 1–9 March 1943.

25   *ibid.,* 16 and 21 April 1943; 18 February 1943.

26   Official notification of Harrison's promotion had been received on 3 April 1943, and his seniority had been backdated to 1 February 1943. NAA A11271, 140/74/P1.

27   *ibid.* CWGC register: Harrison, Flight Sergeant Clifford, 1000251, RAF Volunteer Reserve. 10 April 1943, age 28. Grave 575, St Anne's-on-Sea churchyard.

28   AWM S01651.

29   PR, Bruce Davenport, flying log; 455 Squadron ORB; Lawson, *Four Five Five,* p. 88.

30   AR, Max Roberts, January 2007; McKenzie, *Fred McKay,* p. 81.

31   These totals include those on squadron strength at the time who were killed in action and accidents, and also includes Squadron Leader Catanach and Flight Sergeant Davidson who were taken as prisoners of war.

32   Jeffrey, *This Dangerous Menace,* p. 171; *Dundee Courier and Advertiser,* 21 April 1943.

33   PR, Dick Mason, thanksgiving service, Reverend Dr Fred McKay.

34   AR, Jack 'Jeep' McKnight, 3 June 2006; *Dundee Courier and Advertiser,* 26 April 1943. In total, Dundee's 'Wings for Victory Week' raised £4,160,483, which represented 60 bombers and 352 fighters. It was a great success. *Dundee Courier and Advertiser,* 9 October 1943.

35   AR, Jack 'Jeep' McKnight, 3 June 2006; Jack 'Bluey' Collins, 21 August 2006.

36   AR, Lindsay Patience, 10 August 2006.

37   PR, Dick Mason, thanksgiving service, Reverend Dr Fred McKay.

38   AR, Jack 'Jeep' McKnight, 3 June 2006. PR, Dick Mason, thanksgiving service, Reverend Dr Fred McKay.

Chapter 10   1 Torpedo Training Unit, Turnberry

1   NAA Series A9300, Keith Hand Davenport. Keith was commissioned on 16 January 1944.
2   PR, Phil Davenport, unpublished memoir; *The Australasian*, 8 April 1944.
3   *CCR,* vol. II, no. 1, May 1943.
4   455 Squadron ORB; PR, Bruce Davenport, flying log; Headquarters, *CCR,* no. 11, March 1943.
5   NAA A11271 146/P1.
6   Clune, *Land of Hope and Glory*, p. 261.
7   PR, Bruce Davenport, Sheila McDavid's diary, 7–25 June 1943.
8   Jeffrey, *This Dangerous Menace*, p. 78, pp. 120–21.
9   Jack 'Bluey' Collins, who was in Butch O'Connor's crew, thought it must have been about midnight when they were dropped off. AR, Jack 'Bluey' Collins, 15 November 2006.
10 *Dundee Courier and Advertiser*, 27 and 31 May 1943.
11 455 Squadron ORB; AR, Jack 'Bluey' Collins, 15 November 2006.
12 AR, Jack 'Bluey' Collins, 21 August 2006; NAA A11271 104/P1.
13 Whishaw, *That Airman!*, p. 38.
14 AR, Bill McFadden, 21 March 2007; PR, Bruce Davenport, flying log; Whishaw, *That Airman!* p. 38.
15 AWM S01651.
16 *ibid.*
17 The six crewmembers of Wellington HX774 lost their lives when it crashed into the sea on 7 August 1943; the four crewmembers of Hampden X3025 lost their lives when it crashed into the woods on the same day; one crewmember died when Hampden P5341 crashed into the sea on 16 August 1943; the four crewmembers of Beaufort JM557 died when it crashed into the sea on 23 August 1943; and three were killed when Beaufighter JL610 crashed en route from Castle Kennedy to Turnberry on 28 September 1943. National Archives UK Air 29/702 320121 1 Torpedo Training Unit Turnberry ORB.
18 CWGC register: Riordan, Flight Sergeant Alan Douglas, 420489, RAAF. 16 August 1943, age 20. Sec. E. (White) Grave 297, Dunure Cemetery.
19 AR, Ron Warfield, August 2006 and 30 April 2007; Baskerville, R. and Warfield, R. (editors), *'Ditched'. Saved from the Sea*, pp. 175–78.
20 PR, Bruce Davenport, Sheila McDavid's diary, 14, 20 and 24 August and 25 September 1943.
21 *ibid.*, 20–21 September 1943.
22 *ibid.*, 6 October 1943.
23 Obituary, Dr J.W. McDavid CBE, *Ardrossan and Saltcoats Herald*, May 1964.
24 AR, Bruce Davenport, 14 June 2006.
25 AR, Alastair McDavid, 8 March 2008.

Chapter 11   Commanding Officer, 455 Squadron

1 Goulter, *A Forgotten Offensive,* p. 167.
2 Goulter, *A Forgotten Offensive,* p. 206; Lawson, *Four Five Five,* pp. 100; Thetford, *Aircraft of the Royal Air Force since 1918*, pp.140–5.
3 Whishaw, *That Airman!*, p. 47.
4 AR, John Ayliffe, 27 June 2006.
5 AR, Ivor Gordon, 5 September 2006.
6 AWM S01651.
7 Whishaw, *That Airman!* p. 48.
8 Whishaw, *That Airman!* p. 48; AR, Geoff Watson, 3 July 2008.
9 http://www.gazette-online.co.uk: citation *London Gazette*, 10 November 1942, p. 4867.
10 *ibid.*, 20 April 1943, p. 1797.
11 PR, Ian Gordon, Scott Milson, 16 September 1993.
12 Mark Butler, John Pilcher's son-in-law, attests to this long standing friendship. John had told Mark on many occasions that he, Jack and Colin, as well as Lloyd Wiggins, were all on similar wavelengths and shared a close very friendship; the four of them were like brothers. AR, Mark Butler, 2 July 2007.
13 This phrase is Whishaw's (*That Airman!* p. 48) but the sentiment is echoed by John Ayliffe: 'I thought he used to inspire great confidence in you. Some commanders . . . you'd wonder whether they knew what they were talking about half the time, but with him, I had every confidence in him.' AR, John Ayliffe, 27 June 2006.
14 Herington, *Australia in the War of 1939–1945: Air Power over Europe 1944–1945*, p. 247.
15 AR, Ernest 'Blue' Bernau, 20 September 2006.
16 AR, John Ayliffe, 27 June 2006.
17 Whishaw, *That Airman!* p. 48.
18 PR, Ian Gordon, Noel Turner, 3 April 1991.
19 PR, Ian Gordon, Jack Davenport, 4 November 1987.
20 *ibid.*
21 *ibid.*
22 This was Flying Officer Steve Sykes. On 12 September 1944, he dived on a trawler in Den Helder Harbour and left his pull-out a little late. He recalled that he 'collected the mast top with the nose and brought it back lying at my seat'. Quoted by Gordon in *Strike and Strike Again,* p. 102.
23 PR, Bruce Davenport, 'A Wing and a Prayer'.
24 PR, Bruce Davenport, flying log.
25 AR, Ivor Gordon, 5 September 2006.
26 Whishaw, *That Airman!*, p 51–2.
27 Goulter, *A Forgotten Offensive,* p. 181.
28 AWM 65 Radio talk, 4 August 1944.

29   There was one tragic hitch on 29 December 1943 with the squadron's first Beaufighter death. Flying Officer Peter Gumbrell was a passenger on a familiarisation flight piloted by Flight Lieutenant William Toombs from 489 Squadron. The aircraft entered a low speed stall as it neared the ground, crashed into a wall and burst into flames, killing both men. CWGC register: Gumbrell, Flying Officer Peter Stanley, 124722, RAF Volunteer Reserve. 29 December 1943, age 23. Pevensey (St Nicholas) Churchyard. Toombs, William Henry Clements, 414359, RNZAF. 29 December 1943, age 25. Dundee Crematorium, Angus, Scotland.

30   PR, Geoff Watson, Ted Watson's diary, 6 January 1944.

31   Known locally as 'the Eg', Jack was well familiar with its dining room, where he and Sheila had enjoyed quiet meals, and its guest rooms, when propriety dictated that he stay elsewhere when Sheila's parents were away from home. Sheila McDavid's diary, 22 July 1943.

32   PR, Phil Davenport, unpublished memoir; 461 Squadron ORB.

33   AWM S01651.

34   *ibid.*

35   Unless otherwise credited, details of the reception are drawn from PR, Phil Davenport, unpublished memoir.

36   AWM S01651.

37   AR, June Ross, 24 October 2006.

38   AR, Bruce Davenport, 19 October 2006.

39   The telegram was pasted into PR, June Ross, Sheila and Jack Davenport's 'My Wedding Book' but the original pencilled telegram form found its way into the squadron Line Book. Underneath, someone (signature unintelligible to me), has written 'This is beyond me. It would be appreciated if the Winco keep record of his own expenditure for operational and statistical summary.' It seems as if the squadron would prefer not to hear about any 'operational failures'. AWM 64 455 Squadron Line Book.

40   AR, June Ross, 24 October 2006.

41   AWM S01651. Despite the usual trials of any marriage, it was a happy one and when RAAF public relations officer Ken Llewelyn noted to Jack in this interview that Jack and Sheila had had quite a remarkable marriage, Jack agreed emphatically: 'yes indeed, yes indeed' and, looking forward, commented that 'in fact, next January is our fiftieth anniversary'.

42   McGinlay, *A History of Tigh Mor Trossachs (The Trossachs Hotel)*; PR, Peter Ilbery, Ilbery/Miss M.A. Ilbery 13–14, 18 January 1944.

43   PR, Peter Ilbery, Ilbery/Miss M.A. Ilbery 13–14, 18 January 1944.

44   AWM S01651.

Chapter 12   Beaufighter Leader

1   *CCR*, vol. II, no. 8, December 1943.

2   AWM S01651.

3   Gordon, *Strike and Strike Again*, p. 222.
4   AR, Bruce Davenport, 14 June 2006.
5   AWM S01651.
6   Gordon, *Strike and Strike Again*, p vii.
7   Gordon, *Strike and Strike Again*, p. vii; AWM S01651.
8   AR, Wally Kimpton, 5 September 2006.
9   455 Squadron ORB.
10 NAA A11271 11/2/AIR.
11 AWM S01651.
12 AR, Ivor Gordon, 5 September 2006.
13 AR, John Ayliffe, 27 June 2006.
14 His Distinguished Service Order would be gazetted on 14 April 1944.
15 Whishaw, *That Airman!*, p. 59.
16 455 Squadron ORB.
17 Whishaw, *That Airman!* p. 59.
18 PR, Ian Gordon, Jack Davenport, 4 November 1987.
19 *ibid.*
20 Whishaw, *That Airman!* p. 60.
21 PR, Ian Gordon, Jack Davenport, 4 November 1987.
22 Whishaw, *That Airman!* p. 60–1.
23 455 Squadron ORB.
24 I am grateful to naval researcher Peter Beeston who provided this information from Naval Staff Battle Summary no. 29, Operation *Neptune*.
25 Kemp, *Friend or Foe*, p. 52.
26 *ibid.*
27 PR, Ian Gordon, Jack Davenport, 4 November 1987.
28 PR, Bruce Davenport, Jack Davenport, annual Services dinner speech, 1 June 1990. Jack's house arrest did not last long. He was back in the air on 8 May carrying out practice bombing and cine-camera exercises. PR, Bruce Davenport, flying log.
29 PR, Ian Gordon, Jack Davenport, 4 November 1987.
30 Kemp, *Friend or Foe*, p. 52.
31 PR, Bruce Davenport, Jack Davenport, annual Services dinner speech, 1 June 1990.
32 AR, Ivor Gordon, 5 September 2006.
33 PR, Bruce Davenport, Jack Davenport, annual Services dinner speech, 1 June 1990.
34 AR, Bruce Davenport, 14 June 2006 and 28 June 2008.
35 455 Squadron ORB and Ayliffe, 'RAAF Experiences of John Colin Ayliffe', unpublished memoir, p. 24.
36 AR, Dick Mason, 17 October 2006.
37 *CCR,* vol. III, no. 12, December 1944.
38 Whishaw, *That Airman!* p. 63.

39 455 Squadron ORB.

40 NAA A11271 146/P1.

41 AR, Jack (Jeep) McKnight, 3 June 2006; Whishaw, *That Airman!* p. 63.

42 AWM 64, 126/1. History of 455 Squadron.

43 CWGC register: Pettitt, Flying Officer Ivan Alfred, 415780, RNZAF. 14 May 1944. No age details. Panel 263, Runnymede Memorial. Lowcock, Flying Officer Charles Harry, 151519, RAF Volunteer Reserve. 14 May 1944, age 23. Panel 207, Runnymede Memorial.

44 NAA A11271 11/2/AIR.

45 *ibid.*

46 PR, Ian Gordon. Recommendation for Honours and Awards, Flying Officer Ian Hamilton Masson.

47 NAA A9300, Jack Napier Davenport. Of a total of 270 awards made to Australians across the services in the Second World War, only 70 DSOs were awarded to members of the RAAF. Maton, *Gallantry and Distinguished Service Awards to the Royal Australian Air Force in the Second World War,* p. 93.

48 AWM S01651.

49 RAAF Release 535, no. 113, 8 June 1944. The others in the youthful quartet were Wing Commander John Keith Douglas (22), Wing Commander Ronald Norman Gillies (24), and Wing Commander Rollo Kingsford Smith (24). Jack may not have been the youngest of the four, but at that time, and indeed at the close of the war, he was the most decorated.

50 NAA A11271 9/AIR.

51 *ibid.*

52 455 Squadron ORB.

53 *CCR,* vol. III, no. 6, June 1944.

54 Unless cited otherwise, the main chronology of the 13 June 1944 strike comes from the 455 Squadron ORB.

55 Gordon, *Strike and Strike Again,* p. 47; 455 Squadron ORB; PR, Bruce Davenport, flying log.

56 Air Ministry bulletin, no. 14345, 14 June 1944.

57 *ibid.*

58 PR, Ian Gordon, Noel Turner, 3 April 1991.

59 *CCR,* vol. III, no. 6, June 1944.

60 455 Squadron ORB.

61 PR, Scott Milson, Jack Davenport/Arthur Milson, 20 July 1975.

62 AR, Bill Herbert, 1 June 2006.

63 PR, Scott Milson, Jack Davenport/Arthur Milson, 20 July 1975.

64 NAA A11271 107/P1. Jack's recommendation for Flying Officer Matthew Southgate was not successful on this occasion but he persevered and Southgate was awarded a Distinguished Flying Cross soon after.

65 Quoted from Gordon, *Strike and Strike Again,* p. 223.

66 Jack was also responsible for Milson's bar to his DSO. Milson 'was quite modest and he was critical of me when I made my third recommendation for a gallantry award for him, which was for his second DSO—but I had planned every operation which he led . . . when he was CO of the squadron and I know what he did, and later how he did it.' PR, Scott Milson, Jack Davenport/Arthur Milson, 20 July 1975.

67 Whishaw, *That Airman!* p. 116.

Chapter 13   Dangerous work

1 *CCR,* vol. III, no. 7, July 1944.

2 Duff weather blighted armed reconnaissances on 6, 20 and 30 July 1944.

3 This and following 'surprise visit' comment from *CCR,* vol. III, no. 7, July 1944.

4 AWM S00197.

5 *ibid.*

6 *CCR,* vol. III, no. 7, July 1944.

7 455 Squadron ORB.

8 AWM S00197.

9 *CCR,* vol. III, no. 7, July 1944.

10 AWM S00197.

11 Air Ministry bulletin, no. 14728, 16 July 1944. See also Air Ministry bulletins no. 14728, 16 July 1944 and no. 15753, 26 September 1944; and RAAF release, no. 776, 19 September 1944.

12 PR, Ian Gordon, Jack Davenport, 4 November 1987; AWM S01651.

13 PR, Bruce Davenport, 'A Wing and a Prayer'.

14 PR, Ian Gordon, Jack Davenport, 4 November 1987.

15 Both Herington, *Australia in the War of 1939–1945: Air Power over Europe 1944–1945,* p. 368 and the 455 Squadron ORB noted that the rocket head in this experiment was a 25-pound one. PR, Bruce Davenport, flying log for this day notes that he was using a 60-pound head.

16 PR, Ian Gordon, Jack Davenport, 4 November 1987.

17 Lawson, *Four Five Five,* p. 115.

18 PR, Ian Gordon, Jack Davenport, 4 November 1987. It should be noted that, although Jack played an important part in the rocket testing and evaluation trials, members of 455 Squadron also spent much time firing at that beached ship during August 1944, gaining valuable experience and training in the use of rocket projectiles. Ayliffe, 'RAAF Experiences of John Colin Ayliffe', p. 26.

19 PR, Ian Gordon, Jack Davenport, 4 November 1987.

20 All quotes this paragraph, *ibid.*

21 Lawson, *Four Five Five,* p. 51.

22 PR, Ian Gordon, Jack Davenport, 4 November 1987.

23 Whishaw, *That Airman!* p. 82.

24 PR, Ian Gordon, Jack Davenport, 4 November 1987.

25 AR, Ivor Gordon, 5 September 2006.

26 Tunnicliffe, *From Bunnies to Beaufighters*, p. 194.

27 This and comment from Flying Officer Thompson from RAAF release, no. 724, August 1944.

28 Lawson, *Four Five Five,* p. 122.

29 *CCR*, vol. II, no. 1, May 1943.

30 This was an immediate Distinguished Flying Cross. The award of a second DFC is known as DFC and Bar.

31 *CCR*, vol. III, no. 12, December 1944.

32 455 Squadron ORB, 31 August 1944.

33 455 Squadron ORB, 10 August 1944.

34 CWGC register:
   489 Squadron
   Fricker, Flying Officer Douglas John, 171580, RAF Volunteer Reserve. 10 August 1944, age 24. Surrey. 4. D. 19, Kiel War Cemetery. Woodcock, Flying Officer William Robertson, 141844, RAF Volunteer Reserve. 10 August 1944, age 29. 4. D. 20, Kiel War Cemetery.
   455 Squadron
   Jones, Warrant Officer William Thomas, 413618, RAAF. 10 August 1944, age 28. Panel 259, Runnymede Memorial. Brock, Warrant Officer Harold Eric, 408396, RAAF. 10 August 1944, age 21. 10. E. 8, Hanover War Cemetery. Kempson, Flying Officer Leo Albert, 141844, RAAF. 10 August 1944, age 22. 4. D. 18, Kiel War Cemetery. Curzon, Flying Officer Raymond, 152322, RAF Volunteer Reserve. 10 August 1944, age unknown. 4A. G. 13, Hamburg Cemetery. Batchelor, Pilot Officer Geoffrey Edwin, 185232, RAF Volunteer Reserve. 10 August 1944, age unknown. Panel 210, Runnymede Memorial. Morris, Pilot Officer Harold Richard, 179196, RAF Volunteer Reserve. 10 August 1944, age 21. Panel 212, Runnymede Memorial.

35 See NAA A11271 140/101/P1, 140/105/P1, 140/104/P1 and 140/98/P1.

36 Costello's navigator Flight Sergeant Robert Taylor managed to scramble into the dinghy and was later picked up by a German patrol boat. CWGC register: Costello, Pilot Officer John, 421312, RAAF. 6 July 1944, age 21. Panel 258, Runnymede Memorial.

37 NAA A11271 140/101/P1.

38 CWGC register: Billing, Flying Officer John Urban, 2114, RAAF. 1 July 1944, age 28. Grave 13506, Cambridge City Cemetery. Billing's navigator was killed in the same accident: Edwards, Flying Officer Terence Oliver, 426574, RAAF. 1 July 1944, age 20. Grave 13706, Cambridge City Cemetery.

39 NAA A11271 140/99/P1.

40 NAA A11271 140/105/P1.

41 *ibid.*

42 NAA A11271 140/104/P1.

43 *ibid.*

44 NAA A11271 140/107/P1.

4   NAA A11271, 140/74/P1.

46 CWGC register: Collaery, Flying Officer Edward Francis, 402944, RAAF. 29 June 1944, age 29. Panel 257, Runnymede Memorial. Collaery's navigator, Flying Officer Horace 'Vic' Pearson survived and was picked up by air–sea rescue and returned to the squadron.

47 NAA A11271 140/98/P1.

48 Gordon, *Strike and Strike Again*, p. 63.

49 AWM S01651.

50 NAA A11271 140/107/P1.

51 *ibid.*

52 PR, Ian Gordon, Jack Davenport, 4 November 1987.

53 CWGC register: Barbour, Flying Officer William Morgan, 414380, RAAF. 6 July 1944, age 21. Panel 257, Runnymede Memorial. Barbour's navigator also died that day: Dodd, Flying Officer Frederick George, 152529, RAF Volunteer Reserve. 6 July 1944, age 35. 5. C. 3 Sage War Cemetery.

54 NAA A705 166/5/604.

55 PR, Bruce Davenport, 'Australia Remembers: 50th anniversary of the end of the Second World War', produced for the Commonwealth Department of Veterans' Affairs.

Chapter 14   George Medal

1   Air Ministry bulletin no. 15411, 26 August 1944.

2   455 Squadron ORB; Herington, *Australia in the War of 1939–1945: Air Power over Europe 1944–1945*, p. 368.

3   AR, Ivor Gordon, 5 September 2006; AWM S01651.

4   Flight Sergeant Jack Tucker, quoted in Gordon, *Strike and Strike Again*, p. 98.

5   AR, Bill Herbert, 1 June 2006.

6   Air Ministry bulletin, no. 15584, 10 September 1944, no. 27.

7   AR, Ivor Gordon, 5 September 2006. Thompson and Gordon and pilot officers Steve Sykes and Vic Pearson were diverted to Little Snoring.

8   Air Ministry bulletin, no. 15584, 10 September 1944, no. 27.

9   AWM S01651.

10 455 Squadron ORB.

11 AWM S01651. Bill Herbert recalled that Jack pulled Stanley out by the scruff of his neck. AR, Bill Herbert, 1 June 2006.

12 Air Ministry bulletin, no. 15584, 10 September 1944, no. 27

13 455 Squadron ORB.

14 Gordon, *Strike and Strike Again,* p. 98.

15 Air Ministry bulletin, no. 15584, 10 September 1944, no 27.

16 *ibid.*

17 PR, Ian Gordon, Noel Turner, 12 August 1992.

18 PR, Phil Davenport, unpublished memoir.

19 AR, Vivienne Dart, 17 May 2007.

20 *Daily Mirror*, 11 September 1944; *News Chronicle*, 11 September 1944; *Daily Mail*, 11 September 1944; *Daily Telegraph*, 11 September 1944; *Manchester Guardian*, 12 September 1944; *The Sun*, 11 September 1944; and *Daily Mirror*, 27 January 1942.

21 AR, Phil Davenport, 31 October 2007.

22 Throughout his life, Jack displayed a natural diffidence about all of his achievements and, apart from his initial comments to the Air Ministry journalist, Jack did not speak publicly about his rescue of Bill Stanley until 1993. When Ken Llewelyn asked Jack in their 1993 interview: 'In retrospect, do you think it was rather foolish, as a commanding officer of a squadron, a very valuable pilot, to take that particular action?' Jack modestly replied 'I think you are overrating the pilot, but I must admit that the thought didn't cross my mind.' AWM S01651.

23 AR, Cyril Johnson, 2 February 2007. Although he was not there on that day, the clarity of Cyril's account of the events made it seem as if he had been there. Cyril's detailed knowledge of the events was by no means an isolated case. When I spoke to many of those who knew Jack during the war (and many of those who did not know him) almost the first thing I was told was the story of how he had saved Bill Stanley's life.

24 de la Billiere, *Supreme Courage*, p. 355.

25 My thanks to Anthony Staunton for this information.

26 Air Ministry bulletin, no. 16950, 5 January 1945.

27 This and above quote from AWM S01651.

28 *CCR*, vol. III, no. 9, September 1944.

29 PR, Bruce Davenport, flying log.

30 Whishaw, *That Airman!*, pp. 94–5.; 455 Squadron ORB.

31 455 Squadron ORB.

32 Whishaw, *That Airman!* p. 95.

33 Jack told his crews after the strike of the anticipated loss rate. AR, Ivor Gordon, 5 September 2006. Jack may have kept the true expectations from his crew, but Neil Smith recalled 'we reckoned that it was the diciest trip that we would have to do because of the location of the convoy and the flak.' Gordon, *Strike and Strike Again*, p. 108.

34 Clouston, *The Dangerous Skies*, p. 173.

35 *CCR*, vol. III, no. 9, September 1944.

36 455 Squadron ORB, 26 September 1944.

37 *ibid.*, 25 September 1944.

38 CWGC register: Cock, Flying Officer Colin Edwin Abbott, 415510, RAAF. 25 September 1944, age 26. 29. B. 3., Bergen–op–Zoom War

Cemetery. Lyneham, Warrant Officer Alan Robert, 415671, RAAF. 25
September 1944, age 36. Panel 259, Runnymede Memorial.

Chapter 15   Veteran Commanding Officer

1   The humorous author of *CCR* noted the Dutch and German coasts had
    'at last ceased to be happy hunting grounds by day'. *CCR,* vol. III, no.
    10, October 1944.

2   NAA A9300, Jack Napier Davenport. There may have been little notice
    of the transfer to Dallachy, but Jack received even less notice of his new
    posting. He had prepared the movement order to Dallachy on 19 October
    1994 and had included himself in the air party of 24 October. NAA 11271
    4/1/AIR.

3   Jack confided this aspect of his posting to Peter Ilbery years later during
    a squadron reunion. AR, Peter Ilbery, 18 November 2005.

4   PR, Ian Gordon, Jack Davenport, 24 July 1992.

5   PR, Phil Davenport, unpublished memoir.

6   PR, Ian Gordon, Jack Davenport, April 1994.

7   AWM S01651.

8   Gordon, *Strike and Strike Again*, p. vii–viii; PR, Peter Ilbery, Jack Davenport,
    August 1995.

9   Summary of flying and assessments signed by Group Captain Clouston
    23 October 1944 at the completion of Jack's second tour with 455 Squadron.
    This echoes Wing Commander Bob Holmes' 1 July 1943 assessment. PR,
    Bruce Davenport, flying log.

10 AWM S01651.

11 Whishaw, *That Airman!*, p. 63; AR, Ivor Gordon, 5 September 2006

12 PR, Ian Gordon, undated note and letters Bert Iggulden, 10 and 30
    August 1993.

13 Unless credited elsewhere, the following narrative on the squadron crest
    is drawn from NAA A11271, 136/P1.

14 NAA A11271, 136/P1. The public relations officer was Squadron Leader
    Douglas Gillison, who would later write one of the four volumes of the
    RAAF's official Second World War history. Gillison's letter was dated 12
    June: while squadrons were busy carrying out their post-D-day barrages,
    public relations staff were obviously gearing up for potential PR
    opportunities.

15 This and above quotes from NAA A11271, 136/P1.

16 Wilson and Robinson, *Coastal Command Leads the Invasion*, p. 113.

17 AWM S01651. The 'Kangaroo Squadron', or the 'Kangaroos' tags appeared
    in an Air Ministry bulletin announcing the award of Jack's George Medal
    (no. 16950, 5 January 1945) and found their way into at least two news
    articles which, regardless of Jack's laughing protestations that he had not
    heard of them, were from his own collection of news articles, and one

that he had written himself (he did not use the tag; it was in the biog sidebar). Davenport, 'These are the ship-busters', *John Bull*, 20 January 1945 and in an article on page 9 of the 17 June 1944 issue of *The British Australian and New Zealander*. Given the date of this latter article, it appears that Gillison had already made up his mind about the Australiana nickname!

18 NAA Series A11271, 136/P1.

19 The Christmas card was emblazoned with fierce looking pilot and navigator wearing Viking-type helmets and wielding axes as their Beaufighter miraculously flew itself above a satisfactorily busted enemy vessel (they weren't known as ship-busters for nothing). PR, Ian Gordon's research papers.

20 Whishaw, *That Airman!* p. 71.

21 AR, Wally Kimpton, 5 September 2006.

22 AWM S01651. Although he felt no disgust at the fact that this man had succumbed to the strains of operational flying, Jack did note in his interview that 'this bloke didn't endear himself to me'. It says much for Jack that he did not allow a personal dislike for the man to interfere with a decision to treat the case sensitively.

23 AWM S01651. The above discussion of LMF is drawn from Wells, *Courage and Air Warfare*.

24 Whishaw, *That Airman!* p. 53.

25 AR, John Ayliffe, 27 June 2006.

26 Gordon, *Strike and Strike Again*, p. vii.

27 Jack McKnight's recollection in Whishaw, *That Airman!* p. 54.

28 Jack Cox's recollection in Gordon, *Strike and Strike Again,* pp. 58–9.

29 Jack McKnight's recollection in *ibid.*, p. 54.

30 AR, Ernest 'Blue' Bernau, 20 September 2006.

31 455 Squadron ORB, 19 August 1944.

32 AR, Ernest 'Blue' Bernau, 20 September 2006.

33 AR, Bill Herbert, 1 June 2006.

34 Air Ministry bulletin, no. 16950, 5 January 1945.

35 Ilbery and Mitchell had both attended the Sydney Church of England Grammar School and their friendship began in the school's under 14A rugby team. They had joined the RAAF, both hoping to be mustered as fighter pilots. At their initial training, their intake was split arbitrarily in two and Ilbery and Mitchell were sent to separate elementary training schools. They both ended up at Uranquinty for their service flying training but Mitchell was one course ahead of Ilbery and graduated one month before him.

36 PR, Peter Ilbery, Ilbery/Miss M.A. Ilbery, 14 January 1944.

37 PR, Peter Ilbery, Jack Davenport, 25 January 1944.

38 PR, Peter Ilbery, Jack Davenport, 28 February 1944.

39 PR, Peter Ilbery, Jack Davenport, 26 June 1944.

40 AR, Peter Ilbery, 18 November 2005.

41 PR, Peter Ilbery, Jack Davenport, August 1995.

42 AR, Peter Ilbery, 25 January 2006.

43 *ibid.*

44 Mitchell and his navigator Flight Sergeant Ivor Jury were killed during an anti-shipping patrol. It was assumed that they had been shot down by one of the enemy fighters sighted by the Mustang escort. 455 Squadron ORB, 8 March, 1945. Ilbery was on leave at the time and he did not learn of Mitchell's loss until 15 March when he expected to meet him for their commissioning interviews at 18 Group headquarters. PR, Peter Ilbery, Ilbery/Miss M.A. Ilbery, 15 March 1945.

CWGC register: Mitchell, Pilot Officer William Douglas, 422968, RAAF. 8 March 1945, age 21. Panel 283, Runnymede Memorial. Jury, Flight Sergeant Ivor Hilton, 437134, RAAF. 8 March 1945, age 31. Panel 284, Runnymede Memorial.

45 AR, Peter Ilbery, 29 March 2008.

46 *ibid.*, including 'Egersund recollection'.

47 CWGC register: Longland, Warrant Officer George Edwin, 426229, RAAF. 24 March 1945, age 22. A. 9. 3 Egersund Churchyard. Nayda, Flight Sergeant Errol Claude, 419533, RAAF. 24 March 1945, age 22. A. 9. 2 Egersund Churchyard.

48 455 Squadron ORB.

49 AR, Peter Ilbery, 25 January 2006.

50 *ibid.*

51 Air Ministry bulletin no. 16950, 5 January 1945. Jack, however, disagreed. He considered his 'fearlessness' was 'absolute balderdash. One was frequently very scared but you had a job to do and that's what you concentrated on'. AWM S01651.

52 AR, Ivor Gordon and Wally Kimpton, 5 September 2006 and John Ayliffe, 27 June 2006.

53 Whishaw, *That Airman!* p. 97.

54 AR, John Ayliffe, 8 July 2008.

55 Herington, *Australia in the War of 1939–1945: Air Power over Europe 1944–1945*, p. 247.

56 AR, Lloyd Wiggins, 11 December 2005.

57 Milson, *The Earth Brought Forth*, p. 481.

58 Lawson, *Four Five Five*, p. 128.

59 Gordon, *Strike and Strike Again*, p. 112.

60 Herington, *Air Power over Europe*, p. 247.

61 AR, Wally Kimpton, 5 September 2006.

62 AR, Ivor Gordon, 5 September 2006.

63 AR, John Ayliffe, 27 June 2006.

64 PR, Ian Gordon, Jack Davenport, 26 September 1994.

65 PR, Ian Gordon, Scott Milson, 16 September 1993.

66 PR, Scott Milson, Jack Davenport/Arthur Milson, 20 July 1975.

67 As noted by Jack in 'These are the ship-busters', *John Bull,* 20 January 1945.
68 455 Squadron ORB, October 1944.

Chapter 16   War's end

1   PR, Ian Gordon, Jack Davenport, 4 April 1994.
2   *ibid.*
3   *CCR,* vol. III, no. 11, November 1944.
4   PR, Ian Gordon, Jack Davenport, 4 April 1994.
5   Ellwood, 8 November 1944, *CCR,* vol. III, no. 11, November 1944.
6   455 Squadron ORB, 8 November 1944.
7   *CCR,* vol. III, no. 11, November 1944. The outrider tactic was later refined to take advantage of the element of surprise, with scouts flying about ten minutes ahead of the main force.
8   The bulk of this narrative has been drawn from Chapter 12 of Nesbit, *The Strike Wings* with additional detail from Chapter 8 of Gordon, *Strike and Strike Again.*
9   *CCR,* vol. III, no. 11, November 1944.
10 *CCR,* vol. IV, no. 2, February 1945.
11 Bird, *A Separate Little War,* p. 105.
12 CWGC register:
    404 Squadron
    Middleton, Flying Officer Jeffrey, 187929, RAF. 9 February 1945, age 30. British Plot. E. 17. Haugesund (Rossebo) Var Frelsers Cemetery, Norway. Smook, Flying Officer Harry, J/36168, RCAF. 9 February 1945. Age unknown. Panel 280 Runnymede Memorial. Duckworth, Pilot Officer Alan Murray, J/93719, RCAF. 9 February 1945, age 23. Panel 280 Runnymede Memorial. Jackson, Pilot Officer William James, J/92936, RCAF. 9 February 1945, age 27. Panel 280 Runnymede Memorial. Blunderfield, Pilot Officer William Edward, J/92165, RCAF. 9 February 1945, age 23. British Plot. F. 18. Haugesund (Rossebo) Var Frelsers Cemetery, Norway. Myrick, Flying Officer Philip Rex, J/35788, RCAF. 9 February 1945, age 22. Canada. British Plot. F. 15. Haugesund (Rossebo) Var Frelsers Cemetery, Norway. Berges, Pilot Officer Claude Gerald, J/95209, RCAF. 9 February 1945, age unknown. British Plot. F. 19. Haugesund (Rossebo) Var Frelsers Cemetery, Norway. Lynch, Flying Officer Hugh Charles, J/35785, RCAF. 9 February 1945, age 24. British Plot. F. 16. Haugesund (Rossebo) Var Frelsers Cemetery, Norway. Knight, Flying Officer Oswald Wellington, J/36373, RCAF. 9 February 1945, age 27. British Plot. F. 17. Haugesund (Rossebo) Var Frelsers Cemetery, Norway. Smerneos, Flying Officer Charles, J/29021, RCAF. 9 February 1945. Age unknown. British Plot. F. 13. Haugesund (Rossebo) Var Frelsers Cemetery, Norway. Cochrane, Flying Officer Norman Douglas, J/35704,

RCAF. 9 February 1945, age 26. British Plot. F. 14. Haugesund (Rossebo) Var Frelsers Cemetery, Norway.

455 Squadron

Mutimer, Warrant Officer Donald Ernest, 410694, RAAF. 9 February 1945, age 28. British Plot. E. 16. Haugesund (Rossebo) Var Frelsers Cemetery, Norway. Blackshaw, Pilot Officer John Douglas, 432095, RAAF. 9 February 1945, age 20. British Plot. F. 20. Haugesund (Rossebo) Var Frelsers Cemetery, Norway.

65 Squadron

Caesar, Warrant Officer Cecil Claude, 657915, RAF. 9 February 1945, age 31. British Plot. E. 18. Haugesund (Rossebo) Var Frelsers Cemetery, Norway.

13   Survivors taken prisoner of war: Flying Officer Roger Savard, (404 Squadron); Flying Officer 'Spike' Holly (144 Squadron); Flying Officer P.C. Smith (144 Squadron); Flight Lieutenant Bob McColl (455 Squadron); and Warrant Officer Leslie Leonard MacDonald (455 Squadron). All eventually were sent to Stalag Luft 1. Bob McColl was one of Jack's former pupils from Turnberry.

14   PR, Bruce Davenport, Jack Davenport/Captain G.G. Cooper, 31 October 1984.

15   *ibid.*

16   *CCR,* vol. IV, no. 2, February 1945.

17   *CCR,* vol. IV, no. 4, April 1945.

18   The following account of Phil Davenport's 89th sortie and subsequent events is largely drawn from PR, Phil Davenport, unpublished memoir, with supplementation from Phil's account which forms part of the BBC's Second World War People's War archive http://www.bbc.co.uk/ww2peopleswar, and Bird, *A Separate Little War*, pp. 148–51.

19   Phil was not aware there had been a fighter on his tail until after the war. AR, Phil Davenport, comment on draft manuscript, June 2008.

20   Pilot Officer Fenrik Johannes Wollert Loken and navigator Sergeant Stephen Henrik Engstrom were outriders with 333 Squadron and had been tasked with leading the strike force to the target. Bird, *A Separate Little War*, p. 148; http://home.no.net/thsord/mosquito.htm.

21   The Norwegian, Gudmund Hegland, remembered the dinghy was pulled along by a rope tied to it. Phil recalled his wrist was grabbed and they were towed to shore that way. Hegland's recollection in Bird, *A Separate Little War,* p. 150.

22   PR, Phil Davenport, unpublished memoir.

23   *CCR,* vol. IV, no. 4, April 1 and no 5, May 1945.

24   PR, Bruce Davenport, 'Australia Remembers' speech at Elanora Country Club annual dinner, 1995 (draft).

25   AR, Bruce Davenport, 30 March 2006.

26   PR, Dick Mason, thanksgiving service, Dick Mason's eulogy.

27 AWM S01651; PR Ian Gordon, Jack Davenport, 24 July 1992; AR, Bruce Davenport 30 March 2006.
28 PR, Ian Gordon, Jack Davenport, 24 July 1992; AR, Bruce Davenport, 30 March 2006; AWM S01651.
29 PR, Phil Davenport, unpublished memoir.
30 AWM S01651.
31 Goulter, *A Forgotten Offensive*, p. 170.
32 AR, Bruce Davenport, 30 March 2006.
33 PR, Ian Gordon, Jack Davenport, 24 July 1992.
34 Goulter, *A Forgotten Offensive*, pp. 270–2.
35 NAA A9300, Philip Roy Davenport; PR, Phil Davenport, unpublished memoir; NAA A9300, Keith Hand Davenport.
36 AWM S01651.
37 *ibid.*
38 PR, Ian Gordon, Jack Davenport, 24 July 1992. AR, Bill McFadden, 21 March and 31 August 2007.
39 *The Times,* 20 November 1945.
40 *ibid.*
41 *The Argus,* 12 November 1945.
42 *ibid.* states 1000 men but on 14 November *The Argus* states 350 men. As this would probably be the last ship to reach Australia before Christmas, there was some thought that the men had walked off not because of the overcrowding, but because they had wives and sweethearts in England. Even though they could only arrange their partners' transport as war brides once they had returned to Australia, the men wanted to stay in the United Kingdom. This was hotly denied by many, but the thought was very much apparent in official circles. *The Argus,* 11 November 1945; *Australian Women's Weekly,* 1 December 1945. The principal sea transport officer was quoted as saying 'most of them don't want to be demobilised. They have wives and sweethearts and pay here. The trouble has happened before and will happen again.' *The Argus,* 11 November 1945. This opinion was shared by Bill McFadden in AR, Bill McFadden, 21 March 2007 and John LeCorno in Brown, *Skylarks*, p. 84.
43 *The Times,* 20 November 1945.
44 *The Argus,* 14 November 1945, AR, Bill McFadden, 21 May 2008.
45 Brown, *Skylarks,* p. 84 indicates headlines in London's *Daily Mail* included '*Orion*'s Deck H10 was too much', 'Trouble expected on the *Orion*' and 'Rebels' liner returning—engine trouble'. *The Times,* 20 November 1945 reported the Minister of War Transport's statement in parliament. Australian press coverage included *The Argus* 11, 12 and 14 November 1945; and *Australian Women's Weekly,* 1 December 1945. After finally embarking on 11 November, the *Orion* had to turn back because of damage to her machinery. All passengers were dispatched to holding camps to await passage on another ship, on which they ended up spending Christmas somewhere in the middle of the Indian Ocean. *The Times,* 20 November

1945; Brown, *Skylarks*, p. 84. Interestingly, there is another Davenport connection with the *Orion*. In 1950, Sheila, accompanied by her children, returned to Scotland for the first time since migrating to Australia, travelling on the *Orion*. AR, Bruce Davenport, 8 May 2008.

46   NAA A9300, Jack Napier Davenport.
47   This appeared in the supplement to the *London Gazette*, 1 January 1946. There is no record of Jack's MID citation but Lloyd Wiggins, whose MID was also gazetted in the same supplement, believes that Jack would have carried out his work far beyond the call of duty and someone in authority noted it and recommended him for it. AR, Lloyd Wiggins, 28 June 2007. Phil Davenport believes that Jack's MID recognised his good work, his sense of responsibility and his organisational and administrative abilities. AR, Phil Davenport, 7 June 2007.

Chapter 17   Concrete Industries (Monier)

1   AWM S01651.
2   NAA A907 1946/3/11.
3   Pat recalled what 'lovebirds' Jack and Sheila were; they were obviously a love match and were well suited. Pat would often babysit for Jack and Sheila so they could go out, or if they were hosting business dinners. Pat Curnow, 20 December 2006.
4   AR, June Ross, 24 October 2006. Roy Davenport died 2 February 1957. Grace remained a strong and loving presence in Jack's life until her death on 13 November 1975.
5   AR, June Ross, 24 October 2006.
6   AR, Bruce Davenport, 8 May 2008.
7   AR, June Ross, 24 October 2006 and Bruce Davenport, 14 March 2007. Pat Curnow lived across the road from the Davenports. Her parents were Scottish and the Donaghys proved an important source of strength for Sheila, who was homesick: she would often visit the Donaghys and talk about Scotland. One New Year's Eve (which was Sheila's birthday) Sheila came over to wish the Donaghys a happy New Year. She was feeling particularly homesick on this occasion, and when Pat's father sung a little Scottish song, she was moved to tears. AR, Pat Curnow, 20 December 2006.
8   AWM S01651.
9   CBA, *Bank Notes*, March 1946.
10   CBA.
11   AR, Cyril Johnson, 2 February 2007.
12   AWM S01651.
13   *ibid.*
14   'Recco', in his feature on ex-RAAF types 'What are they doing now?' likened building a cottage out of the prefabricated slabs to erecting a toy

with a Mecanno set. And as for Jack's role in providing homes for 'house-hungry people', he considered it 'something of a contrast to ship-busting with bombs . . . he is in truth now engaged in constructive work of the greatest importance, whereas in the war period he was a destructive agent of no mean order.' *Wings,* December 1947.

15 Dawson, *Strength in Concrete,* pp. 7–11.

16 Clem was not wrong. Stanislaus Carroll, his close friend who had been on the board from the early days of Cement Linings, considered Jack had a fine war record and soon developed the highest admiration for Jack as a person, and not just because of his war record. AR, Tony Carroll, 15 March 2007.

17 AR, Lyn Shaddock, 15 March 2007. It is not known exactly when Jack started with Concrete Industries. Lyn Shaddock recalled Jack and Sheila visited almost as soon as they returned to Australia and his father offered the job at about the same time. Jack implies he started soon after he returned to Australia in PR, Ian Gordon, Jack Davenport, 24 July 1992. His Commonwealth Bank employment record, however, states he resigned from the bank on 12 May 1946, with a payment of salary equivalent of service to 4 August 1946, as well as a superannuation payout which, at the time, was paid on leaving the bank. His resignation was noted in the June 1946 edition of *Bank Notes.* CBA; AR, Marina Stanley, 14 and 15 May 2008.

18 AR, Lyn Shaddock, 15 March 2007; PR, Frank Tomasich (Thomas), Jack Davenport, 17 October 1977.

19 PR, Frank Tomasich (Thomas), Jack Davenport, 17 October 1977.

20 AR, Lyn Shaddock, 15 March 2007; Hope Gibb, 20 March 2007.

21 PR, Frank Tomasich (Thomas), Concrete Industries (Monier) Limited 1978 annual report to stockholders and employees, p. 15.

22 Frank also admired the fact that Jack was a 'straight shooter' and nothing escaped his notice. If something came to light in an internal audit, Jack would act on it promptly and never sweep it under the carpet. Jack also entrusted his personal insurance to Frank and one of the funniest things Frank ever encountered was the time he had to organise a policy to cover semen straws for Jack's Charolais artificial insemination breeding program. AR, Frank Tomasich (Thomas), 3 July 2007.

23 AR, Kevin Parnell, 4 July 2007.

24 AR, Lyn Shaddock, 15 March 2007. Jack's faith in Lyn Shaddock's abilities was well placed. When Lyn left the company, he worked for a large building company to learn the industry ropes, went on to form his own building company and eventually moved into entrepreneurial building development.

25 This even extended to the shareholder meetings in the early days where sandwiches would be laid on, senior managers would be available for a chat about their operations, and dividend cheques handed out alphabetically at the end of the day. AR, Tony Carroll, 15 March 2007.

26 Dawson, *Strength in Concrete*, p. 13.

27 *ibid.*, p. 23. PR, Dick Mason, thanksgiving service, Dick Mason's eulogy.

28 AR, Ron and Rosemary Duncan, 14 March 2007.

29 PR, Frank Tomasich (Thomas), Monier 1978 annual report, p. 15.

30 PR, Bruce Davenport, Ron Duncan, Monier farewell dinner, 7 April 1982; AR, Robin Sen, 25 November 2007.

31 AR, Ron and Rosemary Duncan, 14 March 2007; June Ross, 24 October 2006 and 15 June 2008. As Sheila became more involved in Jack's career her isolation lessened, but it was still more than ten years before she felt as if Australia was her home. AR, Bruce Davenport, 8 May 2008.

32 PR, Dick Mason, thanksgiving service, Reverend Dr Fred McKay.

33 In the mid 1950s, Sheila read Betty Macdonald's *The Egg and I*. She enjoyed the rollicking tale and although it humorously evoked life on a chicken farm, she decided pig farming would be an ideal new life for the Davenports. Jack nurtured dreams of his own piece of land but pig farming was not his idea—and he knew it would not be Sheila's—of the perfect rural pursuit. Even so, he took a pragmatic approach to Sheila's announcement. He waited until Sydney had experienced one of its periodic deluges then took her to a piggery. Funnily enough, Sheila was relieved to return home and piggeries and career changes were not mentioned again. AR, June Ross, 15 June 2008.

34 AR, Dick and Mary Mason, 16 March 2007; June Ross, 15 June 2008.

35 PR, Peter Ilbery, Jack Davenport, August 1995.

36 AWM S01651.

37 AR, Jack 'Bluey' Collins, 15 April 2008.

38 AR, Kevin Parnell, 4 July 2007.

39 AR, Frank Tomasich, 13 July 2007.

40 Hope Gibb, Monier farewell dinner, 7 April 1982. Hope was not alone in discovering how often the impossible can be achieved. In 1956, when the New South Wales division of the AFC & RAAF Association decided to hold a clergy-officiated Anzac Day service in the Domain (in opposition to the official service which would be conducted without clergy) it was arranged with short notice and many doubted it could be done successfully and on such a grand scale as eventuated. Jack Davenport, who led the RAAF contingent during the Anzac Day march, had no doubts. Jack was acting state president at the time and had complete faith 'that we could organise such a mighty show in such a short time'. *Wings*, vol. 8, no. 9, June 1956.

41 AR, Lyn Shaddock, 7 June 2008. Most are still in use today and are in generally much better condition than many other buildings of the same era.

42 Dawson, *Strength in Concrete*, pp. 12–18.

43 AR, June Ross, 15 June 2008. Jack enjoyed a generous company discount, but, true to his commitment to ensure company resources were not exploited, he paid for his house. AR, Bruce Davenport, 14 March 2007

44 Dawson, *Strength in Concrete*, pp. 16–17.

45 AR, Dick Mason, 17 October 2006.

46 AR, Lyn Shaddock, 15 March 2007.

47 The company newsletters (variously named *Concrete Industries News, Monier Memo, Monier Staff News, News Line*) show many celebrations of 20, 25, and 30 years' service. PR, Frank Tomasich (Thomas).

48 AR, Tony Carroll, 15 March 2007; Dawson, *Strength in Concrete*, pp. 2 and 11.

49 AR, Lyn Shaddock and Tony Carroll, 15 March 2007; Bruce Davenport, 14 March 2007.

50 One of his great skills was thinking outside of the square. AR, June Ross, 24 October 2006.

51 PR, Frank Tomasich (Thomas), Monier 1978 annual report, p. 15; AR, Hope Gibb, 14 October 2006; PR, Frank Tomasich (Thomas), Monier 1981 annual report and undated special edition of Monier *Staff News*.

52 AR, Ron Duncan, 18 June 2008; Frank Tomasich (Thomas), 20 August 2007. Redlands engineered the takeover bid because Monier had become a major competitor in the worldwide roofing tiles market.

53 PR, Frank Tomasich (Thomas), Jack Davenport, 17 October 1977.

54 AWM S01651. Interestingly, Jack, the consummate planner, with his fine attention to detail, also thought 'I could have planned better, I could have avoided some of the problems that, in fact, occurred. I'm sure I could'.

55 AR, Frank Tomasich (Thomas), 13 July 2007.

56 AR, Hope Gibb, 14 October 2006.

57 ibid; AR, Ron and Rosemary Duncan, 14 March 2007.

58 Ralph Wragg, *The Sun*, 23 April 1974; PR, Phil Davenport, unpublished memoir.

59 PR, Frank Tomasich (Thomas), Monier 1978 annual report, p. 15.

60 AR, Ron Duncan, 18 June 2008 and Bruce Davenport, notes on draft manuscript, June 2008.

61 Parsimonious or frugal, Jack's approach to corporate finances was very much a part of his concept of integrity. Jack's consideration of sensible management was overshadowed in the late 1980s and early 1990s by a period of great corporate excess and stupendous profits which went more into private coffers than company development. He considered such overweening greed to be totally irresponsible. AR, Dick Mason, 16 March 2007.

62 AR, Ron and Rosemary Duncan, 14 March 2007; Hope Gibb, 14 October 2006.

63 *The Australian*, 8 December 1977; 31 December 1977–1 January 1978; and 30–31 December 1978. Jack was one of the early front runners.

64 That year, there were 286 nominations and Jack was not included in the early nominations. Obviously, his supporters were late starters. *The Australian*, 7 December 1978 and 31 December 1978–1 January 1979.

65 Here, nominations were made by institute members. Jack became an associate member of the institute in 1947 and a Fellow in 1963. AR, Ross Moyle, 7 February 2007; *AIM News*, October 1982.

66 AR, Devon Minchin, 4 July 2007.

67 AR, Dick Mason, 17 October 2006 and 16 March 2007.

68 AR, Wilfred Jarvis, 3 July 2007, 10 August 2007 and 8 July 2008.

69 AR, Frank Tomasich (Thomas), 3 July and 13 July 2007.

70 PR, Bruce Davenport, Monier farewell dinner, 7 April 1982.

71 Sheila Davenport, with much pride, told this story to both her children. She was proud of the inherent honesty and integrity that Jack brought to all areas of his life. AR, June Ross, 24 October 2006; Bruce Davenport, 14 May 2008.

72 PR, Bruce Davenport, Monier farewell dinner, 7 April 1982.

73 *ibid.*

Chapter 18 Integrity and humanity

1 PR, Dick Mason, AGL farewell, 6 November 1992.

2 AR, Dick Mason, 17 October 2006.

3 Dick Mason, speech at Jack's farewell from AGL 6 November 1992. During his response, reinforcing Dick's comments, Jack brushed off the high praise and turned to each one in the room, captains of industry, personal friends, family members, and told them how they as individuals had impacted on his life. AR, Tony Carroll, 15 March 2007.

4 AR, Dick Mason, 17 October 2006.

5 *ibid.*

6 Requests were made via major newspapers. AR, Bruce Davenport, 9 July 2008.

7 AR, Dick Mason, 16 March 2007.

8 *ibid.*

9 Jeni Porter, CBD column, *Sydney Morning Herald*, 6 November 1992.

10 Jack was also a founding board member of Note Printing Australia, a wholly-owned subsidiary of the Reserve Bank and played an important part in the successful restructuring of the bank's note printing works. RBA.

11 *Financial Review*, 3 July 1992. As far as Jack was concerned, there was no place for personal politics in his business dealings. Jack was a conservative voter and, at one stage, Prime Minister Menzies had offered him a safe Liberal seat. He declined because of business commitments and because he had no real interest in politics. Although he personally supported the Liberal Party, he admired both Bob Hawke and Paul Keating as well as then secretary of the ACTU and fellow Reserve Bank Board member, Bill Kelty. AR, Dick Mason, 17 October 2006; June Ross, 24 October 2006.

12 AR, Bernie Fraser, 26 March and 1 April 2007. It was a fact of life that, with so many boards on which he sat, representing both public and private concerns, conflicts of interest would arise. If a real or potential conflict arose, Jack would always declare his involvement. In the case of the Reserve Bank board, if a matter arose which would impact on his other

business dealings his position was always that the country came first. AR, Dick Mason, 16 March 2007. When Jack retired as a board member on 29 September 1992, he joined a very select group to have served three terms. Jack's first term was with effect from 16 September 1977. His second term commenced on 16 September 1982 and expired on 15 September 1987. It is not generally known that the terms were not consective as there was a slight delay in Jack's third appointment. The treasurer recommended Jack's reappointment on 14 August 1987 but because of the cancellation of one Cabinet meeting, a subsequent delay in discussion at the next available Executive Council meeting, and the treasurer's illness which delayed signing the appointment papers, Jack was not formally advised of his reappointment until 30 September 1987. AR, Virginia Macdonald, 28 June 2007.

13 AR, Bruce Davenport, 14 June 2006.

14 *ICAC Independent Commission Against Corruption Annual Report to 30 June 1991.*

15 AR, Jack 'Bluey' Collins, 21 August 2006.

16 This was VH-OJA, which is still in the fleet. It initially flew from Seattle, where it had been built, to London and then operated non-stop from London to Sydney. The flight was just over twenty hours, a world record for the longest non-stop flight by a commercial aircraft. The aircraft was fully fitted out and ready to go into service and this record-making flight operated almost the same as any regular passenger flight with some differences: to enhance the 747-400's fuel economy, the fuel was frozen; the aircraft was towed to the end of the runway so it did not have to use fuel taxiing into position; and the flight organisers elicited some air traffic control concessions towards the end of the flight that saved some time and fuel. Apparently, Qantas held this record for some time until Airbus Industrie tried to seize the record by operating an Airbus A340 from Toulouse to Auckland non-stop. This was not a production aircraft as it had been stripped of all its internal fittings, and the 'passengers' slept in sleeping bags in the bare cabin. AR, Steve Heesh, 13 January and 13 March 2007, 14 May 2008.

17 AR, Steve Heesh, 25 January and 13 March 2007.

18 AR, Steve Heesh, 13 March 2007.

19 AR, June Ross, 24 October 2006.

20 Shortly after Jack retired from AGL, the government ceased to have any jurisdiction over the company. AR, Dick Mason, 17 October 2006; Steve Heesh, 13 March 2007.

21 AR, Steve Heesh, 13 March 2007; Marion Hare 11 December 2006 and 12 March 2007.

22 PR, Sir Arvi Parbo, Jack's speech notes Alcoa retirement dinner, 3 March 1993.

23 AR, Sir Arvi Parbo, 15 October 2006.

24 PR, Sir Arvi Parbo, Paul O'Neill/Jack Davenport, 14 April 1993.

25 Jack's sense of humour was apparent in his response to Sir Arvi's speech. Sir Arvi had noted the eventful seven years of Jack's tenure on the board. Jack responded: 'I, of course, had much to do with the great success in my early years but vehemently disassociate myself from the more recent price decreases'. As he had done at his AGL farewell, Jack spoke of the special talents and qualities of each of his fellow board members, summing up: 'As a board you have done a grand job. Much wisdom sits around this board table.' PR, Sir Arvi Parbo, Jack's speech notes from Alcoa retirement dinner, 3 March 1993; AR, Sir Arvi Parbo, 15 October 2006.

26 AR, June Ross, 24 October 2006.

27 AR, Dick Mason, 17 October 2006.

28 As a life member, Jack was not obliged to pay membership subscriptions but, in keeping with his ethos of 'helping', he continued to pay his annual subscription until death. AR, Gordon Johnstone, 21 April 2008.

29 AR, June Ross, 24 October 2006.

30 AR, Barry Brooke, 23 March 2007.

31 *Wings*, vol. 8, no. 10, December 1956.

32 AR, June Ross, 24 October 2006.

33 AR, Doris McArthur, 27 February 2007. This home was the only Monocrete home in Taren Point.

34 AR, Ted Peacock, 5 July 2007. Ted was a consulting engineer with Crooks Mitchell Peacock Stewart which submitted some designs for the prefabricated Monocrete building which Jack's company manufactured. Their business association lasted for many years and every so often, Jack and Ted would meet for lunch to catch up. Ted considered that Jack was a good person to work with and very pleasant natured. Ted admired many things about Jack but one in particular was his propensity to help others out and his lifelong involvement with the air force association.

35 Gordon, *Strike and Strike Again*, p. 192; AR, Bruce Davenport, 1 November 2006.

36 AR, Michael O'Dea, 20 April 2007.

37 *The Australian*, 5 January 1979.

38 PR, Bruce Davenport, RAAF Europe dinner speech.

39 AR, Ron and Rosemary Duncan, 14 March 2007.

40 AR, Dick Mason, 17 October 2006.

41 AR, Ted Sly, 13 December 2006.

42 AR, Dick and Mary Mason, 16 March 2007.

43 *ibid*. The foundation stone was laid on 30 April 1960. The chapel was financed solely by donations and was completed at a cost of approximately $41,000.

44 AR, Dick and Mary Mason, 16 March 2007; Dick Mason 17 October 2006. No doubt Jack used his influence to include a notice for the *Krait* appeal in *Wings*, June 1981.

45 AR, Max Roberts, January 2007.

46 Annotation on extract from The Heart Research Institute's 1995 annual report held by the RBA.

47 Mr Ross Hohnen AM OBE, Honorary Fellow, obituary of Jack Davenport, The Heart Research Institute annual report 1995, RBA.

48 AR, June Ross, 9 July 2008. Sadly, Jack died just months before the doctorate could be awarded.

49 Australian Government 'It's an Honour' website http://www.itsanhonour. gov.au; *Order of Australia* brochure, Governor-General's Office, Government House, Canberra (undated).

50 *Order of Australia* brochure, Governor-General's Office, Government House, Canberra (undated).

Chapter 19   Family and friends

1 AR, Dick Mason, 17 October 2006.
2 AR, June Ross, 13 May 2008.
3 AR, June Ross, 24 October 2006.
4 AR, June Ross, 24 October 2006 and 15 June 2008.
5 AR, Bruce Davenport, 14 March 2007.
6 Jack loved recycling. He was a great hoarder of anything that might be useful one day. After he purchased 'Drumadoon', truck loads of materials from liquidation sales would occasionally arrive to fill the already overflowing sheds. AR, June Ross, 15 June 2008.
7 AR, June Ross, 15 June 2008; *Wings*, vol. 16, no. 1, December–February 1964.
8 AR, Dick and Mary Mason, 16 March 2007.
9 AR, June Ross, 15 June 2008.
10 AR, Bruce Davenport, 14 June 2006; Hope Gibb, 14 October 2006.
11 Jack's country grandchildren accepted the challenge of the wider world. Jane is a soil scientist who worked in the Tasmanian wine industry before moving to the Falkland Islands. Anna, a psychologist specialising in addictive behaviour, runs a practice in Sydney. David studied engineering then gained an MBA. He works part-time in Sydney as a consultant as well as managing the family properties. AR, June Ross, 15 June 2008.
12 *Wings*, vol. 20, no. 3, August 1968; AR, June Ross, 24 October 2006.
13 AR, Dick Mason, 17 October 2006.
14 AR, June Ross, 24 October 2006 and 15 June 2008; *Armidale Express*, 12 March 1971.
15 The properties continue to prosper today with David, the youngest of June and Malcolm's three children, taking on the management with his wife and two young sons. AR, June Ross, 15 June 2008 and Dick Mason, 17 October 2006.
16 AR, Mark Butler, 2 July 2007.

17 AR, Tony Oliver, 19 March 2007. As far as Les Oliver was concerned, both he and everybody else from the squadron regarded Jack in the highest esteem, both personally and as a successful businessman.

18 AR, John Pilcher, 2 July 2007; June Ross, 24 October 2006; Pam Watson, 24 October 2006.

19 AR, Laurie and Doreen Taylor, 6 July 2007.

20 AR, Vivienne Dart, 17 May 2007.

21 AR, June Ross, 15 June 2008.

22 Jack was invited to be president of Elanora in the early 1980s. There was much official as well as administrative work involved and he declined because he was fully tied up with his business commitments. AR, Dick and Mary Mason, 16 March 2007.

23 AR, Dick Mason, 17 October 2006 and June Ross, 15 June 2008.

24 AR, June Ross, 15 June 2008.

25 Keith Daymond was the brother of Jack's wartime friend, Bruce.

26 PR, Dick Mason, thanksgiving service.

27 Jack and Phil remained friends with Jock for many years. Pat Curnow recalled how Jack took the plans to her father, who knew a lot about boats, to look them over. Pat Curnow, 20 December 2006.

28 AR, Phil Davenport, 20 June 2006.

29 *Margaret Rintoul* kept its second place on corrected time. *Waltzing Matilda*'s corrected time was four days, 41 minutes, fifteen seconds. *Sunday Herald*, 1 January 1950; *Daily Telegraph*, 1 January 1950; *Sydney Morning Herald*, 2 January 1950.

30 There were too few bunks for the twelve-man crew so Jack let the more experienced sailors have the bunks. Over the next few months, Phil and Keith planned their months-long voyage to England. Jack was not overtaken by their enthusiasm; he had no intention of leaving his work and family. He did, however, join friends in one of the many sailing boats escorting *Waltzing Matilda* through the heads on Sunday 29 October 1950. As he drew near, he handed over a Christmas cake, calling out his final farewells. AR, Phil Davenport, 20 June 2006.

31 AR, Dick Mason, 17 October 2006.

32 PR, Peter Ilbery, Jack 'Jeep' McKnight, 23 July 1995.

33 AR, Dick Mason, 17 October 2006.

34 AR, Devon Minchin, 4 July 2007; Marion Hare, 12 March 2007 and Hope Gibb, 14 October 2006; PR, Peter Ilbery, Jack 'Jeep' McKnight, 23 July 1995. Throughout his working life, Jack had been scrupulous about responding to his personal and business correspondence. It was no different now and he responded to every card, letter and call. AR, Hope Gibb, 14 October 2006.

35 AR, Dick and Mary Mason, 16 March 2007.

36 AR, Tony Carroll, 15 March 2007.

37 PR, Peter Ilbery, Jack Davenport, August 1995.

38 PR, Phil Davenport, Jack Davenport, July 1995.

39 AR, Ron and Rosemary Duncan, 14 March 2007. Sheila never recovered from Jack's death and struggled with her health as the cancer spread and took hold. AR, June Ross, 15 June 2008.

40 PR, Phil Davenport, Jack Davenport, 21 December 1995.

41 Jack retired as chairman of Volvo Australia Pty Ltd on 31 December 1995, and had recently sat on his final board with Volvo. He was still a member of the board of Note Printing Australia at the time of his death. AR, Bruce Davenport, 4 July 2008; Dick Mason, 17 October 2006; and Virginia Macdonald, 28 June 2007.

42 The following narrative and extracts are from PR, Dick Mason, thanksgiving service.

Epilogue

1 AR, Dick and Mary Mason, 16 March 2007.

2 PR, Bruce Davenport, RAAF Europe dinner speech.

3 AWM S01651.

4 AR, Wilfred Jarvis, 8 July 2008.

5 AR, Dick Mason, 16 March 2007.

6 As well as garnering association support, Jack made a sizeable contribution to the memorial fundraising effort. PR, Peter Ilbery, Jack 'Jeep' McKnight, 5 March 1992; AR, Peter Ilbery, 16 April 2008.

7 PR, Phil Davenport, unpublished memoir; AR, Phil Davenport, 20 June 2006.

8 AR, Dick Mason, 17 October 2006.

9 PR, Phil Davenport, unpublished memoir.

10 PR, Sir Arvi Parbo, speaking notes at retirement dinner for Jack Davenport, 3 March 1993.

Appendix B

1 PR, Bruce Davenport's papers. Jack's speech notes do not indicate where he made this speech.

2 i.e. two-up.

3 This was not just rhetoric. Jack's friend from the Commonwealth Bank and the 30th Battalion, Corporal Anthony Booth, contracted malaria shortly after arriving at Milne Bay. He survived that and another bout, only to succumb to scrub typhus on 9 February 1944.

4 Bluey Collins recalls that, on 455 Squadron's return from Russia the HMS *Argonaut* was subjected to wild, rolling seas and a number of men were washed overboard. The vessel did not stop to rescue them as they would have perished in the icy northern seas within minutes. AR, Jack 'Bluey' Collins, 21 August 2006.

Index